Playboys and Mayfair Men

Playboys and Mayfair Men

**CRIME, CLASS, MASCULINITY, AND FASCISM
IN 1930s LONDON**

Angus McLaren

Johns Hopkins University Press / *Baltimore*

© 2017 Johns Hopkins University Press
All rights reserved. Published 2017
Printed in the United States of America on acid-free paper
9 8 7 6 5 4 3 2 1

Johns Hopkins University Press
2715 North Charles Street
Baltimore, Maryland 21218-4363
www.press.jhu.edu

Library of Congress Cataloging-in-Publication Data

Names: McLaren, Angus, author.
Title: Playboys and Mayfair men : crime, class, masculinity, and
    fascism in 1930s London / Angus McLaren.
Description: Baltimore, Maryland : Johns Hopkins University
    Press, 2017. | Includes bibliographical references and index.
Identifiers: LCCN 2017004265 | ISBN 9781421423487
    (hardcover : alk. paper) | ISBN 9781421423470 (electronic) |
    ISBN 1421423472 (hardcover : alk. paper) | ISBN 1421423480
    (electronic)
Subjects: LCSH: Robbery—England—London—Case studies. |
    Violent crimes—England—London—Case studies. |
    Criminals—England—London—Case studies. | Social classes—
    England—London—History—20th century. | London
    (England)—Social conditions—20th century.
Classification: LCC HV6665.G72 M35 2017 | DDC
    364.15/5209421—dc23
LC record available at https://lccn.loc.gov/2017004265

A catalog record for this book is available from the British Library.

*Special discounts are available for bulk purchases of this book. For more
information, please contact Special Sales at 410-516-6936 or
specialsales@press.jhu.edu.*

Johns Hopkins University Press uses environmentally friendly book
materials, including recycled text paper that is composed of at least
30 percent post-consumer waste, whenever possible.

Contents

Acknowledgments

When I first came across newspaper accounts of the Hyde Park Hotel robbery, I was puzzled to read that the villains had attacked their victim with a "life preserver." For Americans a life preserver (or life jacket) is a flotation device. My difficulty in understanding what the papers meant by the phrase proved once more the truth of the line (often attributed to George Bernard Shaw) "The English and the Americans are two peoples divided by a common language." I soon discovered a "life preserver" in 1930s Britain was a truncheon, or what North Americans would call a "blackjack." Helpfully, the *Oxford English Dictionary* notes that Anthony Trollope and Arthur Conan Doyle often used the term. The life preserver (cudgel, baton, truncheon, cosh, nightstick, or bludgeon) was a short club, heavily loaded with a lead weight at one end and a strap or lanyard at the other. Easily concealed, it was purportedly designed for self-defense, hence the name "life preserver." A single forceful blow could cause concussion and even prove fatal. The type of weapon used in the Hyde Park Hotel robbery was of scant legal importance. Nevertheless my stumbling over the curious term "life preserver" pricked my curiosity and drew me to the case. And as I tracked the jewel thieves through police reports and press accounts, I realized, to my surprise and excitement, that an investigation of the public response to their misdeeds offered a fresh perspective on many aspects of 1930s British society.

But should I devote a book-length study to the misdeeds of wastrels and scoundrels? George Orwell, who warned that the author was besmirched by the material he handled, might well have viewed even the desire to launch such a project as betraying "a kind of spiritual inadequacy."* Friends and colleagues

* So Orwell said of Cyril Connolly for writing *The Rock Pool* (1936). See *George Orwell: An Age Like This: 1920–1940*, in *The Collected Essays, Journalism, and Letters of George Orwell*, ed. Sonia Orwell and Ian Angus (New York: Harcourt, Brace & World, 1968), 1:226.

were more understanding. Taking time out of their busy schedules, Lucy Bland, Stephen Brooke, Brian Dippie, Jack Little, and Nikki Strong-Boag read early versions of the entire manuscript. Adrian Bingham shared his unrivaled knowledge of the interwar press. I owe special thanks to Robert Nye. He not only read several drafts, but his enthusiastic support of the study also lifted my spirits when, like many authors, I reached that stage of wondering whether the project made any sense at all. I am also grateful to Judith Allen, Peter Bailey, Paul Delany, Catherine Ellis, Michael Finn, Matt Houlbrook, Jim Kempling, Kathy Mezei, Tom Saunders, and Tim Travers for peppering me with ideas and suggestions. Terence Greer offered to help with the cover illustration. More contributions came from Susannah and Richard Taffler and Aimée and Michael Birnbaum, who were, in addition, wonderful hosts during my repeated stays in London.

I owe much to the helpful staffs of the National Archives, the Archives of Kent State University, Wellington College Archives, Harrow School Archives, Oundle School Archives, the libraries at the University of Victoria, the University of British Columbia and Simon Fraser University, and the British Library. Jaimee McRoberts at the British Library News Room was particularly considerate. Willi Lauri Ahonen generously translated a Finnish passage for me; Tineke Hellwig and Dick Unger did the same from the Dutch. Jill Ainsley was an imaginative and industrious research assistant, and at the University of Victoria, Karen Hickton has been an ever-helpful departmental secretary. My previous books were all supported by the Social Science and Research Council of Canada, which allowed me to make several overseas research trips. I am happy to acknowledge once more the Council's crucial role in generously encouraging historical research. This study was launched with the funds left over from my last major grant.

And finally, no words can adequately express all that I owe to Arlene, who has supported me in so many ways. One trifling example: I'm embarrassed to think of the number of times I have interrupted her in the midst of writing or reading to "share" with her yet another anecdote relating to playboys or Mayfair men. She not only tolerates these countless intrusions and hears me out; she often has a better notion than I do as to how such material could be most effectively used. It is due to her aversion to the use of the strained or artificial that I do not conclude these acknowledgments—as I had first planned—by lauding her as my "life preserver."

INTRODUCTION

In the spring of 1938 the English author Fryniwyd Tennyson Jesse wrote to her friend Grace Burke Hubble, the wife of the American astronomer Edwin Hubble: "I do not know whether the respectable newspaper which I am sure you and Edwin take, had an account of the trial over here known as the trial of the Mayfair men. Anyway I went to it. It was not an important trial but very interesting as a social phenomenon."[1] Jesse was well positioned to judge. As a self-taught criminologist, she was to edit several volumes in the Notable British Trials Series.[2] London society found the trial of the "Mayfair men" or the "Mayfair playboys" (as they were often called) absolutely riveting. Four young men in their twenties, all products of elite English public schools, and respectable families, had conspired to lure to the luxurious Hyde Park Hotel a representative of Cartier, the famous jewelry firm. There they brutally bludgeoned him and then made off with eight diamond rings that today would be worth approximately half a million pounds. Such well-connected young people were not supposed to appear in the prisoners' dock at the Old Bailey. Not surprisingly, the popular newspapers had a field day in responding to the public's appetite for information on the accused's pasts, their friends, and families. The trial is fascinating, and not simply for what it tells us about four young men's loutish behavior; the contemporary press and public of the 1930s saw that this court case revealed aspects of class, gender, politics, crime, and punishment that had otherwise escaped serious scrutiny.

This sensational robbery and the responses to it reveal several paradoxes. The first, and one that every historian of crime encounters, is that criminals— far from being asocial—are very much products of their society. As F. Tennyson Jesse argued in her popular criminological volume *Murder and Its Motives* (1924): "The criminal and the community are not two separate factors but one and the same thing. Over the gate of every prison there might with truth be carved this paraphrase of some immortal words: 'There but for the grace of God go I.'"[3] The court had the task of individualizing the guilt of the Mayfair men, but the worrying question hung in the air: to what extent were they representative of their class and generation?

A good deal of recent historical scholarship has looked at the issues of crime and punishment to see what they tell us about normative notions of class, race, and gender.[4] Trial reports have proven to be especially vital sources for understanding the lives of the poor, who rarely left their own written accounts. Social historians have repeatedly demonstrated how useful such an approach can be. Similarly, scholars such as Lucy Bland and John Carter Wood have shown how judicial records can be exploited to reveal by what standards women were judged in interwar Britain.[5] Bland in particular highlights the performative aspects of the criminal justice system, in which a woman's guilt or innocence often depended not so much on what she had done as on her ability to present herself in accord with current norms of respectable femininity. In the same way, when the courts dealt with the Mayfair playboys and their acolytes, the judges spent as much if not more time condemning them for being idlers and loafers as for being thieves. In effect the judge and prosecution defended the British class system by strenuously denying, with all the rhetorical skills at their command, the suggestion that either the accused's class background or education in any way fostered the sense of entitlement that led them into criminality. The court directed this message to both the Old Bailey audience and the far larger national and international newspaper readership.

Historians have long noted the obvious theatricality of trials, though court officials publicly did not.[6] When in June 1938 the crown tried a woman in Downham Market, Norfolk, for the strychnine poisoning of her husband, the local interest was so great that women fought for seats in the courtroom. A police officer, in attempting to restore order, made the plaintive plea: "Please be quiet. This is not a theatre."[7] But the women knew better. Likewise, some who attended the trial of the Mayfair men described it as better than any play. The audience was further titillated to hear the judge sentence two of the accused to be flogged. It could be argued that since neither the public nor the newspapers were allowed to witness the whippings, they were not theatrical performances. David Garland effectively counters such a view in observing, "Punishment has an instrumental purpose, but also a cultural style and a historical tradition."[8]

The figure of the playboy poses a second paradox. Women's history pre-dated the writing of histories of masculinity by a decade or two. Feminist historians have traced the public concern in the interwar period that the forces of modernity had endangered young women. Some feared that women would become oversexed, and that, in contrast, the stresses of the regimented work-place could render modern men effeminate, if not impotent.[9] Historians of masculinity, noting these concerns, have tracked the declining trajectory of manliness from the distant Victorian patriarch to the 1920s family-oriented suburban male.[10] British scholars writing in the 1990s noted that the domestication of men was complemented by post–World War I campaigns for their revirilization. Eugenicists and others preoccupied by the specter of demographic decline stressed the importance of sports and physical culture as a way of rein-vigorating men's bodies and minds.[11]

The press referred to the main characters in this study as "Mayfair men" or "Mayfair playboys" or simply "playboys." In the late nineteenth and early twentieth centuries there was a shift away from the cult of rugged masculinity toward a new model of "masculine domesticity." Yet British culture was far from being monolithic and supported both the men who fled domesticity and those who embraced it. The emergence of the playboy complicated matters. Where did one locate such a character—neither rugged nor domesticated—on the manliness scale? The trial of the Mayfair men popularized in Britain the term "playboy." This character represented a new style of masculinity, a style that historians have argued was not supposed to have surfaced until the 1950s.[12] The 1930s playboy was necessarily a different sort of creature from that conceived of by Hugh Hefner in 1953, but in what ways?[13] Sociologist R. W. Connell coined the term "hegemonic masculinity" to describe the social code that ad-vances the ideas and practices promoting the dominance of men and the sub-ordination of women.[14] For the purposes of this study what is most important in Connell's theory is his contention that masculinity is not monolithic, that hegemonic masculinity exists in tension with subordinate, marginalized forms of masculinity. It is here on the margins that we can locate our playboys. They certainly sought to control women, but as the following chapters demonstrate, they pursued a lifestyle that was quite distinct from that of normative British middle-class masculinity.[15]

Of course, men were often wracked by competing desires. Martin Francis points out that in the 1930s some were "attracted by the responsibilities of marriage and fatherhood, but also enchanted by various escapist fantasies (especially the adventure story or war film) which celebrated militaristic hyper-masculinity and male bonding."[16] What Francis does not note is that married, suburban men could also imagine the sophisticated life of the single man-about-town. One of the obvious reasons why the playboy figure received such attention in films, tabloid newspapers, and popular fictions is that he personified the desire to be free of domestic duties, to kick over the traces.

At first glance it may seem surprising that the indolent playboy should burst onto the scene in the 1930s, when so many were desperately seeking work. The decade was dominated by the repercussions of the 1929 crash, with the British economy bottoming out in 1932. Trade fell by half, heavy industry was down a third, and unemployment was over three million. Attempts by the government to impose austerity programs only made the situation worse. When the gold standard was finally abandoned in 1931, the pound lost 25 percent of its value. The devaluation did benefit exporters, and a slow recovery began in 1933. By 1938 people were sick of discussing the economy. Escapist film and tabloid accounts of playboys' antics were so popular in part because the social situation was so dire. This reaction against the shoddiness of traditional politics goes some way in explaining the popularity of two other charismatic womanizers whose political principles were problematic to say the least—Edward VIII and Oswald Mosley. The illustrated weeklies, in keeping the public up to date on the charmed lives of such celebrities, implicitly lauded the playboy lifestyle.

The newspapers referred to the accused in the 1938 trial as the "Mayfair men," knowing that this evocative term would have an immediate resonance for its readership both at home and abroad. Anglophiles around the world could name its boundary—Park Lane, Regent Street, Piccadilly, and Oxford Street. John Buchan, author of *The Thirty-Nine Steps* (1915) and other thrillers, set several of his novels there. "The West End of London at night always affected me with a sense of the immense solidity of our civilization," admits one of his heroes. "These great houses, lit and shuttered and secure, seemed the extreme opposite of the world of half-lights and perils in which I had sometime journeyed. . . . But tonight I felt differently towards them. I wondered what was going on at the back of those heavy doors. Might not terror and mystery lurk behind that barricade as well as in tent and slum?"[17] Buchan was shrewd to use Mayfair as his locale, as it was "familiar to readers all over the world as one of the most well-known and written about districts in London. Mayfair was the seat of diplomatic power, it sat next to political power, and it contained two royal palaces as well as embassies and government buildings. It

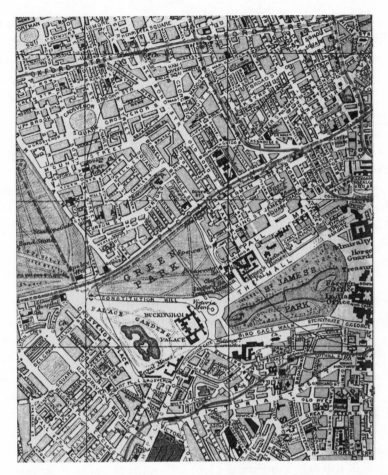

London's West End. *Bacon's Pocket Atlas of London* (London: G. W. Bacon, 1928).
Rare Books & Special Collections, University of British Columbia Library

was also the clubland zone, where Buchan heroes . . . belonged socially, and where young unattached men could encounter adventure."[18]

Some historians who have taken the "spatial turn" argue that the city is not just a locale but a character that, in offering anonymity and freedom from traditional restraints, helps shape the experience of urban modernity. A generation of historians has successfully demonstrated how studies of specific London neighborhoods can reveal much about social attitudes, power relationships, and economic disparities. The vast majority of these studies have focused on poorer neighborhoods. For example, on the East End we have the works of Seth Koven, Ellen Ross, John Marrriott, Gareth Stedman Jones, and Judith Walkowitz; on Soho those of Judith Walkowitz and Frank Mort; and on Holloway a book by Jerry White.[19] Most, if not all, of these scholars were drawn to the subjects living in these locales out of a sympathy and a concern to give voice to the marginalized or, in E. P. Thompson's words, to rescue them "from the enormous condescension of posterity."[20] The lives of the Hyde Park Hotel robbers may not elicit such sympathy, but they do illustrate, in morbidly fascinating detail, the many ways, both legal and criminal, by which members of the upper classes attempted to maintain their privileges and advance their interests. Even conservative writers like John Buchan, who sympathized with such tactics, acknowledged that London's West End was in its own way as mysterious as Whitechapel.

To understand the Mayfair men obviously necessitates locating them in their social milieu. In investigating the upper middle classes, this study risks once more being regarded as unfashionable. We already know more than enough, so the argument goes, about dead, white, wealthy men. Most social historians "study down"—that is, they seek to give agency to the poor, to women, to sexual and racial minorities. Focusing on the crimes and misdemeanors of the upper classes, by contrast, entails "studying up."[21] But far from glamorizing the upper classes, such studying up seeks to understand how they exploited their social advantages. From their families to public school to Mayfair to the Old Bailey, these playboys were supported by networks of friends and kin. They tended to be members of the same clubby elite who had been schooled in places like Harrow and Wellington, spent their weekends in the home counties and their holidays in France, drank in Mayfair and Soho nightclubs, and lived in London's West End. Only their clique could fully decode the sorts of purposely opaque news items so beloved of the *Times*.

The Atherstone (North) met at Shenton and had an excellent hunt from Sutton-Ambion. Going away over the Fenn Lane hounds ran very fast across the brook and over Harper's Hill to Stoke Lodge spinney. Swinging left-handed they crossed the Hinckley road and continued through Wykin to the canal at Higham Thorns, which they reached in 35 minutes. Turning back sharply they hunted more slowly by Wykin Hall and the Stoke Lodge spinneys to the Twelve Acre at Sutton-Cheney, and then crossed the Fenn Lane to Sutton-Ambion where a beaten fox escaped among fresh foxes after a fine hunt of over two hours. Hounds did not find again.[22]

Their pampered lives were proof that the British class system was still firmly in place. In the "London Gazette" and "Court Circular" columns of the *Times* appeared accounts of the elite's accomplishments—their engagements, weddings, dances, presentations at court, appointments, promotions, regimental dinners, transfers, and travels—as well as their occasional losses, including bankruptcies, divorces, and deaths. Such politics of display explicitly promoted a snobbishness and caste consciousness. The middle-class reader would have found it next to impossible to ignore this constant stream of flattering reports of who was doing what in society.

For the historian seeking to trace the emergence of new models of masculinity, the newspapers are an invaluable source. When young men began to call themselves "playboys" it was largely due to their following the media coverage of a number of sensational trials. These cases familiarized the public with a particular lifestyle and in effect served as a vehicle for the performance of new identities. Police reports, trial transcripts, and a range of published primary and secondary sources offer details about the investigation and proceedings, but newspaper reportage represents the best source for gauging the public's knowledge of and reaction to the doings of the West End elite. The *Times*, the leading broadsheet, was the newspaper of record and provides reliable coverage of the most important trials. The tabloids had much larger circulations. Alfred Harmsworth's *Daily Mail*, in the 1920s the world's largest paper, had two million readers by 1930 but was surpassed in turn by Lord Beaverbrook's *Daily Express* on the right and the *Daily Herald* on the left.[23]

The newspaper press was not monolithic. The most obvious difference was that the popular newspapers carried photographs. The broadsheets or quality papers like the *Times* and the *Manchester Guardian* did not, but maintained their traditionally austere design, devoting their front pages to advertisements. In contrast, the tabloids, along with the racy Sunday papers such as the *News of the World* and the *Sunday Pictorial*, depended on photographs and reports of sensational crimes, society scandals, and escapist fantasies to draw a mass readership. They devoted more space to court reporting than to any other category.[24] Observers assumed that the tabloids' gossipy style especially attracted women while the broadsheets' more intellectually demanding articles drew men. The quality papers gave their stories simple titles. The tabloids set out to seduce the reader with sensational banner headlines. The *Times*'s main articles on the Cartier robbery were "Diamond Ring Theft," "Robbery with Violence," "Jewel Robbery Charge," and "Jewel Robbery Sentences."[25] The popular papers responded with "Jeweller's Six Skull Fractures," "Thought He Was Going to Die," "Playboy Gangsters Had Flight Planned," and "Mayfair Playboy Gangster Weeps When He Hears His 'Cat' Sentence."[26] The two types of paper differed dramatically in style, but the content of their coverage of court cases was not that dissimilar.

Periodicals also differed in their political stances, which colored how they reported stories. Most papers supported the Conservative Party. A right-wing publication like the *Daily Mail* raised the specter of Bolshevik and trade unionist plots in the 1920s and applauded Italian and Spanish fascists in the 1930s. The *Mail* attacked scroungers, asserting that the dole produced "soft" men. The left-leaning *Daily Herald* responded that capitalism, in de-skilling labor, was responsible for creating an emasculated, effeminate work force.[27] The conservative press devoted countless column inches to well-off young men who came into conflict with the law. One might have expected the *Daily Herald* to have headlined reports of the disreputable conduct of the upper classes, but unlike its right-wing competitors it played down such scandalous stories, concerned that indulging in gutter journalism would detract from the paper's reputation for seriousness.

Films, too, helped publicize the character of the playboy. In the single year of 1934 there were in Britain an astounding 963 million admissions to the movies. One official report asserted that film was the "most important factor in the education of all classes."[28] Reviewing the movies' depiction of the playboy allows us to test Daniel LeMahieu's argument that in the 1930s filmmakers made a concerted effort to express sympathy for the plight of the working class while still appealing to middle-class consumers.[29]

The book consists of two sections. Part I gives a detailed account of the Hyde Park Hotel robbery and its aftermath. The attack on the Cartier representative, the theft of the diamonds, the testimony of the eyewitnesses, and the spotting of the suspects are described in chapter 1. The question of whether their capture was due to their incompetence or Scotland Yard's brilliance underlies the careful unpacking of the police investigation presented in chapter 2. In chapter 3 I introduce the main characters—John Lonsdale, Peter Jenkins, David Wilmer, and Robert Harley—and review all the information available on the suspects' families, schooling, social networks, and earlier brushes with the law. Within days of the robbery the police had arrested all four. Chapter 4 gives a thorough analysis of the trial of the Mayfair men—a sensation that enthralled London's high society—and the courtroom drama beginning with the accused viciously turning on each other and ending with their convictions. Chapter 5 follows our four felons through prison and their attempts, upon being released, to reintegrate themselves into society and probes the question why the media and the authorities believed some succeeded while others failed.

The first five chapters (about a third of the book) consists of a richly detailed account of the case—of the crime, the villains, their trial, and their punishment. This thick description provides us with an intimate portrayal of the world of the Mayfair men. Without losing track of these micro-narratives, we then turn to the larger picture. After the trauma of the First World War, the 1920s and the 1930s were decades of social, cultural and political renegotiation, a period of uncertainty in which the playboy arose and operated.[30] In part II we examine the social and cultural context in which the robbery was publicly dissected. This particular felony clearly struck a nerve, precipitating discussions of issues that obviously preoccupied the 1930s newspaper reading public. Or to put it the other way around, talking about the crime proved to be a useful way of grappling with such subjects as the emergence of new models of masculinity, the tenacity of social inequities, and the rise of fascism.

The courts sentenced two of the Mayfair men to be flogged. Chapter 6 provides an in-depth analysis of the corporal punishment debate, over which the Mayfair men cast a long shadow. Supporters of the cat-o'-nine-tails presumed it would be used against illiterate ruffians who only understood the lesson of pain, but how was one to respond when old boys of Wellington and Oundle had their backs bloodied? Chapter 7 provides a history of the "playboy" identity, explores the origin of the term, and tracks the ways a modernizing culture popularized a new style of masculinity. It seeks to explain how the anxious, who believed that a man's interest in fashion was a symptom of effeminacy, could at the same time hold him responsible for the unfair treatment of women in courtship, marriage, and divorce.

The 1930s was a period in which a generation of young men and women renegotiated their identities. Feminist scholars have written a good deal about society's alarm at the emergence of the flapper, bachelor girl, or modern woman. Historians have also produced insightful studies on the relationship of the homosexual and the metropolis. They have said little until now about young heterosexual males whom society regarded as behaving badly.[31] To trace the emergence of the playboy as criminal, chapter 8 introduces some additional shady characters. It begins with Victor Hervey, a ne'er-do-well aristocrat, and then compares him to other young men who ended up in the prisoner's dock. They set themselves apart from the middle class by flaunting an interest in fashion, seeking thrills in motorcars and airplanes, abandoning homes for hotels and nightclubs, and pursuing wealthy women. They made half-hearted attempts at securing employment, but preferred to live by their wits. Moved solely by self-interest they graduated from sponging and cadging to outright crime. Yet popular thrillers and films appeared in many cases to justify such predatory behavior. Chapter 9 moves the story away from individual Mayfair men to the class to which they belonged. Having well-off parents, an elite public school education, a place in London society, and an extensive network of friends did not prevent some in the 1930s from feeling relatively deprived, in particular those who proclaimed themselves the "new poor." The benefits the playboys enjoyed—instead of assuaging their cravings—goaded them on to steal that which they felt was their due. The discussion of class leads finally to the topic of politics in chapter 10. In the 1930s, those who debated such important issues as the rise of fascism and the turn toward appeasement often dragged in references to the playboy. Focusing on Lord Kinnoull and Oswald Mosley, both well-known playboys who switched their political allegiances, this chapter seeks to explain why commentators in the 1930s assumed that personal lifestyle choices were often predictive of a person's politics.

With hindsight one can see that the popular press presented the playboy's career as reflecting the experiences of the entire British nation. He emerged in the 1930s, part escapist fantasy figure whose adventures diverted a readership recuperating from the slump, part representative of an elite motivated by the unbridled pursuit of self-interest that led, so the story went, to appeasement abroad and a flirtation with fascism at home.[32] Then came the war, and newspaper references to the playboy all but disappeared. His sort was not supposed to exist in a country fighting a classless "people's war." Before long, however, propagandists saw the usefulness of resurrecting him, showing that the war offered the playboy—as it did the nation—the opportunity of redemption through self-sacrifice.

The ways in which observers commented on the Mayfair playboys evokes anthropologist Claude Lévi-Strauss's notion that some cultural groups found certain animals "good to think with" (*bonnes à penser*)—that is, they served as a vehicle for discussing and dealing with the tensions within the community.[33] Was the playboy "good to think with" for 1930s Britain? Social observers' interest was aroused not because there was a sudden surge in the actual number of hedonistic males but because the concept of the playboy proved useful for those trying to explain, or explain away, disturbing social shifts, particularly those involving relations between men and women.

Though the 1938 Hyde Park Hotel robbery and the responses to it have been long forgotten, there are good reasons for unearthing this episode. I do not intend to rescue the Mayfair playboy from the condescension of traditional historians. Rather, I want to determine why this disreputable character made so many appearances in discussions of crime, class, gender, and politics in 1930s Britain.

The *Daily Express* provided some of the most extensive coverage of the Hyde Park Hotel robbery trial. On the front page of its February 19, 1938, issue it included a bizarre photograph that showed Robert Harley (one of the accused) and five friends at a nightclub. The caption stated that he "was known by many famous people in the West End," but in fact the reader could only recognize Harley in the photo. As the paper explained, "A number of prominent people were there, and at their request the *Daily Express* has had all faces, but Harley's painted out."[34] The doctoring of this photograph graphically demonstrates the lengths to which some would go in seeking to distance the bad behavior of a handful of miscreants from the normal activities of the members of respectable Mayfair society. Countering such crude attempts to airbrush the past, this study firmly locates the Mayfair playboys in their social and geographical milieu.

Part I: The Crime

I N 1929, under the headline "Mr. Edgar Wallace on the Murder Men of Chicago," the *Daily Mail* reported that Britain's most prolific writer of thrillers had gone to the United States to gather material on the lives of gangsters. His apparent hope was that he could reinvigorate his fictions by larding them with references to ruthless "racketeers," victims who were "taken for a ride," or rivals who were "bumped off."[1] Wallace's obvious goal was to exploit the growing British fascination with accounts of American crime. In the 1930s and '40s English readers turned in increasing numbers to the sex and violence ridden American thrillers of James Cain and Mickey Spillane. Progressives such as Richard Hoggart and George Orwell considered this addiction to the hard-boiled school of American crime fiction a tragedy.[2] Such intellectuals could not understand why so many workers found American works refreshingly realistic. They did not appreciate that class-conscious readers judged the classic British detective novel, complete with country estate, bumbling bobby, deferential servant, and bourgeois amateur sleuth, too transparently a defense of the social status quo. Working-class readers felt far more comfortable in the hardscrabble urban worlds of Dashiell Hammett and Raymond Chandler. Workers sensed that the "tough guy" novel in which the legitimacy of the authorities was often questioned, spoke to their concerns.[3]

It was also the case that until the 1940s moviegoers in search of gangster films necessarily went to American movies. The portrayal of gangland was essentially an American enterprise. Some put it down to cultural differences or taste. The United States had crime bosses, Britain had villains. What few people at the time noted was that the British film industry's failure to portray criminal networks was not by chance, it was inevitable, given the British Board of Film Censors' resolute opposition to domestic productions that could be interpreted as in any way glorifying crime. The board had the power to prevent the making of films that depicted minor police indiscretions or momentary criminal successes.[4]

These restrictions help explain why no one produced a film devoted to the Mayfair playboys, despite newspapers around the world giving them extensive coverage. Indeed the British popular press provided the masses with the true crime stories that the film industry failed to deliver. The *Daily Mail* and *Daily Mirror* devoted more column inches to trial reports than to any other topic, and they bulked even higher in the Sunday papers.[5] In focusing on sensational crimes the popular papers of the 1930s were maintaining a century-old tradition, as were their critics, who at best regarded them as regurgitating escapist and distracting pap and at worst inspiring the impressionable to become copycat criminals.

The tabloids especially valued stories of the toff gone bad. Thanks to these popular papers it is possible to trace the careers of the Mayfair playboys from their trial backward in time to their childhood and schooling, their escapades and crimes, and forward to their convictions, punishments, and attempts at rehabilitation. The tabloids provided close-to-verbatim accounts of the leading trials and carried on the policy of publishing the "confessions" of the convicted. Their editors could in addition reprint easily accessible police depositions and witness statements. They customarily did not employ investigative journalists, even for the most sensational court cases.[6] As one historian has noted: "Newspapers often presented such cases as exposing a dangerous underworld to the purifying light of the public gaze, but they rarely undertook that task themselves."[7] Part I of this study responds to this challenge. It provides an overview of the world that produced, sheltered, and ultimately punished the Mayfair playboys. The narrative lays out who these young men were, the harebrained scheme they concocted, and the price they paid.

Chapter I: THE ROBBERY

Monday, December 20, 1937, dawned cold and wintry in London. On Sunday there had been snow at midday; ice and fog made driving treacherous and contributed to the interruption of commuter rail services. There were even delays on several underground routes, but not on the District Line that served Putney. It took little more than half an hour for forty-nine-year-old Etienne Bellenger to make his way from his home at 11 Lytton Grove in this quiet suburb south of the Thames to his office at 175–177 New Bond Street.[1] Bellenger was the managing director of the London branch of Cartier, the world's most famous jeweler. Founded in 1847, the Parisian firm catered to Europe's elite. It particularly prided itself on being the official supplier of gems to the British royal family. Edward VII famously referred to Cartier as "the jeweler of kings and the king of jewelers."[2]

That Monday afternoon, a little before 3:00 p.m., the Cartier offices received a phone call from a guest at the nearby Hyde Park Hotel. A gentleman identifying himself as Captain Hambro stated that he was about to be engaged to a wealthy young woman, and he wanted a variety of expensive diamond rings brought to his hotel suite for his appraisal. The rings had to be "of a certain value"—he cited the figure of £4,000 per ring—because they would represent part of the marriage settlement. Apparently pressed for time, the client rang off with the brusque injunction: "Don't be long."[3] Bellenger immediately selected nine rings and was at the hotel by 3:15.

Why wasn't this extraordinary request—an unknown client asking for thousands of pounds of jewelry to be brought to his hotel room—simply dismissed out of hand? The answer was class. Any suspicions that Bellenger might have harbored were effectively countered in the first instance by where the request originated. The opulent Hyde Park Hotel—ostentatiously flaunting its turrets, balconies, and pillared porticos—was located at 66 Knightsbridge, one

The Hyde Park Hotel

of London's most prestigious addresses. In 1889 investors built the massive red brick structure as a gentlemen's club, then transformed it in 1908 into a grand hotel. Its guests included many of the royals and a wide range of celebrities, including the combative Conservative Party MP Winston Churchill, press baron Lord Beaverbrook, popular author Evelyn Waugh, and Indian nationalist leader Mahatma Gandhi. It boasted richly furnished ballrooms and restaurants, as well as its own private entrance to Hyde Park. Its terrace offered a perfect vantage point for watching the Household Cavalry's morning exercises.[4]

One would naturally assume that a guest at the Hyde Park Hotel would have had his or her bona fides established, but the guest who called Cartier was not just anyone; he had registered as Captain P. L. Hambro of Wimborne Court, Dorset. The Hambros were a well-known financial dynasty. C. J. Hambro, a Danish merchant, established the Hambros Bank in 1839. In the twentieth century, Angus Valdemar Hambro was Conservative MP for South Dorset. His brother Sir Eric Hambro was Conservative MP for Wimbledon and was, coincidentally, on Cartier's board of directors. Sir Charles Hambro, chairman of Hambros Bank, was also a director of the Bank of England.[5] Given the family's social prominence, it is hardly surprising that Bellenger should have responded to a Hambro call with such alacrity.

Once at the hotel, Bellenger found that he had to wait a few minutes as his client was momentarily engaged. At 3:30 the liftman took Bellenger up to the third floor where in the hallway he met the tall young man who called himself Captain Hambro. He led Bellenger to room 305 and introduced him to another young man who acted as his secretary. The formalities concluded, Bellenger presented the nine rings, pointing out their most attractive features. Two of the diamonds were rectangular; seven were emerald cut (that is, octagonal). They ranged in size from 5.06 to 10.69 carats. Smaller diamonds decorated the shoulders of the rings. The settings were platinum. Cartier valued the jewelry at £16,000, approximately sixty-four times a factory worker's annual wage.[6]

The three men compared the brilliance of the gems in the natural light streaming in from the windows and chatted briefly about Cartier's rivals, the jewelers in Hatton Garden, and the general question of the resale value of diamonds.[7] Finally the customer asked to see the gems under a desk light. This obliged Bellenger to turn his back to the communicating door that led to the adjoining room, 309. As he did so he caught sight of the secretary making some sort of signal. In response a third man immediately launched himself from the next room into 305, attacking the jeweler with a weighted cosh, or life preserver. Bellenger turned just in time to catch a glimpse of his assailant, whose features were half hidden by a pair of tinted glasses and a colored handkerchief, covering in bandana-fashion the lower part of his face.[8]

The intruder rained blow after blow down on Bellenger's head, but being a large man endowed with an unusually thick skull, the Frenchman persisted in fighting off his attacker, hitting out at his spectacles. At this stage the so-called secretary yelled, "Come on, finish it quick!" and tackled the jeweler, who, being brought to the ground, received an additional four painful cracks to the skull. The young man who had posed as Hambro simply sat by and observed the uneven fight. Amazingly enough, Bellenger, though he received fifteen blows to the head, never lost consciousness. Nevertheless, exhausted and outnumbered, he gave up the struggle and collapsed on the floor.[9]

At about 4:20, Henrietta Gordon, a housemaid who not only worked but also lived in the hotel, heard some unusual noises—like something being smashed—coming from room 305. She later told the police that she remembered the hour as that was "the time I have to call a titled lady." She alerted Enrico Laurenti, a waiter, who detected what he thought sounded like "muffled laughing." The two domestics listened at the door and initially heard nothing more, but two minutes later the gentleman whom Laurenti had earlier served that day came out of room 305 and, partly walking, partly running, dashed down the hall. A moment later a second man emerged from 305 and strode briskly to the lift. Gordon noted that the second man was laughing, had a fashionable "teddy bear coat" negligently draped over his arm, and "had the most beautiful set of teeth."[10]

Concerned that something was amiss, Gordon and Laurenti knocked on the door of 305. When they received no response Laurenti used his master key to get in. He was shocked to find a large man lying on his back in a pool of blood. The waiter's first instinct was to prevent Gordon from entering. "For God's sake don't come in, get the manager or get somebody." He called the porter to try to apprehend the two men from 305, but they had already fled the hotel. He then phoned the manager, Mr. Burdett, who in turn called the police and a doctor.[11]

In the meantime Laurenti thought it wise to put up a screen by the open door to hide from public view the disturbing crime scene. A small side table with two broken legs lay on the carpet along with a large diamond ring and a ring box. Laurenti picked up the ring and put it and the box on the mantelpiece. In the center of the room lay a man with a split skull whom the maid first thought was dead. Revived, he managed to cry out, "Help, help," and repeated again and again, "They've got my rings."[12] Taking towels from the bathroom, Gordon did her best to clean and comfort him until the doctor arrived.[13]

Dr. Victor Constad got to the hotel along with the police at a little after 4:30. He found Bellenger fully conscious "in spite of the terrible battering he had obviously received."[14] The maid, the waiter, and the doctor lifted him onto a couch. He had received at least a dozen head wounds and manifested the classic symptoms of traumatic brain injury. His left arm was paralyzed, and one side of his face was uncontrollably quivering.[15]

Detective Inspector Henry Hayward of Scotland Yard led the first police on the scene. In the room the detectives found a diamond ring and ring box, a pair of tinted glasses, a Chesterfield cigarette package, a depleted bottle of whiskey, several glasses, and a soda siphon. Bellenger gave a brief if somewhat garbled account of the robbery before being rushed by ambulance to the Beaumont House Nursing Home (off Marylebone High Street), the doctor telling the officers that it was impossible for him to provide a prognosis.

Based on what Bellenger and the hotel staff told them, the police began to sketch out a picture of the assailants. All the witnesses agreed that at the very least three men were involved—the one who called himself Captain Hambro and booked the room, his "secretary," and the man who wielded the cosh. All three, according to Bellenger, were in their twenties and wore dark lounge suits.[16]

The hotel staff had had the most contact with the first suspect, who had arrived at 1:20 that afternoon. They described him as a tall man with a pointed chin and nose. He called himself Captain P. L. Hambro of Dorset and asked for a suite. He stated that he would be staying until Christmas Eve and that his luggage would be arriving later in the afternoon.[17] Reginald Sidney Kelly, the receptionist, recalled the man insisting, "I want a single bedroom and sitting room," but not caring if the suite faced the park or Knightsbridge. Kelly assigned him 305 and 309.[18]

The young man ordered a bottle of Black and White whiskey and a siphon, adding, "And send along some glasses." Since he had no luggage the receptionist asked him to pay for the drink in cash. Kelly was suspicious, in part because he noted that the new arrival kept his gloves on, even when signing the registration form. He told the other receptionist that he thought the client might be a "bogey" or fraud.[19] He certainly was concerned about money. At about 1:45, Enrico Laurenti, the waiter on duty, took the bottle of whiskey to 305. As he was about to leave the guest, sprawled on a couch, asked, "What about my change?" Laurenti pointed out that there was no change, as the pound the guest had given was just sufficient to cover the costs of the drink.[20]

It was that elusive something, the style or bearing of the suspects, that the hotel staff most remembered. James Clarke, one of the liftmen at the Hyde Park, thought he might recognize at least one of the men he took to the third floor at about 2:00 p.m. He was between twenty-four and thirty years of age, five feet ten inches tall, and dressed in a blue-gray, double-breasted overcoat, belted at the back. To Clarke he looked like "a traveler" or salesman, for he did not have "the accent of a cultured and well educated person."[21]

Sloan, another liftman at the hotel, reported taking to the third floor a smartly dressed man, twenty to thirty years of age, about six feet tall, with dark brown, brilliantined hair. "This man spoke like a gentleman and gave me the impression of being rather effeminate."[22]

When Sloan later took Bellenger up to the third floor, William Peter Jefferies, one of the hotel's receptionists, who had been told by his colleague that he was doubtful about the man in 305, accompanied him. In the hallway he found a tall man asking the way to 305. Jefferies told the police he had a pointed nose, wore a blue suit and red carnation, and was "very good looking in an effeminate way."[23] Kelly recalled a man with dark wavy hair, good teeth, wearing a blue pinstripe suit, red carnation, and white gloves, but no hat or overcoat. "He was exceptionally well dressed and walked and spoke rather effeminately. He was well spoken but I could not trace any particular accent."[24]

Henrietta Gordon gave a similar account of the scene. She said that the new guest had taken the wrong direction and she had to direct him to room 305. She described him as a slim, tall man, sporting a red carnation and wearing a blue suit with the trousers riding high. "He was definitely like a pansy boy—a proper 'Sissy.'" His associate, in Gordon's opinion, had a more "gentlemanly appearance."[25]

The men of London's B Division, working from the Gerald Road Police Station, located between Victoria Station and Sloane Square, carried out the police investigation. One of the first acts of the Metropolitan Police was to broadcast a bulletin stating that they sought for questioning three smartly dressed young men.[26]

> Three men; 1st, gave name P. L. Hambro, b. 1911, 6ft., slim build, h. dk. brown (wavy), sharp pointed nose turning slightly to l., pimply face, good looking; dress, blue suit (white pin stripe).—2nd, b. 1902 to 1907, 5ft 10in., medium build, h. brown (brushed back); dress, dk. suit, lt. teddy bear overcoat (buff colour), no hat.—3rd, b. 1917, 5ft 10in., slim build, h. fair; smartly dressed. All effeminate in manner.[27]

Though the police first reported that they sought P. L Hambro and two others for robbery, they soon realized that the chief suspect had merely presented himself as a member of the banking family.[28] They learned in addition from

Angus Hambro that though several members of the family lived in Dorset, Wimborne Court itself did not exist.[29]

Concerned that the suspects might try to leave the country, Special Branch sent descriptions of the three men and the jewels to police detachments at Dover, Folkestone, Gravesend, Grimsby, Harwich, Holyhead, Hull, Newcastle, Newhaven, Southampton, Plymouth, and the port of London, and to the airports at Croydon, Heston, and Lympne.[30] Scotland Yard's Information Room instructed officers to alert pawnbrokers and jewelers about the robbery and have them provide information on any gems offered for sale. To rouse the public's interest, Lloyd's of London, the insurer, offered a reward of £1,500 for information that would lead to the arrest of Bellenger's attackers and the recovery of the rings.[31]

As so often happens with criminal cases, the Hyde Park Hotel robbery, sensationally reported by the press, drew the attention of cranks who peppered the police with misinformation. On December 21, Jack Davies, of Kentish Town, telephoned to say he knew that the robbers would meet that night to dispose of the loot. He dramatically concluded: "I cannot say anymore now as I believe I am being 'tailed.'"[32] That was the last the police heard of him. An anonymous female correspondent had an equally vivid imagination. She wrote to say that she had just seen going into a bookstore on Artillery Row a man who had been connected a few years earlier with a group of robbers. "This man would not be in England unless it would be for some Business," she warned. Having read of the plundering of Cartier she knew he must be involved. "This tall elegant effeminate man usually has a smart suite of rooms in a fashionable square of London & has an extraordinary fascinating manner & if he is with a gang are [*sic*] most dangerous. I know because I met most of them a few years ago while chaperoning an actress. I will not sign my name. It would be too dangerous."[33]

Despite such red herrings, the police owed their most important lead to the actions of yet another private citizen. The breakthrough came when Cyril Smith, a night porter at the Clarendon Hotel in Oxford, informed the local police that on the morning of December 21, at about 6:30 a.m., three men arrived from London in a four-seat, gray saloon Jaguar. Apparently unfamiliar with the car, they had to ask Smith to open the trunk. The youngest of them, though pale and trembling, asked if a suite was available. Two of the travelers registered and the hotel gave them a large room with two beds. Their companion drove off in a northerly direction. Ending his shift at 9:00 a.m., Smith had the chance to read the morning newspaper accounts of the previous afternoon's robbery.[34] Could these three well-dressed fellows, he asked himself, be the men the police were looking for? It was hard to understand why they would have left London at 4:00 in the morning.

Smith reported his suspicions to the local police, who in turn informed Scotland Yard. Inspector Arthur Rolphe of the Oxford police went along to the Clarendon, taking several constables with him. There the maid told him that the new arrivals had had tea in their room but asked her not to put on the light or draw the curtains. Going to the room Rolphe found that the two who had registered as Lammer and Jamieson now identified themselves as John Lonsdale and Peter Jenkins. The former stated that he was a company director and a steward of the Greyhound Racing Association and gave as his address Wimborne, Dorset. Jenkins, a handsome young man, said he was an accountant with Lester Parry and Company at 11 Great Marlborough Street, where he worked with his brother, Gerald Jenkins. When the police turned up, Jenkins was still in bed, and the blond-haired Lonsdale was dressing, but neither seemed obviously perturbed by this unexpected visit. They readily admitted having read about the robbery. On one of the beds lay a copy of the *Daily Mail*, which contained a full account. Their story was that they had been at a Mayfair "bottle party" (an after-hours drinking establishment) the night before and in the wee hours of the morning decided to drive up to Oxford with a friend who was visiting relatives in the neighborhood. He was to pick them up later.[35]

Rolphe left two constables to keep an eye on the suspects while he sought London's advice. At 12:45 the men left the hotel to cash a check and then went to the Mitre Hotel where Jenkins asked a page boy (who later described him as a tall, "very good looking" gentleman) if he could "very quickly" arrange a phone call to Ladbroke 0707; when he got through, a woman answered.[36] The two suspects then attempted to slip out the hotel's back door, but finding the police waiting for them, they finally lost their composure. "We are tired of being chased around like a couple of criminals," complained Lonsdale, "and we are getting the 1:47 train to London. Where can we get a taxi?" They were indeed to return to London, but under police escort. Chief Inspector Leonard Burt in London had told Rolphe that the facts that the men's descriptions matched that of the suspects and that Lonsdale and P. L. Hambro both gave Wimborne, Dorset, as their home address were grounds for insisting that the three visitors be detained, brought back to London, and subjected to a thorough interrogation.[37]

Chief Inspector Burt took the 4:45 train from Paddington up to Oxford where he met the now indignant suspects, who demanded to see their solicitors. Lonsdale was particularly excited, insisting that he be shown Burt's warrant card. What proof was there that he was a policeman? When that ploy failed, Lonsdale asked to see Burt privately. He now told the chief inspector that he was linked to the Secret Service and had important information for the War Office. It was imperative he make calls to London and Paris. When asked who his contact was in the Foreign Office he could only think of a chap in Copenhagen. His final claim was that he was an agent for an arms company—Hermann Zollinger of Limmatquai 94, Zurich, Switzerland. Burt was unmoved.[38]

In the meantime the police located the third suspect, the driver of the car, when a call came in to the Clarendon Hotel for "Mr. Lammer," the name Lonsdale had registered under. It was from a David Wilmer at Blockley 227, the number of Sir John Porter's home near Moreton-in-Marsh, one of the principal market towns in the northern Cotswolds, approximately thirty miles to the west of Oxford. At 4:45 on December 21, Sergeant Thomas H. Smith of the Gloucestershire Constabulary went to Keytes End, Bourton-on-the-Hill, the home of Sir John and Lady Porter. The police had a complicated relationship with the upper classes. One officer recalled in his memoirs of how, in pursuit of a jewel thief, he once had to negotiate with a haughty woman who was offended by his simple request that he be allowed to search her house. "She considered me as though she suspected some fault with the drains."[39] Smith was accordingly cautious. He first had to talk to the Porters and Brigadier Wilmer, David's father. They finally let him speak to David, a young man whose most notable feature was his dark, artificially waved hair. He admitted knowing the other Londoners. "Yes, I know Lonsdale and Jenkins. I brought them to Oxford today." Having cautioned and arrested him, Smith drove Wilmer to Moreton-in-Marsh. He did not seem to understand the seriousness of the situation, asking the constable: "Can we stop at the Chemists. I must get some peroxide. I use it every day to clean my teeth." When the policeman did not answer, he repeated his request.[40] The Gloucester police handed Wilmer over to Inspector Robert Fabian, who had come up from London with Burt. He brought Wilmer back to Oxford that evening. The Gloucestershire Constabulary, who searched the Jaguar, reported finding six gloves, one pair of lady's gloves cut to fit a man, slightly stained with what could have been blood, one jewel case, one piece of flex, and one small metal casing.[41]

In London, the police added Robert Harley as the fourth man to the list of suspects. They knew he had ties to the three other men. This linkage alone clearly did not provide evidence of his involvement in the robbery. Nevertheless, on the afternoon of December 21, Inspectors Fabian and Hayward accosted him at the Queen Street Post Office. "We are Police Officers," declared Hayward. "A jeweler was attacked in the Hyde Park Hotel yesterday and robbed of a number of valuable rings." "I know, I have read about it," replied Harley, a powerfully built, mustachioed man in his mid-twenties. He protested his innocence but, given that he fit the description of one of the suspects, agreed to come to the Vine Street Police Station to provide an account of his movements on December 20.[42]

In Oxford, having missed the last train back to London, the three Londoners and six police officers set off at 11:00 p.m. in two motorcars for the capital. The suspects had driven up to Oxford in a luxurious Jaguar. In order to return them to London, the police, who had at their disposal only one modest Morris 12, had to borrow a car belonging to Superintendent Norman Goodchild of the Oxford police. If the police were embarrassed by their lack of resources they made no mention of it in their report. They also made no explicit reference to the detained men's class. It was nevertheless highly unusual for them to deal with such well-dressed gentlemen. John Lonsdale, Peter Jenkins, David Wilmer, and Robert Harley had been apprehended. The question was: who were they?

Chapter 2: THE INVESTIGATION

In the 1930s the authorities recorded about 80,000 offenses each year in the 700 square miles of London's Metropolitan Police District. Setting aside the Special Branch, the chief constable had at his disposal 1,000 detectives, 150 working out of Scotland Yard. They had access to 60,000 photographs of rogues and over half a million sets of fingerprints.[1] With the news of the attack on Cartier's representative, this elaborate machinery swung into action.

When the police arrived at the Hyde Park Hotel they first spoke to the victim, Etienne Bellenger. Bruised and bloodied, he was understandably confused. He gave a description of his attackers but was not sure which of them had pushed him to the floor. And although he spoke of bringing eight rings to the hotel, he had actually brought nine. He believed all were taken, but the police had found one on the floor during their search.[2] They then interviewed the hotel staff. They searched rooms 305 and 309. Chief Inspector Frederick Cherrill, superintendent of the Fingerprint Bureau of New Scotland Yard, was soon on the scene.[3] By 6:30 he had taken prints off a whiskey bottle, two tumblers, and a siphon.[4] He returned the bottle, one-quarter full, to the hotel manager. That night the officers who rushed to the hotel combed the West End in search of the assailants. Scotland Yard publicized the reward on offer, passed on descriptions of the villains to local police stations, and sought the help of those who traded in diamonds. All these undertakings appeared to have been rendered unnecessary when, the next morning, the Oxford police phoned London to announce that three suspects had been apprehended.

Chief Inspector Leonard Burt, who was later best known for his work on counterespionage and security after the war, was in charge of the investigation.[5] Among his colleagues he had a reputation for being a gifted interrogator, and that was the skill required at this stage of the case. Having detained the likely suspects, the police no longer had to be concerned with detection and capture.

Their goal now was to extract from the suspects a full account of the events of December 20.

The Judges' Rules stipulated that a police officer should first caution before questioning or taking a statement. He repeated the caution when making a formal charge: "Do you wish to say anything in answer to the charge? You are not obliged to say anything unless you wish to do so, but whatever you say will be taken down in writing and may be used in evidence." The rules held that the police were not to cross-examine or question anyone making a voluntary statement. When they charged two or more persons with the same crime, they had the accused read, correct, and sign their statements and exchange copies. The rules stated that the police were not to suggest that the accused had to reply to their confederates' statements.[6]

Burt's best hope was that one or more of the accused would provide a full confession. At the very least he knew, as a seasoned interrogator, that when two or more individuals were charged with the same crime they almost always abandoned their loyalty to each other and sought to save their skins. It was almost inevitable that each would attempt to minimize his own culpability while shifting the blame onto others. Burt's tactic was to separate the suspects, have them produce their self-serving accounts, and then give them each other's statements to goad them into making further disclosures.

In Oxford the three suspects were first asked to give an account of their movements on the afternoon of December 20. The blond-haired Lonsdale reported that he had had a full day: he had brunch at a Lyons' Corner House at 1:00, then went to the Monseigneur Cinema in Piccadilly, met a Mr. Wilby (manager of the Florida nightclub in Bruton Mews), between 3:30 and 4:00 was at the Quebec Hotel on business, then called at his father's place at 155 Gloucester Terrace, proceeded to the Coburg Court Hotel where he made two calls to Paris, took afternoon coffee on the Edgeware Road, and returned home at about 5:45.[7]

Jenkins, the best looking of the three, gave a shorter but equally bland account of his uneventful afternoon in London's West End. He had had a 1:00 p.m. lunch at a Lyons' tea shop on Coventry Street, killed some time wandering about Mayfair, and had coffee at the Kardomah in Piccadilly; from 3:15 to 5:00 he was with his accountant, Lester Parry, then returned to his hotel before going out that evening to Jack's Bar in Mayfair, where he got "pretty tight." He had had dinner on Curzon Street, met Wilmer, and together they went to the 19th Club in Cork Street around midnight, where Lonsdale joined them.[8]

Wilmer was not cooperative and would only state: "I drove down from London to Oxford in my friend's car. My friend being Mr. Blacker-Douglas of 31 Hans Place, London. We started at about 3:30 am this morning and arrived at Oxford at 6:30 am and Bourton-on-the Hill at 8:30 am to stay with my aunt, Lady Porter for Christmas, and I dropped Lonsdale and Jenkins at Oxford."[9] He refused to sign an official statement.

In London, on December 22 at the Gerald Street Police Station, the suspects were more forthcoming. The advice their solicitors offered no doubt played a role. Lonsdale now stated that on December 20 between 12:15 and 12:45 he was at Stewart's Restaurant on Bond Street, where Jenkins, Wilmer, and a man he did not know told him of their scheme to use an expensive hotel room as a front in which by some ruse they would trick a jeweler out of his gems. He warned them that the plan was unwise and dangerous. He would not participate. Nevertheless, that afternoon at about 2:30 out of curiosity he rang up their hotel room. "We have got a bottle up here," Wilmer told him. "You might as well come up and have a drink." He popped in for a few minutes and was relieved to see there was little likelihood of anything resulting from his friends' undertaking.

Lonsdale made repeated references to his supposed involvement in the arms trade. After the drink at the hotel he said he went off to confer with Wilby— "who has been financing me for the sale of Mausers" (rifles)—and on to see his father, who was going to Paris that night "to protect my interests in the deal which I have referred to before." He made some calls to Paris and dined with his father at Bertorelli's near Westbourne Grove. Lonsdale was at a friend's (John Davies of Ivor Court, Gloucester Place) at 11:00 p.m. when Wilmer called. Lonsdale and Davies joined him at the 19th Club. Jenkins and Richard Blacker-Douglas were also there, as was the man who had been at Stewart's, who was now introduced as Michael Harley. Lonsdale stated that Jenkins appeared very nervous and asked for money. Lonsdale refused, telling Jenkins he would only spend it on drink. They all moved on to an after-hours drinking establishment (referred to as a "bottle party") next door to the Florida nightclub. Lonsdale claimed he was now quite drunk and "for no particular reason" opted to go off with the others to Oxford. They arrived about seven, and since it was too early to impose on Wilmer's aunt he and Jenkins took a room at the

Clarendon. At a coffee stall by the train station he saw a newspaper report of the robbery. To his amazement Wilmer and Jenkins now told him they were involved in the affair but had had no idea that it would result in a violent assault. They added that when Harley "who had stayed in the suite unbeknown to them had attacked the man most savagely," they lost their nerve and fled. Harley took all the jewels. What should they do? "Harley had apparently threatened them with physical violence if they did not keep their mouths shut." This explained why they had drunk so much the previous night. But because he too was tired and hungover, Lonsdale claimed he did not fully realize the significance of what he heard, and went to bed.[10]

In Oxford, Wilmer had been taciturn; in London he declared that he was now ready to make a "clean breast of it."[11] His story was that he, Lonsdale, and Jenkins had cobbled together an amateurish plan of peacefully palming a diamond from a distracted jeweler. It was not clear exactly how they would do it. "Our idea was really unformulated and our plan of action was left to chance in that if an opportunity of getting possession of the jewellery did not occur, Jenkins was simply going to say he needed time to consider the matter." The fourth person involved was to help facilitate their escape "and also he had arranged to carry, some adhesive plaster, a fixed strip which he might be able to slip over the man's mouth if he were manoeuvred near the door of the bedroom."[12] But the fourth person's attack on Bellenger was completely unexpected. Neither Jenkins nor Wilmer played any part in the assault. Horrified by the bloodshed, they immediately fled. Indeed, Wilmer claimed that he was so "absolutely terrified" that he had trouble walking normally down the hotel steps.

Later that same day Wilmer made further admissions: First, he named Harley as the fourth man, the man who not only attacked Bellenger but took possession of the loot that same night. "At this time Harley was endeavoring to dispose of the jewellery." Second, Wilmer admitted he was responsible for dumping Harley's weapon at a tube station. "In the taxi Harley gave me the instrument he used wrapped up in the spotted scarf he had covered his face with and told me to hide it in a public lavatory, which I did."[13] He reiterated the argument that he was not fully responsible. "My mind is still very misty regarding my movements after the assault, perhaps due in some part to the whiskey I had drunk and did drink subsequently as well as fright."[14]

In his December 22 statement Jenkins similarly stressed that the crime was not thought out. In his telling it was no more than a drunken lark that got out of hand. One evening at his flat the three friends had all complained of being short of money. They dreamed up a plan to book a hotel room under a well-known name and have a jeweler bring round an expensive engagement ring, hoping that by some scam they would relieve him of it. There was never any suggestion of employing violence; they envisaged a simple confidence trick. Wilmer had included Harley at the last minute, as he supposedly was in contact with a fence. It was otherwise understood that Harley's only duty was to transport the rings. Meeting at Stewart's Restaurant at 12:15 on December 20, they worked out the final details of the operation. Jenkins described how he bought a carnation and took a taxi to the Hyde Park Hotel, where he booked a suite. Wilmer joined him shortly after 2:00 p.m. Harley showed up sometime later. Lonsdale popped in but stayed for only a few minutes. Cartier's representative at first said he was not sure if they could send someone over, but soon telephoned to say that they would.

Jenkins asserted that Harley's attack on Bellenger was completely unforeseen. "The next thing I knew Harley was coming from the bedroom. . . . I saw one of his arms raised with an object in his hand. He looked desperate and I flew out of the place and got on a bus to Knightsbridge."[15] That evening Wilmer phoned him to say something terrible had happened and they should meet at Jack's Bar. Jenkins arrived to find Harley and Wilmer in a taxi outside. They proceeded to the 19th Club, where Lonsdale joined them about 11:00 p.m. They finished the night at the bottle party. Harley had the rings. "I was definitely under the influence of drink but I remember Harley showing me a handful of diamond rings in a café in Curzon Street." Wilmer's advice was to lie low. He was going off to visit his aunt in the country. Lonsdale and Jenkins decided to accompany him as far as Oxford.[16]

By the night of December 22 the police had received a fairly full summation of the Hyde Park Hotel robbery. Lonsdale admitted to consorting with the three others but insisted that he had cautioned them not to attempt anything rash. He did not know a robbery had been committed and knew nothing about Harley's assault until Wilmer and Jenkins informed him in Oxford. The stories that Wilmer and Jenkins told were slightly different. They conceded that they had had the silly notion of acquiring a diamond by some sleight of hand. But whereas Lonsdale said the idea was theirs alone, they included him as one of the architects of the plan. They all concurred, however, that they never envisaged that violence would occur and consequently were terrified when Harley pummeled Bellenger. They had been stupid and drunk. Harley had been vicious. He had wielded the cosh and taken the rings. If anyone were guilty of robbery with violence it was Harley. Where was he?

Robert Honey Fabian, one of the best-known Scotland Yard detectives, claimed the credit for solving what he called in his memoirs "the case of the Mayfair Playboys."[17] He asserted that the morning after the robbery an informant phoned to say that the night before he saw several "geezers" with rings in a café "palled-up with a fence."[18] He didn't know them, but "they looked like proper college toffs to me." From Fabian's photo collection of people on the margins of high society, cut out of the glossy weeklies, the grass, or informant, identified Harley. At 1:55 on December 21, Fabian and Inspector Hayward accosted Harley at the post office in Queen Street, and he agreed to accompany the officers to the Vine Street Police Station.[19]

In his first statement on December 21 the mustachioed Robert Harley (also known as Michael Harley) stated that he had not done much on December 20. He visited his ill brother and left his coat with him. He lunched at Stewart's but saw no one he knew. Between 6:00 and 7:00 p.m. he was at the Spotted Dog, where he bumped into David Wilmer. They had several scotches and then went to some other pubs; he was too drunk to recall which ones. He heard that someone said he looked like one of the robbery suspects, but he had not been at the Hyde Park Hotel in a long time.[20] His account was dutifully recorded, but even as he spoke detectives were finding evidence that undermined his story.

At 4:00 p.m. on December 21 police went to 50a Curzon Street, a block of service flats, apartments that offered hotel services. Harley had rented flat 14 since December 7. In his rooms investigators found an empty Chesterfield cigarette packet that matched the one discarded at the Hyde Park Hotel. Detective Inspector Percy McDouall more importantly discovered in a writing bureau drawer two "life preservers."[21] In Fabian's self-aggrandizing account he and Hayward were the ones who, in searching Harley's rooms, found the cigarette package and a bill for life preservers.[22] He also claimed he knew Harley was associated with Lonsdale and Jenkins.[23]

Peter James Kearney, a valet at Curzon Street, later provided helpful information on Harley's associates. Wilmer had visited Harley on several occasions, the last time being the evening of Sunday, December 19. On Monday, December 20, Harley went out at 10:00 in the morning, returning Tuesday morning. And Harley wore, the valet recalled, a distinctive "teddy bear coat."[24]

In his autobiography Fabian says he knew Harley but does not mention how. Harley was in fact a police informer. When he was formally detained on the morning of December 22 he asked if he could see Fabian privately. He then asked him if he could talk about their relationship. Fabian said he could. At the same time Fabian independently informed his superiors that he had known "Mike Harley" as an informer since October 20, 1937.[25]

The informant (spy, grass, or nose) according to Cecil Bishop, a Scotland Yard veteran, was crucial in real policing, though rarely mentioned in thrillers. One set a thief to catch a thief. Each officer jealously guarded his own informants. The public, most policemen, and the underworld despised such spies, but many felons could find no other source of work and relied on the money paid out of the "Information Fund." Bishop warned that normally they should not be called to testify in person, for in court they were easily discredited. Judges understood that the names of informants would usually not be provided. When giving evidence the police officer would simply say, "From information received, I understood that . . ."[26]

In his second statement Harley placed his actions in this context. If his behavior were suspicious, he argued, it was because he was a police informer. He had called Fabian at Gerrard 2604 on Sunday, December 12, and left a message. He called again on Saturday, December 18, and told him he could alert him to an important event that would occur the following Monday or Tuesday. His account of his movements on December 20 was cryptic. He said that much of the day he attended his sick brother at 22 Wright's Lane, Kensington. Leaving his distinctive teddy bear coat at his brother's, he departed for the Hyde Park Hotel, arriving at about 4:15. He was there for only fifteen minutes. He did not say how, but that evening he came to have the rings in his possession. As it was too late to hand them over to the authorities, he hid them. His plan was to contact the insurers the next day, but as he was coming out of the post office at about 2:00 p.m. on December 22 he ran into Fabian and Hayward, who took him along to Vine Street, where he made his first statement. Harley underlined that he had helped Fabian in a similar situation once before. In the case of the Hyde Park Hotel robbery he insisted that his sole object was to get the insurance money. In other words he simply wanted the reward offered for the return of the diamonds. He now realized that he had acted foolishly and concluded by saying either "We'd better go and get the stuff" or "And now I'll take you to the rocks."[27] In any event, at 2:00 p.m. Burt and Hayward accompanied him to a small, first-floor room at 22 Wright's Lane. There Hayward found hidden behind the waste pipe of a washbasin two sealed envelopes. Inside were eight diamond rings.[28]

The tabloids were to attribute the capture of the four Mayfair men and the recovery of the rings to a "brilliant police investigation." In reality the utter incompetence of the robbers was their undoing. They had neither disguises nor alibis prepared, and no flight plan in place. The *News Chronicle* reported that a pilot offered to fly them to Belgium, but they did not have the £150 he demanded.[29] Most important of all, they failed to do what any seasoned jewel thief knew was essential: have a fence standing by who—paying a small percentage of the true value of the gems—would dispose of the loot within a few hours.[30]

To confirm Harley's role in the robbery Burt had him participate in an identity parade. Burt had the first attempt scrubbed when Harley objected that he was the only tall man in the lineup. After the police found the rings they organized a second parade, at 5:00 p.m. Sloan and Clarke, the lift operators from the Hyde Park Hotel, thought they had seen Harley before, but they were not sure when. Their testimony, complained Burt, was "useless." More troubling was that none of the other witnesses recognized him.[31]

At this stage Burt showed Harley the statements of Jenkins and Wilmer implicating him in the assault on Bellenger. He responded by making a further statement, which attempted to shift the blame back to them. He now admitted that on December 20 he left his flat at 10:45 to meet Wilmer and then went to Stewart's Restaurant to join Jenkins and Lonsdale. It was Jenkins and Wilmer who proposed that he knock out the Cartier representative. "A definite proposition was put to me by both Wilmer and Jenkins that I should hide in a suite and knock him out when they had maneuvered him into a suitable position. As I had anticipated that they had intended only a confidence trick I was naturally taken aback, but I tentatively acquiesced."[32] He pretended to agree, but only so as to know where and when the robbery would take place. In making it clear that he was not going to be the fall guy, Harley sowed further seeds of dissent. "I wish to add that I was not particularly surprised at their suggestion of violence, as, in the previous case in which I assisted Inspector Fabian, Wilmer suggested in front of my brother and another witness that I do practically the same thing to Jenkins to obtain his £655."[33] Harley insisted that he only had gone to the hotel at about 4:30. Entering via the Buttery Entrance, down a passage by the barbershop to the lobby, he ran into Wilmer, who was hurrying to the front exit. They went together by taxi to Green Park

Station and on to Piccadilly, where Wilmer used the toilet.[34] Harley made this statement at 9:30 p.m. on December 22. At 10:00 a.m. the next morning at the Westminster police court Burt showed it to Harley's confederates.

The police were unhappy with the staff of the Hyde Park Hotel for their difficulties in identifying the suspects. This was brought home when the *Daily Mail* splashed photographs of the four accused on its pages on December 24.[35] As a result, on December 27, Reginald Kelly, a receptionist at the hotel, identified Jenkins as the man who had engaged the suite under the name P. L. Hambro.[36] William Peter Jefferies, Kelly's colleague, in reviewing the photos recognized Wilmer as the man who was on the third floor when Bellenger got out of the lift.[37] Thanks to the pictures, Enrico Laurenti identified Jenkins as the first man and thought Harley "resembled" the second.[38] Sloan in a further statement admitted he picked out the wrong man in the identity parade. From the press photos he was now certain it was Jenkins, not Harley.[39] Clarke went to the identification parade at the Gerald Road Police Station on December 22 and picked out Harley whom he remembered having seen at the hotel on December 20. But Harley was not the man he had described in his original statement.[40] Henrietta Gordon recognized Jenkins and Harley in the *Daily Mail* photos but could not identify anyone in the December 22 lineup.[41] Saying that she could recognize the suspect by his teeth, Gordon asked Harley to take his hand away and smile, but she still failed to recognize him.[42]

The police tracked down other witnesses. Jenkins had been staying at the New Clarges Hotel since about December 10. The hall porter stated that Wilmer and Harley had visited Jenkins on December 20, between 10:00 and 1:15. Jenkins was out all afternoon, returning in the evening between 5:20 and 6:00.[43] Greta Vaughn, housekeeper at the Mayfair Hotel, Down Street, Piccadilly, said Lonsdale was a guest there from December 14 to 20, registered under the name of Mainwaring. At around 2:00 p.m. on December 20 she saw him drinking in the lounge with Wilmer and Harley. She had seen this group together on previous occasions. When asked to settle his bill for £3 19s. 6d., Lonsdale said he would pay at 6:00 p.m. To the question, "Can you rely upon that?" he replied, "Absolutely." Overhearing Wilmer wondering aloud if she wanted money, she snapped: "Yes, I do." They left at 2:15. Harley was wearing a teddy bear coat, Lonsdale a navy blue coat, and Wilmer a camel hair coat.[44]

Despite the spotty quality of the eyewitness evidence, within a few days the police believed that they had gathered enough material to warrant the Department of Public Prosecutions going to trial. They had the incriminating statements of the four accused. All were socially well connected but probably had been in-volved in previous cases of fraud and larceny. Lonsdale was a deserter. If he had not participated in the robbery he nevertheless was part of the conspiracy that led to it.[45] There was now bad blood among the accused, and Burt believed that at the very least Jenkins would testify against Harley. Harley had a reputation for vio-lence, but no convictions. He had, in Burt's words, put "forward a fantastic and carefully thought out story of assisting Police and restoring the property to the insurance assessors."[46] The police in addition had physical evidence. They had the hotel registration written in Jenkins's hand. They had found Wilmer and Jenkins's fingerprints on the drinking glasses used in room 305.[47] In Harley's flat, detectives had uncovered two life preservers, with cord attachments iden-tical to the cord found at the Hyde Park Hotel. Burt was pleased to report, "A representative of Messers Gamages, Holborn, will say that at about 2 pm the day of the robbery he sold two life preservers to a man answering the description of Harley."[48]

At Westminster Police Court on December 23, before Magistrate Ronald Powell, the four men were charged with robbery with violence. Powell granted an application to allow Wilmer to see his wife and Harley to see his brother.[49] Because of Bellenger's condition the judge refused to grant bail to the accused. He extended their remand, and they continued to be held in custody at Brixton Prison.[50] In January, Vincent Evans, director of Public Prosecutions, added the charge of conspiring to commit robbery.[51] As there was no evidence of Lonsdale being at the hotel at the time of the attack on Bellenger, his barrister argued that he should be discharged. The magistrate disagreed, pointing out that there was a conspiracy and he was charged with being an accessory before the fact—that is, he had aided and abetted others to commit a crime.[52]

The police were confident that within a matter of days they had tracked down all the Hyde Park Hotel robbers. Others were not so sure. Several infor-mants asserted that Lonsdale's friend Victor Hervey was also involved.[53] Her-vey's name came up in a report Detective Constable W. Chamberlain and Detective Sergeant Heathfield of Kent County submitted to the commis-sioner. An informer told them that Hervey was the gang's ringleader. In De-cember he was supposedly in France or Germany collecting loot from other jobs and was three days late returning. As a result the others panicked and bungled the robbery at the Hyde Park Hotel. Stewart Cappel, eighteen to nineteen years of age, was a friend of the four accused and, along with his sister Betty Cappel, about twenty, visited Lonsdale in Brixton on January 14 or 15.

Stewart, having suspicious amounts of money on occasion, the informant said, was somehow involved in the robbery. The informant was afraid that if the gang found out that Cappel passed on information they would punish him.[54] The snitch concluded by suggesting that if the rings had not yet been located, he could help. A few days later another unnamed informant, being questioned about his link with Lonsdale and Harley, mentioned the relationship between Lonsdale, Hervey, and Stewart Cappel. The authorities knew that Lonsdale and Hervey were involved in delivering arms to the Spanish right-wing rebels. The informant said that Stewart Cappel was also engaged in the scheme and all three could be connected to the Hyde Park Hotel robbery.[55]

Burt set out to squash these rumors. Writing to the superintendent, he said that it was true that Miss Cappel of 26 Basil Street, Knightsbridge, visited Brixton Prison on January 14, but she saw Wilmer and Jenkins, not Lonsdale. Turning to the report of the superintendent of the Kent County Constabulary, who had suggested that Victor Hervey was an accomplice of the four accused, Burt stated categorically: "I know the Hon. Victor Hervey, son of Lord Hervey, very well, and I am aware that he is associated with the four men in custody, but I am satisfied that he is in no way implicated in the matter of robbery which is now before the Court."[56] Despite such assertions, there were some who continued to believe that Hervey's relationship with the Mayfair playboys had yet to be clarified.

The solicitor Reginald Thomas Philip Bennett, of Speed and Company, also played a shadowy role in the proceedings. Wilmer claimed that he spent most of December 20, the day of the Hyde Park Hotel robbery, dealing with Bennett. Harley sought similar cover. On December 30, Horst Robert Leopold Bonsack informed the police that the day of the robbery a man believed to be Harley offered Bennett £100 to support his alibi. According to Bonsack the unscrupulous Bennett had once been struck off the Law Register. He added that Jenkins had been robbed of £600—probably by his colleagues—but had not called the police. Bennett somehow resolved the dispute.[57]

Equally mysterious was the fact that the cash-strapped Harley suddenly came into a sizeable amount of money. In early February the governor of Brixton Prison notified Scotland Yard that Harley's brother had visited the prisoner. A prison officer sat in on the meeting and reported that Harley told his brother (now living at 171a High Street, Kensington) to see Mr. Ellis Lincoln, of 118 Upper Street, Islington—a solicitor who had not until now acted for Harley. He wanted Lincoln to help him open a bank account with £1,000. He asked his brother to contact A. Kramer (Wilmer and Lonsdale's solicitor), who would give him a sealed packet that he was to take to the bank. He was not to tell Harley's current solicitor, Emanuel Garber, anything about this transaction, but he was to reassure Lincoln that it was "perfectly honest money." On the way back to his cell Harley appeared anxious to tell the officer that these transactions were necessary since his old bank asked him to close his account with them.[58] But where did the money come from? What did he do to earn it? Was he being paid to take the fall for the Hyde Park Hotel robbery or, at the very least, not to compromise a wealthy friend?

The police did not pursue such issues. They congratulated themselves on a job well done and split the £80 of reward money provided by Lloyds. Chief Inspector Burt received £21, Detective Inspector Fabian £17, and so on down to Detective Lewis at £5.[59] Burt noted the trial "created unusual interest and publicity."[60] He recognized the assistance provided by the police in Oxford (who were given £20); Moreton-in-Marsh, Gloucestershire; Newbury, Berkshire; and Andover, Hampshire.[61] In London most of the investigation was the work of B Division, with help from Fabian from C Division and Inspector Cherrill of the Fingerprint Bureau. Burt particularly hailed the contribution of Fabian, who was responsible for Harley's second statement and the handing over of the rings. A March report praised the work of both Burt and Fabian. Without their skillful handling of the prisoners, it stated, difficulties would have arisen. What the police meant by this cryptic remark was not clarified. Did it relate to their use of informants? Or aggressive interrogation techniques? The author of the report restricted himself to mysteriously concluding, "The details of it do not and cannot appear on this file."[62]

Scotland Yard's work did not end with the filing of the robbery charges. Between the time of the arrests of the suspects in December 1937 and their trial in February 1938 police and newspaper reporters in Britain and North America continued to collect information on the backgrounds of the four young detainees. The result was a detailed and disturbing portrait of the dark side of London's polite society.

Chapter 3: THE SUSPECTS

In constructing an image of the Hyde Park Hotel robbers the press drew as much from popular notions of the lives of the rich as from police reports: "Four men who gate-crashed parties, night clubs and restaurants. All of good family, all four public school boys, one the son of a general. High life they certainly had—all of them. They followed the sun, they travelled in luxury, they spent thousands of pounds seeking pleasure. They gambled, they bickered over the finer points of rare wines, they were pictured in magazines as fashionable-young-men-about-town."[1] The writers of such gossipy accounts called the suspects "playboys" and projected onto them what they believed to be their audience's desires and fantasies. Readers often found the results entertaining, but a deeper look at the checkered pasts of these four young men on the make reveals more about their possible motives, and about the society in which they operated.

John Christopher Mainwaring Lonsdale was in some ways the most marginal of the four suspects. The twenty-four-year-old Lonsdale—plump, with his blond hair already thinning—had been born in Alberta, Canada, in 1914. Though his ties to the country were tenuous, the Canadian press took a perverse pride in referring to him as a "Calgary native."[2] In fact he came from a well-respected English family whose home was the Further House, Wimborne, Dorset.[3] His grandfather, the Reverend John Henry Lonsdale, had spent some years as a barrister with chambers at 4 Kings Bench Walk before being ordained in 1887 and appointed to the curacy of Wimborne Minster.[4] He had two sons. Arthur, the younger, educated at Radley and Trinity College, Cambridge, was killed at Neuve Chapelle on March 13, 1915.[5] The elder, John Claude Jardine Lonsdale, born in 1889, immigrated to Canada in 1908, when he was only eighteen.[6] Georgina Beatrice, his future wife, had come as a child in 1900. In 1916, John Claude Lonsdale and Georgina Beatrice Lonsdale were living in Macleod, Alberta, with their two-year-old son, John Christopher.[7]

During the war John Claude came back to Britain and enlisted in the Third Battalion of the Dorsetshire Regiment; he was promoted to second lieutenant and later captain.[8] He returned to Canada once the conflict ended. The 1921 census had the Lonsdales living in Ellice, Manitoba. In fact they appear to have been quite peripatetic, which was often a signifier of migrants' inability to establish themselves. Passenger lists document a number of the young John Christopher's trans-Atlantic crossings. The family finally settled in England, John Claude becoming a successful businessman well known in the City.

For whatever reason, John Christopher failed to win the public respect garnered by his father and grandfather.[9] This was despite having every social advantage. He was educated at Radley College (founded in 1847), a prestigious independent boarding school for boys on the southern outskirts of Oxford. He left Radley in 1929, head of the upper modern sixth. He learned French in Lausanne and claimed to have studied for the diplomatic service in Munich, Paris, and Berlin, though he never stated exactly when or where. Similarly, one has to take at face value his boast that at eighteen he worked in Paris as secretary for the American actress Marilyn Miller.[10]

We do know that at nineteen Lonsdale enlisted in the King's Royal Rifles. Apparently garrison life did not suit him, and his father bought him out.[11] In November 1933 he joined the RAF and was appointed an acting pilot officer. He served briefly in Egypt. In 1934 his short service commission was terminated, and he was discharged for overstaying his leave in Marseilles, making false statements, and issuing worthless checks.[12] Under the name of "Trevelyan" that same year he joined the Dorsetshire Regiment, in which his father had served. He once again regretted his decision, but rather than be bought out, he simply deserted. His unit still listed him as a deserter when he was detained in 1937.[13]

Lonsdale drifted into ever more serious forms of criminality. In November 1933 he insured his jewelry through Cox and Kings Insurance Ltd. In January 1934 he put in a claim and received in return a check for £7 8s. 6d. at the No. 4 Flying Training School, RAF, Abu-Sueir, Egypt. But in February, now living in Paris, he asked for a stop payment order to be made on the check and a fresh one drafted. When the Hotel Ritz discovered that he had pocketed the cash from the second check and used the first invalidated check to pay his restaurant bill they went after his insurers, who in turn informed the police.[14]

Given Lonsdale's shady reputation it was ironic that his sole financial coup resulted from winning a slander suit. Miss Pamela Blake, the twenty-year-old daughter of Lady Twysden, of Nea House, Highcliffe was the defendant. The case went to trial on June 17, 1936. Norman Birkett, regarded by many as Britain's most formidable barrister, represented Lonsdale. He charged that on March 6, 1936, Miss Blake—portrayed in the press as a "young society girl" or debutante—told a girl at the Florida nightclub in Bruton Mews, Mayfair, that Lonsdale had a venereal disease. "Moon (which was the pet name of another girl) is going out with John Lonsdale, who has the——." On March 7 at the bar of the May Fair Hotel she went on to assert that Lonsdale had inherited the complaint from his father. "He (the plaintiff) has hereditary——. That is why——[another girl] dropped him."[15] In the witness box, Lonsdale adamantly denied that there was any truth in the allegation. He presented himself as indifferent to any financial compensation but driven by an honorable desire to curb destructive gossip. "There is too much loose talk going on in Mayfair. Reputations are ruined by the lightest whisper or innuendo which grows alarmingly as it is passed on."[16]

Birkett stressed that Lonsdale's conscience compelled him to take legal proceedings. He insisted that his client was not seeking a large monetary reward; he simply sought the vindication of his honor. Nevertheless, a meaningful penalty had to be provided, Birkett asserted, as Lonsdale's reputation had been severely damaged.[17] For a businessman like Lonsdale, who claimed to be the assistant secretary to the International Exchange and Clearing Corporation Ltd., a financial house in the City, such a disparaging attack could entail real costs.[18]

No defense was offered. Pamela Blake's solicitors, Joynson-Hicks and Company, had written to Lonsdale's solicitors on April 17: "She desires through us to convey to your client her unqualified apology for any pain which her words may have caused him. She is also prepared to do all that she can to put the matter right, and with this end in view, is agreeable to signing any proper form of apology and withdrawal you think fit which your client can show." In court her counsel added: "I ask you to bear in mind that this girl is only 20 years of age, and however much one regrets that she should publish such slanders, you cannot expect a person of that age to have the restraint and wisdom of people of more advanced age."[19] The sitting judge was not impressed. In his summation, Lord Hewart said that it would be difficult to imagine anything more disgusting or repulsive than Blake's statements. She now admitted that there was not a word of truth in the disgraceful allegations. He concluded his stern lecture in awarding Lonsdale £500 damages.[20] Lonsdale would meet Birkett and Hewart again in less happy circumstances two years later. For the moment, however, he was triumphant.

Miss Blake married a few months later.[21] Though Lonsdale won his slander case, in so doing he lost a marriage. He had launched his suit in April 1936. On May 1, 1936, the press employed the traditional formula in announcing that "a marriage had been arranged" between John Lonsdale, son of J. C. J. Lonsdale of Wimborne and Mrs. Lonsdale of Paris, and Evelyne, younger daughter of Mr. and Mrs. Mervyn Wolseley of Sutton Park, Guildford.[22] Miss Wolseley initially supported Lonsdale. The press quoted her as saying:

> I knew John was innocent of all the nasty things that were said about him and I was determined to clear his name. He knew nothing of the beastly rumours until I told him and we immediately started to trace them to their source. I believed John so completely that when he proposed to me after he had started the action, I accepted, knowing full well his honour would be vindicated in the courts. It is unfortunately true that Mayfair is a hive of gossip and I hope that the action in which John has succeeded will help towards putting an end to such scandal mongering.[23]

Her parents were undoubtedly unhappy to see the sexual health of their future son-in-law made a subject of tabloid discussion. The trial in mid-June took its toll. On June 27, the *Times* carried the announcement that the Lonsdale-Wolseley marriage would not take place.[24]

Lonsdale had other projects on the go. He appears to have learned to fly in the RAF. Like many wealthy young men in the interwar period, he regarded the airplane as offering new technological powers that the elite had to recognize and embrace. He was associated in some way with the right-wing National League of Airmen, established in 1935 by the press baron Lord Rothermere, publisher of the *Daily Mail* and a fascist sympathizer. Rothermere's plan was to use a group of young pilots, led by Norman Macmillan and Montague Smith, to impress on the public the need to catch up to Germany in the race for air power.[25]

In 1936 Lonsdale met the Honorable Victor Hervey, a rich and notorious ne'er-do-well. The two young playboys discovered that they not only had similar interests in flying and conservative politics. They were also both excited at the prospect of the money that could be made in gunrunning to the combatants in the Spanish Civil War. A detailed account of their undertaking is provided in chapter 10. Here it only has to be noted that they failed completely. Hervey incurred enormous debts. He was declared bankrupt at the age of twenty-one, to the tune of £124,000.[26] Lonsdale, needing to ferret out some means of surviving, fell back on fraud.

Lonsdale spent most of 1937 in France. Some of his activities came to the notice of the authorities. In November 1937, Rudolph Slavik, a barman at the Hotel George V, complained to the Paris police that Lonsdale had used a bad check to defraud him of 1,000 francs. When he heard of Lonsdale's arrest in England, he appealed to Scotland Yard for assistance but was informed that Lonsdale, who was awaiting trial, had "no means." Therefore nothing could be done about the check stamped "returned R.D." ("Refer to Drawer," meaning payment suspended).[27]

Élie Lévy made a more serious charge. Lévy, a Parisian jeweler, asserted that Lonsdale had swindled him out of a ring worth 85,000 francs. The Paris inspector general wrote to the commissioner of police in London that on December 10, 1937, a warrant had been issued obliging Lonsdale (who now called himself a journalist) to appear before the juge d'instruction près le Tribunal de la Seine. Following the crime the police detained his "maitresse" Madame Souriat Chardanoff (née Chakoff). Lonsdale was freed "sous caution"—released on bail—but before the judge could rearrest him, he had left for London.[28] Élie Lévy never received compensation, but he and his family did manage to escape France in 1944.[29]

December 1937 found Lonsdale back in England. On his return he at times went under the name "Mainwaring" so as, he insisted, to avoid entanglements in Hervey's bankruptcy proceedings. Despite his many career disasters and encounters with the law, Lonsdale still maintained the image of living well. He boasted that his life of dueling, arms smuggling, gambling, and socializing with internationally known actors made the adventures of the average "thriller" look tame in contrast. Reporters recalled him dining at the Savoy and the San Marco.[30] For a fraudster, appearances are everything. When the police arrested Lonsdale, the well-dressed young man had on his person a mere two shillings, nine pence.

On his return to England, Lonsdale had contacted David Wilmer, whom he had known for close to two years. Wilmer, who was the most socially well connected of the four, came from a military family. His father, Brigadier-General

Robert Paul Harley, J. C. M. Lonsdale, and Peter Jenkins.
Evening News, Feb. 16, 1938. © The British Library Board

Eric Randal Gordon Wilmer, was born in India in 1882, the son of Colonel J. R. Wilmer of the Indian Army. Eric Wilmer enlisted in 1900, served in World War I, and spent many years thereafter in India. In 1935 he was replaced at Poona and retired to England.[31] Much of his time was subsequently taken up by his duties as secretary of the War Commemoration Fund and other charities supported through Artillery House.[32]

In 1910 at Ticehurst, Sussex, Eric Wilmer married Marjory, the daughter of Major-General Richard Worsley. The local press listed the names of the guests and the jugs, sauceboats, picture frames, inkstands, ashtrays, toast racks, candlesticks, sugar sifters, saltcellars, egg holders, scent bottles, salvers, tea sets, cigarette boxes, sugar bowls, and coffeepots—all in silver—given as presents.[33] Marjory's sister, Edith Dorothy Worsley, married Sir John Scott Horsbrugh-Porter, son of Sir Andrew Marshall Porter.[34] Horsbrugh-Porter was an important figure in Gloucestershire.[35] In May 1935 he led the jubilee festivities honoring the twenty-fifth anniversary of George V's coronation, and in January 1937 he helped organize the celebrations in Bourton-on-the Hill for Edward VIII's coming to the throne.[36] The Wilmers were part of this comfortable social circle linked by marriage, politics, and professional interests. Their invitation to the marriage of Major Edward Latham and Lady Gwendoline Jellicoe, daughter of Earl Jellicoe, Admiral of the Fleet, at Langham Place was one indication of their elite social standing.[37]

Eric and Marjory Wilmer had two sons and one daughter. Their daughter, Thea, married Lieutenant Richard Jenner-Fust of the Royal Navy. He was killed in action in the Second World War; his two brothers were reported missing and assumed dead. In 1951, Thea wed Captain G. F. Spooner of the Royal Air Force, a leader of the British Schools Exploring Society.[38]

The Wilmers' two boys attended Oundle School in Oundle, Northamptonshire. Founded in 1556 by the Worshipful Company of Grocers of the City of London, it promoted games and strong ties with the Church of England. John Whitworth, the future Air Commodore, was there at the same time as David Wilmer. Other notable old boys included Cecil Arthur Lewis, cofounder of the BBC, and Joseph Needham, the scientist and historian.

Frederick Clive, the Wilmers' younger son, entered the school in September 1930, giving the family's address as 26 Cheyne Row, Chelsea. He went on to officer training at Sandhurst and then served in the Second World War. The Oundle School magazine, the *Laxtonian*, listed him as one of the prisoners of war whom the Japanese released in 1945.[39]

David Wilmer, the eldest son, was born in London, October 6, 1913.[40] When he entered Oundle in 1927 he gave as his father's address The Senior Officers School, Belgaum, India. At school he played cricket and boxed as a featherweight, losing the sight in one eye as the result of an accident.[41] After leaving Oundle in July 1930 he supposedly went on to study at Neuchâtel and Heidelberg, but these universities have no record of his registering as a regular student.[42] Friends later reported that he also was a chorus boy in the 1932 production of *The Miracle*, a musical starring Lady Diana Cooper, the famous society beauty.[43]

David Wilmer broke with family tradition in not going into the military. The *Times* reported that he worked briefly as a clerk and then as a trainee for an advertising agency, where he was to earn the handsome sum of £500 a year. He apparently did not allow business to get in the way of pleasure, squandering his allowance of £6 a week in drink and dancing.[44] In July 1937 his employer fired him, "it being thought undesirable that he should frequent night clubs."[45] Nevertheless the *Daily Express* still portrayed him as "a highly paid advertising agent living in Charles Street, Berkeley Square."[46] There is little evidence of his holding a regular job. There are, however, many reports of the active involvement of this "debonair playboy" in London society.

Described by the police as about five feet ten, slim, and "smartly dressed," Wilmer was proud of his success with women. Presumably he had his hair waved to increase his attractiveness. But if he presented himself as a playboy, he was willing to try marriage. In October 1935 the press announced that David Wilmer had married Hilary Inez Elizabeth, elder daughter of Mr. and Mrs. John White of 20 Thurlow Place, SW7.[47] Hilary was only eighteen. The newlyweds were happy for a few months, but in January 1936, according to her, "He then went out late at night and went away at week-ends." She asserted that he was promiscuous and boasted of it to her. He treated her terribly and could not be trusted "financially or otherwise." Finally he wrote stating that he would not return to her, and she had him watched. The public were outraged that Wilmer deserted his wife just before the birth of their child, but appearances could be deceiving. The divorce law at the time required that one party had to be guilty and one innocent. As the courts refused to recognize amicable separations, the husband customarily played the role of the villain. Accordingly in February 1937 Wilmer sent his wife a letter and an incriminating hotel bill indicating that in January and February 1937 he had committed adultery in a hotel in the Strand.[48]

Hilary Wilmer was emotionally involved with Patrick Gamble. Surprisingly enough, Wilmer was to use his estranged wife's lover in constructing an alibi for December 20. Wilmer was to claim that he spent the day of the robbery collecting papers "relating to a Mr. Patrick Gamble's prospects under his grandfather's will—taking these to Messers. W. H. Speed & Co., Solicitors of Sackville Street, and discussing the possibility of raising some money for Mr. Gamble on his expectations with Mr. Bennett, Principal of the firm."[49]

Wilmer knew how he could use charm to ingratiate himself in the eyes of his social superiors. Having had some experience in advertising no doubt heightened his appreciation of ways to curry favor. At the same time he had a nasty streak that expressed itself in physical attacks on social inferiors. On

December 26, 1936, Wilmer and a friend, Anthony Lyon-Clark of Egbury Grange, St. Marybourne, near Andover, got drunk. At the Chequers Hotel in Newbury they came across a dance. When they tried to enter they were informed that it was a private party. Enraged at being refused entrance, Wilmer "struck an official in the face breaking his false teeth." The schoolmaster who was the victim of the assault did not make a formal complaint as he was promised the matter would be settled out of court.[50]

The Boxing Day celebrations were not yet finished. At about 2:00 a.m. Wilmer and Lyon-Clark turned up at an inn, the Three Legged Cross in Crux Easton, on an isolated stretch of road south of Newbury. They roused Fred Greenaway, the licensee, to tell him that their car had skidded and gone into a ditch. He had to help them get it out. Greenaway, a fifty-five-year-old veteran recovering from pleurisy, refused and suggested they go to the nearby village of Highclere for help. They left. Thirty minutes later they returned and this time demanded accommodation. Greenaway, speaking to them from an upstairs window, refused to come down and let them in. Once again Wilmer found such insubordination maddening. He smashed one of the inn's windows and threatened to continue: "if you don't let me in I'll smash every——window in the place." Opening the door to confront the attackers Greenaway found himself hit in the face and ribs. Wilmer admitted punching him, but Greenaway believed he was hit with something heavy like a spanner. Wilmer elsewhere boasted of carrying a knuckle-duster.[51] Greenaway's wife ran for help and the police arrived. Wilmer told them that Greenaway had pushed him and in response he had instinctively lashed out, not realizing the publican's age.[52]

Wilmer was charged with assault and willful damage. The case was to be heard on February 26, but the day before the hearing Greenaway went into a meadow with a shotgun and took his own life.[53] The case was adjourned until April 2. The inquest heard that Greenaway was worried about the upcoming trial and his mind was possibly unbalanced. His wife stated that he was chiefly concerned about getting a young gentleman into trouble. His doctor agreed that while the innkeeper had suffered no serious physical injuries, the prospect of testifying depressed him. As a result of there being no victim, the court withdrew the assault summons and instead charged Wilmer with willful damage. His legal counsel presented him as a hard worker, and employers provided supportive references. Wilmer was convicted at the Kingsclere Petty Sessions of willful damages for which he was fined £5, plus £2 10s. for damages and £16 15s. 6d. costs.[54] It is not possible to say exactly what lessons Wilmer drew from

DAVID WILMER *aboard a yacht during a recent holiday.*

David Wilmer. *Evening Standard*, Feb. 18, 1938.
© The British Library Board

these brushes with the law. One could surmise, however, that he might well have concluded that with money and luck the most difficult situations could be resolved. This was a view obviously shared by the other three suspects.

At twenty-one, Peter Martin Jenkins was the youngest and, despite a few pimples, the best looking of the four detainees. A review of newspaper reports and civil records allows one to sketch in the backgrounds of Harley, Wilmer, and Lonsdale. Jenkins's autobiography, *Mayfair Boy* (1952), in some ways makes the task of tracing his early years much easier.[55] His book has to be used with caution, however, as he clearly had a selective memory and set out to produce a self-serving account.

Peter Jenkins was born in St. John's Wood, London, September 13, 1916. Walter Martin Jenkins, his father, was a successful wool merchant, earning in the late 1920s, so his son claimed, the enormous sum of £30,000 a year. Cobb and Jenkins tweeds were sold around the world out of its head office at 11 Great Marlborough Street, a building erected for the company in 1910 to the design of the architect E. Keynes Purchase.[56]

The Jenkins family had a London residence at 1 Duchess Street, W1, just off Portland Place, but Peter's happiest memories were of their country house, "High Chimneys," a grade II–listed building (as of 1950) in Burgess Hill, West Sussex. In this handsome eighteenth-century red brick farmhouse his mother oversaw a large staff of domestics, including a chauffeur who drove the family Rolls Royce.[57] The Jenkins lived well. When Joan, the only daughter, married, she had her reception, Peter proudly recalled, at the Hyde Park Hotel.[58]

The family's money made it possible for Peter to attend Harrow, one of England's most exclusive independent schools. Located in Middlesex, to the northwest of London proper, this famous institution was founded in 1572 by John Lyon under a Royal Charter of Elizabeth I. One of the original nine public schools that were defined by the Public Schools Act of 1868, its famous old boys included several prime ministers (among them Baldwin, Peel, and Palmerston), many foreign statesmen, members of both houses of Parliament, and numerous princes and maharajahs.

Peter Jenkins was at Harrow from 1930 to 1932. He then spent some time at a more modest institution, Hurstpierpoint College.[59] It is possible that because of some infraction, he was encouraged to make the move. He made no mention of the latter school in his autobiography, preferring to dwell on the socially influential friends he made at Harrow. He did appear to be more candid in regretting that he let down his old school. He justified himself to a degree, arguing that if he had not applied himself to his studies, it was because he believed that his father's wealth guaranteed that he would always be taken care of.

He finished school in 1934. Unaware of his father's financial problems, which had their origins in the 1929 crash, he began learning the wool trade. The story that he told repeatedly thereafter, and one the press was only too happy to retell, was that having been brought up in luxury, he was totally unprepared when his father admitted to having lost most of his money. The family suddenly had to cut back on expenses, moving to a flat at 40/44 New Cavendish Street. Walter Martin Jenkins died soon thereafter, in December 1934, and his wife Evelyn followed in 1935.

In the spring of 1935, the *Times* carried a notice asking creditors and others with claims on Jenkins's estate to submit their demands.[60] Peter, only nineteen at the time of his parents' deaths, was far from being penniless.[61] His father left a sizeable inheritance, although probably not the £52,000 Peter claimed. He found that £5,000 had been placed in trust for him, his father obviously having doubts about his ability to handle money. Only when he turned twenty-five was he to have unfettered access to the bequest.

Peter did not wait. He moved into a flat in South Bruton Mews, close to the Florida nightclub, and plunged into a hectic round of partying. By his own account he attended all the main events of the 1935 season—Ascot, Wimbledon, Henley, and the Eton-versus-Harrow cricket match at Lords. A reporter who interviewed Jenkins in 1937 found him at 8:00 p.m. dressed in silk pajamas and a silk dressing gown. He was drinking brandy and attended by a French secretary. He instructed the journalist: "Call me a Mayfair playboy." Though recently robbed, he claimed that money was of little importance to him. He took pleasure in stating that he had just returned from the Riviera, where he spent up to £100 a week.[62]

The image he had of himself in dressing gown and pajamas was, in his words, "quite worthy of Cecil Beaton."[63] In comparing himself to a well-known bisexual society photographer, Jenkins presented himself as a follower of fashion. At the same time he confessed to worrying about being considered "effeminate."[64] Accordingly, he flaunted his patronizing of Dorchester chorus girls, west London brothels, and Soho striptease bars. He became, he reports, a "Deb's Delight" but was indifferent to the daughter of a baronet chasing him. Unfortunately, the woman he loved viewed him simply as a "dissolute young playboy."[65] This was, of course, the role he embraced. Presenting himself as tragically heartbroken allowed him to justify his launching himself into another hectic round of drinks and parties, a clichéd "mad endeavour to forget."[66]

Jenkins lived with friends and at expensive hotels and flats on money obtained from reversionary interests under his parents' wills.[67] That is to say he mortgaged away much of his inheritance.[68] He called himself a "financier." The reality was that he briefly worked as a stockbroker's clerk but left with a bad character due to his drinking. Piling up debts, he soon gained a reputation for not paying his bills. Pursued by creditors, banned from bottle parties, nightclubs, and hotels, he was constantly on the lookout for easy ways of making money.

For a self-proclaimed playboy like Jenkins, marriage to a wealthy heiress, preferably an American, was an obvious way to attain financial stability. In his autobiography Jenkins refers several times to an unnamed woman whom he hoped to marry. Just before the Christmas of 1937 he told friends that he was about to be engaged to Eleanore Foster, a rich American actress who, he asserted, was worth £100,000 a year.[69] To back up his story he showed cables from her and pictures of them together on the Riviera. When journalists questioned Foster, she made it clear that though she had been photographed with Jenkins on the beach at Cannes, she knew him only slightly and they certainly were not engaged. She indignantly denied sending him any cables.[70]

When sponging off friends and family failed to cover expenses, Jenkins turned to minor forms of fraud. In 1936 he was arrested for false pretenses at the Café de Paris and for writing six bad checks; at the police court additional instances were taken into account, and as a first offender he was bound over for obtaining credit by fraud, to wit illicitly taking drink and lodgings, worth £46.[71] Jenkins was himself a victim of fraudsters. In October 1937 friends told him that huge profits could be made in purchasing armaments on the black market and reselling them to General Franco of Spain. To purchase airplanes Jenkins gathered together £685 in notes that he left in his Grosvenor Street flat when he went to meet his contact at a Jermyn Street restaurant. The hours went by, and the contact failed to appear. Jenkins finally sensed that something was terribly wrong. He rushed home to find all the money gone. He had been double-crossed. Never having met the supposed middleman, and not knowing where the planes were coming from, there was little he could do.[72] Striking the pose of wealthy young man about town, he told a reporter who covered the story that the money was of little importance. In reality he was enraged, and hopeful that Robert Harley, a new friend to whom he had been introduced by Wilmer, was the sort of ex-military tough who could help him get it back.

The press described Robert Paul Harley as standing out in a crowd due to his slight American accent, "rather piercing eyes, jet black hair, slight moustache and aquiline nose."[73] At twenty-six he was a bit older than the others, but he came from the same social milieu. Like Wilmer he was the son of a much-decorated army officer.[74] Henry Kellett Harley joined the British army in 1890 and was sent to India, where he was involved in the Chitral Expedition of 1895. In Africa, he participated in the Egyptian Army's 1898 campaign in the Sudan and in the Boer War of 1901–1902. Having retired from the 7th Hussars in 1909, he returned to the colors to serve in France and Italy during the First World War. Promoted to the rank of colonel, he died at the relatively young age of fifty-three, in 1920.[75]

In 1899 Harley married the Honorable Margaret Holland, daughter of the first Lord Rotherham (William Holland), a Manchester industrialist who entered politics as a Liberal MP. In 1910 Asquith made him a peer.[76] Before divorcing in 1908 the Harleys had one son and one daughter.[77] In 1910 Harley married Esther (or Thella), daughter of Henry Blustin (or Blustein), a Jewish businessman from Kovno, Russian Poland.[78] They had three sons. The youngest, Dennis, was born in 1915 in Maidenhead.[79] Peter, the eldest, born in 1910, followed his father's example in serving the empire.[80] At Wellington College from 1923 to 1925, he went out to New Zealand in 1926, returning to England in the mid-1930s.[81] He worked for the Mauritius Police Force in the 1940s and then the Nigerian Police Force until the 1960s.[82]

Robert, born in 1911, followed his older brother, attending Wellington College from 1925 to 1927. Located in Crowthorne, Berkshire, Wellington was an independent boarding school, built as a monument to the Iron Duke. Opened in 1859, its original mandate was to educate the sons of army officers and those in the colonial service. Some found its military atmosphere to be off-putting. The novelist George Orwell (who attended briefly in 1917) described the school as "beastly."[83] Esmond Romilly—tagged by the press as Winston Churchill's "red nephew"—at age sixteen ran away from Wellington College and castigated the school's military ethos in *Out of Bounds: The Education of Giles and Esmond Romilly* (1935).[84] The actor Robert Morley, who famously declared, "Show me a man who has enjoyed his school days and I will show you a bully and a bore," went on to muse that "the only reason for me visiting Wellington would be to burn it down."[85]

The Harley family had social pretentions but, due to the father's early death, lacked the financial resources to sustain them. After Wellington, the seventeen-year-old Harley worked briefly as a junior clerk. In 1930 his mother paid for his passage to Canada. The idea was that he would learn how to farm. He soon grew tired of rural life, however, and enlisted in the Princess Patricia's Canadian Light Infantry.[86] In 1919 the regiment had been selected to form part of Canada's peacetime army, to be called the Permanent Active Militia. The Regiment's headquarters were established at Fort Osborne Barracks in Winnipeg, Manitoba. Harley (#20990) served for three years.[87] When the news of his arrest broke, Canadian papers noted, "Harley was well known amongst Winnipeg's cricket fraternity a few years ago and enlisted in the Princess Pat's regiment."[88]

He returned to England in 1935 and made a surprisingly advantageous marriage. The press reported that in Battle, Sussex, on March 22, 1936, Robert Harley had wed Freda M. Wightwick. Freda's father was Lieutenant-Colonel Herbert Milner Wightwick, seconded to the Indian Political Service and officiating resident (or magistrate) at Jaipur. The family had spent many years in the Raj. Passenger lists document Freda in 1913 (at age two) and again in October 1928 (at age seventeen) sailing to India. Harley was obviously "marrying up." Freda moved in the best circles and as a debutante had been presented at court.[89] Her brother, John Wightwick, was to wed Audrey Idris, the daughter of Sir Trevor Wheler, Baronet.[90]

The marriage began well enough. The young couple chose as their honeymoon to sail on board the *Queen Mary* to New York City. There they were feted by American friends. In July the *New York Times* reported that a luncheon was given in honor of Mrs. Michael Harley of London by Miss Laura E. Marden of Glen Head, Long Island.[91] To make the family complete, on January 20, 1937, Freda and Robert Harley, of Newdigate House, Bexhill-on-Sea, announced the birth of a daughter, Philippa.[92] Nevertheless, due to Harley's recklessness, the marriage soon floundered. Discovering that Harley was living with another woman, Freda left him in March 1937 and sought a divorce. At first glance it appeared that her chances of success were low. The existing law held that normally a divorce could not be granted to those who had not been married for at least three years.[93]

Having abandoned the security of both marriage and the military, how was a young man with expensive tastes supposed to survive in the harsh economic climate of the 1930s? Harley liked to spend money and fancied himself a playboy.[94] The truth was he had no settled profession. After leaving the army he had a number of odd jobs including, some said, private tutor and member of a traveling circus.[95] The *Evening Telegraph* reported that when he returned to Canada in 1936, "he worked for a year with a television agency."[96] What this means is unclear as until 1952 there were no television services in Canada. Journalists also said he had the notion of selling "television telephones" and "aerial bomb blueprints." It was true that in England he occasionally posed as an American and, when broke, acted as a compère at certain nightclubs.

Harley described himself at other times as a newspaperman. The *Times* agreed that he did some literary work but insisted that he was no journalist.[97] It is worth noting, however, that a passenger list shows that on April 8, 1936, Harley arrived at New York City on board the *Europa* with his friend William Aitken, who was a well-known newspaperman.[98] Harley occasionally called the *Daily Express* with tips, telling them, for example, about Peter Jenkins being robbed. He similarly acted as a police informer, willing even to turn on friends, whom he referred to as "poor dumb-bells." While serving in the Canadian army, he claimed that he used a whippet tank to quell Communist protestors.[99] He also told tall tales of working for the US Secret Service, having his life threatened, and needing to carry a revolver. A reporter described Harley as "powerful, tall, his thick black moustache accentuating the pallor of his face."[100] His speaking with an American accent was a common affectation. In a 1938 novel a character explains the particular inflections of a pimp. "That's because, for the last fifteen years or so, anything that looks big talks with an American accent."[101] Attempting to exploit the reputation of being a hard man who was familiar with guns and New York gangs, Harley was not embarrassed by his nickname, "Killer." The moniker apparently referred not to his being a murderer but to his participation in a particularly nasty fight outside a nightclub.[102]

The reality was that Harley was no master criminal. Prior to the Hyde Park Hotel robbery he had been accused of a series of petty crimes. He was given to skipping out on his rent and other minor forms of swindling. In December 1937 he was charged with obtaining £29 by fraud, but the case was adjourned sine die pending the result of the Cartier case.[103] Perhaps the saddest document in Harley's police file was a letter written to the clerk of the court by a Miss Woolrich. Harley owed her seven shillings for the newspapers she had provided him while he was living at 58 Upper Berkeley Street in November 1937. He had suddenly disappeared, and she did not know what to do. She apologized for taking up the official's time and acknowledged that for some, seven shillings was nothing, but as a small trader, she "respectfully" pointed out, it did matter to her.[104] The authorities did not reply to Miss Woolrich's pitiful query. They obviously felt, however, that it was well worth filing away, for it shored up the argument that Harley, broke and desperate, was prepared in December 1937—like his confederates—to risk involvement in a criminal conspiracy.

When the police assembled their files on the Hyde Park Hotel robbers, the picture that emerged was of four young men who prided themselves on coming from good families, of having attended elite educational institutions and, when in need, of being able to call on extensive networks of influential friends. Most observers assumed that those enjoying such social advantages might, while youths, sow some wild oats but would inevitably go on to become pillars of the community. In the case of the Mayfair men that did not appear to be true. Was it possible, asked the popular newspapers, that their being accustomed to a life of privilege, instead of nurturing a respect for others, implanted a dangerous sense of entitlement that ultimately led to their committing robbery?[105]

Chapter 4: THE TRIAL

In February 1938, James Agate, London's leading theater critic, went along to the famous Courtroom Number One of the Old Bailey to witness the trial of the Mayfair playboys. As he wrote in his journal, he found their performances unsettling: "A horrid glamour about the whole affair. I am naturally fascinated by criminals, whose dreadful jauntiness haunts me for days."[1] His fellow spectators were less sensitive; he overheard some say appreciatively that the trial was "better than any play." "Many brought sandwiches and flasks for surreptitious use in the courtroom to avoid losing their places at lunch time."[2] Heightening the contrast between the "jewels and ermine" of the fashionably dressed audience and the sordid crime of which four young men were accused, the popular press explicitly presented the trial as theater.

The sensational Hyde Park Hotel Jewel robbery trial, in which the chief actors are Mayfair men and the Lord Chief Justice, drew an eager crowd of fashionable people to the Old Bailey. Hours before the doors opened, as in the case of some popular theatre, well-dressed men and women in furs waited in a long queue, and seemed oblivious to the driving sleet of a particularly unpleasant February morning. But admission was, except in a few cases, by ticket only, and extra police on the doors strictly enforced this ukase. Among the privileged spectators in court were the Duke of Rutland, Viscountess Byng, the Countess of Oxford and Asquith, Lady Hubery, Lady Travers Humphreys, and that keen criminologist, Sir Seymour Hicks. Rarely, has the grim Old Bailey presented such an opera-night appearance. The dock, with its four perfectly groomed and tailored prisoners, was perhaps the most startling contrast of all with the customary drab scenery. Mayfair savoir-faire survived even the Ordeal of the Old Bailey. All the accused seemed completely self-possessed and at ease until the final scene, when the Lord Chief, in a few brief scarifying sentences, dealt out their punishment. Even the West End veneer was not equal to that grim "curtain."[3]

Some papers called it the most shocking trial in over a decade. The newspapers wanted to bolster their circulation, so it was of course in their interest to play up the importance of what was revealed in court. Nevertheless, the number of journalists and politicians who subsequently referred to the trial made it clear that the court case had become a flash point in subjecting the lives of a particular cast of young men to public scrutiny.

At the end of January a magistrate committed the four to trial. The Lord Chief Justice (Lord Hewart) set the contest to begin February 16.[4] The blond-haired John Lonsdale was charged with conspiracy to steal and accessory to stealing; the three others with conspiracy to steal and robbery with violence. Robert Harley alone was charged with "receiving eight diamond rings." He and Lonsdale pleaded not guilty to all charges; David Wilmer and Peter Jenkins pleaded guilty to the conspiracy charge but not guilty to robbery with violence.[5]

The trial judge was Gordon Hewart, Lord Chief Justice of England. He had been the Liberal MP for Leicester from 1913 to 1922, entered the House of Lords in 1922 as Viscount Hewart, and served as Lord Chief Justice from 1922 to 1940. Though author of the famous dictum "It is not merely of some importance but is of fundamental importance that justice should not only be done, but should manifestly and undoubtedly be seen to be done,"[6] he was not a particularly distinguished lawman. He had a reputation for boorishness in court, which was aggravated by his poor health. In February 1938, though suffering from a bad cold and forced to consume a steady diet of lozenges, Hewart soldiered on.

The prosecution was led by G. B. McClure, prosecuting counsel to the Treasury from 1928 to 1942, when he became judge of the Mayor's and City of London Court.[7] In the current case he was supported by another future judge, Henry Elam.[8] Each of the defendants had his own lawyer. Wilmer was represented by Norman Birkett, Harley by Bernard Gillis, Lonsdale by F. Ashe Lincoln, and Jenkins by Christmas Humphreys. The newspapers said little about the make-up of the jury except to note that it included three women.[9]

The crown's case, as made by McClure, was that Lonsdale had the idea of how to carry out the robbery, Jenkins made the necessary arrangements, and

Wilmer and Harley did the dirty work. Central to the prosecution's case was the assertion that the four not only conspired to steal. Three had committed robbery with violence. For them now to claim that they hoped the theft could be achieved peacefully was patently ridiculous. Given that they intended to seize and forcibly carry off a jeweler's diamonds, they had to have expected to meet with resistance, and consequently their recourse to violence was inevitable.[10]

For the benefit of the jury, McClure described the robbery, reviewed the statements made by the accused in Oxford and London, and cited the findings of the police. The crown then called witnesses. Bellenger was obviously the prosecution's key witness. His quick wit made him a favorite of the tabloids. When asked by McClure if he was concerned, while at the hotel, that Jenkins or Wilmer would run off with his precious rings, he won a laugh by responding: "No. All I was afraid of was a dud cheque."[11]

Bellenger identified the mustachioed Harley as the man who attacked him. He acknowledged that his assailant wore dark glasses and a bandana but asserted that he recognized him by "the line of his hair." He firmly refused to accept Gillis's suggestion that his identification of Harley was based on a photograph he saw in a newspaper. Similarly, Humphreys failed when he tried to have Bellenger say that Harley appeared "desperate," as Jenkins had claimed. Bellenger asserted that, on the contrary, Harley was "as cool as can be."

Bellenger also identified Wilmer as the man who pushed him to the floor. Birkett sought to cast doubt on his testimony by implying that in his confused state the jeweler's memory would likely be faulty. But Birkett proved to be no match for Bellenger. When the barrister asked: "How many blows do you think you had received before you say Wilmer said: 'Finish it quick?'" Bellenger tersely replied: "I was not counting them." The courtroom again burst into laughter.[12]

The crown introduced material evidence—the gloves, spectacles, and handkerchief—found in the hotel room. All of the accused denied recognizing any of these items. The police had also kept the glasses and whiskey bottle used in 305. Cherrill testified that the prints on the tumbler in the bathroom were Wilmer's; those on the tumbler in the sitting room were Jenkins's; those on the bottle belonged to both Jenkins and the waiter Laurenti, and only the waiter's were on the siphon.[13] A third glass bore no fingerprints. Detectives believed the man who had drunk from that glass was wearing the gloves that were left behind. McClure directed Harley to try them on. "An excellent fit, are they not?" noted the Lord Chief Justice.[14]

MR. ETIENNE BELLENGER

Mr. Etienne Bellenger. *Daily Telegraph*, Feb. 16, 1938.
© The British Library Board

The crown did not produce the most damning evidence against the accused. The four men provided that material themselves in their vicious attacks on each other. The trial provided a classic example of what is known as the "cutthroat defense," a situation in which two or more individuals faced with the same charge conclude that only by betraying their colleagues can they hope to save themselves.

That the four accused conspired together to carry out a theft appeared to be a given. The central question that remained was who had assaulted or assisted in the assault on Bellenger. Each of the four emphatically denied responsibility. Three of the accused testified against Harley. He was therefore the target not only of McClure but also of the barristers representing his erstwhile friends. It was their goal to ensure that he be held solely responsible for beating the jeweler. A tabloid's headline summed up Harley's view: "'Others Lied to Save Their Skins,' One Tells Court."[15]

Harley was in the witness stand for two hours. Bernard Gillis, a fairly competent barrister who went on to become a circuit court judge, represented him. Led by Gillis, he produced his account of his activities on December 20. He met Wilmer at 11:00 a.m. at his hotel. They had breakfast in Bond Street and were joined by Jenkins and Lonsdale. They then proceeded to the bar of the Mayfair Hotel. The judge at this point took the opportunity of openly expressing his distaste for such wastrels.

Mr. Gillis: How long were you there?

Harley: I think we had two drinks.

The Lord Chief Justice: Is that supposed to be a measure of time? (Laughter)[16]

Harley continued, stating that he and Wilmer then went to the Spotted Dog Club until about 2:00 p.m., when Harley returned to his brother's. Later in the afternoon he took a bus to the Hyde Park Hotel, where at about 4:15 p.m. he ran into Wilmer, who was just leaving.

Gillis called two witnesses to confirm Harley's account of his movements. Reginald William McBride, an accountant, stated that he saw Harley on December 20 at 4:30 p.m. crossing Kensington High Street. McBride had known Harley before he went to Canada.[17] Another acquaintance of Harley's who testified was Miss Toby Barry, described in the press as "a dance hostess" and "a pretty blonde actress." They had known each other for a few months. When Harley was on remand in Brixton she visited him and he gave her the name of his solicitor. In court she declared that on the afternoon in question she was on a bus passing the Hyde Park Hotel. She saw Harley in his distinctive beige coat entering the building at about the time he had mentioned.[18]

In response to Gillis, Harley swore that though he entered the hotel he was never in rooms 305 or 309, never in the bathroom, and never struck Bellenger. Harley stated he and Wilmer left the hotel and went by cab to Green Park, then by tube to Piccadilly. But because of all the drinking his memory was hazy. That night he joined Jenkins at the Mayfair Hotel, and they went once more to the Spotted Dog. They also had a drink at a club on Cork Street. At midnight all four met up. At this point, Harley said, his three friends finally told him of the theft; though surprised, he volunteered to dispose of the booty.

That night he came into possession of the gems, which he hid at his brother's flat at 4:00 a.m.

Harley said that he had anticipated something like robbery with violence would take place. "It was suggested to me that I should join Wilmer and Jenkins, Lonsdale not being present, in an attempt to remove jewelry from a man they proposed to get up to a room in a hotel to be decided upon."[19] Why, asked Gillis, did he appear to go along with this criminal undertaking? So that no one else would be brought in on the scheme. His plan was to use the "pretext" of disposing of the rings to return them to their rightful owner and obtain the insurance reward.[20] Even so, he told the court, he doubted his friends would succeed in the proposed robbery. In essence Harley portrayed Wilmer and Jenkins as having hatched a plan that required the use of physical force that they were now trying to attribute to him. As he had said in an earlier statement, he did not want to cause trouble for "these boys," but they were making false claims, and he had to defend himself.

Gillis had Inspector Fabian called as a witness to confirm that Harley was a police informant.[21] The detective testified that Harley had first contacted him on October 20 and they had exchanged information about six times between October 21 and December 12 by "telephone appointment."[22]

Harley was then subjected to a rigorous grilling by both the prosecutor and the other defense lawyers. Birkett (who represented Wilmer) in cross-examination sought to expose the contradictions in Harley's story. He had stated that from previous conversations he knew something big was to occur, but he could not tell the court what these talks were about. At Stewart's Restaurant a plan was sketched out. Birkett asked: "Was there a suggestion of violence?—Correct. Who was to carry that out?—I was." And what about Bellenger? Wilmer told him to "knock him out."[23] Harley claimed that he did not directly say he would. Birkett seized on Harley's admission that he and his friends discussed the theft at least a week beforehand. It followed that it was not the sort of last-minute, spur-of-the-moment undertaking that all the accused had earlier claimed. Moreover it meant that Harley had had the chance on December 18 of informing Fabian of what was to occur two days later.

At the same time, Birkett sought to minimize Wilmer's guilt by portraying him as acting abnormally. He put it to Harley that when he and Wilmer left the hotel, Wilmer was so overwrought that he told the cab driver to go off in four different directions.

Birkett: "You must have thought you were in a taxi with a madman."
Harley: "It did rather look like it."[24]

Birkett was, of course, alluding to the fact that such nervousness was to be expected since the two men were fleeing the scene of a robbery, a robbery of which Harley claimed to be ignorant. Yet all the diamonds ended up in Harley's hands. How and why was this the case? Birkett pummeled Harley, asking sarcastically if his goal had been "to assist in the administration of justice." Harley, floundering, replied: "To a certain extent it was." If so, Birkett insisted, why had he hidden gems he knew were stolen? Asked how he heard of the plan and if he had not encouraged it, Harley denied having earlier met Lonsdale or hearing his story of how in Paris a similar brilliant theft had been carried out. Birkett suggested that in fact Harley drew from his own experience in preparing for the robbery. "Did you say that Messrs. Cartier had sent a man down to Bexhill-on-Sea with jewelry for you to examine, that he carried it in a belt, and came out on to the golf-links where you were playing?" And had he not suggested having a girl play the part of the fiancée? Harley continued to deny Birkett's insinuations, but he was forced to concede that he was correct when asked: "Would you agree that the most contemptible thing in this world would be to save your skin by lies which involve other people?"[25]

Humphreys (who appeared for Jenkins) then took his turn. He began by insisting that Jenkins had not been part of the conspiracy, but Harley replied that Jenkins was not adverse to committing crimes. At the Charing Cross Hotel, two and a half months earlier, he had spoken about using force to extort money from an uncle living in the country. When Humphreys asked if it were not true that the plan in the Hyde Park Hotel case was to avoid violence and simply for Jenkins or Wilmer to throw him a ring, Harley curtly replied, "That is the first I have ever heard of it."[26]

The four defense teams varied in quality. Wilmer obviously had enough family money to be defended by the best—Norman Birkett assisted by W. W. Fearnley-Whittingstall and E. White. Birkett had represented Lonsdale in the Blake slander trial but had far more famous clients. In 1929 he had represented Clarence Harry whose huge frauds shook the stock market; in 1932, Lady Mountbatten in her libel action against the *People* for its reporting of her affair with a black man; in 1933, John Maundy Gregory, compromised by the Lloyd George honours scandal; and in 1936, Wallis Simpson, whose divorce of her second husband raised the possibility of her marrying Edward VIII.[27]

With Birkett's promptings, Wilmer presented his account. His story was that on December 19 he ran into Lonsdale at a bar called French Jack's. They had not seen each other in more than six months. That night Lonsdale came to Wilmer's flat, as did Jenkins. Lonsdale then told them about a simple but daring theft he had read about in *Paris Soir*.[28] An enterprising thief established his reputation as a wealthy spendthrift. His key investment was renting an expensive two-room suite. He then had a jeweler bring around some precious stones. Not knowing that the adjoining room had a second door that opened onto the corridor, the victim allowed his supposed client to take a diamond with him when he went into the bedroom to get his checkbook. Gem in hand, he simply walked out the door and was gone, while the dimwitted jeweler sat patiently waiting for his return.[29]

Wilmer testified that "in fairness to Lonsdale" he had to stress that Lonsdale only told his friends about the Paris thief's trick as a matter of interest; he did not suggest they should copy it.[30] Nevertheless they were all inspired to do something similar. Lonsdale left Wilmer's at 11:00 p.m. and so missed Harley, who "accidentally" dropped by a bit later. Wilmer told him about Lonsdale's tale, they both laughed, and, according to Wilmer, one of them said it should be tried in London.[31] The next day they finalized the details of their scheme and immediately set it in motion. Though they were not seasoned professionals, they appear to have exaggerated how carelessly they made last-minute changes to their plan. The defense clearly felt that there was something to be gained in presenting the robbery as the misguided lark of a few drunken young men rather than a consequence of their cold calculations.

While Wilmer admitted having helped plan the surreptitious appropriation of a diamond, he maintained that what actually occurred was not of his doing. He realized, once Bellenger had arrived at room 305, that spiriting away one of his rings would be impossible. He went into 309 and told Harley to leave. Wilmer denied giving any "signal" and protested that no one was more surprised than he when Harley burst in and assaulted the Cartier representative. Wilmer said that neither he nor Jenkins "raised a finger" to harm him. In response to Birkett's leading questions Wilmer explicitly denied tackling Bellenger and saying, "Finish it off, quick." On the contrary, Birkett presented his client as appalled by Harley's behavior. "The attack on Mr Bellenger was an unspeakable outrage which ran counter to every decent English tradition."[32]

Wilmer claimed that he was astounded by the brutal assault he had witnessed. In a haze, he stumbled from the room with a ring in each hand.

Having lost his head, in the street he got into a cab with Harley, to whom he gave the two rings. Harley in return gave him his scarf and weapon, with the order to dump them in a lavatory. Not finding the Green Park tube station suitable, they finally disposed of the evidence at the Piccadilly tube station. That night Wilmer went out on the town to drown his sorrows. He remembered Harley's answer to the question of why he did it: "He said he was sorry he had done it; he must have been crazy."[33]

Birkett was one of the most skillful lawyers of the time, but as his own clerk reported, defending Wilmer was a hopeless task, given the lack of extenuating circumstances.[34] The court was soon apprised of the holes in his argument. As Wilmer had mentioned that a lack of money drove him to contemplate robbery, McClure asked if he was hard up. Wilmer replied, "Not particularly" and admitted to spending an average of £6 a week on cocktails, restaurants, and nightclubs.[35] Gillis (Harley's barrister) pointed out that Wilmer, in his first statement to the police, mentioned the possible use of adhesive tape to gag the victim. He ceased to refer to such tape when he realized (no doubt after talking to his lawyer) that the law regarded the employment of such a restraint as a form of violence. The justification of his not guilty plea to the charge of robbery with violence was thereby undermined.[36] In addition Gillis accused Wilmer of lying when he said he told the man in the adjoining room that the theft was to be called off and he should leave. His seeking to offload onto Harley the entire burden of guilt was, Gillis stated, too transparently self-serving. So too was his claim that he lost his head. The judge interjected that as confused as Wilmer claimed to be, he still took his coat and two rings and left via the bedroom, not the drawing room.[37]

Since he was not charged with robbery with violence, the court had only to determine whether Lonsdale's discussions with his three friends amounted to making him an accessory to stealing. F. Ashe Lincoln, a well-known barrister, led Lonsdale through his testimony.[38] Lonsdale stated that he had arrived in London from Paris in December, going under the name of Mainwaring to avoid a High Court claim for money, due to his having signed a bill for a friend who had gone bankrupt. The story of the Paris theft, he averred, was true, and he only met "Mike" Harley on December 20. Why did the others use the name Hambro and a Dorset address? Lonsdale conceded that, as he lived in Dorset, he might have suggested these, but that did not mean he imagined they would actually be employed.

Lonsdale testified that he opposed the other men's plan to attempt by some trick to obtain a diamond, but out of curiosity he rang up the Hyde Park Hotel and went round for a drink between 2:30 and 2:40. Once there he learned that Wilmer had phoned Cartier's. "I told Wilmer that I thought it was a very stupid thing to have done, and told him to ring up Cartier's and put the man off. I then said that I wanted nothing more do with him. I then left the Hyde Park Hotel and did not go back."[39] Despite being angry with his friends, Lonsdale joined them for drinks that night. Their behavior was unusual. "Jenkins was more than nervous. He had driven himself into a condition when his nerves were completely gone."[40] But until they got to Oxford, Lonsdale insisted that he had no inkling that they had stolen the Cartier's diamonds. Why then, asked Ashe Lincoln, did he accompany Wilmer and Jenkins to Oxford? Lonsdale replied that he had no idea. Being very tired and drunk he went "for no particular reason." McClure made it clear that the crown did not believe him.[41]

In cross-examination McClure sought to portray Lonsdale as someone who had been involved in other criminal conspiracies. He even suggested that Lonsdale's story of the brilliant Paris theft was really autobiographical. Lonsdale maintained that he had been in Paris for an armaments deal. He insisted the story was not about him. Nevertheless, McClure had Lonsdale admit knowing Élie Lévy in Paris. He denied, however, McClure's suggestion that on November 6, 1937, he had swindled Lévy out of a diamond ring.[42]

The well-known barrister Travers Christmas Humphreys—son of Richard Travers Humphreys of the Court of Criminal Appeal—was Jenkins's representative.[43] He led Jenkins through his testimony, which Jenkins began by portraying himself as a victim of circumstance. Raised in luxury, Jenkins had seen his world fall apart with the loss of the family fortune and then the deaths of his father and mother. He was unemployed. Engaged informally to a New York woman, he had hoped to visit her at Christmas, but in October the £1,000 he had raised on a beneficial interest under a will had been stolen. He was now "penniless."

Jenkins said that he, Wilmer, and Lonsdale met on the night of December 19. "We were all fairly short of money and were trying to think of a way of making some fairly quickly." McClure pointed out that Jenkins did not seem to appreciate how crass he sounded. "Those were strange words to be used by young men of decent birth and education."[44] In any event Jenkins stressed that he and Wilmer were enthralled by Lonsdale's story of the Parisian fraudster.

Why not try the same thing in London? Wilmer had said that his friend Harley, who knew how to dispose of stolen property, should be included. On Monday morning all four met together for the first time. Jenkins stressed that there was no well-worked-out plan. They hoped at best to grab a diamond and run. He agreed that Lonsdale was not happy with the scenario and said he wanted nothing more to do with it. Like Wilmer, Jenkins claimed that they had made no provision for what to do if the plan proved unworkable. This was simply another way of saying that Harley acted on his own in attacking Bellenger. "Amazed" by the unexpected bloodshed, Jenkins stated that he was so "frozen" in terror that he could not intervene. He followed his first impulse, which was to run away, crying out to Wilmer: "For Christ's sake, come quickly."[45] Jenkins claimed that he cursed Harley for having put them all in a terrible position, but that night he met up with him and the others and was shown the diamond rings. He attributed his erratic behavior to being drunk.

In cross-examination, Gillis (Harley's lawyer) implied that Jenkins was lying in saying that the use of force had not been envisaged. Jenkins held his position. He also took the opportunity to refute Harley's assertion that he (Jenkins) had tried to get hold of his uncle's money. He had to admit, however, to having been bound over in June 1936. McClure noted that Jenkins had been convicted of six charges of swindling, four of which were asked to be taken into consideration.[46]

In defending Harley, Bernard Gillis had the most challenging of assignments. He took some comfort in concluding his duties by insisting that though all of the accused betrayed their friends, the prosecution had failed to make its case.[47] The Lord Chief Justice did not share this view. In the two hours he took in summing up, the judge made it abundantly clear that he regarded all four guilty as charged. Could the jury, he asked, doubt that there had been a conspiracy or that Bellenger had been robbed and assaulted? The defense attorneys might talk of sympathy, but what sympathy had the young men shown? "Can you forget that the defendants . . . left that jeweller on the floor of that sitting-room in a pool of blood, left him in circumstances in which, but for the inquisitiveness of a chambermaid and a waiter, he might have conceivably died?"[48] The judge noted that though Lonsdale was not present at the assault, he was an accessory. His expectation of receiving a share of the proceeds was reflected in his behavior. In any event was there any doubt that the conspirators had the jeweler place himself where he was most susceptible to attack, that they knew they would face resistance, and that they followed a plan that required violence? The Lord Chief Justice ended his diatribe by challenging the jury to do the right thing. "If it could in any respect come to a result favorable to any of the accused you will, of course, do so. On the other hand, if soberly and calmly on this evidence you find your minds impelled to certain stern conclusions, I am sure you will not flinch."[49]

Under such clear instructions the jury only needed fifty-six minutes to find Lonsdale guilty of conspiracy to steal, but not guilty of robbery. Ironically, the jury accepted the argument that being a swindler made it unlikely that he would have resorted to violence.[50] The other three were found guilty of all charges.[51] The judge congratulated the jury on coming to the "only reasonable conclusion." Addressing the four directly, he observed that much had been said of their education, though if they were truly educated he would have been even more severe. "But probably all that is meant is that somebody has spent money in providing you with certain conventional opportunities of education, the results of which are not impressive."[52] They were just lucky, he opined, that they had not been charged with murder.

It was at this stage that some of the spectators realized that they were not simply observing a theatrical matinee. Fryniwyd Tennyson Jesse wrote a friend:

> On the last day, when the Lord Chief was going to sum up, all the doors were locked as he would not have people creeping in and out of court. My seat was next to a pillar and the Sergeant, who by then was a dear friend of mine, came up to me and said: "Miss Jesse do you think you could squeeze this gentleman in beside you?" So, ever obliging and polite, I said "Certainly" and the man squeezed in and sat between me and the pillar. The Judge summed up and he and the jury retired and the Sergeant came over again and spoke to this man, saying, "Can you tell me if any of the family relatives of the prisoners are in court?" The man said "I don't know. Jenkins' sister has been here the whole time but I have not seen her this afternoon." The Sergeant went away and I turned to the man and said "I had no idea relatives came to this sort of thing. How dreadful for them!" "Well," he said quietly, "I am one of the fathers." I never had a more awful moment. I felt hot to the ends of my hair.[53]

The Lord Chief Justice proceeded to the sentencing.[54] He sentenced Harley to seven years penal servitude (with two of hard labor served concurrently) and twenty strokes of the cat-o'-nine tails; Wilmer to five years of penal servitude (with two of hard labor served concurrently) and fifteen strokes; Jenkins to three years of penal servitude (with two of hard labor served concurrently); and Lonsdale to eighteen months penal servitude with hard labor. Lonsdale's subsequent attempt to appeal his sentence failed.[55]

Lonsdale, "sleek and icy cool," took his sentence like a trooper; Jenkins sweated and trembled. What shocked the public was the Lord Chief Justice sentencing two young men of respectable families to be flogged. Wilmer was blind in one eye, which the judge seems to have taken in consideration. "I have a report from the medical officer that you are fit for the cat-o'-nine-tails," said the judge, "and you must receive fifteen strokes from the cat-o'-nine-tails." A journalist described Wilmer, on hearing these words, as being close to tears. His father could only watch. "Brigadier Wilmer, stiff and soldiery, saw his son turn down to the cells."[56] The *Daily Mail* described the brigadier staggering from the court, protesting that the sentence was far worse than expected and that his son would be incapable of surviving a flogging.[57] When the judge meted out twenty strokes to Harley, the women in the court gasped. Maintaining his role as a hard man, Harley "just turned away with a grin."[58] Once he was back in his cell he momentarily lost his composure, but when his brother arrived he managed to put on a smile. A reporter overheard him say: "It's pretty stiff but I can take it."[59]

Under such headlines as "Saville Row Suits to Prison Grey," the tabloids gleefully portrayed the traumatic transformation that imprisonment entailed. The felons would be stripped and scrubbed with yellow soap. Coarse prison garb replaced their twenty-five-guinea suits and silk shirts. For the initial two weeks they would sleep on bare boards. Breakfasts consisted of porridge, tea, and bread. Neither salt nor sugar was provided; slivers of cheese or margarine had to be bargained for. Cockroaches rather than cocktails would accompany a typical dinner of sea pie (made of cheap cuts of pork rather than fish) washed down with enamel mugs of weak cocoa.[60]

Etienne Bellenger was in court when the sentences were read out. A reporter asked for his response. "Mais non," he replied. "I have nothing to say."[61] But to another journalist, who referred to the brutal flogging to which the young men would be subjected, he responded: "I am not sorry for them. Why should I be?"[62] He was still recovering from his wounds. Though having the occasional headache, by April he was back at work and indulging in his favorite recreation—horseback riding. He attributed the restoration of his health to a three-week holiday in the south of France under the watchful eye of his wife.[63] Etienne Bellenger was still his firm's London managing director in 1942 when he placed Cartier's offices in New Bond Street at the disposal of General de Gaulle, leader of the Free French.[64]

The trial of the Mayfair Playboys helped precipitate a series of public discussions on societal changes in interwar Britain. Here it suffices to offer only one example of how the reports of the robbery supposedly influenced behavior. King George VI, whose coronation had taken place the previous May, kept himself abreast of developments. Given that Cartier was known as "the jeweller of kings and the king of jewellers," it was hardly surprising that the monarch took an interest in the case. He told a judge that he warmly supported the punishments inflicted. He regretted, however, that as a result of the trial there had been a decline in public trust. As an example he pointed out that it was the custom when the royal family needed to provide jewels as presents to buy them from Cartier. Shortly after the Hyde Park Hotel robbery, the palace asked that they send a man around with a selection of gems. "And what do you think?" the king asked indignantly. "They sent up two men. *Two* men! I could see they were not going to trust *me*!"[65]

Chapter 5: THE AFTERMATH

In his comic novel *Decline and Fall* (1928), Evelyn Waugh's lead character, being a former public school boy, finds the prison regime surprisingly familiar. "Anyone who has been to an English public school will always feel comparatively at home in prison. It is the people brought up in the gay intimacy of the slums, Paul learned, who find prison so soul destroying."[1] It is unlikely that the four Mayfair men found this joke very funny. Their experiences did differ, however, and the newspapers played up the comparisons and contrasts in following them from incarceration to release and their attempts at reintegration into society. The press not only drew the appropriate moral lessons from this coverage, but it also succeeded in creating a place for the playboy in the British imagination.

On June 2, 1939, a photograph appeared in the press of John Lonsdale, his blond hair noticeably thinner, enjoying his first breakfast at his Chelsea flat after being released from Wandsworth Prison. Sentenced to eighteen months for conspiracy, he had earned full remission for good behavior and served only fifteen months. Some wondered why an ex-felon warranted the attention of news reporters. The *Times* was so disgusted by the interest that the popular press took in such people—famous only for being famous—that its editorialist devoted a sarcastic column to the subject under the title "The Morals of Mayfair."

> Whatever the reason, a cursory glance at the columns of some of our contemporaries will show that the better sort of crime (as estimated in terms of circulation) has moved westward from Alsatia [an archaic term for a sanctuary for lawbreakers in the City of London]. . . . In an age whose philosophy moves steadily towards the recognition of publicity as the summum bonum, his chosen habitation should gratefully recognize him as the savior of society. But for [Mayfair

Man] Mayfair would, in a journalistic sense, have to be regarded as a depressed area. . . . The delightful feature of the Mayfair Man is that not only is he dishonest, but, if not rich himself, he has rich relations. No wonder he has put Mayfair on the map again; no wonder that, during his enforced absences from that modish region, the hearts of readers are kept palpitating with thrilling details of the daily routine ordained for him by the prison commissioners, and that on his return to his service flat he finds it crammed with reporters, eager to observe and proclaim to the world exactly what he eats for breakfast.[2]

Other papers carried photographs of Lonsdale and his fiancée, Stella Clive, in advertisements for a confessional article by him entitled "Good-Bye Piccadilly: The True Story of a Mayfair Playboy," which was to appear July 10, 1939. The breathless blurb gushed: "He was a playboy. The bright lights of the West End attracted him. He looked for and found the gay life. He went to expensive nightclubs, lived in expensive hotels. 'I was a playboy—now I've learned my lesson,' says John Lonsdale. He tells the real inside secrets of the West End racket in to-morrow's *Sunday Chronicle and Sunday Referee*."[3]

Lonsdale did his time in Wandsworth Prison. Built in 1849, and serving as the hanging prison of south London, it was the largest penitentiary in England. In addition to Lonsdale, it briefly housed in 1938 a stateless refugee, Nicholas Sidoroff, whose story won the interest of the press. He claimed that his family, which had several estates in Russia, had fled the Bolshevik revolution of 1917.[4] Carrying a League of Nations passport, Sidoroff returned to his homeland in 1933 to see what remained of his family's properties. When the Soviet authorities confiscated his travel documents and prepared to conscript him into the army, Sidoroff fled. Wandering across Europe, he finally reached England in 1936. Having entered the country without papers, he was charged with contravening the Aliens Order. In November 1938 he told the Marylebone Police Court that Mr. John Graham Gillam DSO had offered him a job.[5] In addition, Stella Clive, Gillam's secretary, said she would marry Sidoroff. The romantic story of this "dark-eyed English girl" seeking to save an impoverished aristocrat had obvious appeal.[6] They did not actually become husband and wife, but Sidoroff assured a journalist that "the promises we have made to each-other are as solemn and as binding as a formal wedding ceremony."[7] In any event, the court sentenced Sidoroff to a short stay in Wandsworth Prison, where he became friendly with John Lonsdale. (Sidoroff, it would turn out, was himself a con man.)[8]

While visiting Sidoroff at Wandsworth, Stella Clive ran into Lonsdale, whom she said she had met once at a party three years earlier. Under the headline "His Jail Visitor to Be His Bride," the press reported in the summer of 1939 that Lonsdale was to marry the twenty-six-year-old Stella Edith Howson-Clive. He praised her: "She has been a brick." She reciprocated: "If Johnnie is allowed to settle down and forget he was ever in prison, everything will be all right. I think we can both say it was a case of love at first sight."[9] Shortly after he was released, they married, on July 14, 1939, at the Kensington Registry Office.

Stella appears to have loved several men at first sight. Ironically enough, Lonsdale, an admirer of fraud artists, in marrying Stella Clive found himself entangled with a person who was even more duplicitous than he. Stella had had several affairs and had given birth to Sidoroff's child in October 1937. And her bizarre behavior during the war puzzled many. In January 1940 she went to Paris, where Lonsdale's mother, Georgina, had been living for some time.[10] Stella visited John, who had enlisted in September 1939 and was stationed in Nantes with the Royal Engineers. In February 1940 he returned with his unit to England, but she remained in France and was in Nantes when the Germans occupied the city in June.[11] More than a year later, in the winter of 1941, she arrived in London from Lisbon, claiming that she had been tortured by the Germans but was willing to return to France to recruit underground agents. On November 11, Guy Liddell (in charge of counterespionage for MI5), wrote in his diary: "We have an extremely interesting case which centres round Stella Lonsdale, the wife of John Lonsdale, the Mayfair Boy. . . . She gave a number of other details which according to SIS [Secret Intelligence Service] are substantially correct. It will I think be necessary for us to obtain the fullest possible facts from SIS before we shall be able to establish how far Stella can be regarded as genuine."[12]

British intelligence officers initially provided Stella with comfortable accommodations and were considerate in their questioning.[13] What they did not anticipate were her prevarications and inexhaustible supply of lewd stories. The most hardened interrogators of MI5 were shocked, one declaring: "Much of Mrs Lonsdale's conversation cannot possibly be submitted in a report owing to its indescribably filthy nature." An intelligence officer reported: "She is without any doubt at all a woman whose loose living would make her an object of shame on any farm-yard." "Her mind is—simply and frankly—a cesspool," an interrogator observed. "Without going into details, she held forth for 40 minutes on the difference in love-making of a Frenchman and an Englishman. On another day she expatiated on the theme of animals. She apparently knows not the meaning of decency or reticence. She is sex-fanatical."[14] By December 1941, MI5 concluded that Stella was "thoroughly unreliable and untrustworthy and almost certainly a German agent."[15] In July 1942 the Security Service had her arrested for withholding information useful for the war effort and sent to Aylesbury Prison and then to Holloway Prison, where she remained until 1945.[16]

According to a 1946 report produced by Chief Inspector Fabian, Lonsdale was not suspected of returning to his old shady practices.[17] He had enlisted in the army after the war broke out in 1939, but he did not remain in uniform for long. Having joined the Bomb Disposal Squad of the Royal Engineers, he was discharged as medically unfit, which perhaps represented a return to an ingrained pattern. He had abruptly left all the other military units he had entered in the 1930s—the King's Rifles, the RAF, and the Dorset Regiment.

When exactly John and Stella Lonsdale divorced is not clear. By 1943 they had certainly ceased to live as a married couple. In 1945 she was released and became enamored with the eugenicist and fascist George Henry Lane Fox-Pitt-Rivers, who was, one historian has opined, "somewhere between eccentric and dotty."[18] He went so far in publicizing his fascist opinions that Churchill—a cousin—had him interned during the war under defense regulation 18B.[19] Stella took his name by deed poll, and when he died in 1966 he left his estate to her.[20]

Lonsdale's life—in comparison to Stella's—appeared positively prosaic. He married twice more. In 1944 he wed Betty F. Fuller in Chelsea. The marriage did not last. In 1949 he married Dorothy I. Page (née Walton).[21] In 1952 they were living at 7 Somers Mews, W2. Otherwise little is known of Lonsdale's activities after his release from prison. How he earned a living is a puzzle. Sometime in the 1940s he became a traveler for the South Counties Oil Company, Kings Road, Chelsea. In December 1949, he filed for bankruptcy.[22] In August 1956 the *London Gazette* reported that the "release of trustees" had occurred—that is, the liquidation had been completed.[23]

If Lonsdale were the most successful of the Mayfair playboys in avoiding further conflicts with the law, Peter Jenkins was the least successful. Young and good looking, he never gave up the notion that the wealthy men and women of the milieu that he inhabited had in some sense a duty to share their bounty with him. In looking back on the 1938 trial he could only feel sympathy for the "four foolish and very frightened young men," not for their victim.[24] He resented being denied bail and hurt that his creditors pursued him even behind bars. He did not appreciate having received a relatively light sentence and was genuinely puzzled that the Lord Chief Justice should have mistaken four "drunken young sots" for a band of criminals. His greatest humiliation occurred, however, when "Kitter," the Reverend D. B. Kittermaster, who had been his housemaster at Harrow and was now a Borstal chaplain, came to visit. Jenkins claimed that his one cause of remorse was the feeling that he had let down his school.[25]

Along with his confederates, Jenkins was held initially at Brixton Prison and then, because he was only twenty-one, at the Youths' Prison at Wormwood Scrubs. He was relatively lucky in being able to spend most of his three-year sentence at Wakefield Prison, in West Yorkshire, a "model" penitentiary that sought to help prisoners win back their self-respect by providing rooms instead of cells and allowing them to work unguarded.[26]

Jenkins was released May 10, 1940. In his autobiography he says that his intention was to be a patriotic and law-abiding citizen. He applied to enter the RAF, but once he was identified as one of the Mayfair men, he was told that his services were not needed. An unfortunate accident then foiled his attempt to enlist in the army.[27] As Jenkins saw it, an unsympathetic society pushed him back into the arms of the London underworld. He makes no direct reference to his second brush with the law, but Chief Inspector Fabian reported that on January 27, 1942, Jenkins was sentenced to sixteen months in prison for larceny.[28] The exact details are not available. All that Jenkins admits to in his memoir is that he was hired as a cosmetics salesman and was unaware, so he claims, of the business's illegal practices until they were exposed by the journal *John Bull*. During the war there was an active black market in cosmetics that escaped health and safety regulations. The result was the sale of products that were ineffective, if not actually harmful to the skin.[29] The courts fined several guilty companies, and a few individuals, Jenkins included, were imprisoned.

Like many other good-looking con men, Jenkins attempted to exploit wealthy women. In 1937 he had pursued Eleanore Foster in hopes of marrying up. The tabloid press of the 1930s was full of such stories of heiress hunting. In 1945 Jenkins not only robbed a young woman, but he added insult to injury by tarnishing her reputation. This was his third brush with the law in seven years. Coincidentally, G. B. McClure, who had led the crown's prosecution of the Mayfair men in 1938, presided as judge over the June 1945 Old Bailey trial in which Jenkins (now twenty-eight) was charged with breaking and entering and receiving stolen property. The popular papers described Mrs. Jill Austin, the victim, as a twenty-four-year-old, fashionably dressed, long-haired beauty. She was living in Linden Gardens, Notting Hill Gate, London, and was the daughter-in-law of Vice Admiral Sir Francis Austin, of Gosport.[30]

The crown's case was that Jenkins and Austin had been on "friendly" terms. He knew where she kept the key to her flat. One night in March they went to a pub in Bayswater. She returned home to find her £500 mink coat gone. At a club in Mayfair she asked him about it. In a taxi they had a fight, and she testified that he said, "Now you jolly well won't get your mink coat."[31] The police, being informed, staked out a house in Craven Terrace, Lancaster Gate, Paddington, and intercepted Jenkins as he left with a package that proved to contain a fur coat.

The evidence against Jenkins appeared overwhelming, but he refused to enter a guilty plea. His version of events was that he was introduced to Austin at a Mayfair bar in 1944. They were soon intimate. He knew that her coat had disappeared, but it was not his doing. While out on a walk he had by chance found a fur coat lying between two telephone boxes near Marble Arch. He was about to take it to police when he was arrested. Most importantly, Jenkins insisted that the coat he found was not Austin's and if she were not so vindictive she would admit it.[32]

Recognizing the obvious inadequacies of his defense, Jenkins instructed his lawyer, Derek Curtis-Bennett, to "produce certain documentary evidence" to reveal Austin's true colors.[33] The *Times* refrained from reporting the unseemly tactics employed by Jenkins's counsel to undermine Austin's credibility. The *Daily Mail* gave a full account under the headline "Pictures Embarrass Pretty Woman." It reported that Austin testified that when she was in a taxi with Jenkins, he had said, "If you want me to get your coat you must let me kiss you." Curtis-Bennett, going on the attack, retorted: "You are telling deliberate falsehoods. Have you ever stayed at a hotel with him and slept with him?" She replied, "I have never slept with him."[34] The lawyer then handed her an envelope and asked whether she recognized the two photographs it contained. She "flushed" as she took out pictures that showed her half-naked. She said a friend in the country had photographed her. Bursting into tears, she insisted that Jenkins had not taken the photos.

Jenkins might have momentarily enjoyed Austin's discomfort, but attacking her character was a tactical blunder. It meant that now the crown could explore his past, and in particular alert the court to the role he had played in the Hyde Park Hotel robbery. Having G. B. McClure sitting on the bench could only underscore in the minds of the jury the linkage of the two crimes. In the end it found him guilty of receiving stolen property and not guilty of breaking and entering.

Jenkins was convinced that he was being punished once more for the 1937 crime. Before being sentenced he rashly attacked the judge: "Your summing up was a speech for the prosecution. I don't consider I have had a fair trial. As you know, you were concerned in the Hyde Park case. That coat is not Mrs Austin's coat. Any reasonable jury would have thought so. . . . I have given my lawyers notice to appeal."[35] In his autobiography, written seven years later, Jenkins sought to present himself as more temperate. In the book, he took a quite different view of the role McClure played in his trial: "I must say that he was most scrupulously fair throughout."[36] The extent to which he sought to rewrite his past is even better demonstrated by comparing his 1945 attack on Jill Austin with his 1952 assertion that he would never stoop to such a "despicable act" as exploiting a vulnerable woman.

In any event, in June 1945 Jenkins found himself in Wandsworth Prison. His appeal was rejected in July, and stretching before him lay a long sentence. "Playboy Gets Three Years," read a typical headline. Chief Inspector Fabian, who kept track of such recidivists, when asked about Jenkins, told his superiors: "He is a thoroughly unscrupulous scoundrel and will in my opinion continue to be so."[37]

The time he spent in Wandsworth appears to have made Jenkins more rather than less reckless. Released on May 30, 1947, he went straight to Covent Gardens for breakfast and then to the Savoy bar for lunchtime drinks with disreputable old friends. In his autobiography he asserts that he was still planning a further appeal of his 1945 conviction but needed at least £3,000 to do so. Having exhausted all legal channels, he concluded that only by returning to crime could he raise the necessary funds. With hindsight he had at least the grace to admit that his decision—to rob to prove that he had not robbed—was motivated by "crass stupidity."[38]

He must have known he was being watched. In July 1948 the police arrested him while he was in the process of casing a black marketeer's house in Muswell Hill. He was charged with loitering with intent and bound over for twelve months. Undeterred, he pressed on, responding positively when an acquaintance asked if he could locate a buyer for Sir Joshua Reynolds's famous

1787 unfinished oil painting of Georgiana, Duchess of Devonshire, valued at £5,000. Once he did, a prowler broke into the Earl of Carlisle's flat in Marsham Court, Westminster, and cut the picture from its frame. On September 10, Jenkins went to Pinner with his partner to pick up the canvas. Arrested as he was driving away, Jenkins was convinced that once again he had been set up. He was taken to the nearest police station, which, as luck would have it, was in Harrow on the Hill. From his cell window, he claimed in his book, he could see his old school's first-eleven cricket pitch.[39]

On September 14, Jenkins was charged at Bow Street Police Court with breaking and entering. Remanded, he was sent off once again to Brixton Prison. On October 13 the papers announced that Peter Martin Jenkins, thirty-two, salesman of 23 Kendall Street, Paddington, and Harry Mann, thirty-four, fruiterer of no fixed address, were being tried for receiving a valuable oil painting, knowing that it had been stolen. "You both have shocking records," declared the common sergeant, Mr. H. L. Beazeley, who presided. Indeed, with seventeen previous convictions for breaking and entering, stealing, and receiving, Mann had spent most of his life in prisons and Borstals. As made clear in such headlines as "Judge's Comments to Old Harrovian" and "Playboy Is Sent Back to Prison," the press was, as usual, more interested in the toff. Both men were found not guilty of breaking and entering but guilty of receiving, and they were sentenced to four years of penal servitude.[40]

On February 6, 1949, Jenkins was transferred from Wandsworth to Dartmoor, Britain's most infamous prison, isolated on the bleak Devon moors. It had been built in the nineteenth century from local granite, and prisoners were expected to carry out some of their "hard labor" in the nearby quarry. Jenkins described it as a terrible place with brutal guards, tiny cells, and damp walls constantly dripping with moisture. Nevertheless, he ended his 1952 autobiography with the assertion that thanks to the close friendship of one fellow inmate and the counsel of two Catholic priests, he was no longer "convict, ne'er-do-well, and social parasite." He vowed that a new Jenkins was in the process of replacing the old. A poet and author would "rise once more to a position worthy of a son of that great school which gave him the equipment to lead a decent life."[41]

His subsequent behavior could lead one to believe that the "school" he referred to was Dartmoor, not Harrow. He was incorrigible. Released in June 1951, Jenkins had, as his 1952 autobiography would demonstrate, some success as a writer. A. W. Cockburn, the deputy chairman of the London

Sessions, was impressed. "I will give you one more chance," he said, in conditionally discharging Jenkins in November 1952 after he had pled guilty to stealing a trunk.[42] But leniency did not appear to work. In April 1955, Jenkins was in court again and given a seven-year sentence in Manchester for obtaining a car and £500 on false pretenses. In August 1959, while out on day parole from Pentonville Prison, he was picked up and questioned by the police regarding a Leeds robbery.[43] He pled guilty to receiving two fob watches and was conditionally discharged. That October, under the headline "Freed Playboy Makes a Promise," the press reported his last public appearance. In the course of twenty years he had pled guilty or been convicted on seven occasions and seen the insides of at least six prisons. The now forty-three-year-old Jenkins swore that all he wanted was peace and quiet. The bright lights of Mayfair no longer tempted him.[44]

The corporal punishment to which Wilmer and Harley were subjected garnered worldwide attention and did more than even the robbery itself to assure their notoriety. Following his flogging in Wormwood Scrubs, Wilmer, like Jenkins, served his sentence in Wakefield Prison. But whereas prison authorities released Jenkins in May 1940, it was another three years before they freed Wilmer. Month after month, prisoners had to endure the humiliation of near-constant surveillance and the imposition of mind-numbing routines. Nevertheless, Wakefield prided itself on being a leader in prison reform. Inmates were encouraged to learn a trade that would allow them to improve their job prospects. An October 1938 article on the prison reported that "Wilmer and Jenkins, two of the Mayfair playboys sentenced for their complicity in the Hyde Park Hotel jewel robbery, are at Wakefield. They are earning a few pence a week respectively, and are well behaved."[45] The *People* stated that the warders were prescient in allowing Wilmer and Jenkins to play cricket: "Both have become changed men."[46] Despite such glowing reports it is easy to imagine the shock these ex-public-school boys must have first experienced in contemplating what was on offer. One journalist, in reviewing the regulations the four Mayfair men had to learn before heading to their respective prisons, noted: "As none of them is trained in trade, they will have to sew mailbags until they leave for their new prisons. There they will be trained in shoemaking, tailoring, or some similar job."[47] Harrow and Oundle had obviously not prepared them for such work.

Their time in prison had different effects on the four. Because he was in Wandsworth in 1938, Lonsdale met and married Stella Clive, whose tumultuous life would shadow his for several years to come. In Jenkins's case the years he spent behind bars—far from having a reformative effect—apparently left him less able than ever to pursue an honest living. Wilmer was from the outset better socially situated than his colleagues, and if prison taught him anything it was the value of a supportive network of family and friends.

A review of press references to Wilmer before the 1938 trial reveals the variety of social circles to which he had access. To drive from London to Oxford following the robbery in the early morning of December 21, Wilmer borrowed a car from his friend Richard Blacker-Douglas, of 31 Hans Place, Knightsbridge. The society pages carried many accounts of Blacker-Douglas at music receptions, memorial services, dances, and marriages.[48] He was born in 1912, the son of St. John Stewart and Nina (née Pulteney) Blacker-Douglas. His grandfather was Lieutenant-General Sir William Pulteney, Gentleman Usher of the Black Rod in the House of Lords from 1920 to 1940. Yet high status did not signify high intelligence. According to Charles Bonham-Carter, his chief of staff, Pulteney was "the most completely ignorant general I served during the war and that is saying a lot."[49]

Another well-placed friend of Wilmer's, whose parties he attended, was Miss Helen Chetwynd-Stapylton of 41 Grosvenor Square. She married Captain Michael Edward Adeane of the Coldstream Guards at St. Mark's, North Audley Street. Adeane served in Canada from 1934 to 1936 as aide-de-camp to the governor-generals Earl Bessborough and Lord Tweedsmuir, then as the assistant private secretary to George VI, and finally as private secretary to Elizabeth II, who in 1972 was to make him a life peer.[50]

In prison Wilmer was cut off from his social network. The most concrete example of his newly marginalized status came when his wife, Hilary Inez Elizabeth Wilmer, of Basil Street, Knightsbridge, successfully sued for divorce.[51] She had launched her suit in 1937, but Wilmer had been arrested before it was completed. He had abetted her claim that he was an adulterer by providing a compromising letter and hotel bill as evidence that he had had relations with a woman in a hotel in the Strand in January and February of 1937. Given that the existing law stipulated that to obtain a divorce either the husband or the wife—but not both—had to be at fault, matters were somewhat complicated by Hilary confessing that she too had a lover. Using his discretion to minimize her lapse, a judge granted Hilary a decree *nisi* (a conditional divorce) and custody of their child in March 1938, just as Wilmer was beginning his prison term.[52]

Wilmer had an entrée into elite social circles through his wife's lover, Patrick Henry Noel Gamble.[53] Some were no doubt surprised to hear that Wilmer mentioned Gamble in constructing an alibi, claiming that he spent most of December 20, the day of the Hyde Park Hotel robbery, collecting papers "relating to a Mr. Patrick Gamble's prospects under his grandfather's will."[54]

Although Gamble was the son of the Very Reverend Henry Reginald Gamble, the Dean of Exeter, he participated in what could be described as marital musical chairs.[55] Gamble had divorced his first wife, Lady Mercy Gamble, the younger daughter of the Earl of Warwick, in 1935.[56] She was the respondent in an undefended suit in which Gamble (identified as an estate agent) alleged her adultery with Richard Maurice Marter, late of the Sixteenth Lancers, stepson of General Disney Fasson and son of Captain William Maurice Marter. The judge also heard Mrs. Angela Geraldine Lizzie Marter (niece of Lord Blyth) allege her husband's adultery with Lady Mercy Gamble. He granted decrees *nisi* to both petitioners.[57] Gamble and Lady Mercy had married in 1933 at the Chelsea Register Office. In 1932 her first husband, Basil Dean—the well-known actor, film producer, and founder of Ealing Studios—had divorced her on the grounds of her adultery, citing Patrick Gamble as the co-respondent. Such celebrity divorces provided the tabloids with a ready supply of accounts of the tribulations of the upper classes.

Wilmer won his release from prison sometime in 1943. He had no further encounters with the police, but observers refrained from pronouncing him reformed. The author of an April 1944 article on the Mayfair men cautiously stated, "Wilmer has not been free long enough for his behavior to be appraised."[58] In a 1946 report, which he submitted to his superiors, Chief Inspector Robert Fabian asserted that though Wilmer had not yet been charged with any crime, he was suspected of sharp practices. "Does no work, but is an habitué at many bottle parties (after hours drinking clubs) etc." Fabian went on to note that Wilmer had attempted in two important ways to distance himself from his past. First, he changed his name by deed poll to "David Hamilton." Second, "He is stated to [have] recently married Barbara, daughter of Lord Phillimore."[59]

Though Fabian was correct as concerns Wilmer's change of name, it was Pamela—not Barbara—Phillimore who was to become his wife. Born in 1918, she was the daughter of a cavalry officer, the late Captain Paul Phillimore of the 17th (Duke of Cambridge's Own) Lancers.[60] Having lost her parents and being in line for a sizeable inheritance, she obviously attracted many admirers.

Her coming out in 1936–1937 can be followed in the Court Circular. Her life, like that of other debutantes, was a constant round of dinners, dances, wedding celebrations, and charity balls.[61] Her cousin, Mrs. Aspinall, helped her organize her parties where the Duke and Duchess of Norfolk headed the guest list. The Baroness Beaumont presented her at court.[62]

A central purpose of the London season was to marry off as many debutantes as soon as possible. The fact that Pamela Phillimore took some time in selecting a mate aroused the interest of the press. The *Daily Mail* ran a story titled "Changed Her Mind Twice," noting that when sixteen she had dropped a wealthy American suitor and now had broken a second betrothal. The official notice appeared in the *Times* of November 13, 1937: "The marriage arranged between Mr. Michael Clifton and Miss Pamela Phillimore will not take place."[63] The disappointed suitor claimed he would seek solace in Africa: "I shall either enter a monastery or join the Foreign Legion." In fact, he shot elephants.[64]

Pamela Phillimore was a ward in Chancery until February 1939. She marked the occasion by throwing a cocktail party for more than two hundred guests to both celebrate her coming of age and to announce her forthcoming marriage, in March, to Gilbert A. W. G. Cockburn. The tabloids were relieved to report, "Heiress Weds at 21."[65] Journalists were not the only persons fascinated by the young woman's wealth. A year later, under the headline, "Heiress Beauty Robbed," reporters provided an account of how thieves had ransacked her house in Bryanston Square, W1, and made off with £7,000 worth of jewels and furs.[66] It was not her only loss. Her marriage to Cockburn appears to have ended a year or two later.[67]

David Wilmer was released from prison sometime in 1943 and returned to the family home at 20 Victoria Grove, W8. In July 1944 he changed his name by deed poll to David Hamilton.[68] In March 1945 one David Hamilton married Pamela Cockburn (née Phillimore) in Chelsea.[69] In 1947 they were living in Lingfield, Surrey, which was in keeping with his past interests. Lingfield, like Newbury (one of Wilmer's old stomping grounds), had a racecourse. Despite his troubled past Wilmer had apparently succeeded, thanks to his network of friends and family, in reintegrating himself in his old social set and as a result largely escaped the surveillance of policemen, journalists, and historians.

Robert Harley received the longest sentence and the largest number of lashes. Given that he was the most violent of the four Mayfair men, he also drew most of the press attention. He was portrayed as a larger-than-life character—"the mustached American," the man in the teddy bear coat, the "ringleader" of the gang, and the "boastful, half-Polish son of a colonel."[70] The oldest and biggest of the accused, he was said to have bragged that he could take a flogging. Apparently it was true. "He suffered his punishment manfully," declared the *Star* in reporting his flogging at Wormwood Scrubs. "The whole prison admired him for his courage."[71] This was not the sort of story the defenders of corporal punishment wanted to hear.

From Wormwood Scrubs, Harley was transferred to Maidstone. Whereas Lonsdale spent less than a year in Wandsworth Prison, and Jenkins and Wilmer passed their time in the modernized Wakefield Prison, Harley had to endure close to six years in the antiquated Maidstone Prison. Built in 1819 of grey limestone carved from local Kent quarries, it was by the 1930s much in the need of refurbishing. Although a committee had pondered the question of providing its prisoners with some practical training, nothing was done before the war. Like his fellow inmates, Harley was set to sewing mail bags and weaving cocoa mats, for which meaningless work he was paid seven pence a week.[72] For the incarcerated even small amounts of money represented power. In May 1940 the press reported that Harley's mother—Mrs. Esther Thella Harley of Harrington Gardens, SW7—had been fined £5 at Maidstone court. She had been found guilty of breaking prison regulations in smuggling money into Harley—two 10 shilling notes and twelve pennies. A similar summons was drawn against his brother, Dennis Harley, of Romney Court, Shepherds Bush, but was withdrawn.[73]

Harley's name continued to appear in the papers through 1938 due to his wife pursuing divorce proceedings. The public recalled that Harley had married Freda Margaret Wightwick on March 22, 1936, in Battle, Sussex. The marriage was not a happy one. Freda left him in March 1937 after finding out that he was living with another woman. In February 1938, Harley's solicitor, Emanuel Garber, visited him in Wormwood Scrubs to discuss how to respond to Freda's suit.[74] The press took an interest in this divorce case because it not only involved a notorious criminal. It was also one of the first suits that took advantage of the "hardship and depravity" clause of the Matrimonial Causes Act of 1937.

Following his divorce in 1939 and the fining of his mother in 1940, the press lost interest in Harley. Only four years later, in April 1944, as the date of his release neared, did reporters remind the public of the life that he had led and the problems he would now likely face. A syndicated article entitled "Romance in the Clink; or, What's to Become of London's Playboy Raffles?" appeared in newspapers across the world. In addition to photographs of Harley, Wilmer, Wormwood Scrubs, and the ancient triangle on which they were lashed, the essay carried an illustration of a veiled woman who purportedly was a constant visitor at Maidstone.[75]

Employing traditional redemptionist rhetoric, Harley was quoted as saying he was a changed man. "Before Scotland Yard caught up with me, I went through over a million dollars in a few years. And I must say, I enjoyed the spending of it. However, I know now that Mayfair life is futile. When I'm out of jail I shall try my best to get away from its contaminating connections." If he did avoid conflicts with the law it would be due, so the story went, to the monthly visits of his anonymous female friend. But was any of this true? Riddled as it is with errors, little credence can be given to the accuracy of the article. The purple prose in which it is written is of some interest, however, in that it reveals the sorts of stories the popular press believed would sell. An account of the typical working-class thief could not compete with the romantic tale of Harley, ringleader of a "robber gang," who fleeced the "dowagers and debutantes" who feted him, the cool desperado who, returning from "the gilded haunts of the Cote d'Azur," planned as his "masterstroke" the robbing of Cartier.

Harley was released in the spring of 1944. Chief Inspector Fabian noted in a 1946 report that Harley had a job, was married, and had become the father of a little girl.[76] The officer was nevertheless skeptical. "Recently, however, I have seen him in the company of undesirables and there is no doubt in my mind he will shortly be in custody for fraud."[77] Despite such suspicions, neither the police nor the press had any reason to make any further references to Harley, and he slipped from their sight.

In his 1944 essay on crime literature, George Orwell asserted: "A duke who has served a prison sentence is still a duke, whereas a mere man about town, if once disgraced, ceases to be 'about town' for evermore."[78] On the face of it, his argument makes sense; those having great wealth never had to be overly worried about their reputation. But what of the disgraced arriviste or compromised playboy? Did society forever shun them? The fear that this would be the case presumably explains why Wilmer and Jenkins changed their names. Yet the Hyde Park Hotel robbers appear to have picked up the threads of their old lives. Once they were out of prison, Lonsdale and Harley remarried, continued to live in West London, had no subsequent brushes with the law, and seem to have settled down. Though Jenkins ultimately proved to be an incorrigible criminal, it has to be recalled that when he had finished his first stay in prison and his reputation as a Hyde Park Hotel robber was still fresh in the public's mind, he was immediately involved with Jill Austin, the daughter-in-law of a vice admiral. Wilmer was the most successful of all. He married an heiress and moved from Mayfair to leafy Surrey.

None of these young men were, however, ever completely "free." They could not ignore the fact that references to their criminal conspiracy remained a commonplace. More importantly, the image of the playboy or Mayfair man, which they helped to crystallize, would, as the next chapters demonstrate, play an intriguing role in society's changing views of sex, class, crime, and politics in twentieth-century Britain.

Part II: The Context

Alarmed by a young man's lack of scruples, an interwar diarist confided to his journal: "For some hereditary or physiological reason his normal mental development stopped dead when he reached adolescence." The writer wondered if it were a case of what doctors called "arrested development."

> If this theory is true, it would account for many of his vagaries of conduct, and for his often childish outlook on life—though I hasten to add that that outlook was often bewilderingly characterised by a shrewdness, a power of penetration, which hardened men of the world might envy. It would certainly account for the fact that, as I have already said, it was quite useless to expect him to appreciate any general rules of behaviour; his only yardstick in measuring the advisability or non-advisability of any particular action was, "Can I get away with it?"—an attitude typical of boyhood.[1]

Such an appraisal might describe Lonsdale or Jenkins, Wilmer or Harley. In fact, these few lines were Sir Alan Lascelles's portrait of Edward, the Prince of Wales and future king. As assistant private secretary to Edward, Lascelles was aghast at having to witness at first hand the prince's selfish and vulgar pursuit of pleasure. American newspapers explicitly referred to Edward as a "playboy." Practicing a form of self-censorship, the British press turned a blind eye to his moral failings. Lascelles's observations are particularly relevant to this study. They remind us that the Mayfair men's callousness was not all that idiosyncratic. If the playboys, and the prince, lacked a conscience it was due in part to an upper-class culture that imparted to its children a grotesquely inflated sense of entitlement. Where the Mayfair men differed from the other members of their class was in finally going too far.

Commentators turned the story of the Mayfair men to the purpose of better understanding the emergence of new models of masculinity, the tenacity of social inequities, the relationship of crime to punishment, and British responses to fascism. The authorities tried to use the trial to demonstrate that crime did not pay and that all were equal in the eyes of the law. When social observers broached the subjects of "playboys" and sex, they advanced similar cautionary tales, with the intent of using the specter of rogue masculinity to curb female sexuality. But those who read such reports were not simply cultural consumers. They reinterpreted for their own purposes—at times with radical intent—the portrayal of playboys carried in films, novels, and newspapers. Did the appearance in the metropolis of the modern ne'er-do-well inspire a new sort of sensationalist reporting, or did sensation-hungry journalists invent the playboy? In either case, the provocative behavior attributed to playboys and Mayfair men captured the public's imagination.

Chapter 6: PAIN

"Lash for Robbers." "20 Strokes of Cat." "Mayfair Men on Trial." "Cat for Two Mayfair Men." "Prison Warders Lash English Playboy." Headlines across Europe and North America hailed the sentences doled out by Lord Chief Justice Hewart. It was no surprise that the trial of the Hyde Park Hotel robbers made worldwide news. Well-off young men, of respectable families, educated in the nation's most elite schools, were not supposed to be subjected to punishments tailored for their social inferiors. Some were satisfied that the sentences demonstrated the even-handedness of British justice; others protested that the court should have taken into account the culprits' backgrounds. At a house party a woman asserted that it was outrageous that the "cat" had been used on public school boys. Chief Justice Hewart, who was present, angrily replied, "Scoundrels, all of them! They are lucky. They might easily have been on a capital charge. The fact that they are public school boys makes their crime all the worse. They should have known better."[1]

The popular press agreed, playing up the contrast between the sordid crime and the social eminence of the four. One account described them as "fashionably dressed and well-spoken men."[2] In another they were "young dandies of fashionable Mayfair."[3] The tabloids had a long experience in pandering to their expanding readership with tales of toffs gone bad. The case of the "Mayfair playboys" was exceptional because it entailed four young gentlemen carrying out a vicious crime and a judge sentencing two of them to be flogged, which, apart from hanging, was the most brutal form of punishment available by law. The tabloids were transfixed by the prospect of the lash, normally reserved for working-class brutes who only understood the language of pain, being used to bloody the backs of sophisticated men-about-town.

The debate over the morality and efficacy of corporal punishment had been going on in Britain for over a century. By coincidence, a report of the

Committee on Corporal Punishment appeared just weeks after the Hyde Park Hotel trial. Normally the popular press would have ignored such a dry document, but because the court had sentenced Wilmer and Harley to be flogged, journalists gave it unprecedented attention.[4] The irony was that for the next two decades both the supporters and opponents of corporal punishment would try to turn to their advantage the story of the Mayfair men, the most atypical of felons subjected to the lash.

Harley and Wilmer were initially held at His Majesty's Prison Wormwood Scrubs, located in inner west London.[5] Though they did not appeal their prison sentences, they asked the Home Secretary for the commutation of their flogging.[6] A petition opposing the sentences was signed by the Dean of Canterbury, Dr. Hewlett Johnson; the Dean of St Paul's, Dr. W. R. Matthews; the Reverend P. T. R. Kirk, vicar of Christchurch, Westminster; Dr. L. P. Jacks, Unitarian minister; Professor John MacMurray, Grote Professor of Mind and Logic at University College, London; Edward Glover, psychoanalyst and criminologist; George Benson, Labour MP for Chesterfield; and Clara D. Rackham of the Howard League. Flogging, they insisted, was not effective. Those who did approve of such sentences were not ensuring the safety of the community; such people's satisfaction only lay in knowing that pain would be inflicted.[7]

The question of the flogging of the Hyde Park Hotel robbers surfaced in Parliament. In the House of Commons, Thomas Kennedy, a Labour MP, asked if the home secretary would consider remitting the flogging of Wilmer and Harley. In addition, he and George Ridley wanted to know when the committee on corporal punishment would present its report. In replying, Geoffrey Lloyd insisted that the Home Office could not interfere with court sentences. He did say that the report had been received but was not yet published. Not content with this simple factual statement, Sir Archibald Southby paraded the back-bench Conservatives' adulation of discipline by asking, "In view of the cowardly attack on an inoffensive citizen, will my honourable friend see that these criminals receive the punishment they richly deserve?" This sally won "ministerial cheers" from one side of the House and from the other George Ridley's query if Southby "did not consider that this was a barbaric and sadistic form of punishment."[8] MPs' views of the issue varied according to class loyalties and political persuasion. In discussing corporal punishment Labour MPs presented themselves as humanitarians and Conservative MPs as disciplinarians.

In March the question of the Mayfair men and the "cat" surfaced once again. In response to a Labour member asking if the convicts had yet received any of their strokes, Sir Samuel Hoare, the home secretary, reported that the wardens had carried out the full sentences on March 1. Far from being sated, Tory MPs pushed for an extension of such punishments. Sir Gifford Fox asked if the Home Office did not agree that sabotage and the giving away of official secrets should similarly be punished. Frederick Pethick-Lawrence countered by inquiring if the home secretary had noted the sadistic influence such acts had on the public and whether he would consider ending such punishments. His assertion elicited ministerial cries of "No!"[9] Godfrey Nicholson insisted that press speculations and deplorable parliamentary questions like Pethick-Lawrence's resulted in the "cat" garnering unfortunate publicity. The Conservatives once again used the issue of punishing playboys to burnish their reputation as defenders of law and order.

Once the Home Office refused to commute the floggings of Wilmer and Harley, the press devoted even more column inches to the disgusting details of the administration of corporal punishment. The papers initially asserted that Wilmer and Harley would be moved from Wormwood Scrubs to Maidstone Jail and only be subjected to a whipping after they were settled. In fact they were both flogged as soon as their appeals were denied. The popular press thoroughly covered the fate of Wilmer, the first to be scourged on March 1.[10] Though some held that only three strokes were given at a time, spaced out every three weeks, Wilmer received his full fifteen at once while still at the Scrubs.[11] "Two burly warders swinging alternately laid 15 strokes of a nine-thonged 'cat-o'-nine-tails' on the bare back of a Mayfair playboy in prison today," wrote one reporter. "His hands stretched above his head and tied to a triangle, the youth was flogged while a doctor stood by ready to halt the beating if necessary."[12] Newspapers in Europe and North America gave accounts of Harley's ordeal. Asserting that he was appalled by this cruel form of punishment, the editor of *Le Populaire*, a Parisian paper, went on say that such tortures gave birth to unhealthy interests that were unworthy of a civilized nation.[13]

The press based its accounts of the floggings on a perusal of the published regulations. In prison before sentencing, a medical officer determined if the prisoner were fit enough to be flogged. For example, in 1932 a judge spared two men found guilty at the Devon Assizes of robbing women after they produced medical certificates that testified to their having been wounded in the war. An appeal court revoked the sentence of six strokes imposed by the 1935

Carmarthen Assizes on a miner whose health was dodgy. Lord Hewart's biographer claimed that the judge had never before the Hyde Park Hotel trial passed a flogging sentence, but at the 1937 Kent Assizes he came close when enraged by the case of a thirty-five-year-old man who had beaten a sixty-nine-year-old woman. After sentencing the man to five years in prison, he added that if the cad were not unfit "he would have had a severe flogging that he would have remembered all the rest of his life."[14]

If the medical officer declared a prisoner fit, the court specified the number of strokes, twenty-four being the maximum. Warders strapped the prisoner to a triangle or easel by his hands and feet, screened his head, and protected his neck and loins. The prison governor, a male nurse, the prison doctor, and a senior warder who counted the strokes witnessed the lashing of the prisoner. The doctor could at any time halt the proceedings if he believed that continuing them posed a serious danger. The warders received two shillings sixpence and a half day off work for doing the job.[15]

The *Sunday Pictorial* published what it claimed to be an ex-felon's experience of being flogged.

> Never mind what I got it for. Never mind my name. I'd heard the Beak order me flogging. I knew it was coming. Well, one morning, my Dartmoor cell door opens and the screw (warder) tells me to put on my trousers, and nothing else. There's a couple more outside—in case I am going to get rough. What's the use, I do as I'm told. Between the three of them I'm marched along the iron gallery outside my cell, down to the floor of the hall. There I see the triangle, ready, with the straps on it. The old man, the quack, and the chief screw (governor), medical officer and chief warder are waiting. There's a couple of attendants from the hospital, and three young screws learning the job. They don't waste time. The old man reads out the number of strokes (from a Home Office order authorizing the flogging), and the minute he's done I am grabbed, shoved face-first against the triangle. Both my feet are strapped—my wrists are strapped, too, hauled up on a pulley rope so I'm stretched full. A canvas strip is buckled over the back of my neck so the lash won't get me there. All very quick, see? I don't know which warder has the "cat"—you're not allowed to know. I hear something as though he is swinging it back behind me. I bite my teeth and start to get ready, but I am not quick enough. It comes sooner than I expect, like a smash with a ton weight, right across the bare back that cuts and burns in fierce. It bangs a yell out of me, for I am not ready. I hear the chief shout out "One." Somehow that makes

"Le chat à neuf queues dans une prison de Londres." *L'Illustration: Journal universal,* Sept. 3, 1910. © The British Library Board

me murder angry. Then it comes again. Too quick. You see, the first crack kind of knocks you silly, so you can't time the rest. After three the quack was in front of me, looking close. But he must have reckoned I was all right, because I got three more. Then they unstrap me, carry me back to my cell. Listen—the "cat" has nine tails of cord nearly three feet long, knotted at the ends. They're on a handle a couple of feet long. The screw that wields it is chosen for strength— he gets half a dollar and a half-day off the job. Them tails leave your back all covered in red snake-lines and torn about a lot, too. You get a mattress and pillows to rest on, and the quack rubs in stuff and binds you up. But you never lose the marks. It takes a week before you try and fetch a deep breath afterwards.[16]

Opponents of corporal punishment claimed that few men were able to stand more than five strokes at a time without collapsing.[17] And fear of the dreaded cat-o'-nine-tails even drove some desperate criminals to suicide. In 1930, James Edward Spiers, serving a ten-year sentence for armed robbery, jumped from Wandsworth prison's second gallery before the group of justices of the peace assembled to witness his receiving fifteen lashes.[18] In a 1934 case the coroner concluded: "It appears here, on the man's own statement, that he was suffering very bitterly in mind, especially at the thought of the flogging. That no doubt preyed on his mind to a great extent. It is open for anybody to suggest that that mode of punishment is too barbarous in these times. On the other hand, some people would say that the statement of the deceased and the fear shown in him absolutely justified that particular form of punishment. However, that is purely a matter of academic discussion."[19] Given the suicides, George Bernays in 1934 demanded that an inquiry be made of "this horrible form of punishment." The home secretary initially rebuffed this request, optimistically citing the decline in the use of the cat as evidence that the problem was solving itself.[20]

By chance, the trial of the Hyde Park Hotel robbers took place just as a wave of opposition to the use of the "cat" and other outmoded forms of punishment was cresting. Wilmer's whipping, claimed the press, sparked a letter-writing campaign by reformers. The debate was followed across the English-speaking world. The *Toronto Globe and Mail* headed one account with the headlines: "Shaw and Churchmen Protest Lashes Vainly: 15 Strokes Inflicted upon Young Man-about-Town Robber—Public's Appetite for Pain Said Filled" and later "English Opinion Split on Cat O' Nine Tails."[21] A Jamaican paper headed its version with "Is the 'Cat' Necessary? Controversy in England as to Whether This Form of Punishment Should Be Meted Out or Not": "Cause of the controversy was the recent conviction of four Mayfair men for robbery with violence. The four were sent into penal servitude—two in addition being sentenced to receive strokes of the dreaded cat-o'-nine. Daily prominent London dailies reproduced letters from many prominent persons in the United Kingdom, some protesting against administering of the 'cat' and some seeing no reason why flogging should not be administered for certain serious crimes."[22] Appearing on the same page as accounts of the opening of the Mayfair trial was a report of a speech Sir Samuel Hoare, the home secretary, gave to the Howard League for Penal Reform. He lauded those seeking to modernize the law. "The people who had made the changes were not faddists, sentimentalists, and cranks, but men and women who realized the grim facts of the problem." These reforms were all part of Hoare's new Criminal Justice Act, which would, he predicted, eventually mean less crime.[23] Central to his reform campaign was the 1938 Cadogan report, which called for a radical curtailment of corporal punishment.

Corporal punishment, commonly employed by the courts in the eighteenth century, had declined in the nineteenth century.[24] This evolution reflected in part what Michel Foucault later identified as a shift in the attention of the penal authorities from the body to the soul.[25] Nevertheless, occasional panics, aroused by what were regarded as particularly heinous crimes, led to parliamentary acts that reintroduced corporal punishment.[26] They included the Treason Act of 1842 (sparked by a threat to Queen Victoria), the Vagrancy Act of 1824, the Garrotters Act of 1863, the Vagrancy Act of 1898, and the Criminal Law Amendment Act of 1912 (resulting from the White Slave Panic).[27] There were, the defenders of these acts asserted, brutes, bullies, and cowards who only understood pain.[28] Prison wardens were also allowed by law to employ flogging to punish serious cases of inmate indiscipline.

Nevertheless, in the interwar years judges were less and less likely to include strokes of the cat in their sentencing. Though a handful of men on the bench—like Mr. Justice Day in Liverpool and Mr. Justice Darling in Kent—were prone to demand the whip, fewer and fewer judges handed down sentences of corporal punishment. Yet most judges favored the retention of such an option and bristled when reformers pointed out that English courts were backward, whipping and flogging having been outlawed in every civilized country except for the British dominions.

To respond to such criticisms and to assist the home secretary's program of judicial and prison reform, in May 1937 the government set up a departmental committee, chaired by Edward Cadogan, a Conservative MP. Its mandate was to determine the effectiveness of corporal punishment in the United Kingdom. Its first task was to establish the actual numbers of floggings. It found that many of the old laws sanctioning the "cat" were moribund and could be easily removed from the statute book. For example, no one had ever been charged under the Treason Act of 1842, and the Vagrancy Act led to only four cases of flogging between 1926 and 1935. The Criminal Law Amendment Act (a spawn of the 1912 White Slave Panic) resulted in eleven pimps being flogged in the first year, but between 1913 and 1935 there were only twenty-five similar cases, of which fifteen occurred in the first three years. Robbery with violence was the one offense that resulted in a large number of sentences of corporal punishment levied against adults.[29] Its provisions were contained in the Garrotters Act of 1863 and updated by the Larceny Act of 1916.[30] Robbery with violence cases actually dropped from 1,414 (1904–1913) to 656 (1926–1935), but the percentage of felons sentenced to be whipped rose from 4.3 to 35.8 percent.[31] Between 1900 and 1935, judges subjected a grand total of 466 offenders to the "cat."[32]

Did whipping work? Most policemen and judges believed that it did. It was popularly held that no one was ever flogged twice. This was not true. The committee was familiar with the story that the lash had ended an outbreak of garroting (robbers strangling their victims) that took place in London in the 1860s.[33] Investigation proved that in fact the number of such crimes increased after the passage of the Garrotters Act. Judges insisted that the 1908 crime wave in Cardiff was squelched by fourteen floggings. The subsequent high level of recidivism demonstrated that they had had no apparent effect.[34] Some asserted that the flogging permitted by the Criminal Law Amendment Act of 1912 ended pimping in Scotland. In fact, there were no floggings there between 1912 and 1922, yet cases dropped from forty-seven in 1913 to seven in 1922. Similarly, there were relatively fewer robberies in Scotland (where there was no flogging) than in England and Wales (where there was). Moreover, in England between 1921 and 1930, 55 percent of those flogged (142) for robbery reoffended, versus 43.9 percent of those not flogged (298).[35] To be generous, the committee was willing to concede that flogging made little difference regarding a felon's subsequent career choices, but the more critical witnesses argued that the lash produced bitterness and resentment that increased the likelihood of convicts committing more serious crimes. Rather than repressing crime the punishment tended to fuel it.

Although politicians and newspapers frequently argued that sex crimes should be punished by floggings, the committee noted that experts doubted the efficacy of using the lash in such cases. In practice judges shared this skepticism, since of the 974 men convicted of "attempts to commit unnatural offences (includes importuning, assaults with intent to commit unnatural offences and indecent assaults on males)" only twenty-five were flogged. Courts increasingly recognized that homosexuality was a "psychological abnormality" that could not be cured by beatings. And most young male prostitutes were, the committee stated, not really homosexuals and could be best reformed in a Borstal, or youth detention center. It also pointed out that pimping—living on immoral earnings and procuring—was rarely prosecuted. Courts recognized the injustice of the law that regarded the husband or lover the same as a woman's pimp. The threat of the cat was further discounted since a large portion of the men found guilty of procuring were physically unfit to be punished. Consequently, since 1912 the Criminal Law Amendment Act resulted in only thirty-two floggings, with twenty-two of these in 1913–1914.[36]

The Cadogan committee's report was published a few weeks after the Hyde Park Hotel robbery. It stated that the statistics demonstrated the futility of employing corporal punishment, and that in countering attempts at reform, use of the "cat" posed the danger of making matters worse. Recommending that all corporal punishment of adults outside of prison be repealed, the report concluded: "Corporal punishment is purely punitive; and is out of accord with those modern ideas which stress the need for using such methods as penal treatment as give an opportunity for subjecting the offender to reformative influences."[37]

The press noted that the public's interest in the topic of corporal punishment was clearly sparked by the Mayfair case.[38] The *Spectator*, a conservative weekly magazine, observed:

> The Report of the Committee on Corporal Punishment appeared at a most opportune moment; it should help to decide finally a long controversy which recently has been brought to a head by the sentence passed on the "Mayfair men." The Committee recommends that corporal punishment should be completely abolished for all court offences, and should be retained only as a means of maintaining prison discipline. The Committee's grounds for this conclusion are as interesting and important as the conclusion itself; for while its recommendations will please all who are already convinced of the barbarity of this form of punishment, the Report should also persuade those who hitherto have believed in its deterrent effect. After examining carefully all the evidence the Committee concludes: "We have been unable to find any body of facts or figures showing that the introduction of a power of flogging has produced a decrease in the number of offences for which it may be imposed." This conclusion leaves the defence of corporal punishment in the hands of those who believe in purely retributory punishment, without any deterrent or reformative value, and even they must make logically an exception in the case of juvenile offences; thus there should be no strong opposition to the immediate adoption of the Committee's recommendations. The Committee's own adoption of the principle that purely retributory

punishment is not justifiable should have a good effect on public opinion, and the administration of the law; the sooner this principle is generally applied, the better.[39]

A letter to the editor of the *Spectator* went further, linking the lash to state terror.

SIR,—As an ordinary citizen, I feel I must beg a space in your columns to voice a strong disapproval of the flogging sentences in connexion with the recent Mayfair robbery case. I shall, of course, be accused of being a "sentimentalist" and reminded that sympathy is due to the victim and not the perpetrators of the crime. I certainly concede that sympathy to the victim, and am the very last to condone acts of violence, but as a reasonably civilised human being I must indeed ask myself whether in this year of grace a.d. 1938, the infliction of torture on the bodies of criminals for crimes of violence can be morally justified. We are frequently expressing indignation at acts of cruelty in other countries on unfortunate offenders convicted under their respective codes, but are we any better? It seems that the Continental label of hypocrisy is as true in this as in other matters. There is no difference in substance between methods used now and those used in former days, except a more refined method of infliction—for according to a description given by one who had undergone flogging, the act is carried out with a technique and milieu like that of an operating-theatre perverted to the function of causing agony, the avoidance of oblivion and any fatal effects resulting from the lashing. That this form of punishment is merely the expression of sadistic impulses latent in all of us, and which we can legally satisfy upon suitable scapegoats, is a self-evident fact upon analysis. The relish with which such sentences are reported in our yellow Press further confirms my contention. Embryonic as the stage of psychology still is, we now know enough to "debunk" Victorian self-righteousness. . . . At the present time many States have fallen back into making the inflicting of bodily pain a recognised instrument of policy and terrorisation, and the darkening veil of passion and prejudice seems to be engulfing what little light of intelligence and reason we have developed in European civilisation. Sadism, mass emotion, self-righteous indignation are exceedingly powerful psychic forces, responsible for many social evils.[40]

Though reformers were in the main pleased with the Cadogan report, they were annoyed that it defended the continued use of the "cat" in prison. This appeared to be illogical. The committee had found that whipping had no deterrent value, so some, including Sir Stafford Cripps, asked why it was retained in prisons.[41] Nevertheless, most critics lauded the report for its use of facts and statistics to counter the myth of the efficacy of corporal punishment.[42]

In the interwar years George Benson, Labour MP for Chesterfield and head of the Howard League for Penal Reform, led the campaign against the lash.[43] Benson likened flogging to the death penalty: "Savage penalties have very frequently been tried for the purpose of supplementing ineffective police work. If, for various reasons, the police were inefficient and had captured only a small percentage of criminals, and the authorities, in order to supplement that weakness in detection, increased the severity of penalties on such as are caught, that policy invariably proved a failure."[44]

The league stressed that the various flogging acts were the results of social panics bordering on hysteria, that there was no evidence of whipping having any deterrent value, and that such savagery was almost unique to the United Kingdom.[45] Others made the point that impoverished criminals had little "choice," so retribution was useless.[46] Class made a difference. Sir Christopher Robinson reported that writing a letter to the conservative *Telegraph* opposing the lash led to his being bombarded with violent denunciations by members of the upper classes, including women furious at idea of being denied the pleasure of reading about and discussing the "cat."[47] John Parker suggested that the moneyed were accustomed to accept corporal punishment by years spent in elite boarding schools, "particularly Eton." "To-day, only the very rich still feel a strong desire to preserve the right of buying the very doubtful privilege of birching for their offspring. . . . The ordinary decent Englishman's view . . . is that birching should be abolished."[48] George Bernard Shaw agreed on the influence of environment. "The man who has graduated from the flogging block at Eton to the bench from which he sentences the garrotter to be flogged," wrote the dramatist, "is the same social product as the garrotter who has been kicked by his father and cuffed by his mother until he has grown strong enough to throttle and rob the rich citizen whose money he desires."[49]

Benson, in arguing that the floggers' preoccupation with sex crimes revealed their unseemly psychological motivations, picked up on a theme developed at the end of the nineteenth century. The exaggerated hatred that "normal" men so vociferously declared against the "abnormal" had disturbing sexual undertones, which those in the campaign against flogging could not help but notice.[50] The Humanitarian League, with the support of intellectuals such as Edward Carpenter, Henry Salt, and George Bernard Shaw, led the opposition.

Salt declared that it was ironic that conservatives presented the lash as a puri-
fier of morals when the "psychopathic side" of the question was so obvious.[51]
Shaw, in an 1898 lecture entitled "Flagellomania," asserted that flogging was a
form of debauchery, a mania based "on a sensual instinct" and a "special dis-
order of the imagination."[52] He returned to the issue in 1912, noting that those
who favored the lash ignored or pretended not to know that the desire to flog
or be flogged was a vice. Raids on brothels always uncovered whipping para-
phernalia. The 1912 act, he declared, was "not a legislative phenomenon but a
psychopathic one."[53] Prominent clergymen and liberals joined in the Mayfair
men's appeal against their flogging after Shaw wrote to newspapers that
"the transient pain to the flogged men is not worth considering in comparison to the gratification and encouragement it has given to all our sadists and
flagellomaniacs."[54]

The psychotherapist Edward Glover gave a psychoanalytical gloss to such
accounts of the sexual excitement experienced by the censorious, but by the
1930s laypersons were also discussing issues of unconscious motivation. "My
excuse for this letter is the immense and sensational publicity given to the
'Mayfair' flogging sentences," began a March 1938 letter to the *New Statesman
and Nation*, Britain's leading left-of-center weekly magazine. The writer went
on to argue that an immoral punishment like whipping debased the community. And such a barbaric custom had its disturbing sensual side. He was shocked
to discover that even "girl typists" were now discussing it. The linkage of pain to
pleasure was obvious, for shops selling smut, contraceptives, and aphrodisiacs
also displayed books on flogging. "The obvious object is to create a market for
the other articles."[55] In the next week's issue of the *New Statesman* came a report
that a Paris company was seeking to recruit women authors to write short stories
on corporal punishment. It suggested that works on the whipping of schoolgirls,
slaves, and wives ("matrimonial chastisement") would sell.[56]

Did whipping deter others? The committee found scant evidence to support such a contention.[57] For this reason the civil servants in the Home Office
saw no need to extend the practice. Yet every year the vengeful in and outside
of Parliament demanded an extension of flogging to sensational cases that had
excited their indignation. "For the man who peddled drugs," declared Sir Archibald Southby, "there was only one punishment—'the cat.'"[58] The "cat"
could end the smash-and-grab assaults of the "motor bandit," said some, just as
it had stamped out garroting.[59] Blackmail also warranted a whipping, declared
the Common Sergeant, as it was the "most cowardly offense."[60] Sir Ernest

Wilde felt that the purse snatcher was as bad.[61] Sir Robert Gower, enraged by reports of a man who had beaten a dog to death, sought flogging for cruelty to animals.[62] Sir Thomas Moore told the story of louts pulling the feathers off a live sparrow. "There was no means of showing the meaning of pain to such fiends unless it was inflicted on their own hides."[63] Disciplinarians repeatedly demanded that a taste of the "cat" be dealt out to those guilty of any of a motley collection of crimes including incest; sodomy; rape; demanding money with menaces; assaults on wives and children; cruelty to animals; assaults with razors, bayonets, and broken bottles; and the use of exploding or corrosive substances.[64] Save for the crude desire to meet violence with violence, these crimes were not linked in any logical fashion. Critics noted, however, that it was hard to imagine any middle-class individual being involved in such activities. "If flogging is to be retained as a form of punishment," declared George Ridley, "I see no reason why the list of offences for which that punishment should be applied should not be rationalised in the light of modern conditions. I see no reason, in that case, why share-pushing, tax-evasion, fraud at the expense of poor and unsophisticated people, animal hunting and blackmail should not be added to the list."[65]

Under the heading "Bringing Back the Cat," one paper hailed the sentences imposed by the Lord Chief Justice in the Mayfair robbery case. The writer asserted that there had been too much "coddling" of villains.[66] Sir Reginald Coventry at the Worcester Quarter Sessions took up this line. He claimed that reforms threatened to turn prisons into rest homes where "people can have comfort they would not enjoy in their own homes; where they will be entertained and generally live a type of life which for many of them will be a great improvement upon the life they have at the present moment." Given that humanitarians now threatened to end flogging—despite every judge's opposition—the "professional garrotters of Liverpool and Cardiff" could look forward to being spared the only thing they feared.[67] In a withering reply, Edward Hemmerde, recorder of Liverpool, noted that the social conditions of the poor had to be truly terrible if prison life were better. His main point was the notion that flogging eliminated garroting was a myth, a myth propagated by the same sort of reactionaries who in 1881 had opposed the termination of whippings in the army and navy.[68] The *Spectator* piled on:

> The observations on corporal punishment made by Sir Reginald Coventry at Worcester Quarter Sessions on Monday were reported at length, which is hardly

a kindness to Sir Reginald, for they were not wise remarks. He "knew it had been said that corporal punishment did not cure people, but they would have difficulty in finding any men ever coming back for a second dose." It is not clear what steps Sir Reginald has taken to look for such cases; he might perhaps consult the report and minutes and evidence of the Home Office Committee on Corporal Punishment on the point. He invoked in support of his contention "the professional garrotters of Liverpool and Cardiff, who could look forward to being spared the only punishment which deterred them—the cat o' nine tails"; this is a subject on which more seems to be known at Worcester than at Liverpool or Cardiff. The wisdom of the abolition of corporal punishment is admittedly an arguable question, but the evidence worth hearing on the subject is that of persons, such as prison governors, who are in a position to see what the effect of flogging on a man really is. High Court Judges, who pass a flogging sentence and have no concern with its execution, are little better qualified than, say, bankers, to pronounce on its penal value. Having heard evidence from every quarter, the Home Office Committee reached a unanimous conclusion, and the Home Secretary was fully justified in adopting it.[69]

Despite such sarcastic attacks, the defenders of flogging presented themselves as realists and their opponents as sentimentalists. One wrote, "I cannot find sympathy either for the cruel 'crook' who receives a beating, or for the exaggerator who bleats of the temporary minor suffering undergone by these *beasts*."[70] Another, in arguing for whippings to counter such "abominable offences" as blackmail, asserted, "In comparison with such a result, it would seem that the welfare of so debased an individual is not worthy of consideration."[71] The conservative press portrayed the reformers as out of touch with public sentiment. "When a judge, ordered a flogging for the jewel thieves, known as the 'Mayfair Playboys,' there was much public criticism to the effect that the punishment was not in accord with modern humanitarian principles in dealing with criminals. A survey concluded during the week, suggests that recent criticism did not reflect public opinion, as only 44 per cent, of those approached expressed the opinion that flogging should be abolished."[72]

Defenders particularly disliked being accused of taking a perverse pleasure in inflicting pain. F. O. Taylor tried to reverse the argument, asserting that to accuse of sadism those who employed corporal punishment was a sign of "an unhealthy mind." He insisted that his headmaster, though he inflicted severe pain on his charges, was no sadist.[73] The psychiatrist Robert Armstrong-Jones (grandfather of the Earl of Snowden) agreed. The whipping of children, far from being cruel, was a kindly way of saving boys from their innate desires to steal and lie. Pain acted as a deterrent and was nature's response to the violation of its laws. The sexual side of the issue, he suggested, was something dreamed up by elitists. "It is the perverted imagination—or may it be called the 'intellectual narcissism'?—of a Freudian to discuss sadism and masochism (the love of self-torture) as aspects to be considered in the administration of Justice."[74]

Defenders of the "cat" went so far as to claim that those subjected to flogging in time came to realize its benefits. Often such assertions were accompanied by the revelation that the writer had been "made a man" by the punishment that he himself had received at boarding school. A Marlborough Police Court magistrate stated that sailors, seeing the need of the lash to maintain order at sea, requested its employment.[75] Harold Arthur Frere, late superintendent of prisons in British Guiana, pushed this line of argument to laughable lengths.

Sir, Mr. Shaw must know that "like cures like"—"similia similibus curanter." Therefore it follows that the only punishment which has any meaning for the man who has committed an act of brutality is the "argumentum ad hominem," or to take it out of his skin. I have witnessed, during my 25 years' sojourn in the East and West Indies, hundreds of floggings, and not once have felt any maudlin sympathy for the victims of the lash—though I have often shuddered at the crimes for which they were being thrashed. Flogging is a deterrent, not only to the brute but also to others who may be inclined to commit acts of violence and cruelty, it cured garroting in this country and the use of the knife in Barbados. People in their sense do not argue with sharks or alligators, nor should we use gloved hands when dealing with human brutes who assault women and children and lay violent hands on their fellow-creatures. I have been "slippered" by my father, thrashed by my schoolmaster, and not been brutalised. Nor have I ever felt the slightest desire to use violence except in self-protection. Flogging in our prisons (home and colonial) is not the brutal thing it is made out to be by the would-be reformers, who, for some unearthly reason, always sympathise with the bully rather than with his victim. It is salutary; it is performed in the presence of the prison surgeon, who stops the flogging if the brute faints, from fear rather than from pain. I was once deputed to carry out a flogging upon a "buck nigger," a man with a magnificent physique. After he had received his two dozen lashes with the "cat" and was taken down from the triangle, he merely shot out his arms and cried "Rule Britannia" and from that day behaved like a lamb.[76]

In a 1939 discussion of corporal punishment the leftist MP Denis Pritt declared that the only defenders of flogging were Adolf Hitler and the Conservative Women's Conference.[77] This sally was not literally true, but it captured the essence of the social polarization revealed by the debate. Yet at the same time the popular press exploited the stories of lashings that the upper-class broadsheets shunned. The newspaper reports of the sentences that Chief Justice Hewart doled out were, as a number of commentators complained, all too often transparent appeals to the masses' voyeurism, class resentment, and schadenfreude. The respectable press declared itself appalled by the tabloids' sensational accounts of corporal punishment.[78] The consensus of the respectable, claimed the *Evening Telegraph*, was that flogging was a "degrading and brutalizing form of punishment."[79] The *New Statesman* pointed out that the Sunday papers were "stuffed with sadistic material" pertaining to the floggings.[80] In an editorial the *Times* noted that the Cadogan report was timely: "It happens to be published at a moment when special circumstances lend it adventitious weight. Certain recent sentences of corporal punishment have given occasion for the wanton and mercenary incitement of the public appetite for the most morbid details of the physical process—an appetite supplied with as little regard for truth as for decency. When an institution may expose the mind of the people to a repetition of such nauseous assault, there should be a double welcome for the proof that we can do without it."[81]

The quality newspapers and weekly magazines on both the left and right recoiled from the sensationalism of the "yellow press." The *Spectator* expressed its disgust at the latter's vulgarity.

> The so-called Mayfair men who were recently sentenced at the Old Bailey to flogging as well as imprisonment were guilty of a brutal crime, and if the use of the "cat" were either redemptive or deterrent it would be justified here. But the real scandal, and the decisive reason for the abolition of this penalty, is the loathsomely degrading treatment of the subject in a section of the daily Press. In the interval between delivery of the sentence and the infliction of the penalty readers of certain journals have had laid before them detailed accounts of the manner of a prison flogging and the physical results of it, while on Wednesday at least two papers, the *Daily Mail* and the *Daily Express*, published what purported to be actual descriptions of the flogging that had taken place the day before. The

value of their versions is sufficiently demonstrated by a comparison of the two. According to the *Mail* Harley and Wilmer "took their full flogging without a whimper. Harley received 20 strokes, Wilmer 15." The *Express* alleges that Wilmer "received five strokes and then collapsed." It reported, a little less categorically, "statements" that "Harley received six strokes before he collapsed and was taken to hospital." Whatever the intention of such descriptions (and whether they correspond with fact or not), they can appeal only to sadists or people who find utter beastliness congenial. The one redeeming feature is the prospect that such journalistic exhibitions will do more than anything else to bring the infliction of the "cat" by judges to an end.[82]

Flogging might not change Mayfair men, wrote a contributor, but it made money for the penny papers.[83]

Having played up the notion that the Hyde Park Hotel robbers sentenced to be flogged were young dandies, the press set its own expectations for the punishments' drama. Although journalists were not allowed to witness their scourgings, they nevertheless produced accounts of what *must have* occurred. Little imagination was required to recognize the dramatic possibilities of a scene in which a working-class warder used the "cat" to break the spirit not of some crude ruffian but of a supercilious upper-class playboy.[84]

The Cadogan report eschewed questions of morality and focused simply on the ineffectiveness of corporal punishment. Its call for reform was a symptom of a changing social landscape in which the Labour Party was slowly increasing its power while elements within the Conservative Party and the civil service grew ever more concerned with allaying the hostility of the working class.[85] Given the class discrimination inherent in corporal punishment it was ironic—though predictable—that the only prisoners whose punishments the public recalled were those of the Mayfair men. The story colored the discussion of flogging for another two decades.

The government accepted the recommendations of the Cadogan committee and included them in the Criminal Justice Bill, which Sir Samuel Hoare presented for a second reading on November 10, 1938. Most of the criticism of the bill came from the Conservative government's own MPs. Sir Alfred Beit tried to use the example of the Hyde Park Hotel robbery to defend flogging.

There are some crimes for which reform is not enough, those which are grossly revolting to the public conscience. A very good example of this type of crime was that committed earlier this year and known in the popular Press as the crime of the Mayfair men. I think a case can be made out for some measure of retribution in those circumstances. I hope that it will be possible in Committee for adequate safeguards to be given that the same protection at least will be given to the public as it is now proposed to give in very special cases to prison officers.[86]

Labour MPs responded that disapproving of flogging in general but approving of it in particular cases was illogical. To follow such a line of reasoning would always result in retribution winning out over reform. George Ridley went on to reply dramatically to Beit.

In connection with the Mayfair case I had an extraordinary experience, and I have the permission of the people concerned to relate it to the House. A young society woman, a friend of the injured man, went to the court, filled almost with vindictive indignation against the crime. She sat through the trial, and more and more found unbearable what she described as the evident and indecent pleasure which the infliction of the punishment gave to some people in the court. She was nauseated by it, and, finally, used every effort she could to save the assailants of her friend from the brutality of the "cat."[87]

Whether or not this unlikely story was true is not important. What is interesting is how parliamentary debaters projected onto Mayfair men their own concerns. Both sides in the flogging debate attempted to use the same case to support their opposing arguments.

By June 1939 the bill had passed through committee stage, but it was too late to go to the Lords, for the war intervened. The Labour Party was swept in to power in 1945 and turned to a long list of overdue reforms. It reintroduced the Criminal Justice Bill of 1938, which received almost unanimous support. Though there was a general consensus that the old penal system based on deterrence had to be replaced by one infused with a modern reformative spirit, nevertheless the issue of flogging was, in the words of the *Times*, still "contested with passion."[88] And once again the debaters sought to turn the story of the Hyde Park Hotel robbers to their own purposes. Captain Arthur Marsden, in giving a potted history of the 1938 bill, asserted that flogging had reformed Wilmer and Harley.

However, the war intervened, and [the bill] was not put to the vote of the whole House, but what influenced the House and the public at the time was the incident of the "Mayfair boys" assault and robbery case. Now the Home Secretary has told us that some of those boys, or young men, came back on further charges—but not charges of violence. That is the point. Some of those who got the "cat" certainly came back on further charges, but not robbery and violence, which really proves the point that flogging of that description is a deterrent to violent crimes. I think it is the wish of the people generally that for certain crimes some form of corporal punishment should be retained.[89]

A week after Marsden's speech Mr. Justice George McClure, who ten years earlier had been the crown prosecutor in the Hyde Park Hotel robbery, sentenced a carpenter to eight years' penal servitude for robbing two sisters, aged eighty and seventy-seven. McClure took the opportunity of lamenting the loss of the lash. "In a fairly long experience in these courts I have never heard of a more brutal case than this. Anyone who listened to the evidence may well wonder why the punishment which this offence carries, so far as corporal punishment is concerned, is about to be abolished. If ever there was a case for that kind of punishment this is that case."[90] Despite such last-ditch appeals the Criminal Justice Act received royal assent on July 30, 1948.[91] There were reasons for reformers to celebrate as well as to reflect. In the ten years since 1938, when the bill was first introduced, 310 men had been subjected to floggings—so the rate had actually increased.[92]

Judges refused to accept defeat. They lamented their loss of discretionary powers and in the 1950s kept up the pressure on the Home Office to reintroduce the whip.[93] In the Commons, James Chuter Ede, the home secretary, had to face the assertion that since flogging had ended, the number of women "coshed" had greatly increased.[94] Though the numbers of violent crimes were in fact down, there were always some, as the *Manchester Guardian* noted, who felt greater severity was needed.

> There is a section of opinion in this country which habitually turns to the cat-o'-nine-tails whenever there is a run of well reported crimes. Eleven years ago, one of Mr. Ede's critics of this week wanted us to flog the misguided Irishmen who left bombs in London railway stations. We were once urged to fight car bandits and window slashers with the "cat." Indeed, at one time or another the courts have used the "cat" with intensest zeal to fight gangsters in Liverpool, pimps in Glasgow and Manchester, assaults on drunken sailors in Cardiff. The result was always the same; people were glad to feel that "something is being done," yet in no case was flogging the key to victory.[95]

With the election of a Conservative government in 1951, hopes for a return to flogging blossomed once more, as did references to the Hyde Park Hotel robbers. Inspector Fabian, the officer who took the credit for arresting the Mayfair men, now presented himself as an expert on the deterrent value of the "cat," and Wilmer and Harley were once more used to advance a political agenda. Under the inflammatory headline "Only the 'CAT' Holds Back the Brutes," Fabian wrote:

> I know. It was I who sent the four Mayfair playboys up before the judge for brutally beating and robbing a jeweller in the Hyde Park Hotel and two of these young society men got the "cat." One got the maximum—20 strokes. And the other got 10. It sent a shudder through England to read about it. Remember? Well, I had a drink with both men when they finished their prison sentences. It was not my idea. They came to see me. One of them said: "Would you like to see what all the fuss was about?" He wanted to show me what the "cat" had done to him. Now I believe—as do most senior police officers—that an official should know exactly what he is doing, the full consequences of his acts. I think judges should be as familiar with the grim interiors of prisons as they are with the barristers' robing-rooms. And I was glad to agree to look at this young fellow's back. I felt that, however shocking the sight, it would help me better to understand my responsibilities as a policeman. We went into a private room. He pulled his shirt off. "There," he said, "on the right shoulder blade, Mr. Fabian." Yes I could see it. The scars looked like smallpox marks. No better and no worse. He said, "There it is. That finishes me. You'll never see me inside prison again." "It was so bad?" I asked. He nodded. "The pain wasn't so bad. Not nearly as bad as I'd expected. But to be strapped up there to this easel thing, and whipped like a dog, with the chief warder counting 'one . . . two . . .' and the prison doctor peering into your face from a hand's width away to see how you're taking it—well, I found myself thinking what kind of animal had I become that this was the only way civilised society could pay my score? To be whipped like a donkey? No—I'm going away where nobody knows about this—I'm going to start the slate clean." He did, too. Both of these Mayfair boys did. And that is why I have been careful not to use their names in telling you this story. Because they are names to be proud of again. The names of men who made their mistake, took their punishment, became wiser and repented.[96]

Fabian's story is too good to be true and contains some obvious errors, such as the number of strokes Wilmer received.[97] Nevertheless it has to be admitted that Fabian knew how to craft an effective narrative.[98] After retiring from Scotland Yard in 1949 he became a crime writer for the *Empire News and Sunday Chronicle*. In the fall of 1954 the BBC began to televise its first police series, *Fabian of the Yard*, based in part on the detective inspector's memoirs. An actor played his part, but at the end of each program the real Fabian would step forward and somewhat woodenly draw out the moral of the story in the same way as he did in the above piece on the Mayfair men. Similarly, the defenders of flogging, being unable to produce hard evidence to support their stance, had to rely increasingly on rhetoric and personal testimony. It might be said that if the Mayfair men or playboys had not existed, the floggers would have had to create them.[99]

Their trial helped to popularize the discussion of corporal punishment; their purported reformation justified it. The trial also marked the emergence of the playboy as the representative of a hedonistic 1930s subculture. The popular press played a key role in creating such celebrities, pandering to the conflicting desires of its vast readership to both applaud and condemn the sophisticated self-centeredness of cynical young men at play.

Chapter 7: **MASCULINITY**

The 1938 Hyde Park Hotel robbery trial broadcast the notion that a new type of modern man had appeared—the playboy. Few men embraced this role, but the playboy was not as marginal a figure as one might assume. Indeed, the evidence suggests that this evocative persona appeared as a result of changes in British culture, particularly in gender and class relations. References to the playboy—in effect a new cultural category—popped up in literature, film, and political discourse. Such was the power of the concept that, despite the condemnation of moralists, young men began to call themselves playboys. What did the word "playboy" mean? What did it stand for? The discussion of the playboy often tells us more about the preoccupations of his critics than the playboy himself. Those who worried about modernization in particular found him to be a useful vehicle for the expressions of their cultural concerns. Historians have produced insightful surveys of early twentieth-century society's fear that women's sexual attitudes and behaviors were changing.[1] Tracing the discussion of the playboy allows us to follow purported shifts in what it meant to be a man in 1930s Britain.

Today the term "playboy" is so closely associated with Hugh Hefner's magazine that it is difficult not to assume that it always meant the well-off, well-dressed man who pursues personal pleasure, who is, or at least has fantasies of becoming, a seductive womanizer. This privileging of his sexual side is a fairly recent development. In the seventeenth century, according to the *Oxford English Dictionary*, "playboy" simply meant a boy actor. Ben Jonson in *Love Restored* (1612) referred to the "rogue play-boy that acts Cvpid."[2] By the nineteenth century it could mean a man who shirked responsibilities and sought pleasure. In Ireland it also meant hoaxer or trickster; the teller of tall tales. J. M. Synge in his classic comedy, *Playboy of the Western World* (1907), popularized the use of the word in English, but the French translation—*Le Baladin du monde occidental*

(The buffoon of the Western world) gives a better sense of the main character's personality. Christy is a lucky, irresponsible lout to whom villagers attribute a romantic past. Women hail him: "You're the walking playboy of the western world." He is not the seducer but rather the happy recipient of their mistaken affections. He is still a "boy" and portrayed as rather dim: "[I]t's great luck and company I've won me in the end of time—two fine women fighting for the likes of me—till I'm thinking this night wasn't I a foolish fellow not to kill my father in the years gone by."[3] In Ireland "playboy" was a translation of *buachaill báire*, literally meaning a hurling player, and by extension "a young man who plays games with those around him and scores points off them."[4]

Between 1919 and 1924, Egmont Arens, a fixture of New York City's Greenwich Village artistic scene, published a small magazine titled *Playboy: A Portfolio of Art and Satire*. Contributors included writers Djuna Barnes, E. E. Cummings, Ben Hecht, and D. H. Lawrence; artists Georgia O'Keeffe and Rockwell Kent; and photographer Alfred Stieglitz. In the first number Arens made it clear that he was using the word "playboy" in the traditional sense that stressed playfulness. "Our America is ingrown with Seriousness. Our Art pulls a long face and strikes a pose. Our connoisseurs find their inspiration across [the] sea in faded thoughts of other generations. . . . PLAYBOY is to be a passing record of those who are ALIVE NOW. A Portfolio of Youth. A vessel of Adventure. A magazine given over to Joyous gestures. A Companion of Laughter. A Minstrel of freedom."[5] For most, "playboy" had more negative connotations, meaning a man who, because of his immaturity or lack of seriousness, could not or would not be a productive adult male. In 1923, D. H. Lawrence damned a popular novel as "pretty piffle—just playboy stuff."[6] In Mazo de la Roche's novel *Whiteoak Harvest* (1936) a character states, "No matter how hard I worked I was looked on as a sort of playboy who couldn't do a man's job."[7] Journalists who described William Orpen as "the Playboy of painting," L. P. Jacks as "the Playboy of the philosophical world," or Jack Jones as "the Playboy of Parliament" were referring to these men's apparent playfulness and lack of seriousness; they were not implying their cynicism or promiscuity.[8] Americans employed the term more widely than did the British, but they also maintained for some time the same stress on immaturity.[9] When, in one of his famous fireside chats Franklin Delano Roosevelt attempted to whip up patriotic fervor, he asserted, "From Berlin, Rome, and Tokyo we have been described as a Nation of weaklings—'playboys'—who would hire British soldiers, or Russian soldiers, or Chinese soldiers to do our fighting for us."[10]

Given its pejorative coloring, the British avoided using the term when reporting on the pursuits of Edward, the Prince of Wales. "David," as his friends called him, led a louche life that had all the markings of the classic interwar playboy.[11] A pampered child who as a youth dropped out of Magdalen College, Oxford, and served briefly in the army, he became in the 1920s an idle man-about-town, a habitué of nightclubs. The deferential British press would not refer to his womanizing despite the fact that those in elite circles knew he had had a string of mistresses, including Freda Dudley Ward, Thelma Furness, and Wallis Simpson.[12] The American press felt no such compunction. When the *New York Times* described him as "maturing," it expressed the hope that a more serious individual was replacing the "sportsman and the royal playboy." In 1935 the paper was less confident. "The Prince of Wales will be 41 in June. His playboy days—a decade-full of magazine articles have assured us—are over." In 1936 the *Washington Post* reported that the forty-one year-old bachelor, once a "world playboy," was now king.[13]

If new models of masculinity emerged in the early twentieth century, so too did new models of femininity. Writers in the interwar decades who spoke of changing gender expectations were primarily talking about women. The Great War, which had required thousands of women to enter the masculine world of factory work, shattered the notion of separate spheres. Commentators who sought to reestablish old gender norms argued that women were duty bound to give up their jobs and return to their domestic duties. Working-class women regarded such demands as unfair. Many could not hope to be wives and mothers given that so many young men who could have been their mates had died in the trenches of northern France.

In April 1928 the government lowered the voting age of women from thirty to twenty-one, which in creating the "flapper vote" established the political equality of the sexes. Young women raised the ire of the judgmental in adopting fashions that reflected a desire for independence. "The post-war fashions showing off women's figure as free, young and slim with short hair and skirts, the wearing of cosmetics, smoking in public, the vogue for dancing, were all part of the new image."[14] In fact, women were marrying at an ever younger age. In a new world of romantic consumerism they were supposed to marry for love, though the press continued to announce that upper-class parents had "arranged" the marriages of their daughters. The propertieds' greatest fear was that their child would make a "mésalliance"—that is, marry someone they considered socially inferior.

Experts set sexual standards. Some women's magazines called for sex education to rescue the naïve from the ignorance that the Victorian social purity movement had inculcated. Marie Stopes in her books and lectures boldly set out to eroticize marital sex while the writers of the tabloids' "agony aunts" columns instructed women on how they could maintain romance in their marriage. Such advice only appeared to add to the domestic duties of those wives who regarded intercourse as chiefly ensuring male pleasure.[15]

With the 1930s slump, family size fell to an all time low. Pronatalists blamed women. Though Stopes, who had established the first London birth control clinic in 1921, claimed some of the credit, larger cultural forces were at play.[16] Given the rising cost of children, the big family was no longer economically viable. Even the Anglican Church admitted in 1930 that contraception might play a positive role in marriage. In 1937, Alec Bourne's challenge to the law against abortion led a judge to rule that to protect the life of the mother doctors had the right to take all measures necessary.[17] Those who opposed any form of fertility control trotted out the insulting argument that chaos would soon result as fear of pregnancy was all that prevented many women from plunging into a life of promiscuity. A "bad girl" won her label by her sexual activity, a "bad boy" by his criminal behavior.

The popular press debated every aspect of the young woman's life—her sexuality, fashions, vocations, and entertainments.[18] Its view of women was riddled with contradictions. It wanted them to be modern, yet respectful of traditions.[19] It denigrated those who insisted on working outside the home, while at the same time it lauded efforts by business and government to recruit thousands of women into white-collar work. Despite having lectured women that their natural place was in the home, conservative papers like the *Daily Mail* applauded women flyers and sports car drivers who risked their lives in international competitions. Movies and novels presented young women with similar dilemmas. Were they to identify with the passive, innocent girlfriend or the active, knowing gold digger? Who would they fantasize about: the dutiful, dependable gentleman or the irrepressible playboy?

The playboy, both in reality and as a fantasy figure, represented an evolution or devolution in masculine identity.[20] In the nineteenth century, experts from a variety of fields responded to the disturbing social changes accompanying industrialization and urbanization by making extreme claims for sexual incommensurability. In the 1930s the ideal English woman was still the wife and mother. The ideal English man came from a good family and attended a good public school. In both institutions he learned the values of restraint and self-control.[21] He became a productive, thrifty, and rational citizen. In presenting the breadwinning worker or ex-soldier as hero, the most popular British films and novels of the interwar period reinforced this message, linking masculinity, economy, and nation.[22] True manliness was necessarily manifested in physical fitness and patriotism.[23] Conservatives denounced the dangers of unregulated desire and exalted the need for physical and psychological discipline. They played off the manliness of the gentleman against the effeminate "other"—be it the woman at home or the subject native abroad.[24]

Commentators assumed that the individual man's self-control was the basis of social stability.[25] This was an old idea. What was new was the unprecedented importance the twentieth-century middle classes accorded the domestic sphere. Bourgeois men increasingly accepted love and sexual passion as the foundation of marriage, which, with the advent of birth control, was no longer necessarily linked to procreation.[26] Stopes won international fame for both defending contraception and stressing the duty of men to sexually satisfy their spouses. Middle-class masculinity accordingly was marked by a decline in naked aggressiveness and a turn to the comforts of the suburban home, a shift reflecting in part a reaction to the bloodletting of the First World War.[27] But what emerged in the early twentieth century as the "traditional" style of British masculinity—based on respectability, reserve, and decorum—was challenged in the interwar years by the advocates of individuality and unabashed hedonism.[28] Journalists presented the playboy as adhering to more adventurous modes of behavior and so acting as a dashing counter to domesticity. They presented Lonsdale as an international arms dealer, Harley as an associate of American gangsters, Wilmer as a knuckle-duster-wearing tough, and Jenkins as a West End sophisticate.

Those who noted the appearance of the playboy took it as a given that he was the offspring of a consumerist culture. The Victorians had assumed that men were producers and women consumers. Those who adopted this separate spheres argument asserted that a man's sense of self-worth derived from his productivity. In creating or making goods he provided for the needs of his family and his community. Theorists conversely coded consumption as feminine and necessarily antithetical to healthy masculinity. Political economists asserted that consumption posed a real social danger. Just as doctors claimed that men who spent too much of their "vital fluids" undermined

"Gay nights in the West End." Peter Jenkins, *Mayfair Boy*
(London: W. H. Allen, 1952)

their health, economists warned that bankruptcy awaited a nation addicted
to overexpenditures.

The heroic model of man as producer slowly declined, and the nineteenth-
century hard, disciplined style of masculinity gave way to the more flexible
twentieth-century male consumerist model.[29] The evolution first occurred in
the United States, but in Britain the same process of young men becoming
more open about their role as consumers took place.[30] Initially, conservatives
lampooned male domesticity and the consumerism with which they assumed
it was entangled. Comic publications such as *Punch* portrayed housebound,
middle-class husbands as effeminate weaklings. Their status as "real men,"
satirists asserted, declined as their interest in tawdry consumer goods grew.

Despite such sniping, a generation of thinkers called for a reappraisal of
consumerism. Discovering that in a modern economy demand was as important as supply, that having increased numbers of purchasers was essential to

the smooth functioning of the market, economists begrudgingly began to re-
vise their view of the consumer. By the 1920s the stimulation of demand lauded
by Keynes began to challenge Malthus's call for thrift.

The middle classes had, of course, long demonstrated their status and identity by conspicuous consumption. Writers justified men's greater visibility in
the market by insisting that there were still important gender differences in
buying patterns. Women's consumerism was focused on the home, the domestic, whereas men made purchases for public use—guns, motorcars, and property. Women, argued misogynists, were preoccupied by flighty fashions; men
bought goods for reasons of utility and practicality.

The advent of modern masculinity was closely aligned with the emergence of this consumer culture. Whereas the heterosexual masculinity of the
Victorian was based on a belief in the primacy of character and restraint, his
twentieth-century counterpart performed his masculinity through his physi-
cality and personality. His choice of consumer goods played a central role in
this performance. A man now expressed his masculinity by demonstrating
good taste. This concern manifested itself in men paying more attention to
their appearance, a preoccupation stereotypically associated with women. Indeed, the dandy and the fop blurred gender boundaries. Moralists particularly
condemned homosexuals for their purported penchant for display and effeminacy, attributing to them the supposed female traits of self-indulgence and
irresponsibility. Commentators located the playboy—known for his excesses,
for playing rather than working—in this borderland. He emerged at a time
when society was redrawing the lines between the public and the private. He
could be viewed as a follower of the new model of masculinity that was progressive inasmuch as in embracing "feminine" consumerism it blurred the
conservatives' sharp lines of sexual incommensurability. At the same time his
lifestyle was patently narcissistic and exploitative. Only members of the middle
and upper classes could afford to play the role.[31]

A sociologist notes: "Ironically, though, it was during the 1930s—a decade
that saw the most severe economic depression in American history—that the
'consuming male' took fuller form."[32] Similarly, in England the same years
that saw record-high unemployment also witnessed elite males' unprecedented
interest in fashion and appearance. Those who continued to exalt hard work
and postponement of gratification as the hallmarks of masculinity claimed
that they were countered by increasing numbers of young men—dandies,

men-about-town, playboys—only too ready to parade their narcissism and hedonism.

The playboy, as a rebellious figure, at first glance seemed out of place in the depression of the 1930s.[33] Yet in some ways his appearance was not that surprising. For more than a century each generation had produced its counters to the advocates of male diligence, thrift, and self-discipline. Osbert Sitwell pointed to London's "long line of fops, macaronis, dandies, beaux, dudes, bucks, blades, bloods, swells and mashers."[34] The Mayfair playboy was part of this tradition of dissident, nonproductive masculinity.[35]

The Hyde Park Hotel robbers personified this self-indulgent style of masculinity. Jenkins offered in his autobiography a picture of himself as a disciple of Cecil Beaton.[36] A well-connected, Harrow-educated society photographer who knew how to flatter his wealthy subjects (even those who thought him a "pansy"), Beaton presented indolent masculine beauty as worthy of celebration. Nevertheless the dramatist Noël Coward—"the playboy of the West End stage"—was the one person who did more than anyone to popularize this style of masculinity. Indeed, it has been suggested that Coward first invented himself as the "languid decadent."[37] The 1920s were, for the social elite at least, a welcomed age of frivolity after the carnage of the Great War. Coward made himself "the embodiment of glamorous, dissipated, slightly shocking '20s chic."[38] The 1930s saw the appearance of two of his wittiest comedies, *Private Lives* (1930) and *Design for Living* (1932). His string of successful plays influenced the way men dressed and talked. According to Cecil Beaton, "Hearty naval commanders or jolly colonels acquired the 'camp' manners of calling everything from Joan of Arc to Merlin 'lots of fun,' and the adjective 'terribly' peppered every sentence. All sorts of men suddenly wanted to look like Noël Coward—sleek and satiny, clipped and well groomed, with a cigarette, a telephone, or a cocktail at hand."[39]

All the characters in Coward's plays are idlers. Their virtues consist of being charming, economically independent, and good-looking. Orson Welles, in reviewing Coward's *This Happy Breed*, labeled the playwright a "Mayfair playboy" and charged him with being guilty of "perpetuating a British public school snobbery."[40] Other critics said that in search of publicity, Coward self-consciously played the role of the indolent playboy. He sought to defend himself, claiming that he was the victim of reporters' vivid imaginations: "My metamorphosis into a 'Mayfair Playboy' many years later was entirely a journalistic conception."[41] It did not really matter which account was true. Thanks to him the playboy had become a subject of public debate. One journalist went so far as to accuse Coward of creating the sort of culture in which young men would assume that their need for money gave them the right to steal. "Some years ago Noel Coward wrote a satiric sketch for a C. B. Cochran revue, entitled 'Children of the Ritz.' Into it he put all the ennui, the soul destroying boredom and 'laisser-faire' which in part was responsible for the destiny of the four young Mayfair men sentenced at the Old Bailey for their part in the £13,000 Hyde Park Hotel jewel robbery."[42]

Because Coward thought that the Lord Chamberlain's Office would not allow *Design for Living*'s depiction of a ménage à trois, he did not stage it in London until 1939. At the same time, the British Board of Film Censors welcomed films about playboys, but only as long as they eventually saw the evil of their ways and were rehabilitated.[43] Just such characters appeared in many of the American films that swamped Britain in the 1930s. Some in Britain worried that their failure to produce their own matinee idols was another symptom of the decline of British manliness. In 1934 *Film Weekly* asked, "Why is it that British leading men, with very few exceptions, are either too old or too effeminate? Have we no young men who are good to look at without being sissies?"[44] In September 1937 the *Yorkshire Evening Post* reported that Metro-Goldwyn-Mayer had been looking for vigorous young men to act as undergraduates in the film *The Yank at Oxford*, but few regular extras proved to be sufficiently young and virile.[45]

Comic writers who made the Mayfair man the butt of their humor adopted a lighter tone. According to George Mikes, "In the old days the man who had no money was not a gentleman. Today, in Mayfair, things are different. A gentleman can have money or borrow money from his friends; the important thing is that even if he is very poor he must not do useful work. . . . Always be drunk after 6.30 pm."[46] In Nancy Mitford's *Highland Fling* (1931), Walter's days are occupied with taking his fiancée to Cartier to buy a large emerald and arguing with her over which nightclub to attend. Thinking of marrying, he has the radical idea of getting a job. "Besides, why shouldn't I do some work? If you come to think of it, lots of people do."[47] But he finds that with all the taxis he has to take and meals in town he has to eat, working is too expensive, and he gives it up.

Alarmists took a more pessimistic view. Journalists referred to "Mayfair's worst four hundred," meaning the scroungers and gigolos who lived off friends,

"Glamorous days on the Riviera." Peter Jenkins, *Mayfair Boy*
(London: W. H. Allen, 1952)

filled bars, and seduced heiresses. The press claimed this soft generation of
lounge lizards (male sexual predators), film fans, and effeminate young men
had to be hardened and strengthened.[48] In Richard Aldington's novel *Death of
a Hero* (1929) the reader is told that in the army one met real men, "not boudoir rabbits and lounge lizards."[49] In the 1930s a university rector challenged
his students "to bear themselves as becomes a hardy and historic race. The day
of the lounge lizard, of the years of the joy ride and cocktail are drawing to
their close. Enough of languor and decadence."[50]

Given the humiliation and heartbreak suffered by millions of unemployed
men and women during the economic slump, some protested that writers and
journalists were paying far too much attention to the minor problems of a
pampered few. In *The Rock Pool* (1936), Cyril Connolly portrayed the squalid
lives of a colony of moneyed young people. In his review of the novel, George
Orwell gave Connolly good marks for candidly describing their "drinking,
cadging and lechering." Nevertheless he primly concluded that the author was

besmirched by the material he handled. "Even to want to write about so-called artists who spend on sodomy what they have gained by sponging betrays a kind of spiritual inadequacy."[51]

Such fulminations reflected the unhappiness felt by some in the face of the appearance of what they regarded as a "less manly" model of masculinity.[52] A crop of sexually ambiguous leading men—Fred Astaire, Cary Grant, William Powell, Leslie Howard, and Ronald Colman—dominated the cinema.[53] The new style of masculinity had some of what were taken to be "feminine" traits, such as self-indulgence. English dandyism had long been associated with a consumerism that the middle classes usually coded as feminine.[54] Moralists raised the alarm that men, in interesting themselves in fashion, were becoming "la-di-da-ish" or "effeminate."[55] There was a certain irony in that Coward—a homosexual—cultivated an androgynous look in dress and self-presentation that was taken up by young heterosexuals.

One manifestation of their demand for information on clothes and fashion was the appearance in 1935 of Britain's first men's magazine, *Men Only*.[56] Starting out with the assertion "We don't want women readers," the magazine initially ran short essays on predictably masculine subjects such as beer, dogs, and motorcars, but some may have detected an effeminacy in the advice column "The Well-dressed Man" and the risqué cartoons. The editor attempted to scotch such suspicions by including photographs of female nudes. The first to appear was John Everard's "Gretel," in the June 1937 issue. To the magazine's surprise and delight it was deluged with letters asking for more. Thereafter it regularly ran "artistic" black-and-white pictures from such pioneering nude photographers as Everard and Horace Roy. Readers would insist, of course, that they bought the magazine mainly for its articles.[57]

Even before journalists coined the term "Mayfair playboy," they had familiarized their readership with the type. In 1931, Trevor Allen referred to the effeminate loafer who sponged off friends and occasionally (like Harley) made money by passing on information to the police or the press.

> An elegant young man of the "mother's spoilt darling" type, who moves in Mayfair when he is not in Soho: stylishly dressed with a touch of effeminacy in his make-up, and all the talk of the cocktail parties and the flashier clubs of the Bright Young Things. There is some mystery about his origin; he is supposed to derive from a good family on the shady side! He certainly has an entree to the lighter side of Mayfair which he puts to good—or bad—use in sundry ways. The

Underworld has its liaison officers who "tip it the wink" or retail it a spicy bit of scandal for a consideration. What happens to the casual bit of information after he has retailed it is of no importance to him. He just pays one or two pressing bills—usually the tailor's—and goes to another cocktail party or gets an invitation to the Opera or the Ballet or a fashionable First Night. Nobody asks him how he lives, for he moves in an Overworld in which everyone has money of some sort, somewhere, without having to work for it or explain its source. So long as he can keep on friendly terms with his tailor and his laundry he need not worry about much else. If he cannot afford to buy the smart society weeklies he can cadge them from a friend or run over them at a friend's house, see them he must, but he would never condescend to be seen entering a public library.[58]

Allen fell back on the mother-blaming trope to explain the emergence of the playboy; others used it to explain homosexuality.[59] The two characters tended to blur in the public's imagination.

The first police bulletin sent out after the December 21 assault on Bellenger succinctly described the suspects: "All effeminate in manner." Why had the Hyde Park Hotel staff so portrayed the four young men? It was not just because they were good looking and smartly dressed or had brilliantined hair and good teeth. Reginald Sidney Kelly, the receptionist, said of Jenkins: "He was exceptionally well dressed and walked and spoke rather effeminately." Henrietta Gordon agreed: "He was definitely like a pansy boy—a proper 'Sissy.'"[60] Yet for what it is worth, we know that the four all pursued women and all married, some several times. The truth is that we do not know their sexual orientations. It is nevertheless revealing to recall that in this time of shifting styles of masculinity some might mistake the sophisticated man-about-town for the homosexual. Both were known by their purported penchant for display and effeminacy. Both were the butts of comedians who sought to win cheap laughs from working-class audiences in condemning effeminacy as dirty, unmanly, and indecent.[61] The press followed suit in referring to the floggings of the "effete" felons.

Why would some think the Mayfair playboys were gay? Many regarded a man's attention to fashion as a marker for homosexuality.[62] The tabloids noted which men appeared in court wearing brown suede shoes.[63] According to Robert Graves this was a fashion adopted by "the 'Pansy' or the homosexual beauty."[64] Wilmer had his hair waved. This new style obviously disturbed some because commentators felt obliged to write that men who had their hair waved were not *necessarily* effeminate.[65] Others regarded Harley's sporting a garish teddy bear coat as a provocation.[66] The alcoholic novelist and London dandy Julian MacLaren-Ross, who also flaunted a "teddy-bear coat," recalled being challenged by his mates in the army: "What kind of pansy would have the neck to go round in such a get-up."[67] The rougher sort had difficulty in understanding that one could be flamboyantly turned out yet otherwise still be conventionally heterosexual.

How did one explain the apparent paradox of society regarding playboys as being both effeminate and nonetheless sexual predators who posed a threat to women? The implication that effeminate men were only a fortuitous step or two away from homosexual activity tapped into the old notion that homosexuals were sexually insatiable, based on the assumption that homosexual relations, being a deviation from the real thing, were not "satisfying" and therefore required constant repetition or fresh encounters.

Of all of the Hyde Park Hotel robbers, Peter Jenkins went furthest in discussing male sexuality. He devoted the chapter of his autobiography entitled "Do You Believe in Fairies?" to a discussion of homosexuality. Suggesting that it was due to a hormone deficiency, he argued that it required a medical remedy; persecution only increased misery. He declared that he knew a good deal about "queers" and was trying to learn more about lesbians. Wanting to visit a lesbian club he was told he would have to pass as gay, so a female friend "got busy on my rugged features with the contents of her vanity bag." He claimed that he was "disgusted" by the makeover, but it worked. Though some women at the club recognized him, they did not raise the alarm as they must have thought—mistakenly, of course—that he, too, had "queer tastes."[68]

Jenkins went so far in attempting to distance himself from "queers" that he raised the very question—what was his sexual orientation—he was seeking to finesse. He was more candid in his autobiography's concluding chapter, where he explained that it was only because of the companionship of a young man that he had survived his years in Dartmoor Prison. "Fortune favoured me in one respect only during my stay at Dartmoor—my friendship with a young ex-sailor and budding artist, who was my constant companion during two years of infinite suffering, and who was a continual source of encouragement to me in this work." Jenkins lauded George's creativity and brushed aside the idea that he was a hardened felon. He had been led astray. "He is just a young man who foolishly strayed into crime after the excitement of the war had abated and he could no longer use that outlet for his adventurous young spirits."[69]

It was, of course, not simply the playboy's effeteness that bothered commentators. It was the threat that he posed to women. The nervous regarded his appearance as a symptom of a broader crisis in gender relations manifested in changing standards of sexual behavior. Although the British press of the 1930s would not describe the Prince of Wales as a playboy, it increasingly employed the word when accounting for a subset of idle and seductive males. In England the use of the term spiked in the late 1930s, thanks to the notoriety of the "Mayfair playboys." During the trial of the Hyde Park Hotel robbers, and years later, all four of the accused not only embraced this persona; they played a part in creating it. This character became a new recruit in the sex wars. Moralists stressed the sexual aspects of the playboy, using the term interchangeably with bon vivant, womanizer, Don Juan, and Casanova. The anxious used him as a sort of scare figure, citing him as the cause of many of the current problems encountered in courtship, marriage, and divorce.

Sali Löbel, a Romanian actor and dancer, and leader of the Every Women's Health Movement, divided men into categories:

> I don't know which is the worse—the playboy or the cad? I think the cad has it— for the worse. You know the playboy quickly—he just plays—and makes little pretence at anything else. When he *has* money he spends it freely, when without he spends someone else's. He is lavish when he loves you, and he *can* love, BUT does not love you long. He is indolent, self-centered, and entirely vain, though the latter failing makes him fastidious, his saving grace. Yes—he has a saving grace! He is the despair of those who bore him and the despair of the woman who is unfortunate enough to want a permanent alliance with him. But it all just passes over his immaculate head—for his egoism builds no other world but his.[70]

Her advice was simply to avoid him.

The trial of Harley and his confederates gave commentators the occasion to denigrate not just four felons but the social milieu from which they emerged. An article entitled "'Mayfair Men' Still at Large," which appeared just after the Hyde Park Hotel robbers were locked away, expressed the hope that their punishment would serve as a deterrent for other young men and as a warning to young women. The latter had to be alerted that they were at risk of falling prey to such "pests." Unfortunately, many had a weakness for bad boys. "The modern girl, being what she is, insists on her own latchkey and a great deal of freedom. She thinks that she is an excellent judge of character. Maybe she is, and yet time and again she is prone to prefer the more exciting company of these Mayfair men to the worthy if duller friendship of young men who work in their father's offices, or at any rate, work."[71] The playboy's "slick sophistication" appeared to be an irresistible lure for debutantes and innocent youths. These layabouts, the article asserted, hung out at nightclubs and bars, passed bad checks, and trawled for rich girls. They had no manners, avoided work, and sponged on their friends. The worst drifted into criminality, though most did not go beyond "second rate pilfering, mild blackmail, confidence tricks, dud cheque changing and eternal borrowing."[72]

Accounts of the Mayfair playboys almost always noted that Wilmer and Harley succeeded in courting, marrying, and then abandoning debutantes. The question was posed: if playboys could ensnare, exploit, and cast aside women who came from good families and had been presented at court, who was safe? In the summer of 1938, under the headline "They Are Called 'Young Mayfair': One Meets Delightful Cads in Society London," by "Ex-Deb," an Australian newspaper carried the following warning:

> MOTHERS, beware! If you have a daughter who is going to London, or perhaps one who is there now, you cannot be too careful. Your daughter is going to be launched in "society" by one method or another. The question is, in just what society are you going to launch her? . . . From just such a set as this came the four young Mayfair men of the Bellinger [*sic*] jewel robbery, so much featured in the English newspapers. These four young men, all of good family and education, were sent to gaol for long stretches, with strokes of the "cat" thrown in. One of them, David Wilmer, had previously deserted his 18-year-old wife just before the birth of their child, but this fact did not come out in the newspapers. From this same set came another young man (Hervey), also in headlines some months ago. He was the son of one of the members of the House of Lords, a retired British Minister abroad. He (the son) was an amusing creature, immensely popular with parents and chaperones. All the same, he went bankrupt at the age of 21, to the tune of £124,000, gunrunning in Spain.[73]

Such sensational accounts reflected the fears that many wealthy parents must have felt at a time when young women were demanding more freedoms.[74]

In some of the more louche social circles he frequented, David Wilmer met two adventurous young women with famous fathers: Jenny Nicholson, the daughter of the poet Robert Graves, and Sarah Churchill, daughter of the future Conservative prime minister. In the eyes of their distressed families the two young women, in seeking to lead independent lives as chorus girls, were meeting—at drinking bouts and wild parties—too many unsavory men like Wilmer. Their parents were clearly not happy with their daughters revealing their navels and singing, "How low can a chorus girl go, before she is called a so-and-so?"[75] The Churchills' worst fears came to pass when twenty-two-year-old Sarah fell in love with Vic Oliver (Victor Von Samek), an Austrian-American comedian who was seventeen years her senior and appeared in the same C. B. Cochran review, *Follow the Sun*. When they eloped, her close friend Jenny, described by the tabloids as a "London cabaret girl," told the press that they were sailing aboard the *Bremen* to New York City where they planned on marrying.[76] Her brother Randolph Churchill, who voiced the family's concern about both the age disparity and the fact that Oliver's divorce of his first wife had not yet been finalized, pursued them. Much to Churchill's regret they wed on Christmas Day 1936.[77] The marriage only lasted a few years.[78]

Sarah had given a letter explaining the situation to her mother, which she asked Jenny to deliver.[79] When Jenny gave the story to the press, the Churchills were understandably angry. To make amends, Robert Graves aided her in writing an apologetic letter.[80] The men with whom the eighteen-year-old Jenny was associating equally distressed him. Pat Moran, her lover, gave her gonorrhea and possibly got her pregnant. Graves met Moran and his friend Tony Wheeler at the Spotted Dog, a Mayfair pub, in November 1936.[81] The hard-boiled Wheeler warned Graves that Jenny was at risk. In December, Graves told Nancy Nicholson that Jenny had been pressured by Moran, who "deliberately tried to force marriage by blackmail."[82] A year later Graves's brothers called to warn him that Jenny might be linked to the Hyde Park Hotel affair. His diary entry for Thursday, December 23, 1937, reads: "John and Philip both rang me up (inspired by Charles, I suppose) about Jenny's alleged connexion with David Willmer [*sic*] & the other 3 who did a jewel robbery-with-violence in a Knightsbridge hotel. Jenny has not had anything to do with them for months."[83] Which, of course, means that earlier she did socialize with them. The journalist Patrick Rankin lamented that young women were strangely attracted by the slick sophistication of such Lotharios. He claimed that a mere four days before he was arrested, Wilmer had called him to ask for the address of his niece.[84] Rankin was pleased to report that he had refused to help.

Jenny Nicholson's lover, Patrick Moran, was an old boy of Cheltenham College. He described himself as a journalist, but the police knew him as a

Mayfair playboy. His name appeared in the press in December 1939 when he was charged, along with John Topham (educated at Rugby and Cambridge), with stealing a £350 mink fur coat from the actress Diana Ward (also known as Diana Colgrave). Found guilty of conspiring to defraud a pawnbroker, Moran, age twenty-four, was sentenced to ten months in prison. His twenty-year-old fiancée, Elizabeth Mary Saunders, like Jenny Nicholson a "show girl," was bound over.[85] Moran had four previous convictions for motoring offenses and passing bad checks. A police officer testified: "I know him as a Mayfair play-boy and I have seen him almost nightly in clubs and hotels. He is an associate of well known Mayfair men, some of whom are serving long sentences of imprisonment."[86]

Little is known of Moran's friend Tony Wheeler. As noted in chapter 3, a police informer claimed that Charles Anthony Wheeler was a criminal associate of Stewart Cappel, but Wheeler seems to have done little more than indulge in the sort of vandalism not untypical of young men of his class. The members of Oxford's infamous Bullingdon Club in effect institutionalized such loutish behavior. Along with two old Etonians, Wheeler was arrested and charged in 1932 with having thrown bricks through the windows of the Imperial Service College in Windsor. As his only defense was that he had been drunk, the court found him guilty of malicious damage and levied a fine of £30 plus costs. Having given up such escapades, in 1936 he made a most advantageous marriage. His bride, Edith Dawkins, was the daughter of Major Arthur Dawkins and Lady Bertha Dawkins (née Bootle-Wilbraham), who from 1907 to 1935 had served Queen Mary as Woman of the Bedchamber. The dowager queen herself topped the list of those giving wedding presents.[87]

Moralists who wanted to portray the dangers posed by male "pests" could do no better than point to the fates of Jenny Nicholson and Sarah Churchill, but the cautionary tale of the inevitable unhappiness that resulted when independently minded young women pursued unreliable young men was often told. When Wilmer's wife divorced him, the two witnesses who testified on Hilary Wilmer's behalf were Elizabeth Pelly and Betty Patricia Cappel. Elizabeth Pelly was the granddaughter of Queen Victoria's secretary and the indulged daughter of Arthur Augustus William Harry Ponsonby, who, as Baron Ponsonby, led the Labour opposition in the House of Lords from 1931 to 1935.[88] She married John Denis Cavendish Pelly in 1929 and divorced him in 1932 after he admitted committing adultery with a "woman unknown."[89] The classic "Bright Young Thing" of the 1920s, Elizabeth Pelly had by her endless partygoing, excessive drinking, and deadly car crashes attained celebrity status. She was loved by the tabloids and inspired Evelyn Waugh to sketch out the character of the self-destructive Miss Runcible in his novel *Vile Bodies* (1930). Less than a year after testifying at the Wilmer divorce proceedings Elizabeth died of alcohol poisoning.[90]

When a Canadian paper announced Pelly's death it referred to her as London's "playgirl number one." North Americans used the term "playgirl" from the 1920s onward. An American paper described a murdered young woman in 1939 as a "Mayfair play girl," whereas the British press simply called her a prostitute. Film commentators might label as a "playgirl" any woman manifesting a degree of independence. She could be a hard-bitten gold digger like Kay Francis in *Play Girl* (1941, dir. Frank Woodruff) or a woman trying to save a man from a gold digger like Barbara Stanwyck in *Breakfast for Two* (1937, dir. Alfred Santell); an independent young woman like Margaret Lockwood in *The Lady Vanishes* (1938, dir. Alfred Hitchcock); a "wild and wealthy" socialite like Joan Crawford in *Letty Lynton* (1932, dir. Clarence Brown); or a worldly wise Mayfair young woman like Anne Crawford in *Millions Like Us* (1943, dir. Sidney Gilliat and Frank Launder).[91]

The newspapers were full of stories about Elizabeth Pelly's antics. Relatively little was known about Betty Cappel aside from the fact that she was the daughter of Commander Norman L. Cappel of the Royal Ulster Rifles and that her brother had been at Charterhouse School from 1934 to 1937. The police noted that Betty, about twenty years of age, and her brother Stewart, eighteen, were friends of the four Mayfair men. She visited Wilmer and Jenkins in Brixton Prison on January 14 or 15, 1938, a few weeks before their trial.[92] Wearing a diamond bracelet and earrings, Hilary Wilmer also came to see her supposedly estranged husband. Interestingly enough, Cappel gave as her home address 26 Basil Street, Knightsbridge, which was the same as Hilary Wilmer's.[93]

The second time Betty Cappel came to the authorities' attention was in June 1939 when the police charged her, along with Paul Mitchell (a friend of Jenkins) and Harold White, with conspiring to defraud and forging a check for £630. The crown decided to regard Cappel as Mitchell's dupe, and she in turn testified as a witness for the prosecution.[94] Despite her admitting that she cashed the incriminating check, Mitchell, a well-known twenty-three-year-old Mayfair playboy, gallantly insisted that Cappel had nothing to do with the fraud. At the same time, James Burge, his lawyer, sought to blacken the reputation of the victim of the criminal conspiracy, a Mr. Sutherland.[95]

Mr. Burge—have you been to more bottle parties apart from Smokey Joe's (the nightclub)? Yes, three or four. Questioned as to what he did in Paris when he went there with Mitchell, Sutherland said he met a girl from the "Folies Bergère" at a bar and danced with her. Mr. Burge—Is it true that you were having a "binge"? No. I am suggesting that you were not such an innocent young man as you would lead us to believe: I suggest that you hang around as many bottle parties in the West End as you can. No.[96]

Cappel was represented in court by the skilled barrister Derek Curtis-Bennett. He depicted Cappel as an innocent, dark-haired girl blinded by her love for Mitchell—a touching portrayal that the press rebroadcast. Mitchell's lawyer argued in turn that his client was blinded by the bright lights of Mayfair, a view summed up in the *Daily Mail* headline: "23, 'Ruined by West End Life.'" According to Burge, Mitchell "had been living the life of a Mayfair playboy, with its cocktail parties and bottle parties. He had made genuine efforts to get work, and he had endeavored, without success, to obtain a commission in the R.A.F."[97] The judge was not sympathetic. He noted that the two accused men had both gone to good public schools. They now chose to associate with fellows who lived by their wits, and at best were "share-pushers" and at worst con men. Alluding to the Hyde Park Hotel robbers, the judge reprimanded Mitchell for being "an associate of four young men who were recently convicted at the Central Criminal Court."[98]

Portraying Mitchell as "a Mayfair playboy, an associate of undesirable characters and frequenter of doubtful nightclubs," the judge made it clear that he was more disgusted by the life that the accused led than by the crimes he had committed. "We have had constant talk of Turkish baths, where apparently some of them sleep, of meetings in bars in London, and of cocktail parties."[99] He sentenced Mitchell to twenty months in prison. He directed the jury not to convict Cappel. Having apparently learned her lesson, she returned to her family and, unlike Elizabeth Pelly, had the time to salvage her reputation. In November 1944 the press reported that "a marriage had been arranged" for Betty Patricia Cappel, elder daughter of Commander N. L. Cappel, and Flight Lieutenant John Blackford, only son of Air Commodore D. L. Blackford, RAF, British Embassy, Washington. A year later the *Times* announced that a son had been born to Mrs. John D. Blackford (née Betty Cappel).[100]

For centuries British wealthy families had attempted to protect rich heiresses from ruthless adventurers.[101] The playboy was in some ways simply the twentieth-century incarnation of such schemers. The popular writer Beverley Nichols joked about it, in claiming that in the 1930s a young man asked him if he knew any rich women. "I observed him with disapproval. I naturally assumed that he wished to become a gigolo. Times were so bad that this was a profession which, it was rumoured, was shortly to be officially recognized by the universities."[102] In fact the young man was a dress designer looking for customers.

Like many other good-looking con men, Peter Jenkins targeted wealthy women. He had hopes in 1937 of marrying up by wedding the wealthy American actress Eleanore Foster. The tabloid press of the 1930s was full of such stories of heiress hunting. Paul Mitchell, a friend of Jenkins, described in the papers as a "young sportsman," pursued the Hollywood film star Mary Carlisle in London and then, by 6,000-mile telephone calls, after her return to California. She was quoted as saying "she hardly knew him and couldn't very well marry a stranger."[103] At the very least Mitchell forced himself on public's attention by his public courtship. In April 1936 one tabloid wrote, "Mayfair Man off to Hollywood—to Propose." Journalists reported that the contradictory accounts of his success had the screen colony "dizzy."[104]

That gambit having failed, Mitchell turned his attentions to Anne Godwin Turner. He later admitted that he only married her for her money. Anne was equally hardheaded. She was to inherit £15,000, payable on her wedding day. As both were minors in July 1936, they had to forge the consent of their parents in order to marry. Once they left the registry office, Anne took off her wedding ring and gave Paul £1,500. He went abroad and did not see her again for four months. By 1938 he was once again penniless and living with his mother.[105] He had not only lost a small fortune on the Stock Exchange, but he was under probation in connection with a share-pushing scam.[106]

Anne had been equally reckless. After having gone through £8,000 to £9,000 pounds in the space of two years, she began to write bad checks. In July 1938 she was found guilty of obtaining credit and clothing by false pretenses—that is, by issuing eighty-seven bad checks. As a condition for being placed on probation she had to enter a Church of England home for girls.[107] On December 21, however, she was before the courts once more. She and Patricia Mallory, a twenty-three-year-old drug addict, pleaded guilty to obtaining two coats by fraud. Three days earlier they had absconded from a church home in Spelthorne, Surrey. F. Ashe Lincoln, Anne's counsel, succeeded in making the case that she had already suffered a good deal in marrying a scoundrel and dissipating her inheritance. The judge agreed that since she had a good family in Jersey who could look after her, she was a suitable case for probation.[108] The courts were less sympathetic when it came to dealing with her mercenary marriage. In May 1938, Anne, now twenty-two, launched a summons for a separation from her husband on the grounds of cruelty and desertion. She had Peter Jenkins subpoenaed as her only witness, and the police brought him to London in handcuffs. Though smartly dressed in a double-breasted light blue suit, he failed to impress the court. Anne was disappointed to find that her summons was rejected. That she had to call on someone as notorious as Jenkins to appear as her sole witness spoke to the weakness of her case.[109] Nevertheless, Paul Mitchell appears to have held a grudge against Jenkins. In October 1940 at a party presumably held to celebrate Jenkins's release from prison, Mitchell struck him with a champagne bottle. Jenkins ended up in hospital; Mitchell was sentenced to a month in jail.[110]

Dedicated readers of the trials of Anne Turner could only conclude that this young woman's rebelliousness was the cause of her misfortunes. If she had only followed the dictates of her parents, all would have been well. Associating with a well-known playboy was her first mistake. She had only herself to blame for the loss of her inheritance and her reputation. Ironically, she was left yoked to the unreliable young schemer who was supposed to have aided her in gaining her freedom.

Jenkins played a key role in yet another trial that revealed how playboys used and abused young women. In December 1938, Sylvia Doris Leggi sought an affiliation order at Clerkenwell Police Court against John Clotworthy Talbot Foster Whyte-Melville Skeffington, twenty-four, son and heir of Lord Massereene and Ferrard. He was the epitome of the wealthy young man-about-town. He had attended Eton, owned estates in Ulster and England, and loved fast cars—he drove in the 1937 Le Mans Grand Prix—and pretty women. Leggi testified that she met Skeffington on November 16, 1937, at a cocktail party at the Florida nightclub. She was working as a photographer's model at the time. He swept her off her feet, giving her £10 a week for lodgings, buying her a £169 silver fox coat, and sending her letters in which he called her "my sweet white nymph."[111] But by the end of the year the relationship had soured. They quarreled at Christmas while in Paris. In March 1938, Leggi followed him to New York, where she discovered that she was pregnant.[112] When she told Skeffington he threatened that if she caused trouble there would be consequences. Frightened, she signed a note in April freeing Skeffington of any responsibilities. In August 1938 she gave birth to a baby girl at the Royal Bucks Hospital, in Aylesbury, and in December—despite her earlier promise—was demanding financial support from "the only man in the world" who could be her baby's father.[113] The tabloids loved the story, a typical headline reading, "Viscount's Heir Sued by Girl."

Bernard Gillis, Skeffington's counsel, responded by attacking Leggi's morals, pointing out that within four days of their meeting she was going to country hotels with him and accepting his money. Gillis also produced evidence that at the Chelsea Arts Ball of December 30, 1937, Leggi told a friend she was out to get something big from Skeffington. Gillis's central strategy, however, was not to deny that his client had intercourse with Leggi but to argue that so too did other men, in particular Peter Jenkins.[114]

Gillis called three employees of the Dorchester Hotel who testified that they recognized her as staying at their West End establishment with Jenkins, November 17–23, 1937. A Dorchester attendant recalled going "to valet" Jenkins and seeing Leggi dressing in the same room. A waiter and a reception clerk also saw them together. There was more. "It so happens that there was ample ground for fixing these two persons in the memory of the hotel staff," said Gillis. "The reception clerk had the greatest difficulty, and very little success in collecting the bill."[115] The valet stated that Jenkins claimed the night after his arrival that he had lost his checkbook and would have to run a tab. In fact, Jenkins and Leggi ran off without paying their bill, and the hotel seized their luggage. Solicitor Reginald T. P. Bennett testified that on November 30 he acted for Jenkins in settling an account of between £50 and £70 at the Dorchester in order to have the luggage released.[116] The luggage problem clinched the defense's argument. Magistrate Kenneth Marshall dismissed Leggi's appeal, cruelly adding: "I entirely agree that this is not a case of a young and innocent girl, but quite clearly an immoral girl."[117] The court refused to grant her an affiliation order. This was not a surprise; in 1936 there had been 24,895 "illegitimate" births, but only 4,349 women were successful in obtaining affiliation orders.[118] Adding insult to injury the court awarded Skeffington fifteen guineas cost.[119]

A mere three months after the papers ran headlines such as "Girl's Case against Peer's Son Fails," Skeffington married Annabelle B. K. Lewis, whose father, Henry D. Lewis of Combwell Priory, Hawkhurst, Kent, was a Jewish mining magnate and chairman of Lewis and Marks Limited, a South African mining company.[120] The fact that a peer's eldest son had been cited in a paternity suit did little to diminish his eligibility as a marriage candidate. Nor did a lack of common sense. In April 1938, Skeffington appeared before the Bankruptcy Court, which determined that he possessed £4,300 and owed £10,252. His debts largely stemmed from his having lost £16,000 in backing an unsuccessful theatrical play. He did not take the situation seriously, preferring to treat the proceedings as a joke. "The Official Receiver—Have you been bankrupt before?—Good heavens, no! I have not had time. I am only 25."[121]

The Skeffington trial, to be fully appreciated, has to be placed in context of the shifting relationship of the sexes in the interwar years. The increased unchaperoned interaction of young men and women obviously alarmed traditionalists, but in the main observers applauded women's growing independence. One sign of this was the decline in the number of women who sued men who had jilted them. "Modern Eve Scorns Claims for Breach of Promise," declared the *Daily Mail*. But the same paper would report, under the headline "Traps for Men," Conservative MPs' claims that mercenary single women sought to attribute their pregnancies to wealthy men.[122] These male MPs were concerned that the current marriage reform bill not only extended the grounds for divorce but also made provisions for assisting women seeking affiliation orders. In contrast, Irene Ward, a female Conservative MP, hailed these proposals. "I particularly welcome that Clause in relation to affiliation orders, because it must be obvious that the unmarried mother is in a particularly defenceless position in obtaining evidence of the means of the man concerned with her case."[123] Skeffington won his case because his lawyer successfully portrayed Leggi not as a weak woman deserving protection but as a modern manipulative, designing female—a gold digger.[124] Such women "are seen bedaubed by every colour of the rainbow," asserted a barrister in a 1935 court case. "In the hotels of the Continent and Mayfair, in the cabarets and night clubs of Europe, there are such people selling themselves for money, the sale being sanctified by formal marriage or not."[125]

The Mayfair playboys were not only involved in cases of courtship and seduction; they also were entangled in the divorce law, which in the late 1930s was going through a major reform. Both Robert Harley and David Wilmer's names continued to appear in the papers through 1938 due to their wives pursuing divorce proceedings against them. Hilary Inez Elizabeth Wilmer, of Basil Street, Knightsbridge, had launched her suit in 1937, but Wilmer had been arrested before it was completed.[126] As noted in chapter 3, Wilmer had abetted his wife's claim that he was an adulterer by providing her with evidence he had had relations with a woman in a London hotel. In March 1938, just as Wilmer was beginning his prison term, a judge granted Hilary a decree *nisi* and custody of their child.[127] The decree *nisi* did not end the marriage. It simply indicated that the court agreed that the petitioner was entitled to a divorce and could apply for a decree absolute.

In the case of Harley, the newspapers reminded the public that he had married Freda Margaret Wightwick on March 22, 1936, in Battle, Sussex. The marriage was not a happy one. Freda left him in March 1937 after finding out that he was living with another woman. In February 1938, Harley's solicitor, Emanuel Garber, visited him in Wormwood Scrubs to discuss how to respond to Freda's suit.[128] The press took an interest in this divorce case because it not only involved a notorious criminal but also was likely to be one of the first suits that would take advantage of the "hardship and depravity" clause of the Matrimonial Causes Act of 1937.

Divorce reform was much in the air in 1930s, though only a tiny percentage of the population was directly concerned. There were on average no more than four thousand divorces a year. Victorian divorce law had been glaringly inequitable, allowing a husband to divorce his wife simply for being unfaithful whereas a wife could only divorce her husband if in addition to having committed adultery he had engaged in bigamy, rape, sodomy, bestiality, incest, cruelty, or desertion.[129] The 1912 report of a royal commission called for sweeping changes and a small step forward was made by a 1923 law that allowed the woman—like the man—simply to invoke the adultery of their spouse when seeking a divorce. Women petitioners increased from 39 percent in 1923 to 63 percent in 1925.[130] Nevertheless, the law, in insisting that adultery was still the only sufficient cause for divorce, had the unintended consequence of rewarding hypocrisy and punishing candor. One party had to demonstrate guilt; the other innocence. Amicable separations were not allowed. The authorities did not accept desertion as warranting the ending of a marriage. Mr. Justice Swift cited the case of a couple separated for sixteen years, both of whom had happily made new partnerships. To regularize their situation—that is, to obtain a divorce—one of the spouses was required to commit adultery, or at least claim to have.[131] As a consequence of such ludicrous requirements it was almost impossible for any except the well-off to obtain a divorce. Money was needed to pay for the solicitors, the detectives, the witnesses, the hotel staff, the anonymous third-party (usually a woman), and the associated court fees.[132]

The predictable result of such a law was collusion—the orchestration by the couple of a "hotel divorce," in which a husband's sexual misconduct was faked. But if a couple were found to have colluded, the divorce could be denied.[133] The King's Proctor had the unseemly task of seeking evidence that would deny a decree absolute to those who broke the restrictive rules. Even Wallis Simpson, the mistress of the Prince of Wales, was worried that the story she and her husband concocted when seeking a divorce between October 1936 and May 1937 might unravel. If couples were worried, judges were bored. Having to hear the same obviously prefabricated story over and over again, they declared themselves weary of such "fictions," or what Lord Chief Justice Hewart called "rubbishy cases."[134]

The success of A. P. Herbert's comic novel *Holy Deadlock* (1934) reflected a heightening of interest in divorce reform.[135] Herbert was elected in November 1935 as an Independent MP for Oxford University and elicited wide support in his campaign for liberalization of divorce law. The public was increasingly of the opinion that the institution of marriage was not honored but brought into disrespect by laws that trapped spouses in unhappy unions. Even the Church of England recognized the need for change.[136] The bill that Herbert introduced in February 1936, after much amending, received royal assent in July 1937 and was in force in 1938. Cruelty, insanity, and desertion for three years or more were now included as grounds for divorce. Immediate divorce was available for cases of adultery by either party. As a sop to conservatives, the bill stipulated that divorce could only be sought after three years of marriage, but exceptions were allowed in cases of "hardship" and "depravity." Sir Boyd Merriman, president of the Divorce Division of the High Court, claimed that the new law worked well, pointing out that that there had been 6,800 petitions in the first nine months of 1938, compared to 3,700 the previous. Alarmists regarded rising divorce numbers far less benignly, but petitioners often only sought the formalizing of an existing separation.[137]

It was in this changing legal climate that the Harleys came to court in July 1938. The press noted that with the easier rules a rush had been expected, but there were only 1,233 petitioners in the Trinity law sittings. (There were, however, twenty-six insanity pleas.)[138] Freda, represented by S. E. Karminski, argued that given the misconduct of her husband she had no choice but to sue for divorce.[139] Sir Boyd Merriman expedited matters. He permitted Freda to offer a written address rather than testify in person, and he allowed the divorce to proceed even though three years had not yet passed since her marriage.[140] He presumably took the imprisonment of Harley into consideration in reaching his decision. Freda was granted a decree *nisi* with costs, and custody of her child. The decree *nisi* was made absolute in February 1939.[141] The court dealt with the case in a matter of minutes and made no mention of the name of the woman with whom Harley committed adultery. She must have been someone of some importance, however, as Walter Frampton, holding a watching brief, represented her in court. Working with the solicitor Theodore Goddard, Frampton had two years earlier assisted Norman Birkett in obtaining Wallis Simpson's divorce.[142]

Hilary Wilmer was not as lucky. In the spring of 1939 the papers reported that the King's Proctor was intervening in the Wilmer divorce suit.[143] The proctor only investigated a small number of petitions for divorce, but the majority of those examined were denied. When the case was heard in November, the proctor opposed having the decree *nisi* made absolute on the grounds that evidence had emerged indicating that Hilary had condoned her husband's adultery and had herself slept more times with her lover, Patrick Henry Noel Gamble, than she had first admitted. Condonation was by law an absolute bar to divorce, and the Wilmers unfortunately appeared to have had an unusually amicable separation. Wilmer and Gamble seemed to be friends, and Wilmer had even named Gamble in constructing an alibi for the day of the Hyde Park Hotel robbery.[144]

The proctor was not concerned with the robbery. What triggered his disquiet was the discovery that Hilary and Gamble had a cottage at Henley-on-Thames, which they shared on occasion with Wilmer. Two servants claimed that the supposedly irremediably divided couple actually slept in the same bed a few times. The shocked judge opined that "nobody could deny that a situation in which a petitioning wife was dining, dancing, and merry-making with her respondent husband in the house of which another member of the party was paying expenses was not ordinary social intercourse."[145] Nevertheless he conceded that it would be cruel to tie her forever to a cad who never acted as a real husband and was now in prison. In contrast, Patrick Gamble was a gentleman who wanted to regularize their relationship by marrying her. The judge stressed that given the erratic behavior of the Wilmers, the King's Proctor's intervention had been completely justified, but he concluded that the court regarded the testimony of servants as unreliable and would accordingly demonstrate its mercy in not rescinding the decree *nisi*. A week later the decree was made absolute.[146]

The moral that the judge drew from the proctor's intervention was not that the law was antiquated but that only by chance had Hilary escaped being compromised by her playboy ex-husband. She had been altogether too friendly with him. "No one," declared the judge, "who was not a fool could fail to realize what a tremendous weapon she was putting into the hands of a man like that."[147]

Although the handful of cases examined in this chapter can make no claim to be representative, they do provide some sense of the perspective commentators took in the 1920s and '30s when accounting for many of the shameful situations in which risk-taking women found themselves. If the adventurous were sexually compromised, if they were seduced and abandoned, if some gigolo had only married them for their money, if even their recourse to divorce was lost, it was likely due, judges and journalists agreed, to their having been victimized by some cad, bounder, or playboy. Such an approach was not as fairminded as it might first appear. Faulting women for their naïveté on the one hand while castigating men for their duplicity on the other allowed the censorious to individualize each problem and ignore the systemic nature of gender inequality. Women were doubly victimized, first by society and then by some man. The difference was that the playboy only posed the woman a potential or possible risk; the constraints of an inequitable society were inescapable.

The playboy represented a new style of hedonistic masculinity. There were of course continuities with other, earlier forms of dissident masculinity such as the rake and the cad. The chief difference was that the popular press had described the latter in condemnatory language, whereas it tended to pore over the exploits of the playboy with rapt attention, if not obvious envy. Young men who would have been insulted if called gigolos or womanizers proudly described themselves as "playboys," which signified—not always truthfully—their dedication to worldly pleasures, success with women, amused indifference to middle-class counsels of restraint, and an apparently effortless ability to live well. In reflecting changing class and gender relationships, the playboy was a creation of interwar societal shifts. At the same time he was not simply a symptom of changing mores; he was both a cause and effect of the modernizing of British attitudes toward sexuality and consumerism.

The playboy of the 1930s might in some ways be regarded as the male counterpart to the flapper of the 1920s. The playboy was usually upper or upper-middle class, as were the Bright Young Things, but the flapper could in theory be from any class. The press portrayed both as seeking to free themselves from many traditional social restraints and candidly confessing to devoting themselves to the pursuit of pleasure. Both adopted an androgynous look, women by having their hair cut in a boyish crop, men by aping Noël Coward's air of indolent sophistication. Of course, only a tiny number of upper-class men and women had the wherewithal to play such roles. The movies, mass-circulation newspapers, and popular novels were primarily responsible for constructing and popularizing these personae. Writing about the playboy offered one a way of broaching shifts in gender relations. For moralists his appearance signaled the danger of men choosing to be idle, effeminate consumers. Similar news stories warned that young women's struggle for independence could result in their ending up as seduced chorus girls or the accomplices of thieves. In novels such as Michael Arlen's *The Green Hat* (1924) and Norah C. James's *Sleeveless Errand* (1929), the authors presented the emancipated woman as ultimately having to pay for violating gender norms. In a similar fashion, those who portrayed the playboy usually had him eventually repent for his prodigal past.[148] The dissimilarity was that moralists had no difficulty in using the playboy character to warn young women of the dangers posed by men; they were far less successful in employing the flapper to make men wary of women. Major social changes might have undermined traditional gender expectations, but the sexual double standard still prevailed.

Chapter 8: CRIME

In a trilogy of novels set in interwar England, Patrick Hamilton presented as his antihero Ralph Gorse, a consummate womanizer and opportunist. Though beguiled by this playboy, his female mark senses something amiss. "She now believed that he was a 'gentleman.' His blue suit, his hat, his manner and success at the Metropole, his old-school tie—all these had practically convinced her. Also she thought she liked him. He had dash, and she had laughed a good deal at his 'Silly Ass' act. But still there was just something wrong which made her suspect and *not* altogether like him."[1] Many writers of the interwar period explored the unsettling notion that in an increasingly anonymous world the cad or bounder could obtain the wherewithal to pass as a member of respectable society. The detective stories of Margery Allingham, for example, are replete with such con men.[2] Facts, of course, are often stranger than fictions. The popular newspapers tapped into their readers' fascination with real-life criminals—retired or reformed—by running what purported to be their autobiographies. Dismissing these narratives as "fantasy, formula, or fluff," moralists condemned such publications for glamorizing crime and pandering to the worse instincts of their readership.[3] Undeterred, the tabloids published similarly sensational accounts of the playboy.

In putting together a composite picture of the "Mayfair playboy," journalists, novelists, and moviemakers produced a fantasy figure—not so much the portrayal of an actual modern male as a screen on which the hopes and fears of a generation of young men and women could be projected. He was a potent and easily manipulated construct. On the positive side he was an entertaining, fun-loving, sophisticated rival to the dependable if staid suburban male. Conversely, he could be idle, hedonistic, irresponsible, and untrustworthy, representing British culture's fear that the war had unleashed the forces of greed.[4] The negative connotations of this style of masculinity predominated.

If gender roles were blurred, if males were becoming narcissistic, if young men unembarrassedly sought lives of idleness, much of the responsibility could be attributed to this new role model. In the 1930s observers credited many slick, male sophisticates with having less creditable intentions. Writers did not, of course, simply make up the playboy. They were first inspired to use this new classification when reporting on the activities of men-about-town. The person interacted with the label and, following a looping effect, young men began, by a process of self-invention or self-fashioning, to describe themselves as play-boys.[5] Which appeared first—the playboy or the idea of the playboy—is impossible to say.

Victor Hervey embodied the popular conception of the "Mayfair man" as the individual who moved from ethically dubious to patently illegal acts. Press coverage of the three-day Victor Hervey trial, which took place in July 1939, a little more than a year after the sentencing of the Hyde Park Hotel robbers, confirmed the tabloids' linkage of crime and the playboy. The courtroom audience included the ex-king and queen of Siam and the American actor Douglas Fairbanks Sr. In the prisoners' box stood one hardened professional thief and three well-dressed and well-connected young men. The press hailed Hervey as the "'Dress Suit Bandit' of Mayfair."[6] The crown described him as an "associate of persons convicted in the Hyde Park robbery case."[7] The three with whom he shared the prisoner's dock had equally tawdry pasts. Geoffrey Coop, twenty-four, had been to a public school and met Hervey at Sandhurst. Coop won a commission in the infantry, but after he wrote several worthless checks, his superiors asked him to resign. Once his family allowance ended he got by as a salesman, and then as a private in the Royal Army Ordnance Corps. After deserting he idled away his time writing songs and poems.[8] George Hering, twenty-three, also a product of a public school, was married but separated. Previously charged with taking money under false pretenses, he lived by his wits and as "Peter Proud" wrote as a freelance gossip columnist. William Goodwin, a thirty-year-old expert working-class burglar (or housebreaker), who had four previous convictions, and had only been released from prison in May 1937 was what the British called "an old lag" and very much the odd man out. Journalists gave him scant attention; Victor Hervey dominated the proceedings.

Victor Frederick Cochrane Hervey was the nephew of Frederick Hervey, the fourth Marquess of Bristol and the son of a former British minister to Peru, Lord Herbert Hervey. A British aristocrat, he bore some of the vices of his forebears, particularly an inflated sense of his own importance.[9] His parents provided him as a youth with the extraordinarily large allowance of £1,000 a year, though they otherwise abandoned him. As a consequence, claimed journalists, he never developed any self-discipline. He briefly attended Eton, from 1929 to 1931, when the headmaster asked him to leave.[10] Eton having proved unsuitable, in February 1934 he entered the Royal Military College at Sandhurst. In less than a year the commander advised his father to have him withdraw as he was "temperamentally unsuited to be an officer."[11] At the age of nineteen, he became a "share-pusher," or stock salesman. He claimed to have made a fortune on the market, but he lost as much, if not more, in setting up a company to make films. Reflecting his cinematic interests, Hervey was much given to striking dramatic poses, especially that of the adventurer. He carried a swordstick. In September 1935 the West London County Court fined him £17 for slashing a taxicab with just such a weapon. He was probably not unhappy when counsel referred to him as a "modern D'Artagnan" (of *The Three Musketeers*) leading "a number of other bright young people" on nightly escapades.[12]

At age twenty-one Hervey embraced the role of heroic gunrunner, founding the armaments firm Hervey Finance Corporation Limited to supply arms to General Franco and the Falangists in Spain. Profits failed to materialize. On March 22, 1937, the London Bankruptcy Court summoned Hervey to appear before it, as his liabilities far surpassed his assets. He told the bankruptcy hearing that he would be able to pay his debts once he received a £30,000 commission owed him by the Spanish dictator. The court delayed proceedings on the understanding that his armament firm would soon be able to pay off its creditors.[13]

John Lonsdale also had the idea of exploiting the civil war that was ravaging the Iberian peninsula. In the latter part of 1936, he visited the Spanish republican and rebel armament buyers and claimed to have received orders from both. Recognizing their mutual interests, Hervey and Lonsdale decided to work together, but given that both gave spurious accounts of their activities, it is unclear whether they actually sold any arms at all. It was well known, however, that their attempt in the spring of 1937 to purchase guns and munitions in Finland was a fiasco. The expenses Hervey accrued left him—with liabilities of £123,955 and assets of £6,668—bankrupt. It came out in court that he spent £5,827 a year and had hosted "some sort of drunken orgy."[14] With an enormous inheritance awaiting him, Hervey was unabashed by his financial failures. Indeed, he appeared to take pleasure in the notoriety he had gained by both his shady business activities and the spivs and ex-cons with whom he consorted.[15] Recruiting a number of acolytes he took on a new role, presenting himself in the guise of a sophisticated jewel thief and gang leader.

The news that the police had arrested the heir to the Marquess of Bristol for conspiring to steal and for breaking and entering burst onto the pages of the tabloids in April 1939. The crown charged Hervey, Hering, Coop, and Goodwin with two thefts. The first charge was that the gang had, over the Easter weekend, stolen from Pauline Daubeny ten rings, a tie-pin, three brooches, two necklaces, six bracelets, and a mink coat valued at £2,500.[16] Knowing that Daubeny would be in the country visiting the family of his accomplice George Hering, Hervey had his men break in and strip her Queen Street flat of valuables.[17]

Michael Walter, who was on the margins of Hervey's gang, testified against his colleagues.[18] He told the police that on Good Friday he heard Hervey and Hering discuss which friends would be out of town over the weekend and whose homes could be looted. Having been told that Daubeny would be away, Hervey said, "Right, we will have that." When Walter protested, the gang told him to keep his mouth shut. Hervey in fact introduced him to three ruffians; if he squealed, they warned, he would get "the broken end of a bottle in your throat."[19]

The gang's second success more or less replicated their first. They robbed a wealthy young woman—Mrs. Gabrielle Burley—who was personally known to them. Michael Walter had met Mrs. Burley (of Park Lane) on Boat Race Day; he in turn introduced her to Hervey and Hering. They all noticed her jewels. On April 11, Walter heard Hervey say, "We must have Mrs. Burley's rings and clip." Walter and Mrs. Burley spent the next day in the country. After cocktails at her flat that evening, they proceeded to the Ritz cocktail bar, where they met Hervey and Hering, then went on to Grosvenor House and finally had supper at Quaglino's.[20] At about one in the morning Mrs. Burley begged Walter to take her to a notorious nightclub, but he protested it was "not quite the proper place to take a lady." "I suggested that as she was so bottled she had better come and have dinner with me alone, as it was no good having a drinking party."[21] Nevertheless all four went on to the Nest Club, in Kingly Street, off Regent Street.[22]

Walter testified that Hervey told him: "We can get her jewellery tonight. I can fix The Nest."[23] Walter claimed that he had no intention of participating in a robbery but admitted he did nothing to prevent it. His excuse was that he and Mrs. Burley were both so drunk that they could hardly walk. They had had three bottles of white wine before they got to the Nest. At the club, which was a "bottle shop," someone provided their table with two bottles of rye whiskey. After the drinking and dancing, Mrs. Burley was soon half asleep. Hervey knocked her handbag containing her diamond ring onto the floor and prevented Walter from retrieving it. Bill Goodwin, sitting at a nearby table, picked it up, quickly pocketed the contents, and returned it. In the meantime Hervey slid the watch and the two platinum and diamond dress-clips off his dozing companion. Telling Walter, "The job's done," he left with Hering.[24]

How Hervey expected to get away with the brazen theft of £2,860 in valuables was never made clear. Discovering in the early morning hours that her jewels were missing, Mrs. Burley was initially so embarrassed by her own behavior that she dithered before going to the police. Once she did, they in turn prevailed upon Walter to assist in the April 17 arrest of Hervey and Hering at Victoria Station. The crown opposed allowing Hervey to be let out on bail, arguing that there was a good chance he would flee, especially as he had his own plane. The judge did in fact grant bail, which allowed Hervey to visit Hering in Brixton prison and warn him of the dangers of testifying against his friends.[25]

As the evidence against Hervey and his associates was overwhelming, his counsel, Norman Birkett, as a last resort set out to undermine the credibility of Michael Walter, the crown's chief witness, by portraying the unemployed young man as a gigolo. "Mr. Birkett: Do you find it a very expensive matter to lead the kind of life you were leading at these hotels?—I did, but I very rarely had to pay."[26] Walter's reputation might have suffered, but his testimony was still damning. In his summing up, the judge made it clear to the jury that he was revolted by the actions of both the gang and their chief victim, Mrs. Burley. "You may think that all the persons in the case are loathsome. That includes the woman in the matter, whose mentality is such that her idea of pleasure is to attain a state of semi-drunkenness, and then publicly parade her degradation. But she, like everyone else, is entitled to the protection of the law."[27] Having made that grudging admission, the judge did reserve a barbed reprimand for Hervey. "How low you have stooped, you alone know."[28] The jury took only eighty minutes to reach its verdict. All four men were found guilty. In passing sentence, the judge lamented the fact that the trial had ex-

Victor Hervey and Michael Walter. *Daily Sketch*, May 17, 1939.
© The British Library Board

posed "the craft and guile that had been used by men of education."[29] He sentenced Coop to nine months imprisonment, Hering and Goodwin to two years, and Hervey, as ringleader, to three years.[30]

The judge criticized Hervey for misusing his talents, but the convicted felon was not above exploiting his newfound notoriety for financial gain. He assisted the *Sunday Dispatch* in immediately producing a series of "tell-all" articles. On July 9 appeared "At 21 I Dealt in Millions" and on July 16 "The Inside Story of the Arms Racket." The advertisement for the installment of July 23 gave some sense of Hervey's inflated view of himself:

A Gun-Runner's Thrills!

Under fire in the Spanish war zone . . .

An escape from death—by inches . . .

Travelling with £5,000,000 of gold . . .

Hit by Spanish antiaircraft fire . . .

Landing half-a-million pounds' worth of guns at Barcelona . . .

Victor Hervey son of a Lord, nephew of a Marquis, Mayfair Playboy and eminent figure in the Arms Racket, was sentenced in the recent sensational Old Bailey trial. Now he tells his own thrilling experience.[31]

In fact there is no evidence that Hervey dealt in millions or was a successful arms dealer or was ever in Spain during the civil war. All his confessions appeared to be the romanticized, self-serving fictions of a convinced fantasist.

Hervey was initially detained in Brixton Prison. After the trial he spent a short time in Wormwood Scrubs before being transferred in September 1939 to Camp Hill Prison on the Isle of Wight. The author of a recent history of the British security services states that with the outbreak of war in September 1939, MI5 (the security service) took over Wormwood Scrubs as its temporary headquarters. The move was so sudden that the intelligence agents found some convicts still in residence. "Prisoners remained in several of the cell blocks and were sometimes seen exercising in the yard. 'Don't go near them,' one of the warders warned female staff. 'Some of them ain't seen no women for years.' Other prisoners, however, had. The ex-public-school 'Mayfair Playboys', who had been imprisoned earlier in the year for robbing high-class jewelers, had danced with some of the Registry staff at debutantes' balls during the London season. The Playboy's leader, the twenty-two year old Victor Hervey, the future sixth Marquess of Bristol, was later said to have provided some of their inspiration for the 'Pink Panther.'"[32] It's a good story, but the author mixes up two different criminal conspiracies. The anecdote indicates how easy it was (and is) to confuse the Hyde Park Hotel robbers of 1937 with Hervey's 1939 gang. The same names popped up in the two trials. John Lonsdale linked the two groups. Norman Birkett defended both Hervey and Wilmer. As their names were so similar, some later took Hervey to be Harley and mistakenly declared Hervey the last man to be publicly flogged in Britain.[33]

The reading public was sufficiently familiar with the notion of the West End gentleman thief that in P. G. Wodehouse's *Quick Service* (1940) it understood why a butler would warn his mistress about a house guest. "A suggestion which has been advanced by a friend of mine to whom I confided the circumstances is that he is one of these Mayfair men who, having recently pulled off a big job, is using the Hall for what is termed a hide-out."[34] Similarly in *The Mating Season* (1947), when Bertie is mistaken for a burglar, a woman describes him as: "A dressy criminal though shopsoiled. . . . One of those Mayfair men you read about, I suppose."[35] In turning to less-well-known "Mayfair playboys" and "Mayfair men" of the late 1930s, it becomes apparent that many observers regarded them through the filter of the Hyde Park Hotel robbery. A review of their criminal trials reveals that they in effect all followed a similar script. Some young men embraced the role to such an extent that they explicitly declared themselves to be Mayfair playboys. In other cases journalists applied the label of "Mayfair man" to otherwise run-of-the-mill delinquents, whose stories were shaped to fit a specific procrustean bed.

What were the traits of the typical Mayfair playboy? First, he came from a "good," that is to say upper-middle-class, family. One of the press's first employments of the phrase "Mayfair playboy" was in August 1937, when referring to Richard Vyvyan Dudley Beaumont, the twenty-two-year-old son of the Dame of Sark. Under the headline "Mayfair 'Playboys' Sailing round the World 'Tired of Debs and Debts,'" the press reported:

> Six self-styled "Mayfair playboys" will begin a world tour in a 50-feet yawl on the week-end. They say that they are "fed up with debs, and debts," and want to show that they are able to do manual work. The party consists of Dick Beaumont, son of the Dame of Sark, a racing motorist and airman, and boxing champion of his school, who is the navigator and captain; Bill Patterson, a Rugby star and cousin of a South African millionaire; Ronald Gaunt, a nephew of Admiral Sir Guy Gaunt, and grandson of the founder of Geelong College (Victoria); Dick Harrison, the Australian "crash stunter" for the films; Arthur Cortez, who claims descent from the famous Spanish explorer; and Paddy Ryah, who played cricket for Canada against Australia, and later took up tea planting in Ceylon.[36]

Planned as a result of a get-together in a Mayfair cocktail bar, the adventure soon went awry. The police arrested Beaumont on his yacht at Southampton for writing a worthless check for £15 7s. 10d. When Beaumont, "described as of no occupation," appeared at Bow Street Police Court, the magistrate refused to allow bail. As more serious charges were pending, Beaumont had to spend a week in Wormwood Scrubs.[37] James Burge, his lawyer, stated that the spoiled young man, used to every comfort in life, had now learned his lesson.

But Burge went on to brazenly blame businesses for providing credit too easily. "One does not want to criticize hotels, but it is a temptation to a young man who finds it easy to run up expenses amounting to £15 in a stay of three days. Both in Cambridge and Mayfair one finds that young men do this sort of thing." Burge expressed the pious hope that Beaumont would seek farm work abroad and so avoid "this sort of extravagance." As he could pay off his debts, Beaumont was simply bound over by Sir Rollo Graham-Campbell, the magistrate. He said that he would make no order for Beaumont's supervision "because I understand he has relatives who can look after him."[38] Apparently their supervision was insufficient. Less than a year later Beaumont pled guilty to obtaining credit by fraud at the London Casino and asked that other offenses be taken into consideration. The court sentenced him to three months hard labor.[39]

If indebtedness became overwhelming, the Bankruptcy Court located on Carey Street offered the man-about-town one last line of defense. One account of the court listed among its varied clients "the playboy who squandered his patrimony and thinks jauntily that 'Carey Street' is an easy out."[40] In fact, as the writer stressed, bankruptcy entailed real costs and loss of reputation. Unlike Victor Hervey most Mayfair men were not independently wealthy. That was the obvious reason why some turned to illegal activities. In May 1939 the newspapers described Hugh Grayson Edwards as a Mayfair playboy. He came to the public's attention when a court sentenced him to twelve months imprisonment for breaking and entering. He led a curious life, and the police declared that his account of it was remarkable. At age two he had been adopted by a wealthy barrister who in 1932 bequeathed him £3,000. Calling himself a "typical Mayfair playboy," the thirty-year-old Edwards related how he spent his entire inheritance on drink and pleasure.[41] Finally he turned to crime. In his defense he argued that despite a public school education he always felt that as an adopted child he was something of a misfit. "No doubt the money left him had turned his head," concluded one reporter.[42]

If young men from respectable families drifted into crime, the reason was, most commentators agreed, because they lacked discipline. One journalist cited a policeman who said that the playboys were war babies—they had lost their father to the fighting or their parents separated after the war. They were delicate and avoided games in school. "Life has been made especially soft for them. Perhaps that is why they seem to be immoral in every way."[43] The question was what to do with them. At one time "remittance men" (sons paid to live abroad, some of whom were an embarrassment to their families) were sent overseas, but with the economic slump the colonies and dominions would no longer accept them. Similarly the Spanish Civil War meant that the island of Majorca could no longer serve as a dumping ground for "these social misfits."

In the interwar decades the psychologically inclined tended to blame inadequate mothers for their sons' homosexuality. It comes as no surprise to find such experts similarly linking the playboy to poor parenting. John Bowlby, the eminent psychiatrist who developed what was known as "attachment theory," devoted his career to highlighting the role early emotional deprivation might have in producing delinquents. He pointed out that the courts and the press, in seeking to explain the motivations of the "Mayfair men," fell back on the old clichés that since they came from well-off families and went to good public schools, they had no excuse. Bowlby protested that the family milieu in which they had been raised had not been investigated, but it clearly had to have been of some importance. Unfortunately Bowlby based his hypothesis on his belief that at least one of the Mayfair men had, as an infant, lost both parents, a supposition that was simply not true.[44]

Others pointed out that if there appeared to be a spurt in the number of delinquents who came from well-off families it was because the popular press exploited the public's interest in upper-class bad boys. Reports of "toffs" and "nobs" misbehaving were always guaranteed to outsell mundane stories of workers' misdemeanors. For that reason, argued an editorial in the *Times*, calculating journalists subjected the younger sons of peers (or Hons) to special scrutiny.

> But the real hardship is dependent on the popular, and probably accurate, journalistic assumption that only the misdemeanors of a Younger Son [of an aristocratic family] are news. It may be suspected that the actuaries of evening paper circulation know one Younger Son on the bills to be worth two Mayfair Men. Hence the tendency of younger sons to become involved in smash-and-grab raids, motor accidents, and the divorce court. They go bankrupt or are salvaged financially by their elder brothers: they get involved in night-club brawls in foreign countries and have to be rescued by the Foreign Office. . . . They never seem to rescue drowning women, stop runaway horses, or make a fortune.[45]

Wealth and status might well win a young man the sympathy of a judge and jury, but such prejudices had always been countered by the popular appetite for moralizing accounts of the decline and fall of the proud and pretentious.

The public loved stories of toffs getting their comeuppances. The popular papers of the interwar years exploited such scandals, but both their desires to attract a family readership and their fear of England's harsh libel laws countered inclinations to muckrake. If the police charged a person with an offense, that person, of course, became fair game. Otherwise journalists generally followed the directives of press lords such as Beaverbrook and Rothermere (who had their own affairs) to respect the privacy of the discreet.[46]

According to court and newspaper reports what might be described as the "playboy's progress" began with his relying on a family allowance. When that ended or proved insufficient he cadged or borrowed from friends. He continued the age-old aristocratic tradition of postponing, if not paying, his bills, of skipping out of hotel and restaurant charges.[47] It was a short next step to writing bad checks and from there to fraud. In condemning such stratagems, commentators spoke of young men "living by (or on) their wits," meaning being a fraud, cheating, taking advantage, and seeking to make money in a clever, usually dishonest, way.

In 1929 the novelist Evelyn Waugh wrote a series of comic essays entitled "Careers for Our Sons," in which he surveyed the restricted employment options available to the middle class in the current economic slump. He dryly concluded that crime offered many advantages, particularly robbery with violence. Suggesting that one carry a hammer and wear a bandana, he sketched out a scenario that sounded remarkably like the attack on Etienne Bellenger: "Another crime which is committed with astonishing frequency is to go into Cartier's and say: 'I am Lord Beaverbrook. Please give me some diamonds.'"[48]

The depression of the 1930s swelled the numbers of those who had to have recourse to a variety of expedients to survive. In Dorothy L. Sayers's *Murder Must Advertise* (1933) when Lord Peter Wimsey dons a disguise to work in an advertising agency, a secretary senses he is not exactly whom he claims to be: "One of the new poor, I expect. Lost all his money in the slump or something." A colleague replies: "I expect he's been one of those gilded johnnies who used to sell cars on commission, and the bottom's dropped out of that . . ."[49] In another whodunit, Ngaio Marsh envisaged some cash-strapped elitists toying with the notion of turning to crime. "Well, the twins were saying at breakfast yesterday that they thought the only thing to be done was for them to turn crooks and be another lot of Mayfair boys."[50]

Often as not a journalist was responsible for determining if a fraud artist was labeled a playboy. For example, in April 1938 the press reported the trial of

Patrick Alan Adamson. The newspapers could have identified him simply as a London accountant but opted for a more sensational slant, presenting him as a thirty-one-year-old Mayfair man-about-town, and playing up his friendships with David Wilmer and Peter Jenkins, two of the men serving sentences for the Hyde Park Hotel jewel robbery. One of Adamson's previous schemes was to sell gramophone recordings of the Duke of Windsor's abdication speech. The police now charged him with defrauding Sir Victor Chetwynd, an alcoholic who, living abroad, had asked Adamson to manage his affairs in Britain. They had opened a joint banking account in London, and using his power-of-attorney, Adamson stripped it, taking nearly £1,000. The tabloids added the incriminating detail that he was thereafter often seen in West End restaurants and hotels. Found guilty of theft, he received a twelve-month sentence. Ironically enough, he had invested the purloined funds in a film company that was set to produce a series of short films entitled "Crime Doesn't Pay."[51]

The Hyde Park Hotel conspirators, unlike most other Mayfair men, crossed the line separating simple theft or fraud from robbery with violence. Magistrates claimed that these crimes were not isolated incidents. "It is not unusual these days to find young men of good social standing who are guilty of all sorts of violence," declared Mr. Dummett at the Bow Street Police Court when sentencing three men in their twenties. They were charged with assaulting a policeman after having been ejected from the Café Royal, on Regent Street. One of the accused was an adopted Conservative candidate for a Scottish constituency. He insisted, when asked, that he had gone to a good public school. Nevertheless, in fining one and placing two on remand, Dummett castigated them for behaving "like utter cads and toughs of the worst description."[52]

Having told their readership how playboys obtained their money, the press provided colorful, if not fictional, portrayals of how they spent it. The best known of the playboys, like Lonsdale, Jenkins, and Hervey, produced detailed accounts of the luxurious lives that they had led. All these stories tended to sound the same and were obviously tailored to fulfill the fantasies of a voyeuristic reading public, hence the continual references to staying at expensive hotels, dining at exclusive restaurants, holidaying on the Riviera, and so on. Paul Mitchell was one of the press' favorites. In June 1936, the papers reported on his attempts to wed an American actress; "Mayfair 'Play-boy' in Hollywood?" read one headline. A year later he recalled the perquisites of the good life: "Just a year ago I was living at the Dorchester Hotel at the rate of £300 a week. I lit a cigar with a ten-pound note every night. I sent a dozen bottles of champagne to the follies girls. Now at 19, I am looking for my first steady job. Almost straight from Bradfield public school [Bradfield College] I stepped into the arms of the Mayfair racket. I thought I was being clever. Others knew I was merely green. I introduced them to my wealthy, titled friends. For that I was given all the money and fun I wanted."[53]

One of the chief sources of the playboy's "fun," reported the press, was his pursuit of the thrills associated with high-speed driving and flying. In 1935, under the headline "Playboy Lord Freed in Auto Death, Feudal Pageantry Revived in Trial," the *Daily Mail* recounted the case of twenty-eight-year-old Edward Russell, Lord de Clifford. His was the last trial to be carried out by the House of Lords. Russell's father had been killed in a road accident, and his son's 1928 maiden speech in the Lords was aptly devoted to the subject of road safety. However, in August 1935, Russell, driving his supercharged Lancia on the wrong side of the road, killed an oncoming driver. As a supporter of Sir Oswald Mosley and the British Union of Fascists he did not believe the regular courts would treat him fairly and demanded, as was his right, to be tried by his peers in the upper chamber. Unsurprisingly his cronies found him not guilty.[54] The Russell case led journalists for years to come to link the words "playboy" and "road accident."

The young playboy Anthony Marston who accidentally kills two children while speeding through a village—"I had my licence suspended for a year, Beastly nuisance"—is the first to die in Agatha Christie's classic whodunit *And Then There Were None* (1939).[55] In the interwar decades it was a commonplace that the playboy's reckless driving was a sign of his indifference to rules and regulations. Valentine Cunningham has noted that the poems, plays, and novels of the 1930s were dotted with references to the "obsessively doted-on aids to speed, a motorbike, a racing-car, or airplane."[56] The automobile promised youth escape from home and parents. It offered young women a new mobility and young men the seductions of speed, risk, and danger.[57] The car promised to increase women's independence, but in the 1930s women only represented about 12 percent of drivers. Even for the man-about-town the car required a major investment in conspicuous consumption. Advertisements implied that the larger and more expensive one's automobile was, the more successfully aggressive one would be. At an unconscious level driving was sexualized. To possess a car was the first step in possessing a woman. In *Brighton Rock* (1938), Graham Greene referred to a roadster that, even when parked, reeked of its owner's sexual adventures. "A scarlet racing model, a tiny rakish car which carried about it the atmosphere of innumerable road-houses, of totsies gathered round swimming pools, of furtive encounters in by-lanes off the Great North Road."[58] Countering the lauding of fast cars, some sketched out cautionary tales. In *The Devil Is Driving* (1937, dir. Harry Lachman) an American didactic film focused on highway carnage, the playboy son of a wealthy family is responsible for two highway deaths.[59]

Young men's addiction to thrill seeking was particularly evident in the background to the 1938 trial at the Derbyshire Assizes reported under the headline "4 Mayfair Play-Boys Gaoled." Patrick Wakelyn Topham, twenty-four, pilot; David John Beatson Sneddon, twenty-six, independently wealthy; Richard Norman Campbell, twenty-nine, aircraftman; and John Miller, twenty-eight, clerk, pled guilty to breaking in and stealing £330 of jewelry from Samuel Royse, prospective Liberal candidate for the Lough Division of Lincolnshire.[60] The commissioner of the assizes likened the case to the Hyde Park Hotel robbery in that both revealed young men given to drink and short of money, looking about to see what they could cadge.[61] The accused in the Derbyshire case he described as "[f]our idle young men who had been drinking and fooling their way round Mayfair and the West End." The pity was that Topham and Sneddon had gone to good schools. Topham had decided to be a playboy when he left Cambridge, and in three years he burned through a £10,000 legacy. Sneddon regularly spent £2,000 a year. Miller and Campbell, their more modestly situated friends, rather than work "haunted West End night clubs, preferring the company of young men of independent means."[62]

Journalists covering the trial recalled that both Topham and Sneddon were addicted to speed. Topham, while still an undergraduate at Cambridge, was lucky to have been found not guilty of dangerous driving at Folkestone on September 7, 1934, despite being involved in an accident in which his car left a skid mark 132 feet long.[63] A month later his dangerous driving led the magistrate at the Bedford Quarter Sessions to fine him £15 and suspend his license for two years.[64] Though his car crash resulted in six injured and one killed, the coroner had to rebuke him for arriving late to the inquest.[65] Sneddon, like Topham, lost his driver's license but drove anyway. Such was Sneddon's father's sense of shame that he committed suicide the morning before his son's 1936 trial for driving while disqualified.[66] In 1940 Topham was back in court, charged with breaking and entering and theft of a mink coat.[67]

Having a chauffeur-driven Rolls Royce (as did Martin Jenkins's father) signaled that one was firmly ensconced in the upper classes, but young people wanted to drive themselves. References to a passion for reckless driving littered the playboys' biographies. John Whyte-Melville Skeffington, drove in the 1937 Le Mans Grand Prix. Victor Hervey was involved in a motorcar collision in the midst of his 1939 trial proceedings. The arm of his female passenger was broken, and he suffered shock.[68] In the single year of 1945 he racked up seven more driving offenses.[69] Geoffrey Coop, one of Hervey's henchmen, deserted from the Royal Army Ordnance Corps in 1938 because restrictions were placed on him as a result of several motoring charges.[70] Gordon Russell was killed sometime after five in the morning when driving Elizabeth Pelly, a friend of the Wilmers, home from a dance.[71]

Flying was a marker of even higher status. In the interwar years it was not simply a means of transportation but an elite activity.[72] John Davies, a wealthy friend of John Lonsdale, was born without a right arm yet acquired a pilot's license and in the war served as a pilot for the Air Transport Auxiliary.[73] The playboys who took up flying included John Lonsdale, Victor Hervey, Pat Moran, Patrick Topham (who bought and crashed two planes), David Sneddon, the Marquess of Donegal, John Whyte-Melville Skeffington, and the Prince of Wales. James Mollison, a Scottish pilot who set several flying records in the 1930s, cemented the notion that aviation and the fast life were linked by entitling his memoirs *Playboy of the Air* (1937). He embellished his autobiography with accounts of his love of nightclubs, heavy drinking, and romance.[74] Predictably enough, Mrs. Victor Bruce, a pioneering female aviator, attended the Mayfair men's 1938 trial.[75]

Given its elitist nature, flying particularly attracted those on the political right.[76] John Lonsdale joined the National League of Airmen, which Lord Rothermere established in 1935 as a pressure group to goad the government into building up a large air force to match Nazi Germany's.[77] Rothermere's long-term goal was to forge an alliance between Britain, Germany, and the United States in preparation for their inevitable conflict with the nonwhite races.

The censorious had to admit that the thrill of flying appealed to the masculine sense of adventure and could provide valuable skills that would be needed in wartime. No such justifications could be advanced to justify young men's self-destructive pursuit of drink. Yet if the tabloids were to be believed, the playboy chiefly sought his pleasures in an active nightlife. Columnists reported that he had certain specific haunts. "These consist largely of bars, second-rate restaurants, third-rate clubs, and certain bottle parties."[78] The court described Mitchell as "a Mayfair playboy, an associate of undesirable characters and frequenter of doubtful nightclubs." When Topham and Sneddon were being prosecuted, the crown asserted that their "indulgence in drink in West End clubs, association with undesirable persons, and living on their wits" inevitably resulted in their turning to crime.[79] Many trials provided detailed accounts of the drinking establishments patronized by the accused. The four Hyde Park Hotel robbers, for example, testified to having visited the Florida, the Spotted Dog, the 19th Club, and the bar at the Mayfair Hotel. The press pointed out the obvious moral: "Night-clubs lured them to their downfall."[80]

The nightclub emerged after the First World War. The old elite's social calendar continued as ever. Racing at Ascot, sailing at Cowes, and attendance at debutante dances and regimental balls persisted much as they had for decades past, but they now had to compete with new spaces—the nightclub, dance palais, and penthouse.[81] The focus of entertainment slowly shifted from the staid private ballroom to the exciting public nightclub. In the latter, young men and women relished the opportunity of pursuing adventures while consuming that American affectation, the cocktail.[82]

In the 1920s Sir William Joynson-Hicks, the home secretary, sought to restrict the clubs' sales of liquor. He failed to understand that times had changed and in launching his campaign against nightclubs was completely out of his element: "he expected them to be filled with whores and found them crammed with 'society.'"[83] Smart nightclubs included the Embassy, the Kit-Kat, and Chez Victor, followed by the Top Hat, the Oriental, the Bag o' Nails, the Lamp Post, and the Venetian. To enter an exclusive venue like the Ritz one needed money or connections.[84]

In the 1930s, Gordon Halsey, owner of the Florida nightclub, invented the "bottle party" as a way of circumventing the restrictive hours on the sale of drink.[85] A "bottle party" was purportedly private, so restrictions did not apply. One could reserve drinks in advance and receive an invitation to the "party" or buy instant membership at the door.[86] In some clubs the dance hostesses who preordered the drinks illegally doubled the price when selling to the customer.[87] In others the manager added 9 to 12 shillings per bottle.[88] The press estimated that in 1938 there were 170 bottle parties in the West End. Because of their questionable legality the rougher establishments drew a somewhat shady crowd and were occasionally visited by the police. Mario Santini, who ran a bottle party on Frith Street, was raided three times in 1937, perhaps because he also operated a brothel on the same street.[89] In many clubs dance hostesses offered their services as partners or dance teachers. In the larger places they were paid by management; in the smaller they relied on their clients' tips and gifts. The police suspected that some were lured into prostitution. The press referred to their male counterparts as lounge lizards or gigolos.[90]

The puritanical particularly condemned the nightclub as an unsupervised locale pandering to desires for drink and promiscuous socializing. They had earlier attacked hotels and restaurants for similar reasons.[91] They warned that women could be compromised by drinking and partying in public. Sylvia Leggi met John Skeffington at the Florida nightclub. Pamela Blake libeled Lonsdale at the Florida and at the bar of the Mayfair Hotel. Though respectable women would have a male escort when attending a nightclub, such a visit still held out the promise of a chance encounter. Mrs. Burley had the money to patronize the Ritz, Grosvenor House, and Quaglino's but had her heart set on visiting the tawdrier Nest Club.

The Florida, the Nest, and the Bag o' Nails all offered black entertainment. The Florida, in Bruton Mews, off Brook Street, had telephones on the tables, which encouraged flirting. Known first as Toby's Club and then in 1936 as the Old Florida Club, it booked black bands like the Snakehips Johnson Orchestra. In 1938 the African American singer Adelaide Hall and her husband, Bert Hicks, purchased and relaunched it as the New Florida, the first black-owned nightclub outside of Soho.[92] The Spotted Dog was located in the same building. That there was the possibility of a mingling of the races was yet a further reason why conservatives viewed the nightclubs with distaste. One sensational account portrayed them as the haunt of confidence men and "nigger bands," where pleasure-sated white girls died from overdoses of cocaine provided by some "black or yellow parasite."[93] Such alarms probably made them all the more alluring to young people.

Under the headline "Paul Mitchell 'To Give Up Night Clubs,'" the *Daily Mail* reported Judge Dodson's insistence that the playboy "give up night clubs and cocktail bars and settle down to the work of earning your own living."[94] This insistence that young men turn their lives around became a familiar refrain. The broadsheets presented the playboys as but common criminals—indeed, worse than common criminals inasmuch they had every advantage yet nevertheless resorted to robbery. The tabloid press was more sympathetic, publishing, for example, first-person accounts of Lonsdale—"I Have Been a Fool: Confessions of John Christopher Mainwaring Lonsdale"—and Hervey's "A Gun-Runner's Thrills!"[95] Following the reformed or redemptionist script, the playboy would own up to his inadequacies, promise to change his ways, and cite the person (often a woman) whose intervention made his conversion possible. At the same time he would warn other young men to avoid "loose companions" and the temptations of West End nightlife. ⌐

Some playboys who swore that they had given up the fast life were soon back in court. Paul Mitchell was a classic case. After his creditors launched a bankruptcy petition against him in October 1936, the police arrested him on fraud charges.[96] The court found him guilty of obtaining credit from Messrs. Schwab and Snelling, stockbrokers, by means of false pretenses, and bound him over for three years. In August 1937 he was arrested for cashing a fraudulent £25,000 check in Davos, Switzerland. The press identified him as a Mayfair Playboy who played a part in the "introduction racket."[97] In 1938 he made a false application for a passport, and in June 1939 the authorities charged him with being involved in another elaborate plot to defraud.[98] As described in a news story entitled "23, 'Ruined by West End Life,'" he was sentenced to twenty months in prison for fraud and false pretenses.[99] Mitchell had a bad war, being court-martialed twice on charges of false pretenses and escaping from military custody.[100] In 1949 French authorities sentenced him to two months in Santé prison for passing forged £1 notes then told to leave the country. He was angered that many still thought he was one of the Mayfair men.[101] When not in prison he haunted the hotels and bars of Mayfair. His charge sheet listed a string of convictions for passing counterfeit notes and false pretenses. At his last court appearance he was charged with obtaining clothes by false pretenses. Under the headline "West End Playboy Dies in Street Accident," the press reported in September 1953, that the thirty-six-year-old had been run down in Thurlow Place and a coroner's inquest was to be held. Mitchell (also known as Thomas Shaw), having just finished a three-year sentence, had in his short life been convicted nine times and court-martialed twice.[102]

The press intermittently raised the issue of life copying art when it described the Mayfair men as "real life Raffles," referring to the fictional character created by E. W. Hornung, the brother-in-law of Arthur Conan Doyle. Hornung introduced his hero, A. J. Raffles, an indolent and athletic figure, and his loyal batsman Bunny in *The Amateur Cracksman* (1899). Raffles is a clubland hero and cracksman (burglar or safecracker) who enjoys the "romance and peril" of robbery.[103] His adventures are related by Bunny, who had "fagged" (acted as a servant) for Raffles at their public school. The story begins with

Bunny, overwhelmed by debts (though having a flat in fashionable Mount Street) and pondering suicide. In the nick of time Raffles appears, saving Bunny by recruiting him into a life of crime. Raffles justifies his thefts as adventures. "Why should I work when I could steal? Why settle down to some humdrum uncongenial billet, when excitement, romance, danger and a decent living were all going begging together? Of course it's very wrong, but we can't all be moralists, and the distribution of wealth is very wrong to begin with."[104] Breaking into a Bond Street jewelry shop and stripping it of its gems is their first invigorating joint operation.

In 1930 a reformed burglar published the story of his life under the title *Raffles in Real Life*.[105] Eloise Moss has examined how newspapers labeled many burglars between 1898 and 1939 as "real life Raffles."[106] There was, of course, a well-established tradition of the populace lauding the skills and daring of highwaymen and other celebrated thieves, especially those from modest backgrounds who pillaged the rich and spared the poor. The Raffles character was different; he came from the middle or upper classes, and cheap newspapers, true crime texts, and ghostwritten memoirs traced his career.

Hornung's Raffles does not simply steal from anyone. He takes from those who, because of their race, class, ethnicity, or sexual orientation, are not worthy of their wealth. At one point he tells Bunny why they have to steal from such people: "We're getting vulgarly hard up again, and there's an end on 't. Besides, these people deserve it, and can afford it."[107] His victims include Reuben Rosenthall, described as having "a great hook-nose, and the reddest hair and whiskers you ever saw" and a "retinue of Kaffirs" with "black faces, white eye-balls, wooly pates."[108] Hornung's racism is all too obvious. He has Raffles, in preparing for a burglary, congratulate Bunny: "By jove, old boy," he whispered cheerily, "you look about the greatest ruffian I ever saw! These masks alone will down a nigger, if we meet one."[109] Rosenthall has made his millions "on the diamond fields of South Africa," and Raffles feels he has a moral obligation to rob such a grotesque character. Others whom Raffles feels deserved to be robbed include those who "fluked" into wealth and a "young fellow of the exquisite type," meaning a homosexual.[110]

Some have described as "blackguard literature" the works that lauded this new breed of British hero. The term emerged following the appearance of Roger Pocock's *The Blackguard* (1897), with his Canadian Mountie singing the praises of the empire. Minor works in the same genre include C. J. Cutliffe Hyne, *Honour of Thieves* (1895), the central character being a Harrow-educated ex-cowboy.[111] Despite this literature's apparent flouting of morality, it was inherently conservative, the villains always being social or racial outsiders. Blackmail themes figured in many of the stories, the blackmailer often being presented as a Jew or foreigner holding some mysterious bundle of letters that endanger an old English family. In repetitively portraying the vengeful hero's brutal punishment of the lower classes and nonwhites, authors appealed to the sadistic side of their readers. They presented the racial superiority of their white heroes as justifying their dishonest dealings with villains.[112] Pocock's "blackguard" upbraided French Canadians to "talk white": "Get away back to the reserve, or behave like a white man, you mongrel!"[113] Sax Rohmer's Fu Manchu paranoid tales played on fear of the Chinese. In a typical 1925 serial, the writer presented the English hero holding off a gang of Orientals: " 'Back! Stand back, you scum of the black channels,' he snarled. 'Back, or I'll drill you so full of nickel you'll want a steam navvy to lift your damned coffins. Hey! Henri—out of that! Get over with these Chinky rats! Hustle you son of a dog!' "[114] In Raffles's adventures the language was not too dissimilar. Critics rarely commented on such naked appeals to race and class. What readers noted were the portrayals of the hero's coolness and daring. Well-paced stories written in sporting spirit seemed innocent forms of escapism. Even George Orwell, the enemy of authoritarianism, later defended Hornung, claiming there was a "charm" about the Raffles stories; as a gentleman he knew that certain things were "not cricket" or "not done." The creed of "playing the game," believed Orwell, acted as a check on bad behavior.[115] He feared the "anti-gentlemanliness" of the totalitarian age and much preferred the gentleman-burglar Raffles to the heroes of American hard-boiled thrillers in which there were "no gentlemen and no taboos."[116]

One of the first newspaper accounts of the Hyde Park Hotel robbery claimed that a film had inspired the perpetrators. The four youths planned the perfect crime "after seeing a motion picture and improving on the plot."[117] There is no evidence to support such an assertion, but a remarkable number of films in the 1930s did glamorize the jewel thief. It was tempting to believe that if it had not been for these movies, the owners of gems would have had less to fear.

Filmed versions of Raffles came out in 1930, 1933, and 1939. The *Times* critic hailed the 1930 production for capturing "the right kind of boyish delight" the hero had in playing off the police.[118] There was in addition a flood of films featuring what the Americans referred to as "kid-glove crooks." Such transnational influences were obviously important. Britain followed America's pioneering preoccupations with both celebrity culture and the mass media.

A typical American example of a jewel thief film was *Dangerously Yours* (1933, dir. Frank Tuttle), the clichéd story of a female detective falling in love with a thief. One reviewer wearily said of the star, "Warner Baxter interprets one of those slick jewel burglars who are always depriving wealthy dowagers of their diamonds."[119] Similarly, in *Sylvia Scarlett* (1935, dir. George Cukor) the rascally Cary Grant sought Katherine Hepburn's help in stealing jewels from a wealthy family.[120] The most daring of such films was William Dieterle's *Jewel Robbery* (1932), a risqué comedy based on a 1931 Hungarian play about a society woman (Kay Francis) bored by both her dull husband and humdrum lover, being captivated by a charming jewel thief (William Powell). The husband, who calls the playboy a "communist," is himself a banker and therefore presented as a hypocrite. His wife is infatuated with the thief and accordingly appalled by his proposal to leave her "untouched in the suburbs." The film ends with her going off to join him in Nice.[121]

In a few films such as *Night Spot* (1938, dir. Christy Cabanne) and the confusing *Number Seventeen* (1932, dir. Alfred Hitchcock), the jewel thieves were presented as the villains. Perhaps the most original of this ilk was *Smash and Grab* (1937, dir. Tim Whelan) in which a private detective, hired by an insurance company to track down a gang of smash-and-grab jewel thieves, discovers that what looks like a theft is in fact a put-up job to collect insurance.[122]

In a few films a woman turns out to be the thief. *Desire* (1936, dir. Frank Borzage) begins with the traditional gender roles being reversed as Marlene Dietrich, portraying the cool thief, heartlessly uses the naïve Gary Cooper as an unwitting accomplice. Unfortunately the film succumbs to sentimentalism, ending with Cooper reforming and marrying Dietrich.[123] In *Satan Met a Lady* (1936, dir. William Dieterle), the second screen version of *The Maltese Falcon*, a detective has to deal with a lying seductress and a lady jewel thief. In *The Last of Mrs. Cheyney* (1937, dir. Richard Boleslawski), Joan Crawford plays an American jewel thief who worms her way into British society in pursuit of a valuable pearl necklace. The portrayal of the woman as jewel thief occurred less frequently, but it reflected society's growing appreciation (or apprehension) of women's intelligence and talents.

The stealing of jewels appears to have been easier to justify than other sorts of thefts. Why was this? The first reason is that it was a crime that presumably could only be carried out by a superior sort of person—intelligent enough to organize a complicated plan of attack, sophisticated enough to enter the best social circles, and calm enough to serenely undertake the riskiest of gambles. The *Times* critic skewered this view in reviewing *The Last of Mrs. Cheyney*: "Inevitably the introduction of jewel thieves will provoke at least some of the conventional variations from conventional morality. These fascinating and superhuman creatures are always so much more noble than their prey, and so much more sophisticated than those whose manners they imitate; the parasite, in fact, is so much more splendid than its host that by hook or by crook its conduct must be justified. Here, of course, his justification is comparatively easy, though perhaps not altogether fair."[124] In these sorts of films one immediately identified with the dashing master criminal. The plodding police were, in contrast, often objects of ridicule. Far from being sophisticates, the bobby and the inspector were presented as out of place in the homes of the rich. They were, as one commentator cruelly noted, "obviously the sort of people who have to be given lunch on a tray in the library."[125]

The second reason why film jewel thieves could be forgiven was quite obvious. They necessarily only stole from the rich, preying on Bond Street jewelry shops, West End mansions, and country estates. They might not have given to the poor, but at least they did not rob them.[126] The dramatization of their depredations might well have been cheered on by working-class audiences as a veiled attack on the British elites' monopolization of wealth and social power.[127]

The moral to be drawn from the playboy criminals' confessions—both true and fictional—was that crime did not pay. Nevertheless, the public was probably more impressed with the depictions of the pleasures that cool daring and native intelligence had won than by hollow avowals of remorse. The young men who were condemned by the courts had no doubt read stories or seen films that glamorized Raffles and his kind. In reality the Mayfair men were for the most part the feckless sons of respectable families, so lacking in imagination, energy, and intelligence that they stole from friends, colleagues, and nearby West London businesses. Yet the tabloids that condemned them one day romanticized them the next as descendants of that familiar figure, the suave, debonair, gentleman thief. Were such tales responsible for leading some to commit copycat crimes? Moralists in the 1930s debated—as they had for the previous hundred years—the question of what effect fictional accounts had on impressionable minds. They reached no firm conclusion, but both sides agreed that demand for such portrayals never ceased to grow. Newspapers and film companies exploited the hunger for firsthand accounts of criminal activity, and both felons and retired policemen competed for the attention of a mass readership looking for sensational tales.[128]

The vast majority of those who enjoyed accounts of adventurers fleecing the wealthy were, of course, law-abiding citizens who would never engage in crime. They might indulge in the fantasy of not having to play by the rules, but such idle thoughts were harmless diversions. Indeed, it is possible that the entertaining fictional accounts of robbery, which figured in so many films and novels, served a compensatory function and actually prevented real thefts. Yet at some level these stories' appeal had to be related to their conjuring up the notion that robberies not only were inevitable but, given Britain's glaring class disparities, were in some cases justified.

Chapter 9: CLASS

Two hundred years before the trial of the Hyde Park Hotel robbers, William Hogarth depicted the rise and fall of a ne'er-do-well in his famous series of paintings *The Rake's Progress* (1733). Rebecca West, responding to the belief that this type of character seemed to be flourishing once more, produced in 1934 an updated version with illustrations by the cartoonist David Low. George, the central character, having inherited a title and an estate, dissipates his money on parties, cocktails, "lovelies," nightclubs, and gambling dens. The story ends with the debauchee divorced, losing the last of his funds in the crash, and forced to go on the dole.[1] The Mayfair playboys' careers followed similar trajectories but ended even more disastrously. In Hogarth's day fashionable men and women amused themselves by viewing the lunatics in Bedlam. In 1938 the same sorts of people went to the Old Bailey to witness firsthand four young men being sentenced to imprisonment and floggings. Thousands more around the world followed the proceedings through syndicated press reports.

"Society bigwigs today," reported the *Chicago Tribune*, "made a Roman circus out of the trial of four Mayfair playboys."[2] The trial received so much attention in large part because it brought to light stresses and strains within the British class structure.[3] The spectacle of four upper-class young men stealing diamonds was in itself disconcerting, but their behavior appeared all the more outrageous given that in the same year millions of unemployed working-class men and women were stoically enduring privations that West End playboys could not begin to imagine. Accordingly, the trial offered commentators a way of broaching the "condition of England" question. Was society becoming more democratic and egalitarian? Was the power of the social elite declining? Many worried that the robbery was a symptom of a weakening of the existing social contract. Others were angered because the trial demonstrated that,

despite evidence of upper-class criminality, the elite still enjoyed immense social power. Observers from both camps held that in having respectable families, public school educations, money (or access to it), West End residences,
acceptance by London society, and extensive networks of friends, the Mayfair
men enjoyed every advantage of their class. Their turning to robbery thus
only made sense if regarded as a release of the youths' worse "instincts." From
another point of view, however, perhaps their crimes are best understood if
the extent to which the idea of the Mayfair men was socially constructed is
appreciated. Their "advantages," far from acting as restraints, instilled in these
playboys a dangerous sense of social superiority. Their hubris in turn incited
them to seize that which their culture told them was their due.

Did the Mayfair men represent the elite? Was it in decline? Frank Mort
notes that "historians have conventionally defined the years after 1945 as wit-
nessing the near-terminal decline of the English social elites."[4] A decade earlier some believed that the Hyde Park Hotel robbery was a symptom of that
decay. Such scandals appeared to call into question the elite's claims justifying
its privileged status. The popular press played up the notion that the Mayfair
men came from the upper classes, if not the aristocracy. The four dapper
young men were described as "aristocratic both in bearing and lineage, all
were graduates of outstanding British public schools. And one of them was the
son of a high Army official."[5] Another reported: "Fashionably dressed men and
women jostled for seats in Westminster police court today at the hearing of
four 'young men about Mayfair'. . . . All moved in swanky West End society
circles."[6]

In contrast, the *Times* tried to distance the robbers from the establishment.
It admitted that the trial revealed that even a good environment might produce the occasional bad apple, but it insisted that the accused had succeeded in
penetrating no farther than the margins of elite society. "They have naturally
moved among people of some rank and culture, however naturally they may
have gravitated to those fringes of society whose horizon is bounded by bars
and night clubs."[7] The tabloids harped on the theme that the overly ambitious
young men's love of luxury and easy money inevitably led to prison. The Mayfair men were not wealthy, but an enormous gulf separated them from the
lower classes. When asked at the 1938 trial about his financial situation Wilmer
stated unapologetically that he spent about £6 a week—twice the weekly wage
of a male worker in manufacturing—solely on entertainments.[8] In describing
their discussions Jenkins admitted, "We were all fairly short of money and

were trying to think of a way of making some fairly quickly."[9] The four could probably be best described as upper-middle class. Lonsdale and Jenkins's fathers were successful businessmen, Wilmer's was a brigadier-general, and Harley's a colonel. Wilmer and Lonsdale had family money, and Jenkins drew interest on his parents' will. Having lost his father, Harley appears to have been the least advantaged of the four. All managed to live beyond their means by borrowing from friends, writing bad checks, and skipping out on hotel bills. The four may at times have been spongers and bilkers, but they had the cultural capital that won them the attention of the members of the social elite attending their trial, such as the Duke of Rutland and Viscountess Byng.

The upper classes, consisting of perhaps 40,000 people, were defined by their wealth and status. The Great War had been a shock. Between 1918 and 1922 one-quarter of the land in England and Wales changed hands on account of increased taxes and death duties. There was also a shift in influence from land and finance to commerce and manufacturing. Some assumed that financial embarrassment explained why the aristocracy allowed middle-class interlopers like the Mayfair men to enter the best circles. For the same reason the sons and daughters of the upper classes were beginning to enter business and the professions. "No surprise was caused when Mayfair women opened dress-shops in Bond Street, or started Social Bureaux for supplying guides to American visitors," reported Robert Graves. " 'Society', it was generally assumed, had to earn its living like any other class; so 'Society' came to mean 'people worthy of a columnist's respectful mention.' "[10]

Taxes and inflation tested the elite, but if the super rich slightly declined, the numbers of the ordinary rich increased. In the 1938 Sir Halley Stewart Lecture, John Hilton, professor of industrial relations at Cambridge, reminded his audience of the enormous disparities in wealth between the rich and poor. The old saw held that thrift was the basis of wealth, but in fact it was old money that led to new money. Similarly, the cautionary tale of the man of means who, due to lack of foresight, ended up in a dole queue was a fiction. Such cases, declared Hilton, were so rare as to be mythical. "But apart from the rarest personal disasters and tragedies, 'family' in our land stays put. Wealth stays put. Riches to-day have a high margin of safety."[11]

Disparities in income were similarly enduring. The socialist academics G. D. H. Cole and M. I. Cole pointed out that those with incomes of £1,000 a year and up equaled only 1.5 percent of the population but took 22 ½ percent of all earnings, whereas the bottom 87.5 percent received only 58 percent.

Sixty percent of all incomes were under £125 a year and 73.5 percent of families had an income of less than £4 a week.[12] Of 12 million families, 8 million had less than £100 in capital.[13] The disparities were even greater when it came to property holding. The top 1 percent held almost 40 percent of all property, while the bottom 63 percent held only 7 percent.[14] In 1938, 20 percent of the population, according to Hilton, even fell short of obtaining adequate nutrition. These marginals never "had a chance," tumbling into poverty if hit, as they inevitably were, by sickness, job loss, or accident.[15] In *A Night in London* (1938) the brilliant photographer Bill Brandt provided the most memorable graphic illustrations of such class differences. Next to "Late Supper," which captures a well-dressed, apparently bored couple trying to decide what to take from a table loaded with crystal, crisp linens and innumerable meat and vegetable dishes, he placed "Behind the Restaurant," showing a vagrant, under a waiter's indifferent gaze, rummaging for food in the trash cans of a darkened alley.[16]

Despite all the statistics, many conservatives believed in the pauperization of the rich or the emergence of what was known as the "new poor."[17] The phrase was used after the war to describe those on fixed incomes hit by rising taxes, rates, and inflation. According to the alarmist tabloids even a well-off man earning £2,000 a year would soon be impoverished by the steady increase in school fees, taxes, and servants' wages. The *Daily Mail* called for a new political party to represent this endangered portion of the population. On the continent powerful fascist movements emerged as a result of similar fears. In Britain, after the 1920 upturn in the economy, the issue ceased to be a subject of public discussion for close to a decade.[18]

After the 1929 crash it predictably resurfaced. The wealthy were once again shocked, not by actually being impoverished but by a sense of relative deprivation. A potent mix of feeling that others were doing better while they were falling behind and a belief that the respect that they once enjoyed had been lost fuelled the discontent of the propertied. According to the French politician and academic André Siegfried, "In their wounded pride they aggressively refer to themselves as the 'new poor.' "[19] " 'The New Poor' positively boasted of their penuriousness," agreed Robert Graves.[20] Under the headline "Distress among the 'New Poor,' " the *Times* reported that the Professional Classes Aid Council had helped 1,200 highly educated clients in 1931–1932.[21] More worrying were reports that otherwise respectable individuals were seeking to dodge taxes and that others had become contemptuous of the democratic state. Outsiders showed little sympathy. An Australian newspaper coolly mocked the anxieties of the English upper classes:

> London's new poor: 1939 vintage. The new poor are with us again, it seems from the advertising columns of *The Times*. Mink coats which cost £500 are being thrown on the market for half that price; certified gentlefolk and country people desperately are trying to get rid of large houses, oil paintings, Rolls-Royces; a serving cavalry officer appeals to a "patriotic person" to give him an unwanted high-powered or medium-powered car—a Mercedes would be acceptable, he says. The agony column is a mirror of these times, more than ever abounding in pointers for novelists and short-story writers. A refugee must sell four internationally known Hungarian paintings; Royal Academy exhibitors will paint portraits at a quarter of peace-time fees; you may rent for seven guineas a week, furnished, an eighteenth century country house that Dean Swift lived in, now complete with three bathrooms and a garage, and intersected by a trout stream, a "human machine," unwanted by the fighting services ("to the machine's great disgust") announces himself for hire at half his peace time salary of £1,040. And is there an art-loving person who can give a home to a young, "rather unknown" refugee poetess, now working as a maid?[22]

In his "confession" John Lonsdale sought to present himself as yet another member of the "new poor." Why did so many well-educated youths fall into crime? Lonsdale replied that normally they would be in real estate, stocks, car sales, or insurance, but they were hit by the slump. Yet being middle or upper class they had to keep up appearances, which meant living well. He presented himself, strained by social demands and trying to keep pace with his wealthy friends, as "forced" to write bad checks. Indeed, he became a "check chaser," covering one check with another—at one point being £800 in debt.[23]

It was one thing to be rich; it was another to be a member of "society." The *Times* regarded the Mayfair men as interlopers, but the tabloids made much of the fact that the elite had opened its doors to them. News stories referred to "four well-known young Mayfair society men."[24] Journalists noted that the four all had West End addresses.[25] The *Daily Sketch* described "society" flocking to the trial of the four immaculate and debonair youths.[26] Others referred to the expensively dressed friends of the accused who attended the trial.[27] "The little Westminster Police Court room was crowded to capacity for the preliminary hearing. Only one-third of those attending could be seated. Many smartly dressed women were among the spectators."[28] The Mayfair men exemplified how far (and how low) the ambitious young man might go in society by exploiting friends, family, and social connections.

"Society has a thoroughly English conviction of the superiority of the man to whose breeding, heredity, tradition and education have contributed their best," a foreign observer noted, "and it regards itself, on the whole justifiably, as a highly bred class in that sense—not, that is, as constituting a higher type of humanity all round, but as specially developed and trained to be the best possible leaders and governors of the country."[29] High society had at one time exerted both social and political power. Following World War I it no longer had the ability to rule. Society now served a different function. Because of death duties and tax increases, more members of what had been the leisure class moved into business. With the government cutting back on army and navy budgets, not to mention the increases in the cost of living, sons who had previously assumed the right to positions in Parliament and the services had to reconsider their career options. Upper-middle-class families on fixed incomes sought to reduce expenses. Some sold off their mansions and moved into flats. In the future their political power depended on their success in business.[30]

According to Patrick Balfour, "society" had replaced the world once dominated by aristocratic castes.[31] Society nevertheless embraced what was an inherently snobbish culture, sustained as it was by the monarchy. Some of its barriers were dropping, but there was no prospect of them disappearing. "Society now presented a picture of metropolitan glamour which none the less still legitimated the existing distribution of wealth and social esteem."[32] Entry was based on one's kin, schooling, and wealth. The big London houses such as the Devonshire, Dorchester, and Grosvenor ceased to function as political hubs, but society hostesses continued to integrate the old closed landed elite with a more open eclectic elite.

Hostesses like Emerald Cunard were powerful.[33] These gatekeepers reviewed a newcomer's breeding, background, and education. Style and cultural habits were of great importance. One needed capital or, as was the case with the Mayfair men, links to it via relations or friends. "So that although wealth was continually sought after, birth and 'breeding' were treated with, if anything, greater deference. Thus you could be the penniless younger son of a younger son, but if you came of 'good' family it could enable you to marry an heiress from among the newer rich, or get a top job in the Diplomatic Service if you were clever, or in the armed forces if you were not so clever."[34] If accepted, it was said one "moved" in the best circles.

Society's function was to prolong the power of the upper classes by protecting and promoting privilege. The *Times* and *Telegraph* informed their readerships who were the "best people," what degrees or promotions they had won, and when and where they held their weddings, christenings, and funerals. Everything else one needed to know about high society was conveyed by gossip columnists like "William Hickey" (Tom Driberg) and aristocratic journalists, including the Marquess of Donegall and Lord Castlerosse. The popular papers, such as the *Daily Mail, Daily Sketch, Daily Express,* and *News of the World,* in publicizing and glamorizing the doings of society promoted snobbery and caste consciousness.[35] Society in turn used the press to broadcast reports of the cycle of celebrations and social displays that justified its existence.

The popular press was always fascinated by the minutiae of the wealthy, who, it was assumed, represented glamour and style. Despite this fetishization of the elites, stories of their fall from grace, journalists knew, also sold newspapers. If the upper classes dominated culture, they paid the price in having the press broadcast often sensationalized reports of their peccadilloes tailored to entertain a lower-middle-class readership. To be a member of high society, grumbled one writer, meant always talking to some hack or being photographed. "It can only be a question of time before married couples are photographed in bed."[36]

Some felt standards had declined. "Since 'society,' so-called ceased to be a purely leisured class, since the idle rich became the new poor, the term 'London season' has lost the distinctive significance which it bore in the past."[37] Nevertheless the majority of the elite slavishly followed the traditional calendar of events (as did the lower-middle-class tabloid readership) from the presentation at court of debutantes in their coming-out to Royal Ascot to the Cowes Week regatta. Continuing to meet at such events as well as at parties, balls, races, and the opera, London society seemed to have been almost oblivious to the economic crisis the nation had faced. The trial of the Mayfair men served as a reminder that even high society could harbor men whose sense of relative deprivation might lead them into criminality.

Where one lived was as important as how one lived. When the police stopped poet Brian Howard and asked his name and address, he insultingly replied: "I live in Mayfair. No doubt you come from some dreary suburb."[38] The Hyde Park Hotel robbers shared Howard's fixation on their famous environs. This posh, central district of London was bounded by Piccadilly on the south, Regent Street on the east, Oxford Street on the north, and Hyde Park on the west. In December 1937, Harley was staying on Curzon Street; Wilmer at Brook Mews, Davies Street (between New Bond Street and Grosvenor Square); Lonsdale at the Mayfair Hotel, Down Street, Piccadilly (just north of Green Park); and Jenkins at Fleming's New Clarges Hotel, Clarges Street, Piccadilly. It was clearly important for their self-presentation to have a good address, and sacrifices would be made to retain it.

Mayfair had a particular cachet. It had for more than two centuries been in the English-speaking world the synecdoche for wealth. According to Clarence Rook, in the early 1900s one could identify a London neighborhood by its inhabitants.

> Thus, you may know Bloomsbury by its Jews . . . , the "City," by its black-coated business men; Whitechapel, by its coster girls with fringes; Somers Town and Lisson Grove, by their odoriferous cats and cabbages; Mayfair, by its sleek carriage-horses, and also by the very superior maids and butlers you meet in its silent streets. Or, perhaps, by the straw that occasionally fills the quiet square corners, sounding the sad note of Death. I have seen a slum child dying of cancer in a crowded garret,—baked by the August sun,—covered with flies,—in a noisy alley; but only rich people's nerves require soothing at the last![39]

In the mental map of the average Londoner, Mayfair represented luxurious living. It came by its reputation honestly, harboring the townhouses of many aristocrats. The Duke of Westminster, who earned £1,000 a day, or 700 times as much as the average working-class 1914 wage of 30 shillings a week, owned much of Mayfair.[40] Accordingly, in 1935, when Waddingtons obtained the license to manufacture and sell a British version of Monopoly, the most expensive property was inevitably called Mayfair. At the same time because of its restaurants, bars, and nightclubs, the district enjoyed a racy reputation. Young men could still find small flats there.[41] Lonsdale and his friends followed in the wake of the ambitious youths who invaded the district following the war to turn stable lofts into mews cottages and transform storefronts into nightclubs.[42]

James Agate, the theater critic, wrote that for the bohemian, Covent Garden was the core of London, for the Cockney it was the East End, and for the man-about-town it was Mayfair. Accordingly, writers such as Oscar Wilde and P. G. Wodehouse often located their characters there. Despite its reputation as a bastion of old money, novelists portrayed Mayfair as having its mysteries.

E. F. Benson, a prolific homosexual writer, produced in *The Freaks of Mayfair* (1916) a series of humorous sketches, including one about a man regarded as an "aunt."[43] In *Three Hostages* (1924), John Buchan used this district as the locale for a thriller plotting the nefarious practices of a master criminal.[44] Mayfair was most famously portrayed in Michael Arlen's bestseller *The Green Hat* (1924), a melodramatic account of the lost generation of tragic war heroes, adventurous young women, and raffish cads.[45]

For many outsiders Mayfair was a fantasy, a dreamland where they could experience what they most desired. In discussing the 1933 Unemployment Bill, the Labour Party firebrand Aneurin Bevan so indulged himself in a curious assertion: "I was born the son of a miner, and I went underground when I was 13 years of age, inevitably. Down the pit was the only place to go. I was as inevitably made into a collier as I would have been made into a shooter of big game if I had been born in Mayfair."[46] For most people the mention of Mayfair more likely brought to mind the pleasures of urban living, not adventures on the veldt, and the elite's pursuit of foxes and pheasants, not big game.

The war changed Mayfair. In the 1920s taxes and death duties led many aristocrats to sell their London townhouses. The Duke of Devonshire remained in residence in the early 1920s and continued to host balls and presentations. Most of his peers sold off their properties. The great homes disappeared, to be replaced by luxury hotels, though often with the same names, as in the case of the Grosvenor and the Dorchester. Speculators built the Mayfair Hotel on the site of Devonshire House in 1927 to target US tourists.[47] Sir Alfred Beit had Aldford House rebuilt as flats and shops. Well on into the 1930s contractors were demolishing eighteenth-century houses as commerce pushed westward around Berkeley Square.[48] The population and properties changed; the language evolved. "As the period advanced the 'Mayfair accent' changed remarkably," Robert Graves noted, "from an over-sweet rather French lisp to a rasping tone that had traces in it of Cockney, American, and Midland provincial."[49]

Arthur Greenwood, the minister of health in the 1930 Labour government, contrasted the Mayfair man with the slum dweller. "The people who inhabit the slums are much like the people who occupy the benches in this House. It is true that among the slum dwellers there are shiftless people. There are shiftless people in Mayfair, whose shiftlessness never comes to the public eye because they are too well looked after by other people."[50] Greenwood was prophetic inasmuch as the 1938 trial of the Mayfair men was to expose the shiftlessness of a cohort of men-about-town. As a result the term "Mayfair man" took on a darker meaning. In the 1940s *John Bull*, a muckraking Labour-supporting paper, would report that in Mayfair nightclubs members of high society rubbed elbows with criminals.[51] Guy Ramsey's 1938 article "Mayfair: Where Men Live on Their Wits" provided a composite portrait of the ruthless Mayfair man. He borrows cars, wears an Eton tie, cadges drinks, and skips out on hotel bills. He maintains a shaky financial stability by robbing widows and having clubs pay him for bringing in new members. "He gossips in the bored, clipped jargon of the upper classes to maîtres d'hôtel, to waiters, to bar-tenders." He has perfect manners, but if a woman asks him to repay his loans, he can turn nasty. He knows everyone and is seen everywhere. "He works so hard, just not to do an honest job."[52]

When leftists mentioned Mayfair it was often as not to condemn it as the home of the idle rich, but also just because of the association of this district with wealth it was frequently cited by the press when imagining class reconciliation. So under the headline "A Mayfair 'Shop Girl' Engaged," the *Daily Mail* ran a story in 1931 of the engagement of Lord Castlereagh (a product of Eton and Oxford) to Miss Romain Combe. Unfortunately, the implication that this was an example of love conquering all was dissipated when the reporter admitted that the "shop girl" was the niece of the Duchess of Sutherland and had only spent a few months as a Mayfair hair salon receptionist. Though she was no longer employed, a reporter claimed with seeming seriousness that "she greatly enjoyed the experience of being a 'business girl' and getting up at 8 am so as to start work at 9."[53]

Turning to films, one finds similar sorts of escapist scenarios.[54] Strikingly enough, no producer made a movie about the Hyde Park Hotel robbery. The British Board of Film Censors allowed the importation of Hollywood gangster films since they confirmed the notion of a violent American culture, but it would not permit the showing of British films that glamorized crime.[55] The board did allow the working class to be satirized and the upper class to be gently mocked.[56] It was most supportive of films that lauded class harmony. Among the earliest and crudest was *A Romance of Mayfair* (1925, dir. Thomas Bentley), in which a duke's son falls in love with an actress while the duke's daughter is wooed by a socialist MP. Predictably, the class gulf that separates them does not succeed in ruining the affairs.[57] *Mayfair Melody* (1937, dir. Arthur B. Woods) was a "quota quickie" (a film made by Hollywood subsidiaries in response to the 1927 law requiring a percentage of movies shown to be British) in which the daughter of a factory owner discovers the wonderful voice of one of his workers and helps him on to a successful career as a professional singer. Critics noted that the film was enjoyable though Keith Falkner, the popular bass-baritone who played the lead, "never suggests the faintest impression of a mechanic."[58] *The Playboy* (1938, dir. Walter Forde)—also known as *Kicking the Moon Around*—had a similar clichéd plot. A rich young man—abandoned by his gold-digging fiancée when he pretends to have lost his money—befriends a salesgirl who has singing ambitions.[59]

Mayfair screen playboys were gentlemen, far removed from the cads tried in 1938. Jack Buchanan, the Scottish singer, most successfully embodied the debonair, affable man-about-town. In the musical comedy *A Man of Mayfair* (1931, dir. Louis Mercanton), he played the role of Lord William, the epitome of the good-natured English gentleman. The George Formby musical *Off the Dole* (1935, dir. Arthur Mertz) presented yet another gallant Mayfair playboy, in this case rescuing a young woman from her brutal stepfather.

Almost a Honeymoon (1938, dir. Norman Lee) was a broad farce in which a Mayfair playboy—idle and indebted—has twenty-four hours to find a wife so that he can win a colonial appointment restricted to married men.[60] The comic possibilities of denying one's social status were also exploited by the producers of *Fools for Scandal* (1938, dir. Mervyn Leroy), a comedy in which a French count pretends to be a Mayfair cook in order to win over an American film star.[61] Both the domestication of the playboy and the overcoming of class differences were dealt with in *Maytime in Mayfair* (1949, dir. Herbert Wilcox), a British musical comedy. A penniless man-about-town is left a high-class Mayfair fashion salon. His plan is to sell it as soon as possible, but he, of course, falls in love with its manager and settles down to help her in fighting off a rival establishment.[62]

Given these films' lack of originality and their outlandish plots, the question is what viewers made of them. For some they were "palliative fictions" that allowed their audiences for an hour or two to enter a dreamworld of Mayfair townhouses, home county cottages, luxurious hotels, glamorous Riviera villas, and sleek Atlantic liners. For a population still struggling with the blight of unemployment they provided a form of compensation and escape.[63] It is unlikely, however, that working-class movie patrons accepted the films' message that they could look to the upper classes for care and concern. We know that American films were more popular than their British rivals in part because they seemed to be classless, and at the very least were free of irritating upper-class English accents.[64] The most popular movie of 1938 in Britain was *A Yank at Oxford* (dir. Jack Conway), which followed a brash and boastful American encountering the stuffiness of English society.[65] To be pro-American was a way to be anti-upper-class.

The novelist and social commentator J. B. Priestley concluded his *English Journey* (1934) by advancing the notion of the existence of three Englands—Old England, nineteenth-century industrial England, and postwar England—the last, he wrote in a famous passage, "belonging far more to the age itself than to this particular island. America, I supposed, was its real birthplace. This is the England of arterial and by-pass roads, of filling stations and factories that look like exhibition buildings, of giant cinemas and dance-halls and cafés, bungalows with tiny garages, cocktail bars, Woolworths, motor-coaches, wireless, hiking, factory girls looking like actresses, grey-hound racing and dirt tracks, swimming pools, and everything given away for cigarette coupons."[66] Especially around London one encountered a more democratic, accessible society. The elite feared this invasion of American culture.[67] They tended to support a xenophobic, hierarchical society with strong links to agrarian interests. Intellectuals of both the left and right were critical of popular modernism as represented by newspapers, movies, thrillers, and advertising. One means of defense was the embracing of anti-Americanism.[68]

In the courts free rein was given to such sentiments. The press described Harley, the most violent of the Mayfair men, as the "moustached American." His lawyer in his defense played up the idea of Harley being somehow tainted by his time in the United States. "During the last 10 years, years when most young men have the advantage of a home life, this young man has been in America, open to all sorts of temptations and seeing all sorts of things."[69] Although Harley employed that most English of weapons—the life preserver—the tabloid press proclaimed that Britain would not allow importation from America of the "ruthlessness of the gangster."[70] A judge informed another jewel thief who had committed "a most un-English type of crime" that "[w]e are not dealing with the wild West."[71] Similarly, in 1942 two American volunteers in the Canadian army appeared in court, accused of robbing a car driver. The judge who sentenced one to be whipped stated sententiously: "Gangsters are unwelcome in this country."[72]

As the press never failed to point out, not only were the Mayfair men members of London society, but they all came from respectable families.[73] Those who attended their trial heard how they had betrayed both their families and friends. The audience caught glimpses of Lonsdale's and Wilmer's fathers—tragic figures who, having enjoyed successful careers, were unprepared to deal with the humiliating situation in which their sons had placed them. Working-class men and women might have to inform a police court magistrate of conflicts within their family. For the middle and upper classes, such candor was normally unthinkable. Family privacy was one of the essential benefits of privilege. "Keeping a secret, like keeping a servant," notes a historian, "was one of the ways, then, to define the middle class."[74]

The question of whether the Hyde Park Hotel robbery was an isolated incident or only the tip of an iceberg of filial insubordination hovered in the air. The *News of the World* reported that the police were struck by "how many young men and women of excellent parentage and education live as sheer adventurers."[75] They boasted of swindling tradespeople, hotel proprietors, tailors, and even their friends. Determining how common such behavior was remains difficult, but there are a few sources that substantiate the charge. When her parents complained about her excesses, Elizabeth Pelly (or Elizabeth Ponsonby, as she was known) retorted that compared to her friends she was an innocent. "You may complain of my goings-on, but you ought to consider yourselves lucky that I am not like many of the others: I don't forge, I don't drug, I don't shoot, I don't steal."[76]

When the Mayfair men were tried, Peter Jenkins was twenty-three, John Lonsdale and David Wilmer were twenty-four, and Robert Harley was twenty-six. It was easy for the tabloids to present them as representatives of their generation and compare them to the bright young people of the 1920s, born about a decade earlier. The latter were notorious for their raucous parties and public escapades; the Hyde Park Hotel robbery similarly began as a lark, but it almost ended in murder. The two generations were also alike in having to somehow compete with the indelible memory of the thousands of young men who had heroically sacrificed themselves in World War I. On a more prosaic level, both cohorts found themselves looking for work in a country whose economy was weak and jobs scarce. Nevertheless, with the exception of Wilmer, they all gave themselves professional titles: Robert Harley, journalist; Peter Jenkins, financier; and John Lonsdale, estate agent. And even when family money was running out they found ways of keeping up appearances and were able to "dress for the occasion," be it a dance, a theatrical performance, or drinks at a nightclub.[77] To sustain this prosperous façade the four Mayfair men finally turned to crime. There were even more troubling options. In *The Condition of*

Britain (1937), G. D. H. Cole and M. I. Cole noted that in all countries the fascists were recruiting among such "half-gentlemen." "They are most dangerous when economic depression prevents them from finding jobs which satisfy their desire for gentility."[78] The Coles cited Hitler as the classic example.

Under the headline "3 Young 'Mayfair Men' Ordered Flogged and Sentenced to British Prison in Hold-Up," the *New York Times* gave a brief account of the last day of the trial. "All of London has been buzzing over the crime and speculating on what treatment these four sons of respectable rich persons—all public school graduates and entitled to wear the 'old school tie'—would get in comparison with that of the ordinary British criminal."[79] In a leading editorial in the *Sunday Express*, entitled "The Lepers of Mayfair," James Douglas used the same phrase: "They are the product of gentility. They are well born, well educated, and well dressed—the old-school-tie class."[80]

Every account of the Mayfair men noted that they had all been educated in elite public schools. Such observations led to obvious questions. Did their schooling contribute in some way to their criminality? Did it nurture their feeling of being somehow above the law? The schools supposedly inculcated a sense of fair play, built character, and instilled correct cultural manners (that is, aristocratic manners) in upper-middle-class boys. Their defenders claimed that the tone and morality taught to the boys in turn spread to the nation. It was certainly the case that many who could never afford such an education were nevertheless fascinated by it. One sign of this was Frank Richards's (Charles Hamilton) enormously popular series of stories about "Greyfriars," a fictional public school, complete with saintly headmaster and sports-mad students, that appeared in the boys' papers *The Magnet* and *The Gem* for close to half a century. The success of James Hilton's international best-seller *Goodbye, Mr. Chips* (1934) provided further evidence of the appeal that even the fictional portrayal of a second-rate public school held, as long as it harbored a beloved teacher.

The influence of the public schools peaked in the 1930s, but they were not immune to attack.[81] Critics argued that public schools focused on character, not intelligence. They encouraged the belief that one's position should depend not on performance but on family or school connections. They indoctrinated their charges with a ruling-class ideology based on a disdain for trade.[82] The poet W. H. Auden recalled his school's express contempt for the working class. It saw as its purpose the production of gentlemen. In his case it failed. "I was— and in most respects still am—mentally precocious, physically backward, short-sighted, a rabbit at all games, very untidy and grubby, a nail-biter, a physical coward, dishonest, sentimental, with no community sense whatever, in fact a typical little highbrow and difficult child."[83] Yet despite his own failings, Auden enjoyed his time at Gresham's School.

The best-known critics of the public schools were other "highbrow" writers—including Alec Waugh, H. G. Wells, George Orwell, E. M. Forster, Graham Greene, and Esmond Romilly—who had had unhappy school experiences.[84] They accused the public schools of producing snobbery, philistinism, and homosexuality. Authoritarian masters rewarded conformity and suppressed individuality. The resulting products were ignorant and arrogant young men, toughened to mask their feelings, seeking protection in drinks and jokes. Members of all male institutions, they, of course, knew little about women. Most did not go on to university, and given that their impressionable years were those spent in school many old boys were forever entangled in a "permanent adolescence."[85]

The practical value of the public school lay in the contacts it provided and the self-confidence and class consciousness it instilled, which were so crucial to networking once out of school. Determining who was worth approaching was a challenge. The "old school tie" provided one solution in signaling one's status. It bore a code that informed others of one's class affiliation, education, and school. Other ties referred to aspects of life worth vaunting, such as one's club, regiment, or cricket team. The tie thus served to both include and exclude.[86] As a result some seriously argued that the sale of ties had to be controlled. A writer in the Malvern College magazine complained that since the Old Malvernian tie sported bright colors it was being worn by "Negroes in Liverpool docks or by bookies' touts."[87] When Robin Alexander Lyle, a twenty-seven-year-old ship owner and adopted Conservative candidate for a Scottish constituency, appeared in court, the magistrate's first question was: "Are you entitled to wear that tie?"[88] In an article titled "Protect That Old School Tie," one journalist asserted that the "imposter" or "supercad" who wore a tie to which he had no legitimate claim should be prosecuted.[89]

Even the most conservative of old boys recognized that by the 1930s mention of the old school tie often as not raised a laugh.[90] Many equated it to back-scratching and cronyism. Comics derided the mixture of snobbery and sentiment it conjured up. "The Old School Tie," was the most popular song of the Western Brothers, who made a career playing two silly asses on stage and radio.[91] In formal dress and monocles, and with the irritatingly bored drawl of the arrogant upper-class male, they paraded their stupidity by, for example, listing as elite schools Eton, Harrow, Borstal, and Pentonville.[92]

The Mayfair men clearly exhibited the worst traits of the public school. Idlers and spongers, they tried to make careers out of exploiting their networks of friends and acquaintances. Noting that the press was fixated on their elite schooling, Lord Chief Justice Hewart went out of his way to deflect criticism of the public schools. The accused may have attended exclusive institutions, he conceded, but they had not really been educated. Though their parents had invested heavily in their sons' educations, the youths had obviously squandered their opportunities.[93]

Lord Chief Justice Hewart's support was not needed. The reality was that the schools, though under attack in the 1930s, continued to have enormous influence. John Hilton noted that an expensive education guaranteed one a place in the "reserved stalls" of life. One-sixth of MPs had gone to Eton; fifty-two of fifty-six bishops and twenty of twenty-one cabinet ministers had been privately schooled.[94] Thanks to the old boys' networks one's entrée into the army, police, civil service, or colonial service could be expedited. Although Britain was modernizing, its elite still relied on tribal loyalties, school friendships, and family connections. The upper classes assumed that rules and regulations could be bent for the privileged. What was important was to know the right people. In this endogamous society who would vouch for them? Were they "one of us"? Did we "know their people"? The courts, of course, made an example of the Hyde Park Hotel robbers, but it was a case of the exception proving the rule.

Arrivistes, the nouveaux riches, and those whose industriousness smacked too obviously of the world of trade found themselves excluded from the best social circles. The pose struck by the ex-public-school boy and the Mayfair playboy involved the studied appearance of carelessness or nonchalant boredom. André Siegfried attributed England's decline to the fixation on this notion of the gentleman, which held that appearing to be engaged in hard work was unseemly. "A gentleman, we must realize, never strives too much; it is not considered the thing."[95] In 1932, Harold J. Laski, the left-wing political theorist, produced *The Danger of Being a Gentleman*, in which he lamented that in the culture inculcated by the public school the question was always who someone was rather than what they did. This was the culture of the amateur and sportsman. England could once afford this type, but it could no longer govern on the premise that others were inferior on account of class or race.[96]

The public schools also had a few critics on the right. In a 1941 essay, Douglas Reed, an anti-Semitic journalist who believed in a Zionist conspiracy, held the schools responsible for a host of evils.

The old school tie bears more blame for the dreary advent of this war than any other single thing, because it kept all the keys of power in the hands of men unfitted to hold them. Not merit, but money, gave them those keys. For the government of the country, the conduct of its policies, is also "man management," and history can show few examples of man mismanagement more horrid than that of the years 1918–39 in England. The old-school-tie system has the Somme, Passchendaele and Dunkirk among its battle honours, or dishonours, and it also produced those "Mayfair Men," criminals of the most unprincipled kind, who infested the social scene of London in those between-war years. When its virtues are extolled in such immoderate terms, that needs also to be said.[97]

Reviewing the Hyde Park Hotel robbery today, one is not particularly surprised to learn that some expensively educated youths from good families fell afoul of the law. One is taken aback, however, by a minor but nevertheless significant detail in the court record. Cartier's representative did not think it at all unusual, when asked by a supposedly wealthy customer, to carry across London diamond rings worth approximately sixty-four times a worker's annual salary. And it would appear that his view was shared by journalists, the police, and court officials since none of them thought the issue worthy of comment. Apparently one would have to have been naïve indeed to be shocked by the startling contrast of the enormous wealth of the few with the impoverishment of the many. In the 1930s the British took the yawning gulf separating the classes as a basic fact of life.

"Traditional British class society was at its apogee in 1939," asserts historian Arthur Marwick. Others have argued that in 1930s Britain the idea of class was more important than the reality.[98] The Marxist typology might have been simplistic, but class remained at the very least a potent rhetorical construct. Evidence of class warfare, us against them, was found everywhere. It emerged in discussions of every aspect of the lives of the Mayfair men—how they had been raised, what schools they attended, where they lived, with whom they socialized. Each of these aspects could, with hindsight, be seen to have contributed to the young men's sense of entitlement that ultimately tipped them over into criminality. One newspaper summed up the story in the headline "Mayfair Playboys, Too Poor for Luxury Lives, Took to Crime."[99]

There were young men in the 1930s who were fortunate enough to have a "good" family, an expensive public school education, an entrée into London society, and the support of powerful friends who nevertheless felt that they deserved better. The evidence suggests that in the case of the Mayfair men their "advantages" legitimated, at least in their own eyes, their seizing that which they felt society owed them. It is telling that though forced to admit to having moved from lying and cheating to robbery with violence, they never showed any sense of guilt or remorse. Most members of the middle and upper-middle classes were clearly appalled by the behavior of Harley and his confederates, yet many, especially those who regarded themselves as the "new poor," also complained of having been somehow victimized, of having had to unfairly bear the costs of their nation's awkward adjustment to social and economic change. They were further frustrated by the apparent inability of the older political parties to respond to their pleas for aid. The British Union of Fascists' assertion that it was listening and would do something to protect the propertied played a key role in its early successes. Its ultimate failure, argued some observers, was in part due to fascism's association with the playboy.

Chapter 10: **FASCISM**

In his autobiography Oswald Mosley, leader of the British Union of Fascists, devoted several pages to explaining how he determined that his followers should wear black shirts. He recalled wanting something that radiated strength and virility. He then added: "Soon our men developed the habit of cutting the shirt in the shape of a fencing jacket, a kindly little tribute to my love of the sport."[1] Being an inordinately vain man, he could not prevent himself from alluding to both his success as a swordsman and to the devotion he inspired in his acolytes. Mosley obviously did not appreciate that a good portion of the press and public would regard a man so proud of his fencing triumphs, and with such sartorial preoccupations, as being more of a playboy than a serious politician.[2]

We have seen how the media constructed a narrative in which the Mayfair playboy personified many of the stresses associated with changes in class and gender relations.[3] The same is true for the world of politics. Those who debated such important issues as the rise of fascism at home and appeasement abroad sought to shore up their arguments with references to the otherwise apolitical man-about-town. Where did one locate the mythical Mayfair man or playboy on the political spectrum? Given conservatives' parading of their disdain for the idle and unproductive it might be assumed that he was a creature of the left. Most observers no doubt regarded him as largely indifferent to formal politics but nevertheless assumed that logically the self-centered man, devoted to the pursuit of personal pleasures, would necessarily find his natural habitat on the right. Indeed, some on the left argued that the unbridled pursuit of self-interest could in Britain, as had been the case on the continent, lead to fascism. Representatives of the right replied that those who blathered on about the threat of fascism were actually creating the stressful conditions in which political extremism would flourish. Regardless of political stripe, commentators in the 1930s assumed that personal lifestyle choices were often predictive of a person's politics.

Under the headline "Former Playboy of Mayfair Renounced Society to Aid Workers," the *New York Post* announced the death, on March 19, 1938, of the Labour peer Lord Kinnoull (George Harley Hay-Drummond). The *New York Times* reported that he "was at one time known as a Mayfair playboy" and once said that nothing in life was worthwhile except "pour le sport." His devotion to nightclubs, motorcars, and airplanes led to him losing his family's 16,000-acre Scottish estate. Remarkably enough, he gave up his old pursuits, switched allegiances from the Conservative to the Labour Party, and before his early death at age thirty-five won a reputation as a devoted supporter of progressive causes.[4]

Few would have predicted Kinnoull ending up as a supporter of the Labour Party. In 1916, at the age of thirteen, he inherited a Scottish earldom in Perthshire. Eton educated, he sat in the House of Lords as Baron Hay. He first came to public attention in 1922 when, as a minor, he became entangled with a woman six years his elder, described by the press as a previously married former chorus girl. His family scotched the possibility of the nineteen-year-old marrying a gold digger by having the Registrar-General intervene and packing off the boy to South Africa.[5]

His mother's goal was to have him wed an heiress, as the estate he inherited was heavily encumbered. The family's plans all seemed to fall into place when, after a whirlwind courtship, Kinnoull, in December 1923, married Enid Hamlyn Fellows, granddaughter of Sir Frederick Wills, who had made a fortune in tobacco. After the wedding reception at the Hyde Park Hotel the couple set off for the south of France, the press reported, in a "racing car which is the Earl's gift to his bride."[6]

Like many bright young people of the 1920s the couple was addicted to speed. Kinnoull raced at Brooklands, and on public streets they both collected dozens of traffic tickets. In 1926 he committed four driving offenses in two days: causing an obstruction, speeding, and driving without a license. He got off after his solicitor argued that he had been acting as a special constable during the general strike and believed that as such he would not be summoned for minor offenses.[7] Yet the couple was proud to report that Enid had paid a fifty-shilling fine for exceeding the ten-mile-an-hour speed limit in Perth. They boasted that to get Enid in court on time they flew the 900 miles from London to Perth and back again, passing under the Forth Bridge on the way.[8] They were happy to be photographed taking flying lessons and to have their daring mishaps logged. "Lord Kinnoull," the *Times* reported in July 1925, "who made a bad landing at Le Bourget on Tuesday night, and was slightly injured, was removed yesterday from Beaujon Hospital to a hotel." His "touring aeroplane" had flipped over.[9]

Aside from nightclubbing, driving, and flying, the couple seemed to have enjoyed what members of the upper class were supposed to enjoy—London in the season, Scotland in the summer, Egypt or the south of France in the winter. There were, however, causes for concern. In 1925 their infant son died.[10] The earl might have wandered; in any event the couple ceased living together. In 1926, Kinnoull, who had always had trouble handling money, appeared before the Bankruptcy Court having liabilities of £26,972 and assets of £587. He was forced to sell off the furnishings of the family estate in Perthshire and eventually lost Balhousie House as well, largely due to dealing with unscrupulous moneylenders. Mr. Allcorn, the assistant official receiver of the court, asked, "Looking back, do you not think that, although you attribute your failure and insolvency to extravagance in living, an additional cause is your reckless and stupid dealings in these bills?" Kinnoull answered, "Yes."[11] As luck would have it, just as the earl was having to deal with demanding creditors, his estranged wife Enid inherited the bulk of her mother's enormous estate of £1,965,183. It did not save the marriage. Citing her husband's adultery, the countess launched a Scottish divorce action in March 1927; it was granted in November.[12]

On the face of it, Kinnoull was the classic interwar playboy, but at the age of twenty-five he closed that chapter of his life and began another. Twenty-four hours after his divorce became final he announced his engagement to Mary Meyrick, daughter of the most famous nightclub owner in London, Kate Meyrick.[13] Though jailed on multiple occasions for violation of liquor laws at the 43 Club, Kate ran several other venues, including the Silver Slipper, which Mary managed. At Kinnoull's second marriage, in June 1928, the press pointedly reported that none of his family were present, whereas the nightclub world was well represented. Eustace Hoey, the best man, was known as the wine order boss of the West End.[14] Mrs. Meyrick was in attendance despite that the previous week a Bow Street magistrate had granted twenty-six summonses against her and her customers for illegal drinking. She obviously regarded having an aristocrat as a son-in-law as a sign of her success; the respectable took this mésalliance as an example of the dangers posed by the mingling of classes, which the nightclubs encouraged.[15]

Kinnoull did not simply change spouses; he went through a political con-version.[16] In 1929 he ceased to sit in the House of Lords as a Conservative and was formally accepted as a member by the Labour Party.[17] His driving did not improve, but to the surprise of many, he became a hardworking advocate in the Lords for progressive causes.[18] During the general strike of 1926 he, like many wealthy young men, had served as a special constable, protecting prop-erty owners from possible threats by the poor. Though still clearly a member of the elite, in the 1930s he attacked the dangers posed by economic disparities. As Labour junior whip in the upper house he called for the nationalization of all transport and the restriction of hours for truckers. In 1934 he accompanied the unemployed marchers' representatives when they attempted to present a petition to the minister of labour.[19] As the *Times* reported, he opposed the sup-porters of the "means test," who insisted that public assistance be restricted to the unemployed who passed a humiliating screening. "The Earl of Kinnoull said that men who were welcomed in 1918 as heroes were now being treated as criminals. He would agree to no means test. The workers had the right to de-mand work or, if no work were available, to be kept by the State with a decent standard of living without being subjected to the indignity of the means test or the degradation of the Poor Law."[20]

On the continent, fascists had succeeded in exploiting the middle classes' fear of social unrest. Kinnoull raised the alarm that what had happened in Austria and Germany could be replicated in Britain. In 1934 he pointed out that British fascists, employing "Hitler-like" tactics, including the use of uni-forms, barracks, and fleets of steel-sheathed lorries, were already causing pub-lic disturbances. Journalists and ministers had been threatened. Five different fascist parties in Britain competed for attention. Lord Rothermere and the *Daily Mail* offered them some financial support, but Kinnoull pressed the gov-ernment to determine who else provided funding.[21]

Kinnoull came to see how injustices at home were related to injustices abroad. He sought to draw attention to the treatment of political prisoners in Nazi Germany.[22] At the same time he noted that Britain also employed arbi-trary methods of incarceration. In Parliament he quizzed the government on the detention in India of Subhas Bose, an anti-imperialist activist who had never been tried but was held as a terrorist under regulation III of 1818. There were altogether 2,000 detainees in India, which to Kinnoull smelled "very much of Fascism and savours very strongly of the Nazi concentration camps."[23] He demonstrated his support of the Indian nationalists by attending (with

Lord Churchill, another radical peer) India Independence Day celebrations at the National Trade Union Club.[24]

Like others on the left, Kinnoull was especially worried by the Spanish Civil War. In November 1936 he, along with six other British politicians visited Madrid to raise public awareness of the besieged city's plight.[25] He was a member of the Spanish Youth Foodship Committee—as were Aneurin Bevan, Harold Laski, Naomi Mitchison, D. N. Pritt, Lord Churchill, and David Low—whose goal was to raise 100 tons of food and £1,000 in aid. He offered to deliver personally the relief supplies on his converted trawler, the *Mino*. The popular press obviously relished the image of a peer, wearing a red muffler and giving the communist salute, setting sail from Southampton on such a quixotic adventure.[26] In fact, because of government regulations, the consignment had to be sent by regular cargo ship. The newspapers did not have to embellish their account of Kinnoull's life. The true story of how a playboy gave up a life of cocktails and racing cars to turn his energies to improving the social conditions of the working class was remarkable enough.

When the press in March 1938 announced Kinnoull's death it recalled him saying: " 'I have renounced cocktail parties, night clubs, racing and motor cars for political work. My youth may have been misspent, but I don't regret it altogether. Every man has to make a fool of himself at some time, and it is better to get it over while he's young." The nightclubs had provided "contact with life . . . and made me understand and sympathize with human weakness."[27] No one claimed—he least of all—that he was an especially insightful student of British politics. The simple fact is that he was only one of many men-about-town who came to appreciate that the threats posed to Britain at home and abroad meant that life could not go on as usual.

"Today the forces of life and progress are ranging on one side, those of reaction and death on the other. We are having to choose between democracy and fascism, and fascism is the enemy of art." So wrote the literary critic Cyril Connolly, in *Enemies of Promise* (1938). Perceptive middle- and upper-class intellectuals who recognized the coming political crisis were, he asserted, throwing their lot in with the workers. "I think a writer 'goes over' when he has a moment of conviction that his future is bound up with that of the working class. Once he has felt this his behaviour will inevitably alter. Often it will be recognized only by external symptoms, a disinclination to wear a hat or a stiff collar, an inability to be rude to waiters or taxi-drivers or to be polite to young men of his own age with rolled umbrellas, bowler hats and 'Mayfair men' moustaches or to tolerate the repressive measures of his class."[28] It says something of the sense of crisis felt in the late 1930s that a social climber like Connolly made such an avowal.[29] A scholarship boy at Eton and Oxford, he had been dazzled by the elite. He, too, had volunteered as a special constable during the 1926 general strike; now he was declaring his support for the workers. If what this meant in practice remained rather vague, Connolly and Kinnoull reflected a common sentiment on the left that supporting the labor movement was linked to opposing fascism at home and abroad.

As early as 1925 the *Manchester Guardian* pointed out the connections of the playboy, the fascist, and Sir William Joynson-Hicks, or "Jix," the authoritarian home secretary. When the British fascist leader General R. B. D. Blakeney, who blamed the Jews for the Russian revolution, visited Manchester, the paper teasingly noted, "The British Fascists—hasn't someone called them Jix's Playboys of the Postwar World?"[30]

In May 1938 several MPs likened the Hyde Park Hotel robbers to Italian fascists. The occasion was Lieutenant Colonel Charles Barclay-Harvey's defense in the Commons of the government's failure to stop the Italians from invading and occupying Ethiopia. "If we are charged with condoning this so-called crime now," he said, "I would remind those who make the accusation that only a few weeks ago the Press of this country was filled with news about what was known as the Mayfair jewel robbery. Four young men were convicted of a brutal crime and sentenced to varying terms of imprisonment. Some time those young men will come out of prison. Does anyone suggest that because they will be let out of prison that this country will be condoning that crime?" Sydney Silverman pointed out the analogy's obvious flaw. "Does the honourable Baronet suggest," he asked, "that when those four men come out of prison they ought to be left in undisturbed enjoyment of the proceeds of their crime?" Barclay-Harvey offered a petulant response. "Certainly not. That is not the point that I am making. My point is that we are accused of condoning a crime. The fact is that the Italians are in occupation of Abyssinia. We could only eject the Italians from Abyssinia by war, and I am certain that nobody wants to do that."[31] He was led by the logic of his argument to admit that might made right, that the state would punish the playboy turned bully but think twice before standing up to a fascist state.

Such elements of an appeasement policy were hard to sell. In the past the Conservative Party wrapped itself in the flag, supported bellicose policies, and mocked the Labour Party's timidity. Now the roles were reversed, with the left pushing for interventions in Europe and the right opposed. Although few newspapers supported Labour, their presentation of complicated foreign conflicts in an accessible language heightened the pressure on the government. When in 1936 they called Italy's aggression in Abyssinia "robbery" and in 1938 spoke of Hitler's "smash and grab raid" on Austria, they necessarily led readers to ask themselves why the government did nothing.[32]

Those who took the view that the Hyde Park Hotel robbers could be called "fascists," no doubt saw themselves as consciously or unconsciously doubly damning the felons by yoking them to a discredited ideology. There were other commentators, however, who took the opposite view and attacked those whose tactics were to denigrate a legitimate belief system by associating it with criminality. Evelyn Waugh, regarded by many as Britain's finest living novelist, in a March 1938 letter to the *New Statesman* was the first to advance this argument.

SIR,—I am moved to write to you on a subject that has long been in my mind, by an anecdote I have just heard. A friend of mine met someone who—I am sure, both you and he himself would readily admit—represents the highest strata of "Left Wing" culture. The conversation turned on the "May-fair" jewel robbers and the Socialist remarked that they exhibited "typical Fascist mentality." This seems to me an abuse of vocabulary so mischievous and so common, that it is worth discussing. There was a time in the early twenties when the word "Bolshie" was current, it was used indiscriminately of refractory school children, employees who asked for a rise in wages, impertinent domestic servants, those who advocated an extension of the rights of property to the poor, and anything or anyone of whom the speaker disapproved. The only result was to impede reasonable discussion and clear thought. I believe we are in danger of a similar, stultifying use of the word "Fascist." There was recently a petition sent to English writers (by a committee few, if any of whom, were English professional writers), asking them to subscribe themselves, categorically, as supporters of the Republican Party in Spain, or as "Fascists." When rioters are imprisoned it is described as a "Fascist sentence"; the Means Test is Fascist; colonisation is Fascist; military discipline is Fascist; patriotism is Fascist; Catholicism is Fascist; Buchmanism is Fascist; the ancient Japanese cult of their Emperor is Fascist; the Galla tribes' ancient detestation of theirs is Fascist; fox-hunting is Fascist . . . Is it too late to call for order? It is constantly said by those who observed the growth of Nazism, Fascism, and other dictatorial systems (not, perhaps, excluding the USSR) that they were engendered and nourished solely by Communism. I do not know how true that is, but I am inclined to believe it when I observe the pitiable stampede of the "Left Wing Intellectuals" in our own country. Only once was there anything like a Fascist movement in England; that was in 1926 when the middle class took over the public services; it now does not exist at all except as a form of anti-Semitism in the slums. Those of us who can afford to think without proclaiming ourselves "intellectuals," do not want or expect a Fascist regime. But there is a highly nervous and highly vocal party who are busy creating a bogy; if they persist in throwing the epithet about it may begin to stick. They may one day find that there is a Fascist party which they have provoked. They will, of course, be the chief losers, but it is because I believe we shall all lose by such a development that I am addressing this through your columns.[33]

In the 1920s Waugh struck the pose of the apolitical satirist in comic classics such as *Decline and Fall* (1928) and *Vile Bodies* (1930). In fact, embarrassed by his family's middle-class background, he constantly strove to associate himself with the aristocracy and hopelessly pursued a number of society beauties, including Diana Guinness.[34] Hypnotized by the glamour of the landed elite, disdainful of the working class, he was, as one biographer succinctly put it, an "assiduous opportunist driven by a fear of failure to excesses of vindictive snobbery."[35]

Waugh never fully recovered from his first wife leaving him for John Heygate, a BBC news editor and well-known playboy.[36] One result of this betrayal was the inclusion in his novels of raffish playboy characters like Basil Seal in *Black Mischief* (1932) and Tommy Blackhouse in *Men at Arms* (1952). Waugh as a young man was himself a sort of dandy who was fascinated by decadent playboys like the poet Brian Howard. It was not surprising that he took a special interest in the Mayfair men. Moreover, he was well acquainted with the Hyde Park Hotel, using it as retreat when a writing project required an uninterrupted block of time. He was clearly titillated when staying in the very rooms once occupied by the robbers, confiding to his diary September 28, 1942: "On 14th we went to London by the night train. I met Laura and we spent the night at the Hyde Park Hotel in the suite where the 'Mayfair men' attacked Mr Bellinger."[37]

The ending of his first marriage and his conversion to Catholicism in 1930 pushed Waugh well to the right, a trajectory most obviously apparent in his travel writings. In 1935 he reported on the beginnings of the Second Italo-

Abyssinian war for the *Daily Mail*. In *Waugh in Abyssinia* (1936), he defended the imperialist adventure, asserting that the country was "a savage place which Mussolini was doing well to tame." Leftist writers naturally responded. David Garnett dismissed the book as propaganda. Rose Macaulay wondered what was more influential in Waugh's producing this "Fascist tract," his dislike of the League of Nations or his obedience to the Catholic Church.[38]

A 1938 trip to Mexico offered Waugh another opportunity to publicize his conservative views. The title of the resulting book, *Robbery under Law* (1939), made clear his take on leftist nationalization programs. Describing himself as a "partisan of Franco," he declared: "I believe that inequalities of wealth and position are inevitable and that it is therefore meaningless to discuss the advantages of their elimination." According to him, the danger was that the "frivolous and vindictive" demands of trade unions would push the middle class into embracing radical solutions. "Self preservation and patriotism combine to produce Fascism," but it too, he conceded, attracted "cranks and criminals."[39]

Waugh advanced a "blame-the-victim" argument. Fascism, he acknowledged, was in many ways a nasty political ideology, yet it only succeeded when the left threatened to make life intolerable for the propertied. Since Britain at the moment did not face such a crisis there was no fascist movement, but as he argued in his letter to the *New Statesman*, the left labeled as "fascist" anyone or anything it did not like.

Because Waugh's letter succinctly pointed out how a word could be so easily debased, it has been frequently reprinted; the response of the *New Statesman* has not. It is worth being fully quoted inasmuch as its editors made the crucial observation that by a skillful sleight of hand, Waugh had avoided saying anything about the actual activities of Mayfair men that led some to call them fascists.

> Mr Waugh is very enigmatic about the author of the remark to which he objects, but a similar comment was made to us by a friend who based his opinion not upon political bias but upon a conversation he had had with two of the guilty men. Moreover, anyone who, like Mr Waugh, has studied the growth of Fascism and Nazism, knows that among the most active champions of these movements were a number of young men with tastes which a repugnance or disability for work prevented them from gratifying. These, too, did not stop short of either brutal assaults or common dishonesty in their efforts to improve their position,

and they can now be seen alike in Italy and in Germany enjoying the agreeable sinecures which their violence has earned. We do not suggest that the mentality of the Mayfair gangsters is that of all Fascists, but it is a historical fact that Fascism attracted men with just such a mentality and just such an economic position. Finally it will not have escaped Mr Waugh's attention that at least one of the guilty men had been active in selling arms to General Franco. We agree, however, that to call fox-hunting "Fascist" is a gross abuse of language.[40]

As the editors stated, it was highly unlikely that Waugh could have been unaware of the Mayfair men's involvement in the sale of arms to Franco. Moreover, in his "confessions" written for a Sunday newspaper, Lonsdale clearly stated that he joined the British fascists and offered his services as a machine gunner in the Spanish Foreign Legion.[41]

The Spanish Civil War broke out in 1936. In July the army declared itself opposed to the constitutional government. Nazi Germany and Fascist Italy in July and August sent troops to support the rebels. Ultimately there would be seventy thousand Italians and twenty thousand Germans in Spain, as well as a thousand or so Catholic and anti-Communist volunteers. General Francisco Franco emerged in October as the Falangist military leader. Civilian militias had in the meantime formed to defend the republic, which won the assistance of the Soviet Union and the thirty thousand members of the International Brigades.[42]

Public opinion in Britain was overwhelmingly in support of the republic, but the Conservative prime ministers Baldwin and Chamberlain were pro-Franco.[43] Britain and France sought to contain the conflict by placing an embargo on the sale of weapons to either side. The result was the creation of an arms trafficker's paradise, what one newspaper called "El Dorado."[44] Peter Jenkins had hoped to take advantage of the situation. His plan on selling weapons to the Spanish fascists was only scuttled by the robbers who stole his savings. His colleagues were slightly more successful. In 1936, Lonsdale began a gunrunning partnership with Victor Hervey. Lonsdale later boasted that he had once been a member of Franco's Spanish Foreign Legion and that leftists had jailed him during the Asturias revolt. If it is hard to believe his story that he had been sentenced to death by Spanish communists, but by some miracle had escaped, it is quite clear that he and Hervey did seek to profit from the arms trade. A newspaper reporter recalled that Lonsdale was fairly candid that if the price were right he would willingly transport any product. "Guns or oranges," he used to say, "it's all the same money to me."[45] The Honorable Victor Hervey was equally indifferent as to the means or morals required to obtain money.[46]

Their plan was to set up front companies to ship arms from Finland to Spain. Finland had not signed on to the international blockade of Spain and had accordingly become a center of the illegal armaments trade. The Englishmen established their first firm in October 1936. The weapons were to be paid for by the Republicans, but Lonsdale and Hervey intended to double-cross their customers by informing Franco, the Falangist leader, how he might intercept the deliveries.[47] All going well, Lonsdale and Hervey would be paid twice for the same munitions. The problem was that initially a large amount of money was required to launch the operation. In January 1937, Lonsdale was so desperate for funds that he and Hervey borrowed £100 at the astonishing interest rate of 90 percent per annum.[48] The rate was so high because both were considered bad risks. Hervey, having liabilities of £5,692 and no assets, was threatened with bankruptcy.[49]

To finalize their scheme Lonsdale and Hervey made a flying visit to Helsingfors, Finland's main port.[50] There they assembled a vast collection of arms, including 455 Russian machine guns; 35,000 rifles from Belgium, Norway, and Finland; and 130,000 hand grenades from Hull. They allowed the Marquess of Donegall (Edward Arthur Chichester), a pro-Franco columnist for the *Sunday Dispatch*, to accompany them.[51] This was a mistake. In an article published April 18, 1937, Donegal exposed Lonsdale and Hervey's double-dealing and their intention to each make $250,000 from the sale of $10 million worth of munitions.[52] Suddenly the two men, identified as "Victor Hervey, 21 year-old son of Lord Herbert Hervey, former British Minister in Peru, and John Christopher Lonsdale, of Wimborn, known in the West-End as a man about town," found their profiles on the front pages of the world's newspapers and their elaborate scheme destroyed.

A Finnish newspaper published in Canada provided a detailed account of the adventure's ignominious ending.

Helsinki—In late March two young businessmen from England arrived here and signed into a first-class hotel. The young men immediately started looking for connection with potential weapons sellers, and managed to contact two majors, Mikael Gripenber and Spare, Spare being a representative of the Pihkakoski arms factory. After negotiations the weapon buyers, John Lonsdale and

Victor Hervey, who was found out to be the son of Lord Hervey, had sought entertainment by partying in large groups, with no lack of liquor. The buyers were not paying anything towards their upkeep, and after the hotel bill had been growing for days, the hotel started demanding payment. By then, April 8th, the bill had reached 15,000 Finnish marks. The men had promised to pay the bill on the Wednesday of next week, but had left the hotel covertly before that and boarded a ship towards Hull. The authorities returned the men to Finland. A social democrat Member of Parliament has raised a question about the men in Parliament. On Tuesday, Helsinki announced that the Finnish government will be conducting an investigation into the matter, especially as the Marquess of Donegall in London has claimed that Finland is being used as a storage location for a weapons cache worth 10,000,000 dollars, destined for a delivery into Spain.[53]

The question of the British government's view of the matter was raised in the House of Commons. Captain Victor Cazalet asked if attempts had been made to breach the Non-intervention Agreement. Anthony Eden, the foreign secretary, replied:

> I understand that Mr. Hervey visited Finland with two other British subjects, the Marquess of Donegall and Mr. John Lonsdale, at the beginning of March, and that they established connections with certain officers of the Finnish army and with officials of the Finnish arms and munitions factories, declaring that they were buying arms for Brazil. I am glad to have the opportunity of saying that I am satisfied, as a result of inquiries which I have made; that, contrary to reports which have appeared in the Press, there is no evidence that Finnish officers gave any assistance to these gentlemen in obtaining arms for Spain under false pretences. When they were unable to produce any authorisation from the Brazilian Government for the purchase of arms in Finland, all negotiations with them were broken off. I regret that allegations against Finnish officials should have received publicity in this country.[54]

As if to underline the ending of Finland's role as a weapons entrepôt, an enormous explosion in July 1938 flattened the island arsenal of Sveborg, near Helsingfors, killing eight and wounding over a hundred.[55]

Given the broader political context, Waugh appears to have too quickly dismissed the notion that the robbers could be described as fascists. Lonsdale, Hervey, and Jenkins all intended to deliver arms to the conservative forces in

Spain. Lonsdale and Hervey planned on swindling the republican buyers by giving Franco the identity of blockade-running ships, and they both claimed to have actually been in the Iberian peninsula fighting alongside the Falangists. How much of this was true is difficult to determine, but these men clearly presented themselves as supporters of the rebel forces. They acted like fascists, they backed a fascist regime, and they sought to defraud the enemies of fascism. For Waugh nevertheless to have insisted that it would be "stultifying" to describe these men as having a fascist mentality was clearly a case of special pleading.

The "petition" to which Waugh referred was a questionnaire entitled "Authors Take Sides on the Spanish War" (1936), which Nancy Cunard, heiress and political activist, distributed with the assistance of the poets W. H. Auden and Stephen Spender. The organizers of the survey made their sympathies clear, asking respondents if they were for the "legal government" of Spain or for fascism. The starkness of the question provided a reason for Virginia Woolf, Bertrand Russell, E. M. Forster, and James Joyce not to reply. Nor did the cranky George Orwell, who wailed: "Will you please stop sending me this bloody rubbish. This is the second or third time I have had it. I am not one of your fashionable pansies like Auden or Spender. I was six months in Spain, most of the time fighting. I have a bullet hole in me at present and I am not going to write blah about defending democracy or gallant little anybody."[56] Two hundred questionnaires were sent out. Of the 147 who answered, 126—including W. H. Auden, Samuel Becket, Fenner Brockway, Margaret Cole, Cyril Connolly, Arthur Calder-Marshall, Cecil Day-Lewis, Havelock Ellis, Ford Maddox Ford, David Garnett, Douglas Goldring, Victor Gollancz, Geoffrey Gorer, Tom Harrison, Lancelot Hogben, Laurence Housman, Brian Howard, Aldous Huxley, C. L. R. James, Arthur Koestler, Harold J. Laski, Ethel Mannin, and Rebecca West—were for the government. Sixteen—including H. G. Wells, Ezra Pound, T. S. Eliot, and Vera Brittain—were neutral. Five— Waugh, Edmund Blunden, Arthur Machen, Geoffrey Moss, Eleanor Smith— were against.

For the left, Republican Spain represented everything that Mayfair was not; a place where there were no smart clothes, tipping, private automobiles, servility, or polite modes of address.[57] It was something worth fighting for. Waugh took the opposite position. "If I were a Spaniard," he declared, "I would be fighting for General Franco. As an Englishman I am not in the predicament of choosing between two evils. I am not a Fascist nor shall I become one unless it were the only alternative to Marxism."[58] It was the church's hostile response to the emergence of the Spanish democratic republic that led some right-wing Catholics to embrace pro-fascist positions. Echoing Waugh's satiric approach, Douglas Jerrold claimed that the leftist view was that "anyone going near a church is a Fascist today, unless, of course, he is going there quite innocently, in order to burn it."[59] As editor of the *English Review* and director of the publishing firm Eyre and Spottiswoode, Jerrold was among the most active of the pro-Franco English Catholics. Arguing that Spanish republicans had used fraudulent means to take power, Jerrold undertook to provide Franco's forces with money, machine guns, and ammunition.[60]

According to Paul Mitchell, some Mayfair playboys recognized the financial possibilities of offering well-off Catholic women a way to both aid Franco and improve their social status. Accordingly, these young men set up false pro-Falangist charities to bilk the naïve. "Many a wealthy lady on the fringe of society felt that here was the chance that she had prayed for to attain that social distinction which had so far eluded her grasp."[61] When the frauds were finally revealed, the victims were too embarrassed to protest.

Most Conservative politicians in Britain were not passionate about Spain, but a group of right-wing MPs including Captain Victor Cazalet, Henry Page Croft, and Alan Lennox-Boyd were vocal supporters of the nationalists. Some hankered after Spain's return to the old regime; others looked for a modernized state.[62] Lord Phillimore (Godfrey Walter Phillimore of Coppid Hall, Henley-on-Thames) headed the pro-Catholic Friends of National Spain.[63] Convinced that Spanish Christians were being martyred, the society resolved to help crush "the forces of anarchy, tyranny and Communism." In 1939, with Hilaire Belloc, the uncompromising Catholic apologist in attendance, it gave thanks for the triumph of "Christian civilization in Spain."[64]

British fascists were divided in their response to the man-about-town. One faction presented itself as the deadly opponent of such loafers and idlers. The traitor William Joyce (Lord Haw-Haw) took this approach. "Joyce, if nothing else, was an indomitable champion of the working class," states his biographer Michael Walsh, "for whom all his efforts were directed. It was hardly surprising that he was as consistently scathing of capitalists and communists; not to mention the decadent English bootlickers, whom he described as 'the parasites of Mayfair.'"[65] Nevertheless, Joyce was a member of the Right Club, a largely upper-class association united by its anti-Semitism and opposition to a war against Germany.[66] The membership included Prince Yurka Galitzine and his half-sister Pauline Daubeny, who, as noted in chapter 8, moved in the same social circles as Victor Hervey.[67] Her home was the first that he looted.[68]

Curiously enough, a fascist police informant claimed that Victor Hervey was also involved in the attack on Etienne Bellenger. A police inspector reported on January 4, 1938, that he had had a discussion with Philip John Ridout of the Imperial Fascist League (IFL), a "fanatically anti-Jewish organization." Ridout said that a third person told him that the Honorable Victor Hervey was the brains behind the Hyde Park Hotel robbery and that the stolen rings had been flown to Holland.[69] None of this was ever confirmed. The IFL, founded in 1929, had only had a few hundred members. Arnold Leese, its leader, and a rival of Oswald Mosley, shifted its focus from Italian corporatism to German anti-Semitism.[70] Ridout, who was also in the tiny Nordic League, popularized the slogan "Perish Judah." The authorities prosecuted him several times for giving inflammatory speeches that violated section 5 of the Public Order Act of 1936. One magistrate upbraided Ridout that in abusing Jews he acted "like an unutterable cad" and warned that if "this nonsense" continued he would be sent to prison.[71]

On April 4, 1938, veiled anti-Semitic slurs surfaced in the course of a chaotic debate in the Commons. The issue at hand was the government's acceptance of the presence of General Franco's agent in London. In practice if not in theory, this amounted to Britain's according of diplomatic status to the regime backed by the rebellious Spanish military. The opposition, led by Emanuel Shinwell, taunted the Conservatives with not having the courage to acknowledge their change in policy. The pugnacious Shinwell, born in Spitalfields, London, and raised in Glasgow's Gorbals, had a reputation as a firebrand. Elected in 1922 as the first Jewish Labour MP, he had in the general election of 1935 roundly defeated Ramsay MacDonald, prime minister of the National Government from 1931 to 1935.[72] As a supporter of the democratically elected government in Madrid, Shinwell accused the Conservatives of employing half-truths and hypocrisy to justify their Spanish policy. The Speaker of the House was about to reprimand Shinwell for his unparliamentary language when Commander Robert Tatton Bower entered the fray. Considered by even some of his Conservative colleagues as "a pompous ass, self-opinionated, and narrow," Bower could think of nothing better than to shout at Shinwell, "Go back to Poland!"[73] Stunned by this crude anti-Semitic insult, Shinwell crossed the floor, struck Bower "a resounding blow on the left cheek," and gestured for him to step outside. A general uproar ensued, but as both men apologized to the Speaker, no disciplinary action was taken against either. The press reported that the MPs had exchanged an interesting variety of epithets. In the midst of the confrontation one Labour MP unimaginatively yelled across the aisle, "You are an old dog," while a colleague, in gesturing toward Bower, sneered, "That is an English gentleman, a playboy of Mayfair."[74] Sparked by Bower's anti-Semitic outburst, the episode reflected the turn to gutter politics led by Oswald Mosley and the British Union of Fascists.

In the years immediately following World War I, Mosley successfully exploited his glamour, good looks, and youthful vigor to win accolades as the embodiment of the modern British politician. His detractors would eventually highlight these traits in portraying him as a playboy who was bound to fail. Mosley's career was mercurial.[75] On the strength of being a decorated war hero, he was, in 1918, at the age of twenty-one, elected as Conservative MP for Harrow. In 1920 he married Cynthia, daughter of Earl Curzon, viceroy of India (1899–1905) and foreign secretary (1919–1924), confirming his position in high society. In the Commons, Mosley proved to be a spellbinding speaker, though it was difficult to determine what, beyond wishing to prevent another war, he hoped to achieve. Ever restless, he left the Conservative Party to sit first as an independent and then, in 1924, as a Labour MP. When Labour won the 1929 election he put forward an ambitious plan to counter the slump with high tariffs, nationalizations of key industries, and extensive public works. Despite the support of young backbench MPs from all parties, the government cautiously rejected his plan. Embittered, he left Labour to launch the "New Party." Many were attracted by its corporatist economic policies, but it failed to win any seats in the 1931 election.[76] Mosley's response was to move even further to the right, abandon the orthodoxies of democratic politics, and create the British Union of Fascists (BUF), a paramilitary organization. Modeled on Mussolini's success, the BUF particularly appealed to young, lower-middle-class males, offering them the excitement of participating in a radical political experiment.[77] As far as foreign affairs were concerned, the BUF was not especially interested in the Spanish Civil War. Mosley's goal was an alliance of Italy, Germany, France, and Britain, which could counter the mythical, Russian-controlled Jewish Bolshevik League.[78] At home he called for the shielding of industry and the disciplining of labor. Though Mosley claimed to have never attacked Jews "as a people," he voiced the old anti-Semitic slur that the country's economic malaise was somehow caused by a conspiracy of Jewish bankers and communists. The world he hoped to create was one in which elitists like himself would hold sway. *In the Second Year* (1936), Storm Jameson's depiction of a future dystopia, has a character sketch out a view of the society Mosley supposedly sought. "He began describing the England he would create when he and his friends were in charge. It made me wince. It was like nothing more than a fearful sort of public school, with willing fags, a glorious hierarchy of heroes in the persons of himself and his Volunteers, and floggings for the unwilling or rebellious. For the rest, all stout and jolly together, and daring the other nations to come on and be licked."[79]

"The playboy of the summer became the dedicated soldier of autumn."[80] This was the way Mosley portrayed himself as rushing to enlist in 1914. He thus tried to put that youthful image behind him, but hostile commentators continued to represent Mosley as an irresponsible dandy. Their attacks clearly had a role in undercutting his successes.[81] The playboy was the indolent dilettante; Mosley seemed to enjoy effortless success. Before he was thirty he had everything—a supportive family, a glowing war record, intelligence, money, and a striking resemblance to a Hollywood movie star. Such good fortune raised suspicions. Beatrice Webb said he was the most effective speaker in the Commons, that he had "birth, wealth, and a beautiful aristocratic wife," but concluded that "so much perfection argues rottenness somewhere."[82] Many of his colleagues regarded him as a playboy. "Rich and ambitious son of a Tory baronet, with white teeth, metallic charm and a Douglas Fairbanks smile," was Raymond Postgate's succinct summing-up.[83] "Mosley was," a historian has pointed out, "among the very few interwar politicians whose sexual energy and kinetic and physical qualities fostered a celebrity and a body cult."[84] The tabloid press was, of course, central in the presentation of him as a matinee idol. They reported excited girls exclaiming "Oh! Valentino!" at the sight of "Mr. Mosley caressing his miniature moustache with one hand and gaily slapping his razor-like trouser-edge with the other."[85] Such accounts impressed some while leading others to view Mosley as not really a gentleman.

These concerns were picked up in *The Autobiography of a Cad* (1938), in which A. G. MacDonell used the purported memoirs of one Edward Percival Fox-Ingleby to trace the career of a young Mayfair flaneur on the make. He is completely self-centered. His Eton and Oxford education neither impedes his exploitation of chorus girls nor hinders his expulsion of cottagers from his estate. Having become an MP and profited from the war, he nevertheless is still worried by the threat of the masses. He prays that the country will develop a sort of Italian fascism that looks like democracy but really is not.[86]

Leftist writers attributed to Mosley many of the same traits associated with the playboy. He was a dandy who took pains to dress well and was concerned that his Blackshirts be stylishly turned out.[87] He was known to share the obsession with motorcars and airplanes. When a group of Blackshirts decided to honor Mosley, they thoughtfully presented him with an MG Midget.[88] His well-known addiction to speed was easy to spoof. In *Point Counter Point* (1928) Aldous Huxley portrayed the passion of the Mosley-like character's driving. He loves the "power and sense of superiority" given by the car. "It was a powerful machine (for Everard was a lover of furious driving) . . . he shot off with violent impetuosity." Similarly, Patrick Hamilton in *Hangover Square* (1941) presented the mercenary Netta of Earl's Court favoring a vicious fascist because of his criminal past and "for killing a pedestrian with his car while drunk, and this she liked, this stimulated her."[89]

Many members of elite social circles also knew that Mosley followed what was now the classic playboy script of exploiting women. F. E. Smith, who first brought up the idea of Mosley going into politics, finally turned on the man he called "the perfumed popinjay of scented boudoirs."[90] To Ellen Wilkinson, he was the Sheikh, not "the nice kind hero who rescues the girl at the point of torture, but the one who hisses: 'At last—we meet.' "[91] And takes advantage of her. He was a notorious womanizer. A friend left an account that gave a sense of Mosley's ruthless pursuit of bed partners. He informed a shocked Bob Boothby that he had told his wife, Cynthia Mosley, of all the other women he had slept with. Mosley went on to correct himself, "Except, of course, for her sister and stepmother."[92] After Cynthia died, he married his long-term lover Diana Guinness (née Mitford). They celebrated their 1936 wedding in the Berlin home of Joseph Goebbels with Adolf Hitler as guest of honor.

The BUF's popularity peaked in 1934, the *Daily Mail* and *Daily Mirror* initially supporting its protectionist and anticommunist policies. Mosley's use of paramilitary Blackshirts and their well-publicized assaults on opponents at a 1934 rally at the Olympia exhibition center and at a 1936 march down Cable Street in the East End of London confirmed the leftist view that Mosley was aping the thuggish tactics of continental fascists. Once this was publicized, his popularity ebbed away. The violence of the Blackshirts goaded the government into passing the Public Order Act of 1936, banning political uniforms and quasi-military organizations. When the war broke out some of his col-

SIR OSWALD MOSLEY . . .
. . . his black shirt for yesterday's stopped East End march blossomed out into a new and military-looking uniform, with silver buttons in sets of three—a feature of Guards officer tunics, with riding breeches and peaked cap like a police-inspector's Brodrick. Note the badges on the cap, the Fascists' "flash of lightning," and below the axe and fasces of the ancient Romans, which belongs to Mussolini.
The woman is Mrs. Anne Brook-Briggs, organiser of the southern command.

Sir Oswald Mosley. *Daily Mirror*, Oct. 5, 1936.
© The British Library Board

leagues came to regard him as a traitor. In May 1940 the government banned the BUF and finally interned Mosley and several other active fascists under Defence Regulation 18B. How many supported fascism in Britain? In 1940 the left-wing journalist Douglas Goldring pessimistically estimated that they "who, like the flogged 'Mayfair men,' specialize in violence—must be almost as large as the percentage of Germans who believed in Hitler seven years ago." Goldring included "Mayfair girls" who like Unity Mitford "rush across Germany heiling Hitler."[93]

Observers had for years characterized Mosley as a restless, energetic, if misguided, dilettante. His reputation as a pleasure-seeking playboy countered his message that he was a serious politician who had the answer to the nation's economic and political ills. A. J. P. Taylor later concluded: "Mosley was, in fact, a highly gifted playboy. From the moment he modeled himself on Mussolini he resembled nothing so much as an actor touring the provinces in a play which someone else had made a success in London. Watching newsreels of Mosley on the march through the East End recalls the memory of another Londoner. Oswald Mosley aspired to be the great dictator. Sir Charles Chaplin played the role better."[94] This is not to say that fascism's inability to take root in 1930s Britain was simply due to leftists using such terms as "playboy" and "Mayfair man" to attack right wingers.[95] The political and economic conditions that gave rise to fascism on the continent were simply not present in Britain. No political leader, no matter how gifted, could have imposed the BUF on the country.

Mosley's career appeared to provide some support for commentators' belief that personal lifestyle choices often predicted a person's politics. Much like Edward VIII, Mosley took up one of the key roles created by a celebrity culture, that of the young, good-looking, wealthy, athletic, good-natured populist determined to rebel against the constraints of an older generation.[96] If Mosley the playboy had become an ascetic would he have had greater success? It is highly unlikely. A self-denying Mosley would not have been Mosley. Whatever charisma he enjoyed was fueled by the same passions that would eventually bring him down. In any event, with the outbreak of the Second World War the press declared there was no place in Britain for fascists. References to the playboy also seemed to disappear. The journalist Hannan Swaffer's description of the BUF members as "men too silly to work with their heads and too 'proud' to work with their hands" mirrored the tabloid's view of the playboy.[97] In the 1930s the playboy served as a symbol of divisive class and gender relationships. During the early war years patriotic newspapers—viewing such a character as an embarrassment to a nation under siege—no longer considered ferreting out reports of his misdeeds as serving the public good.

The press could not, however, ignore John Amery, profligate son and traitor to his country. Indeed, John Amery, the scapegrace offspring of a distinguished political family, underlined in the public's mind the linkages of playboy and fascist. His indulgent father, Leo Amery, was a friend of Churchill and a long-serving Conservative cabinet minister. John, a classic wastrel who enjoyed every social advantage, repeatedly disappointed his doting parents. He left Harrow, his father's school, with the reputation of being a liar and thief.

While still in his teens he frequented London nightclubs like Mrs. Meyrick's and began his life as a binge drinker.[98]

John's career had all the hallmarks of the interwar playboy. Like other crass young men he regarded involvement in the film industry as a way of meeting attractive women and conning gullible investors. He set up his own shady film company in 1934, when he was only twenty-two, and was bankrupt by 1936. Like other playboys he loved fast cars, and before being banned from driving in 1932 he had collected over eighty traffic tickets. It was telling that after his capture by Italian partisans in 1945 his chief concern was for the return of his Lancia Aprilia. He was on occasion a small-time thief, accused of blackmail and embezzlement, but he was never convicted. The French police did arrest him in 1933 for having used a dud check to purchase diamonds in Greece. His father paid off the jeweler.[99]

Amery did differ from his peers in having a marked penchant for prostitutes, a weakness that resulted in his contracting syphilis at an early age.[100] Even streetwalkers regarded his exhibitionism as perverse. The tabloids first brought him to the public's attention in 1932 when, as a minor, he sought to defy his family by marrying the "actress" Una Wing.[101] They soon separated. His second partner, also a prostitute, drank as heavily as he and died a sordid death, choking on her own vomit. As long as John was in Britain or France he could rely on his father using his money and influence to bail him out of such minor difficulties. Parental assistance was not possible once he plunged into the world of fascist politics.

Like John Lonsdale and Victor Hervey, Amery supported General Franco during the Spanish Civil War. He claimed not only to have run guns to Spain but also to have held a commission in the Spanish army. As he was a congenital liar, his account is open to question. It is clear that he remained in France after the 1940 German occupation and, despite his mother's conviction that he was a "prisoner," freely agreed to do propaganda work for the Nazis.[102] In November 1942, he launched a series of pro-fascist broadcasts from Berlin. These consisted of praise for Hitler and unoriginal anti-Semitic scare stories focused on "the menace of Jewish Communism." He made these treasonous diatribes apparently unaware that his father's mother was Jewish.[103] He further compromised himself in April 1943 by attempting to recruit British prisoners of war into a "Legion of St. George," which would fight for Germany against the Soviet Union on the Eastern Front. As the war wound down he moved to Italy to make propaganda speeches for Benito Mussolini. Italian partisans captured

Amery in Milan in April 1945 and handed him over to the British. Leonard Burt, the same Scotland Yard officer who interrogated the Hyde Park Hotel robbers seven years earlier, and who was now seconded to MI5, brought him back to London. The gravity of his offense clearly escaping him, Amery told the detective: "I don't suppose for a moment they'll bring a charge against me, but if they did, of course, my father would see to it."[104]

The newspapers played up the notion of a deranged prodigal son breaking the hearts of his loving parents. What the press failed to note was that if John had not been born into an upper-class family his youthful escapades would have soon resulted in a magistrate's court labeling him a juvenile delinquent and having him treated or incarcerated. Having the power to protect their son, the Amerys continually intervened to spare him from accepting responsibility for his actions. One unintended consequence was that as a thirty-year-old, he manifested a complete absence of moral sense, guilt, or remorse.

Once back in Britain, for reasons he never fully explained, Amery countered his family's campaign to support him, pleaded guilty to the charge of high treason, and was sentenced to death by hanging. His parents still had hopes of a last-minute commutation, but Sir Frank Newsam, permanent undersecretary at the Home Office, insisted that despite the pressure of such a famous and well-connected family, Amery had to die. If a self-professed traitor were spared, Newsam warned the government, "[i]t would be difficult to convince the ordinary man that Amery had not received exceptional and privileged treatment."[105]

In covering his trial the popular press labeled Amery a "West End playboy."[106] Rebecca West followed this line of argument in *The Meaning of Treason* (1947), her classic account of English traitors. The idiot son, according to her, never grew up. "John Amery continued, into his twenties and thirties, to like glossy, costly automobiles as an adolescent likes them, and as an adolescent he liked glossy, costly women, disregarding the plainest whorishness. And in such automobiles and with such women he delighted to visit those grandiose hotels which delight the immature and revolt the mature as the very antithesis of home."[107] Even John's father employed the playboy metaphor to make sense of his son's brief life, cut short by his hanging in Wandsworth Prison on December 19, 1945. Leo Amery pathetically reported that in the last few days of John's incarceration he "was 'no longer a playboy' but had grown into a 'real man.'"[108]

Epilogue

Britain was not alone in having to deal with outrages committed by young men from respectable families. In the United States the famous Leopold and Loeb trial of 1924 raised some of the same issues evoked by the Mayfair men's court appearances in the late 1930s.[1] Nathan F. Leopold and Richard Loeb—young, rich Chicago Jewish youths (aged nineteen and eighteen) involved in a homoerotic relationship—kidnapped and murdered a fourteen-year-old boy simply for the Nietzschean thrill of committing a perfect crime. Their families could afford Clarence Darrow, America's best-known lawyer and avowed opponent of capital punishment. He shrewdly had the youths plead guilty but argued against their execution. In presenting them as highly intelligent though emotionally deprived, he succeeded in winning them life sentences. What remained unexplained was why such privileged young men should have carried out such a crime.

The British press provided massive coverage of the Leopold and Loeb trial. It inspired Patrick Hamilton, a twenty-four-year-old English writer to use this "Crime of the Century" as the basis for his 1929 play *Rope*. In his adaptation he set the action in Mayfair and presented his main characters as bored and arrogant Oxford undergraduates.[2] They are not Jewish; indeed the dominant of the two—a tall, muscular, blue-eyed blond—resembles a model fascist. The Lord Chamberlain's Office prevented homosexuality from being directly discussed on the stage, but Hamilton made clear his characters' narcissism and effeminacy.[3] The play was an enormous success, first in London and subsequently in the United States. In 1948, Alfred Hitchcock produced a film version of Hamilton's drama, though the locale was now America, where his two smirking playboys shared a New York City apartment.[4]

It is striking that while playwrights and moviemakers exploited the Leopold and Loeb case, they did not see the dramatic possibilities of the Hyde Park

Hotel robbery. It is true that in June 1938 the aspiring writer Julian Maclaren-Ross wrote Val Gielgud, brother of the actor John Gielgud and the BBC radio's director of drama, that he was toying with the idea. "The plays which I am preparing include dramatisations of the Mayfair Men Case and also the Stavisky Scandal—naturally, in fictionised form."[5] The plays never materialized. Yet looking back from 1946, a theater critic credited Hamilton with having created a play that chillingly anticipated by almost a decade the scandalous behavior of the Mayfair men.

> [*Rope*] possesses an almost historical interest. . . . [A]part from being inspired by a similar murder which actually occurred in America, a few years later London was made very acutely conscious of the gang of young men with the highest social pretensions and an almost mystical pursuit of violence. By the late 30s most of them were in gaol after having been caught for various robberies, usually with violence. The chief character of *Rope* and principal villain, Brandon, is most carefully described in the stage directions as "plainly very well-off . . . with clear blue eyes. a fine mouth and nose and a rich, confident and really easy voice . . . with the build of a boxer." The type is only too recognizable and its importance and role in Europe at that time was greater than that of amateur cracksmen. It was very fortunate that in this country Mosley never attained the social importance to attract the Mayfair toughs, whose spiritual home was clear enough. This play then was rather more perceptive than the average, and even in 1929 perhaps the audience felt a disquiet which, if inspired by seeing the play, certainly went beyond its story. Sensitive writers were beginning to feel similarly though few saw the implications . . . and Hamilton at least showed himself in touch, if unconsciously, with the prevailing social currents.[6]

It was hardly surprising that Hamilton, as an avowed Marxist, should have recognized that there were elitists in both America and Britain whose class and upbringing led them to believe that they were above the law.

Fictional portrayals of the playboy, which had all but disappeared during the war, resurfaced in the later 1940s. In Warwick Deeping's *Portrait of a Playboy* (1947), the main character—introduced as a "nasty little bounder"—is eventually reformed by a cool British beauty.[7] Sax Rohmer, the producer of the racist Fu Manchu thrillers, focused on a man-about-town in *Hangover House* (1949). Rohmer, like Deeping a conservative, made his opposition to the welfare state clear by mocking Sir Stafford Cripps, the Labour government minister most associated with rationing. Rohmer describes his hero, the Honorable Peter Faraway as an "English playboy, with enough money (his wife's) to keep on playing with Comrade Cripps on his tail."[8] With the ending of the war the man-about-town reappeared in the streets of Mayfair, and clubland began to function once again.[9] However, the fiscal pressures created by the war and the tax policies of the 1945 Labour government curbed the economic influence of the upper classes. Skillfully mixing nostalgia and snobbishness, Evelyn Waugh concocted *Brideshead Revisited* (1945) as a lament for an age when the owners of stately homes, free of the constraints imposed by a nanny state, could expend small fortunes on their amusements.

A few years later the novelist Ian Fleming (a friend of Waugh's) responded in a different fashion to shifts in the British class system. He was an almost exact contemporary of Wilmer, Jenkins, Harley, and Lonsdale, and his early attempts to find his way in life curiously mirrored theirs. He was born in 1908 at 27 Green Street, Mayfair, the second son of a banker who was killed in action in 1917. As the boy showed little talent for scholarship while at Eton, his mother sent him not to Oxford but to the Royal Military College at Sandhurst. He left under a cloud in 1927. He spent some time at universities on the continent, where he gained a reputation as a playboy. After he failed the Foreign Office entry examination, his mother used her connections to have him hired by Reuters' continental office. Returning to England he proved to have no natural talent for either banking or stockbroking. Fortunately for him, the war broke out and the old boy network continued to function. In 1939 naval intelligence overlooked his lack of qualifications and appointed him as the personal assistant of the director.[10] The rest is history. Fleming would draw on his wartime experiences in intelligence and his own love of fast cars, drink, and women to write the James Bond books. *Casino Royale*, the first, appeared in April 1953. Critics winced at Bond's overweening preoccupation with sex, sadism, and brand names. What they at first overlooked was Fleming's presentation of a new type of playboy, a combination of the old school indolent but entitled gentleman and the ruthless, modern professional. Supposedly classless—though politically conservative—Bond's blatant sexuality clearly separated him from his fictional forebears.[11] Bond was a new kind of playboy, amoral as opposed to immoral, clever, difficult to locate socially and so able to move between classes on an international playing field. Though true to the 1930s playboy's love of speed, he armed himself with a range of new technological gadgets.

The 1938 Mayfair men affair could be regarded as a case study in the long trajectory of a particular kind of dissident masculinity, that of men behaving badly. The respectable regarded such mavericks as posing a social, if not a criminal, menace. If such types were traced back in time one might include the nineteenth-century gents and swells, would-be gentleman who parodied the dress and manner of their betters.[12] Looking forward to the latter half of the twentieth century, the affairs involving John Profumo in 1963 and Lord Lucan in 1974 seemed to fit perfectly the louche playboy mold. Such scandals gave commentators the opportunity to question the prerogatives of males, including their continued adherence to a sexual double standard, and the custom of upper-class men to rally to the defense of their fellows.[13]

Across the Atlantic the November 1953 appearance of the first issue of *Playboy* underlined the middle classes' acceptance of greater sexual libertinism. *Stag*, an already existing men's magazine, blocked Hugh Hefner's original intention to call his new publication *Stag Party*. At the last moment he reluctantly opted for *Playboy*, though his wife, Millie Hefner, "thought it sounded outdated and made people think of the 1920s."[14] The populist Hefner did in fact purge the word of many of its existing associations with the sorts of public-school-educated, upper-middle-class Mayfair men whose careers we have traced. His more socially modest readership was attracted by the claim that the instructions he offered on making the right decisions—be it on clothes, cars, wine, or women—would assist their upward mobility.[15]

The Hyde Park Hotel robbery won the Mayfair men worldwide notoriety. The international press carried reports of their 1938 trial, some papers presenting it as casting an embarrassing light on British mores. The accused, stated *Le Matin*, were four "chenapans" (scoundrels), yet they belonged to London's high society. When they were sentenced, *Le Figaro* solemnly informed its readership that English law followed the vindictive maxim: "Celui qui tue sera pendu. Celui qui bat sera battu." (He who kills will be hanged. He who hits will be beaten.) *El Mundo*, a Puerto Rican paper, related the floggings of Wilmer and Harley to campaigns in the Anglo-Saxon countries like Britain and the United States to maintain corporal punishment.[16] A few newspapers presented the event as a simple entertainment. A Dutch daily, after playfully presenting the robbery and the pursuit and arrest of the felons as a "Drama in Three Acts," concluded with an epilogue: "The source of this lovely story? My childish imagination? No. The memoirs of Hercule Poirot, Geoffrey Gill and their colleagues (in the trade of sleuthing)? No. Hollywood? No. The source of this story is nothing other than the report of a British trial and as everyone knows, at a trial, above all a British trial, nothing other than the unvarnished truth is said. The moral: romance hasn't left the world yet, so read more news-papers and fewer detective novels."[17] The 1938 trial was not in and of itself of any great importance. Indeed, the two best-known British histories of the 1930s present the Mayfair men's court appearance as just one of the many human-interest stories that the popular newspapers used to divert a public de-pressed by bleak diplomatic reports foreshadowing another European war. What was considered newsworthy? In 1937, wrote Robert Graves, "[t]here had been two-way air-mail flights across the Atlantic: how soon, people were ask-ing, would passengers also be carried? Next came the case of the 'Mayfair men,' Harley, Wilmer, and their associates, who were sentenced to be flogged and to serve long terms of penal servitude for having committed a violent jewel robbery in a high-class London hotel. The crime was the more newsworthy because the criminals belonged to an upper-class social set. This was well-featured in the popular Press with a bright spotlight on the administration of the cat and its effects."[18] The tabloids, he tells us, soon sensed their reader-ship's waning attention and quickly turned to a new sensation, the "torso mys-tery case," the chopped up body of a dance hostess having been found at the home of an army officer.

Though his account of the Mayfair men is brief, Graves appears positively loquacious when compared to Malcolm Muggeridge, who devotes a mere ten words to our young men. "Mayfair playboys held the stage, until sentences given, then forgotten."[19] For Muggeridge the trial was an overnight sensation that occurred about the time of the Munich Agreement and before the tragic sinking of the submarine *HMS Thetis*.

Muggeridge was to an extent correct in implying that the details of the Hyde Park Hotel robbery were forgotten, but he was obviously wrong if he meant that the playboy disappeared. Just such a figure dominated one of the most daring of wartime British films—*The Rake's Progress* (1945)—written and directed by Sidney Gilliat, co-written by Frank Launder, and starring Rex Harrison. The film begins with Harrison coolly taking the risky decision of leading an armored patrol across a bridge thought to be mined by the retreat-ing Germans. The cameras then immediately cut to the dramatic newspaper headline "Former Playboy Missing," and a voiceover begins to tell us the story of the irresponsible Vivian Kenway. Likeable though unreliable, we first see him expressing his disdain for rules and regulations that results in his being sent down from Oxford in 1931. His long-suffering father, a wealthy Tory MP, packs him off to a South American plantation. He is hired only because of the old boy network, his knowledge of cricket being of more importance than his knowledge of coffee. Learning that crops are routinely destroyed to keep prices high, his cynicism is deepened. After losing his job due to drink he returns to England to pursue fast cars, whiskey, and women. He has a grubby affair with his best friend's wife and marries an Austrian Jew to get her to England, where he steals her money. As a result of his drunken driving he accidentally causes his father's death. Hitting rock bottom, reduced to selling used cars and hiring himself out as a taxi dancer, he tells a friend, "The 1930s produced us; our type is now obsolete." Luckily for him, he is rescued by the war. He dies a hero, holding a last scrounged bottle of champagne. "He died as he lived," marvels his sergeant. "Drinking champagne he didn't pay for."

The film was a critical and commercial success. The British press lauded this account of a self-centered ne'er-do-well.[20] Though the American censor required cuts to what in North America was called *Notorious Gentleman*, Bosley Crowther of the *New York Times* praised the depiction of the "cold egotistic concern" of the charming but mean main character who, Crowther agreed, was "typical of a class in the decade before the war."[21] What critics failed to mention was that the producers, in framing the story with a depiction of Kenway's self-sacrificing wartime heroics, effectively undercut their indictment of the prewar English elites. Like all good propagandists their message seemed to be that all a playboy needed was the challenge of a good war to be miraculously transformed from cad to charismatic hero. This was not the only fiction to exploit this reformist trope. A number of World War II films "portrayed insouciant playboys redeemed through gallant self-sacrifice."[22] A classic example was *In Which We Serve* (1942, dir. Noël Coward and David Lean), which had Coward starring as the saintly Captain Kinross of the *HMS Torrin*, a man-about-town who becomes a war hero. Indeed, the film shows the entire officer class renewing and reinvigorating itself in response to the Nazi threat. In contrast, its treatment of the working-class crew is casually condescending. Nevertheless, the *Times* declared it a "magnificent" work of cinematic art.[23] And many believed that such transformations were not simple fictions. An American industrialist in a 1943 speech to Empire Club of Canada portrayed the British Empire as reemerging as a warrior nation. "It's the Mayfair playboy turned parachute trooper."[24]

Lonsdale and Jenkins did not exhibit such heroics, but they did serve briefly in the army, and all four of the Hyde Park Hotel robbers emerged unscathed from the conflict. Many of the other young men of their milieu were not so lucky. John Lonsdale successfully sued Pamela Blake for libel. Her brother Arthur Michael Blake married Dianna Tyrwhitt-Drake in December 1941; a little over a month later he was killed in action.[25] A police informer in 1938 linked the young Stewart Cappel to the Cartier robbery. In 1943 the press reported that Captain Louis Stewart Matheson Cappel, age twenty-three, son of Commander Norman L. Cappel of the Royal Ulster Rifles, had been killed while on active service in Italy.[26] Flying a Typhoon on a reconnaissance mission, Patrick Stewart Greville Moran—"Mayfair playboy" and one-time lover of Jenny Nicholson—was brought down by flak and killed August 14, 1944.[27] Major Robin Lyle of the Scottish Horse, who had flaunted his old school tie in court, was killed in Normandy in 1944.[28] When assaulting a pub licensee in 1936, Wilmer had been accompanied by his friend Anthony William Patrick Lyon-Clark. Born in 1913, the son of Major William Lyon-Clark and Helen Lyon Clark (née Holt), the young man was much involved in horse racing. A captain in Queen Mary's Own Royal Hussars, Lyon-Clark was killed in action in France on July 18, 1944, and buried in the Ranville War cemetery.[29] David Sneddon and Patrick Topham received fifteen-month sentences for robbery in 1938 but were released when war broke out in September 1939.[30] Topham, who piloted Lancaster bombers, was awarded the Distinguished Flying Cross.[31] Sneddon (Beds and Herts Regt), a speed addict in peacetime, served appropriately enough as a driver in the Royal Army Service Corps in Hong Kong. The city fell to the Japanese in December 1941, and Sneddon was listed as a prisoner of war.[32] Similarly, Fredrick Clive Wilmer, David Wilmer's brother, was reported missing in Malaya with the Royal Deccan Horse in 1942.[33] The Japanese released him in 1945.[34] If the war changed anyone at all it was Prince Yurka Galitzine, half-brother of Pauline Daubeny, whose home was looted by Hervey's gang. Galitzine, the son of a former military attaché at the Imperial Russian embassy in London and an Englishwoman, was before the war an anti-Semite and active member of the Right Club. He abandoned his racist views when, as an intelligence officer, he discovered in December 1944 the horrors of Natzweiler-Struthof, the first concentration camp to be liberated.[35]

Propagandists presented the playboy's career as mirroring that of the national narrative. He appeared on the scene as a self-serving predator in the 1930s, that "low dishonest decade" that saw many members of the elite embracing appeasement and drifting toward fascism out of a concern to protect their property.[36] Then came the war, which commentators worked into a "social democratic narrative of suffering and social justice."[37] The playboy, like the nation, redeemed himself in a bloody conflict that demanded that naked individualism give way to self-sacrifice and cooperation. Mass Observation might caustically report in 1940 that conservative papers such as the *Express* and the *Telegraph* sought to show that the West End suffered like the East End and "how brave the playboys and girls of Mayfair were, and how kind the West Enders were to refugee East Enders."[38] The government dismissed such carping. The collective heroism of an altruistic generation of young men and women led in turn to the construction of the welfare state.[39] This powerful myth of national solidarity sustained itself by downplaying reports of rapes, lootings, and profiteering. It overwhelmed the odd isolated protest that the rich were not contributing their fair share, that the classes were more divided than ever.

For a new member of the officer class to assert his support for the Labour Party still took real courage. Despite having a reactionary Tory as his commanding officer, Donald Bruce was proud to state that during the war he never hid the fact that he was a socialist. One incident stood out in his memory. "King George VI was coming round to our regiment. So a security wallah turned up and said had I got any dubious characters in the unit, so I said that we had a couple of jewel robbers, Peter Martin Jenkins and another character. 'Oh,' he said, 'I don't mean those. Have you got any socialists?' I said, 'Yes, I'm one,' and he looked a little aghast and said, 'Isn't that a little unusual?' "[40]

Societal shifts would take time. It was certainly the case that despite the optimistic belief in change, normative styles of masculinity and femininity did not relax all that much in the 1940s. The government encouraged women who had been mobilized for war work to return to their domestic duties as soon as possible.[41] There was hardly any appreciable decline in homophobia.[42] Soldiers continued to equate flashy clothes with effeminacy and call conscientious objectors sissies or pansies. The war posed the police with far more serious challenges, yet each year the authorities prosecuted hundreds of men under antiquated anti-homosexual laws.[43] Alan Turing, the brilliant mathematician who broke the Enigma Code, was only the most famous postwar victim. The court having sentenced him to chemical castration, he ended his life in 1954.

During the war the British lauded a particular type of reserved, understated masculinity. They succeeded in constructing a model of manliness—embodied in the temperate, calm antihero—that played well in contrast to the bombastic and misogynistic model embraced by the Nazis.[44] In the early years of the conflict, accounts of the classic self-indulgent playboy seemed to have all but disappeared from the newspaper columns. It wasn't that such hedonists no longer existed; rather, editors felt that such characters had no place in a supposedly classless people's war. Like many others Tennyson Jesse drew the moral that the Hyde Park Hotel robbery revealed the corruption of prewar Britain. "The Mayfair Men, sleek and lizardy, were the sort of young men that are seen at every bar in Paris and on the Riviera, in London, New York and Hollywood—without heart and without bowels. . . . And this is a 'great and civilised country' . . . where such things should not be possible. The Mayfair Men were an example of a society so overripe that it is rotten."[45]

In fact, journalists continued to report some of the behaviors associated with the playboy, but because they were manifested by a courageous military, they were regarded benignly. "Aircrew," observes one historian, "had an especially notorious reputation for reckless driving (usually, although not always, fuelled by heavy drinking), a popular assumption that was so prevalent that insurance companies frequently imposed an additional premium on RAF personnel."[46] The RAF was the most junior of the services and—embracing as it did a technocratic and meritocratic view of the military—the most modern. Nevertheless, Martin Francis has found that while RAF Bomber Command embodied the new masculinity of the "people's war," the fighter pilots who were hailed for having heroically warded off the Luftwaffe in 1940 carried on "old-style, public-school-derived notions of martial masculinity." Flaunting their pursuit of pleasure some pilots had the name of their favorite Mayfair nightclub emblazoned on the side of their aircraft.[47] And despite government assertions that the nation was united as one, class-consciousness did not disappear. "In both Bomber and Fighter Commands, moreover, social distinctions between officers and NCOs, and between the aircrew and ground crew . . . remained deeply entrenched."[48]

In the interwar years a team of British drivers known as the "Bentley Boys" garnered enormous public acclaim for the races they won in France and the glamorous lives they led in London's West End. In his memoirs, written in his eighties, W. O. Bentley recalled, "The public liked to imagine [the drivers] living in expensive Mayfair flats with several mistresses and, of course, several very fast Bentleys, drinking champagne in nightclubs, playing the horses and the Stock Exchange, and beating furiously around racing tracks at the weekend."[49] Historian Martin Pugh refers to the Bentley Boys as "playboys," but in the early 1930s the press did not; the word had not yet entered journalists' vocabulary. It was only a few years later that they began to use this term for a particular type of urban male.

The playboy's entry onto the public stage was both a cause and an effect of the destabilization of conventional gender roles and the redrawing of the lines between the public and the private. The anxious warned that modernity threatened to emasculate men and virilize women. They located the playboy— known for his "feminine" excesses, for playing rather than working—on the borderlands of masculinity.

Tabloid journalists played a central role in popularizing and exploiting the notion that a new type of unreliable young man on the make had arrived. For such writers who catered to the mass readership's interest in toffs behaving badly, the playboys provided a limitless source of sensational stories. At the same time a surprising number of more serious social observers regarded the investigation of the lifestyle of such cynical and self-serving young men a compelling undertaking. They used the figure of the playboy as a cipher to channel wider discussions of generation, gender, class, crime, and politics.

Because so many of the Mayfair playboys were members of the cohort born about 1910, a number of commentators presented the Hyde Park Hotel robbery as a symptom of generational conflict. The Mayfair men came of age just as the depression hit, not the most propitious of times, as Noël Coward noted in "Children of the Ritz" (1932):

> In the lovely gay
> Years before the Crash
> Mr Cartier
> Never asked for cash,
> Now shops we patronized are serving us with writs,
> What's going to happen to the Children of the Ritz?[50]

Journalists had portrayed the high jinks of the Bright Young People of the 1920s as the more or less innocent acting out of a generation scarred by the Great War. This study shows that the tabloids took a gloomier view of playboys, young men produced by the 1930s depression who spurned appeals for economy and sacrifice in favor of a self-indulgent life.

That the flapper symbolized women's quest for independence is a commonplace. What has not been appreciated is that playboys represented the extent to which heterosexual young men might turn against the traditional model of a disciplined, rational, and productive masculinity. Their chroniclers and critics in newspapers, novels, and films fleshed out the portrait of this new type of man. They did not, of course, simply create out of whole cloth a new style of masculinity. There were men who led hedonistic lives long before the press gave them a name, while others, in embracing the role of playboy, engaged in a process of self-fashioning.[51] Even in their confessions such men self-consciously sought to control, or at least negotiate, their identities and, by parading the social networks of which they were part, shore up a newfound celebrity status.

Though the middle and upper classes did not experience anything like the working-class' savage drop in family income during the Great Depression, there were always some on the margins of Mayfair society who suffered from relative deprivation, who imagined themselves threatened by any perceived shrinkage of the precious gap separating the propertied from the impoverished.[52] Playboys like Lonsdale portrayed themselves as the "new poor," deprived by the depression of what they considered their due. Such class preoccupations dominated the newspaper and film dissections of playboys and Mayfair men, but the resulting investigations also reveal a host of other social issues.

Many writers used the trial and punishment of the Mayfair playboys as proof of the efficiency of the police, the fairness of the English court system, and "the just measure of pain" penitentiaries implacably doled out to convicted felons. Histories of corporal punishment have tended to highlight the role of progressives in seeking to end the humiliating and brutal ordeals to which working-class men were almost alone subjected. Their stories have yet to be told. Justice was purportedly blind, yet because of class bias the only prisoners whose punishments burned themselves into the public memory were predictably those of the upper-class playboys.

Even those who debated the issues of the rise of fascism at home and appeasement abroad shored up their different arguments with references to the apolitical man-about-town. Oswald Mosley, leader of the British Union of Fascists, enjoyed a charisma that owed something to his reputation as a playboy. It was poetic justice that his notoriety, which initially served him so well, ultimately undermined his efforts to be taken seriously as a politician.[53]

In the reports of the 1938 trial of the Mayfair men and in subsequent discussions by politicians, journalists, novelists, and moviemakers, the notion of the playboy performed what can be called "cultural work." The robbery and its aftermath did not create the anxieties that some felt in the face of evolving class and gender relations, but for many it crystallized such worries. The trial became a cultural referent, offering those preoccupied by the threats posed by the depression and the social changes accompanying modernization the cause and the occasion to air their concerns. Ironically enough they dragooned the playboy—this indolent, self-centered character, whose guiding principle was avoidance of honest labor—and set him the burdensome task of personifying many of modernity's most worrisome challenges.

Notes

The abbreviation MEPO used in the notes is Records of the Metropolitan Police Office, National Archives, London.

Introduction

1. "Writer Fryniwyd Tennyson (Jesse) Harwood Writes to Her Friend GBH," Apr. 1, 1938, Huntington Digital Library, http://hdl.huntington.org/cdm/ref/collection/p15150coll7/id/5823 (accessed Sept. 16, 2015).

2. Jesse also published novels, plays, a war memoir, and several books on popular criminology. Joanna Colenbrander, *A Portrait of Fryn: A Biography of F. Tennyson Jesse* (London: Deutsch, 1984).

3. F. Tennyson Jesse, *Murder and Its Motives* (London: Heinemann, 1924), 18.

4. William M. Meier, *Property Crime in London, 1850–Present* (New York: Palgrave Macmillan, 2011), 21.

5. Lucy Bland, *Modern Women on Trial: Sexual Transgression in the Age of the Flapper* (Manchester: Manchester University Press, 2013); John Carter Wood, *The Most Remarkable Woman in England: Poison, Celebrity and the Trials of Beatrice Pace* (Manchester: Manchester University Press, 2012). See also Mary Hartman, *Victorian Murderesses: A True Story of Thirteen Respectable French and English Women Accused of Unspeakable Crimes* (London: Robson Books, 1977).

6. Douglas Hay et al., eds., *Albion's Fatal Tree: Crime and Society in Eighteenth-Century England* (New York: Pantheon, 1976).

7. *Derby Evening Telegraph*, June 2, 1938, 1.

8. David Garland, *Punishment and Modern Society: A Study in Social Theory* (Oxford: Clarendon Press, 1990), 19.

9. Billie Melman, *Women and the Popular Imagination in the Twenties: Flappers and Nymphs* (Basingstoke: Macmillan, 1988), 24; Lesley Hall, *Hidden Anxieties: Male Sexuality 1900–1950* (Cambridge: Polity, 1991).

10. Michael Roper and John Tosh, eds., *Manful Assertions: Masculinities in Britain since 1800* (London: Routledge, 1991); John Tosh, *A Man's Place: Masculinity and the Middle-Class Home in Victorian England* (New Haven: Yale University Press, 1999); Angus McLaren, *The Trials of Masculinity: Policing Sexual Boundaries, 1870–1930* (Chicago: University of Chicago Press, 1997).

11. Patrick McDevitt, *"May the Best Man Win": Sport, Masculinity, and Nationalism in Great Britain and the Empire, 1880–1935* (Basingstoke: Palgrave Macmillan, 2004); Ina Zweiniger-Bargielowska, *Managing the Body: Beauty, Health and Fitness in Britain, 1880–1939* (Oxford: Oxford University Press, 2010); Joanna Bourke, *Dismembering the Male: Men's*

Bodies, Britain, and the Great War (Chicago: University of Chicago Press, 1996); Paul R. Deslandes, "The Male Body, Beauty, and Aesthetics in Modern Britain," *History Compass* 8, 10 (2010): 1191–1208.

12. Barbara Ehrenreich, *The Hearts of Men: American Dreams and the Flight from Commitment* (Garden City, NY: Anchor Press, 1983); Frank Mort, *Capital Affairs: London and the Making of the Permissive Society* (New Haven: Yale University Press, 2010).

13. Carrie Pitzulo, *Bachelors and Bunnies: The Sexual Politics of Playboy* (Chicago: University of Chicago Press, 2011).

14. R. W. Connell, *Masculinities* (Cambridge: Cambridge University Press, 1995).

15. On homosexuality as a form of marginalized masculinity, see Matt Houlbrook, *Queer London: Perils and Pleasures in the Sexual Metropolis, 1918–1957* (Chicago: University of Chicago Press, 2005), and Matt Cook, *London and the Culture of Homosexuality, 1885–1914* (Cambridge: Cambridge University Press, 2003).

16. Martin Francis, "The Domestication of the Male? Recent Research on Nineteenth and Twentieth-Century British Masculinity," *Historical Journal* 45, 3 (2002): 637.

17. John Buchan, *Three Hostages* (1924; reprint, London: Thomas Nelson, 1946), 102.

18. Kate Macdonald, "Hunted Men in John Buchan's London, 1890s to 1920s," *Literary London: Interdisciplinary Studies in the Representation of London* 7, 1 (March 2009), www.literary london.org/london-journal/march2009/macdonald.html (accessed Aug. 28, 2015).

19. Seth Koven, *Slumming: Sexual and Social Politics in Victorian London* (Princeton: Princeton University Press, 2004); Ellen Ross, ed., *Slum Travelers: Ladies and London Poverty, 1860–1920* (Berkeley: University of California Press, 2007); Gareth Stedman Jones, *Outcast London: A Study in the Relationship between Classes in Victorian Society* (Oxford: Peregrine Penguin, 1984); John Marriott, *Beyond the Tower: A History of East London* (New Haven: Yale University Press, 2011); Judith Walkowitz, *Prostitution and Victorian Society: Women, Class and the State* (New York: Cambridge University Press, 1980), *City of Dreadful Delight: Narratives of Sexual Danger in Late-Victorian London* (Chicago: University of Chicago Press, 1992), *Nights Out: Life in Cosmopolitan London* (New Haven: Yale University Press, 2012); Mort, *Capital Affairs*; Jerry White, *The Worst Street in North London: Campbell Bunk, Islington, between the Wars* (London: Routledge and Kegan Paul, 1986).

20. E. P. Thompson, *The Making of the English Working Class* (London: Gollancz, 1963), 12.

21. Luis L. M. Aguiar and Christopher J. Schneider, eds., *Researching amongst Elites: Challenges and Opportunities in Studying Up* (Farnham, Surrey: Ashgate, 2012).

22. *Times*, Jan. 4, 1938, 5.

23. Tom Jeffrey and Keith McClelland, "A World Fit to Live In: The *Daily Mail* and the Middle Classes, 1918–1939," in *Impacts and Influences: Essays on Media Power in the Twentieth Century*, ed. James Curran, Anthony Smith, and Pauline Wingate (London: Routledge, 2013), 27–52.

24. Adrian Bingham, *Family Newspapers: Sex, Private Life and the British Popular Press 1918–1978* (Oxford University Press, 2009), 131; Bland, *Modern Women on Trial*, 214–225.

25. *Times*, Dec. 24, 1937, 9; Dec. 31, 1937, 9; Jan. 14, 1938, 11; Feb. 19, 1938, 17.

26. *Evening Standard*, Feb. 15, 1938, 5; *Daily Express*, Feb. 16, 1938, 15; *Daily Express*, Feb. 19, 1938, 1; *Daily Mirror*, Feb. 19, 1938, 3.

27. Adrian Bingham, *Gender, Modernity, and the Popular Press in Interwar Britain* (Oxford: Clarendon Press, 2004), 230, 232.

28. D. L. Le Mahieu, *A Culture for Democracy: Mass Communication and the Cultivated Mind in Britain between the Wars* (Oxford: Oxford University Press, 1988), 228–229.

29. Ibid., 236–252.

30. This has been a theme of the work of Lucy Bland and, in particular, Matt Houlbrook's recent *Prince of Tricksters: The Incredible True Story of Netley Lucas, Gentleman Crook* (Chicago: University of Chicago Press, 2016).

31. On flappers, see Bland, *Modern Women on Trial*; on homosexuals, see Houlbrook, *Queer London*.

32. "Cato," *Guilty Men* (London: Gollancz, 1940).

33. Claude Lévi-Strauss, *The Savage Mind* (Chicago: University of Chicago Press, 1966); Susan Carol Rogers, "Good to Think: The 'Peasant' in Contemporary France," *Anthropological Quarterly* 60, 2 (1987): 56–63.

34. *Daily Express*, Feb. 19, 1938, 1.

Part I. The Crime

1. *Daily Mail*, Dec. 3, 1929, 8.

2. George Orwell, "Raffles and Miss Blandish," in *The Collected Essays* (London: Secker & Warburg, 1968), 3:212–221; Richard Hoggart, *The Uses of Literacy: Aspects of Working-Class Life* (London: Chatto & Windus, 1969).

3. Ken Worpole, *Dockers and Detectives: Popular Reading, Popular Writing* (London: Verso, 1983).

4. Jeffrey Richards, "The British Board of Film Censors and Content Control in the 1930s: Images of Britain," *Historical Journal of Film, Radio and Television* 1, 2 (1981): 95–116; Christine Grandy, *Heroes and Happy Endings: Class, Gender, and Nation in Popular Film and Fiction in Interwar Britain* (Manchester: Manchester University Press, 2014), 188.

5. Adrian Bingham, *Family Newspapers: Sex, Private Life and the British Popular Press 1918–1978* (Oxford: Oxford University Press, 2009), 131.

6. Critics commonly attacked the ethics of such journalists. "If they are 'star' or 'feature' reporters, they have become keyhole Boswells prying on the boudoir activities of film actresses or the bottle-party eccentricities of a Mayfair playboy." *Cooperative Review* 13 (1939): 26.

7. Matt Houlbrook, *Queer London: Perils and Pleasures in the Sexual Metropolis, 1918–1957* (Chicago: University of Chicago Press, 2005), 222.

1: The Robbery

1. The 1938 London telephone directory lists Bellenger's address as 11 Lytton Grove, Putney SW15.

2. In 1934 Prince George, Duke of Kent, went to Cartier to choose a sapphire engagement ring for Princess Marina. *Daily Mail*, Sept. 13, 1934, 11.

3. MEPO 3/902, Dec. 20, 1937, Statement of E. Bellenger; MEPO 3/902, Jan. 5, 1938, Statement of E. Bellenger taken at Beaumont House; see also *Times*, Dec. 22, 1937, 12.

4. Anthony Masters, *Inside Marbled Halls: Life Above and Below Stairs in the Hyde Park Hotel* (London: Sidgwick, 1979).

5. *Who Was Who* (London: A & C Black, 1936), www.ukwhoswho.com/view/article/oupww /whowaswho/U48320 (accessed Jan. 15, 2017).

6. MEPO 3/902, Dec. 20, 1937, 9:25 p.m., Metropolitan Police Telegram.

7. Etienne Bellenger had written on the subject; see "Gems are the Best Investment," *Daily Mail*, June 4, 1936, 14.

8. One account mistakenly states that Bellenger was hit with "a large ornament that was in the room." A. E. Bowker, *Behind the Bar* (London: Staples Press, 1951), 248.

9. *Times*, Jan. 28, 1938, 4; *Daily Telegraph*, Feb. 16, 1938, 6, 7.

10. MEPO 3/902, Dec. 20, 1937, Statement of Henrietta Gordon; MEPO 3/902, Dec. 27, 1937, Statement of Henrietta Gordon. Gordon described a teddy bear coat as having thick short hair, wide lapels, and a belt.

11. MEPO 3/902, Dec. 20, 1937, Statement of Enrico Laurenti.

12. Ibid.; see also *Times*, Jan. 14, 1938, 11.

13. Gordon had her enemies at the hotel. One presumably was the writer of an anonymous letter—signed "Fair Play"—sent to the Westminster Police Court magistrate. The writer claimed that Mrs. Bellenger had come to the Hyde Park Hotel to reward those who had helped her husband. She gave a "present" to Netta (Henrietta Gordon), the chambermaid. Indeed, Netta had been boasting of her need now to go to Lloyd's Bank. The writer asserted that these actions should be exposed as criminal, as it was against the law to approach a witness. See MEPO 3/902, Jan. 6, 1938.

14. MEPO 3/902, Dec. 21, 1937, Statement of Dr. Victor Constad.

15. MEPO 3/902, Jan. 6, 1938, Statement of Nils Lovold Eckhoff. Eckhoff operated on Bellenger to repair the fifteen wounds that had resulted in the severe fracturing of his skull.

16. MEPO 3/902, Dec. 20, 1937, Statement of E. Bellenger. Bellenger stated that "Hambro" had pimples.

17. *Times*, Dec. 22, 1937, 12.

18. MEPO 3/902, Dec. 20, 1937, Statement of Reginald Sidney Kelly.

19. Ibid.

20. MEPO 3/902, Dec. 20, 1937, Statement of Enrico Laurenti.

21. MEPO 3/902, Dec. 20, 1937, Statement of James Clarke.

22. MEPO 3/902, Dec. 20, 1937, Statement of J. W. Sloan.

23. MEPO 3/902, Dec. 20, 1937, Statement of William Peter Jefferies.

24. MEPO 3/902, Dec. 20, 1937, Statement of Reginald Sidney Kelly.

25. MEPO 3/902, Dec. 20, 1937, Statement of Henrietta Gordon.

26. MEPO 3/902, Dec. 20, 1937, 9:25 p.m., Metropolitan Police Telegram

27. *Police Gazette*, Dec. 21, 1937, 1.

28. MEPO 3/902, Dec. 20, 1937, "P. L. Hambro & and 2 Others. Wanted for robbery to prejudice of messers CARTIERS, at the Hyde Park Hotel."

29. MEPO 3/902, Dec. 21, 1937, Deputy Chief Constable to Commissioner.

30. For the argument that there was a need for an "air police," see H. L. Adam, C. I. D., *Behind the Scenes at Scotland Yard* (London: Sampson Low, Marston, 1931), 178.

31. MEPO 3/902, Dec. 21, 1937, Information Room.

32. MEPO 3/902, Dec. 21, 1937, Jack Davies letter.

33. MEPO 3/902, Dec. 22, 1937, Anonymous letter dated Dec. 21, 1937.

34. MEPO 3/902, Dec. 22, 1937, Statement of Cyril Smith; see also *Daily Express*, Feb. 19, 1938, 5.

35. MEPO 3/902, Dec. 23, 1937, Oxford City Police: Arthur Rolphe review of case for Chief Constable.

36. MEPO 3/902, Dec. 22, 1937, Statement of Mitre Hotel pageboy. Ladbroke 0707 was the number of a Miss B. Levensberg (probably Levenberg) of 50 Oxford Gardens, London W10.

37. MEPO 3/902, Dec. 29, 1937, Chief Inspector Leonard Burt overview.

38. MEPO 3/902, Dec. 23, 1937, Chief Inspector Leonard Burt.

39. Robert Fabian, *Fabian of the Yard* (London: Naldrett Press, 1950), 38.

40. MEPO 3/902, Jan. 6, 1938, Evidence to be given by Thomas H. Smith, Moreton-in-Marsh station, Gloucestershire Constabulary.

41. MEPO 3/902, Dec. 24, 1937, Gloucestershire Constabulary.

42. MEPO 3/902, Dec. 22, 1937, Report of Inspector Robert Fabian.

2: The Investigation

1. George Dilnot, *The Real Detective* (London: Geoffrey Bles, 1933), 3–7, 34.

2. MEPO 3/902, Dec. 20, 1937, Statement of E. Bellenger. See also MEPO 3/902, Jan. 5, 1938, Statement of E. Bellenger taken at Beaumont House.

3. His most famous cases are included in Frederick R. Cherrill, *Cherrill of the Yard: The Autobiography of Fred Cherrill* (London: G. G. Harrap, 1954). See also Fredrick R. Cherrill, *The Finger Print System at Scotland Yard* (London: HMSO, 1954).

4. MEPO 3/902, Dec. 29, 1937, Statement of Frederick Cherrill.

5. Burt reviewed his most sensational cases, including those of the traitors Lord Haw-Haw (William Joyce) and John Amery, in Leonard Burt, *Commander Burt of Scotland Yard* (London: William Heinemann, 1959); see also Rupert Allason, *The Branch: A History of the Metropolitan Police Special Branch, 1883–1983* (London: Secker & Warburg, 1983), 124–125.

6. Dilnot, *The Real Detective*, 231–233.

7. MEPO 3/902, Dec. 21, 1937, Statement of John Lonsdale taken at the Central Police Station, Oxford.

8. MEPO 3/902, Dec. 21, 1937, Statement of Peter Martin Jenkins taken at the Central Police Station, Oxford.

9. MEPO 3/902, Jan. 6, 1938, Evidence given by Thomas H. Smith, Moreton-in-Marsh Station, Gloucestshire Constabulary.

10. MEPO 3/902, Dec. 22, 1937, Statement of John Lonsdale taken at the Gerald Street Police Station.

11. Detective Sergeant Tapsell wrote up the confession that Burt witnessed. Tapsell played a small part in one other noteworthy case. In 1935 the wife of a Norfolk magistrate, shocked by Naomi Mitchison's novel *We Have Been Warned* (1935), alerted Scotland Yard. Tapsell drew up a report for the director of public prosecutions on the morality of the book. "(Page) 274 describes carefully the seduction of a man, hitherto moral, by a Russian woman," he warned, and "(Pages) 487–88 contain a discussion between a man and wife as to whether she can get rid of a pregnancy by an abortion." The DPP was interested, but John Simon, the home secretary, had the case shelved in the name of artistic freedom. *Daily Telegraph*, UPI News Services, Oct. 3, 2005.

12. MEPO 3/902, Dec. 22, 1937, Statement of David Wilmer taken at the Gerald Street Police Station.

13. *Times*, Jan. 7, 1938, 9.

14. MEPO 3/902, Dec. 22, 1937, David Wilmer Further Statement.

15. *Times*, Jan. 7, 1938, 9.

16. MEPO 3/902, Dec. 22, 1937, Jenkins statement.

17. Robert Honey Fabian, a detective inspector of C Division, was involved in many famous criminal cases, including the 1947 Alec de Antiquis murder. Retiring shortly thereafter as detective superintendent, he became a well-known crime writer, contributing to the popular BBC TV drama series *Fabian of the Yard* (1954–1956). Martin Fido and Keith Skinner, eds., *The Official Encyclopedia of Scotland Yard* (London: Virgin, 1999), 135.

18. The use of informers was cloaked in secrecy. For a brief reference to a police informer fined for receiving stolen property, see *Times*, Dec. 2, 1938, 16.

19. MEPO 3/902, Dec. 22, 1937, Robert Fabian report. A police reporter stated that in fact Etienne Bellenger recognized two of his assailants from photographs that Superintendent John Sands brought from Scotland Yard's Criminal Record Office. *Evening Standard*, Dec. 21, 1937, 1.

20. MEPO 3/902, Dec. 21, 1937, Statement of Robert Harley.

21. MEPO 3/902, Dec. 24, 1937, Detective Inspector Percy McDouall Statement.

22. Given that Fabian took liberties in all of his accounts, they have to be treated with caution. For example, he tells the story of a robbery very similar to the Hyde Park Hotel case. He states that in 1926 "Augustus Wiley," using a big car and an expensive hotel room to pose as a maharajah's representative, swindled a jeweler. The real story was that Edward Russell Watts, claiming to work for "an exalted personage," convinced a Regent Street jeweler to bring to his hotel a £14,500 pearl necklace. Saying that he had to make a phone call, he took the pearls and fled via a back exit, going by cab to Croydon, where he chartered a plane for Paris. He mailed most of the jewels to a woman and returned to London claiming that he had been drunk. The judge, finding that he was still sober enough to carry out a skilled robbery, sentenced him to thirteen months in prison. *Times*, Sept. 14, 1926, 11; cf. Robert Fabian, *Fabian of the Yard* (London: Naldrett Press, 1950), 55–59.

23. Fabian, *Fabian of the Yard*, 186–188. He also asserted that he caught Wilmer thanks to a "good guess."

24. MEPO 3/902, Jan. 10, 1938, Statement of Peter James Kearney taken at 50 A Curzon Street. He was also present on December 21 when officers searched the room and took possession of a pack of cigarettes of a certain brand. His name is given as Peter James Curie in the *Times*, Jan. 14, 1938, 11.

25. MEPO 3/902, Dec. 22, 1937, Robert Fabian report.

26. Cecil Bishop, *From Information Received: The Reminiscences of Cecil Bishop* (London: Hutchinson, 1932), 39, 40, 42; see also Dilnot, *The Real Detective*, 119, and Howard Vincent, *A Police Code and General Manual of the Criminal Law* (London: Butterworth, 1924), 70, 130.

27. MEPO 3/902, Dec. 29, 1937, Chief Inspector Leonard Burt overview; MEPO 3/902, Dec. 22, 1937, Harley Statement.

28. MEPO 3/902, Dec. 22, 1937, Robert Fabian report.

29. *News Chronicle*, Feb. 19, 1938, 1, 3, 5.

30. *News of the World*, Feb. 20, 1938, 13; Trevor Allen, *Underworld; The Biography of Charles Brooks, Criminal* (New York: R. M. McBride, 1932), 152.

31. MEPO 3/902, Dec. 29, 1937, Chief Inspector Leonard Burt overview.

32. *Times*, Jan. 7, 1938, 9.

33. *Yorkshire Post and Leeds Intelligencer*, Jan. 7, 1938, 10.

34. MEPO 3/902, Dec. 22, 1937, Robert Harley further statement. Some pages pertaining to the night of Dec. 20, 1937, are missing.

35. The prosecutor Vincent Evans stated that the press, in publishing photos of the four accused, might have prejudiced the ongoing identification process. *Yorkshire Post and Leeds Intelligencer*, Jan. 7, 1938, 10.

36. MEPO 3/902, Dec. 27, 1937, Kelly statement taken at Gerald Road Police Station.

37. MEPO 3/902, Dec. 28, 1937, Jefferies statement.

38. MEPO 3/902, Dec. 27, 1937, Further statement of Enrico Laurenti.

39. MEPO 3/902, Dec. 28, 1937, Statement of J. W. Sloan.

40. MEPO 3/902, Dec. 28, 1937, Further statement of James Clark.

41. MEPO 3/902, Dec. 27, 1937, Henrietta Gordon statement.

42. *Times*, Jan. 14, 1938, 11.

43. MEPO 3/902, Dec. 21, 1937, Statement of Clifford Perkins, Hall Porter, New Clarges Hotel.

44. MEPO 3/902, Jan. 10, 1938, Statement of Mrs. Greta Vaughan; *Times*, Jan. 14, 1938, 11.

45. MEPO 3/902, Dec. 31, 1937, Police to Department of Public Prosecution. In handing over the file the police stressed Lonsdale's ties to Dorset and his likely knowledge of the Hambro family.

46. MEPO 3/902, Dec. 31, 1937, Burt's seventeen-page summary of the case for the Superintendant of Criminal Investigation Department.

47. MEPO 3/902, Dec. 29, 1937, Statement of Frederick Cherrill. Cherrill compared the prints on the bottle to those of Wilmer and Jenkins in Brixton Prison. *Times*, Jan. 21, 1938, 9.

48. MEPO 3/902, Dec. 31, 1937, Burt's summary.

49. *Times*, Dec. 24, 1937, 9.

50. *Times*, Dec. 31, 1937, 9.

51. *Times*, Jan. 7, 1938, 9.

52. *Times*, Jan. 28, 1938, 4.

53. The information that the Imperial Fascist League activist John Ridout provided the police is discussed in chapter 10.

54. MEPO 3/902, Jan. 18, 1938, Detective Constable W. Chamberlain and Detective Sergeant Heathfield of Kent County report to Commissioner.

55. MEPO 3/902, Metropolitan police telegrams, Jan. 20 and 21, 1938. Cappel was at Charterhouse from 1934 to 1937. According to the informer, Tony Wheeler was Cappel's partner in crime.

56. MEPO 3/902, Jan. 24, 1938, Letter from Burt to the Superintendant.

57. MEPO 3/902, Dec. 30, 1937, Horst Robert Leopold Bonsack statement. See also Bonsack, Horst Robert Leopold (known as Godfrey Bonsack), Germany, Interior Decorator and Antique Dealer, Flat 17, 51 South Street, London W1, 19th September 1966, in "List of Aliens to Whom Certificates of Naturalisation Have Been Granted by the Secretary of State," *London Gazette*, Oct. 25, 1966, 11492.

58. MEPO 3/902, Feb. 4, 1938, Governor of Brixton Prison to Scotland Yard.

59. MEPO 3/902 C600457, Amounts given to each officer.

60. MEPO 3/902, Mar. 1, 1938, CID report to Superintendent of Scotland Yard.

61. MEPO 3/902, Feb. 24, 1938, Leonard Burt's report.

62. MEPO 3/902, Mar. 11, 1938, Report to the Commissioner.

3: The Suspects

1. *Daily Mail*, Feb. 19, 1938, 9.

2. *Toronto Globe and Mail*, Feb. 19, 1938, 15.

3. But see *Times*, May 15, 1919, 15.

4. *London Gazette*, May 15, 1903, 3112.

5. See *Times*, Jan. 27, 1921, 13, on the marriage of his only daughter.

6. At age eleven he was at Stubbington House School, Crofton, Hampshire.

7. Canada census 1916, Census Place: Alberta, Macleod, 34, Roll: T-21952, Page: 2, Family No.: 27.

8. *London Gazette*, Jan. 15, 1915, 492; *Supplement to the London Gazette*, June 8, 1920, 6419; see also National Archives, WO 339/39840 Lieutenant John Claude Jardine Lonsdale, The Dorsetshire Regiment, 1915–1920.

9. Lonsdale's kinsman, C. J. Lonsdale, had a more predictable career: Radley College Officer Training Corps, Christ Church College, Oxford University BA (1931), on the executive of the Oxford Carleton Club (Conservative Party), and enlistment in the King's Rifles (1935). *Times*, Feb. 11, 1930, 8; Apr. 30, 1930, 11; July 22, 1931, 14; Oct. 16, 1931, 19;

Oct. 30, 1931, 6; Mar. 9, 1935, 23; May 24, 1938, 19; Nov. 26, 1943, 2. In 1938 he was living in Leicester. *The Radleian* 569 (Feb. 1938): 5.

10. *Daily Express*, Feb. 19, 1938, 5. Marilyn Miller was one of the most popular musical stars of the 1920s and early 1930s. Among his many tales, Lonsdale claimed to have fought a duel in France over some woman, possibly Miller.

11. "A soldier who wishes to leave the Army within three months of joining it has a right to purchase his discharge, but after three months, and after the country has spent a very large sum in making him efficient as a soldier, the case is different." HC Deb 17 Nov. 1920 vol. 134 cc2040. To be bought out could cost at least £35.

12. *Times*, Nov. 17, 1933, 20; Nov. 22, 1933, 9; Feb. 21, 1934, 9; *London Gazette*, Nov. 21, 1933, 7542; Feb. 20, 1934, 1158.

13. *Times*, Feb. 19, 1938, 17; *Daily Express*, Feb. 19, 1938, 2.

14. MEPO 3/902, Jan. 14, 1938, Cox and Kings Insurance Ltd to Burt.

15. *Yorkshire Post and Leeds Intelligencer*, June 17, 1936, 6.

16. *Swindon Advertiser and North Wilts Chronicle*, June 27, 1936, 5.

17. *Times*, June 17, 1936, 4; *Ottawa Journal*, July 4, 1936, 18.

18. I can find no evidence of such a company ever existing.

19. *Ottawa Journal*, July 4, 1936, 18.

20. The lesson was drawn that one had to be careful about what one said about the affairs of others. At the time the British newspaper press could not openly discuss the Prince of Wales's affair with Mrs. Wallis Simpson. Indeed, Ernest Aldrich Simpson, her second husband, sued a woman who said he was paid not to oppose Wallis's divorce suit. *Straight Times*, June 29, 1937, 18.

21. On the marriage arranged between Leslie Beuttler, only son of Lieutenant-Colonel V. O. Beuttler, and Pamela, daughter of late commander Blake of the Royal Navy and Lady Twysden, see the *Times*, Oct. 9, 1936, 17.

22. *Times*, May 1, 1936, 19.

23. *Swindon Advertiser and North Wilts Chronicle*, June 27, 1936, 5.

24. *Times*, June 27, 1936, 17; *Nottingham Evening Post*, June 27, 1936, 5. The following year, Ursula, the elder Blake daughter, married John Henry Spencer, only son of the late Commander H. Spencer, RN. *Times*, Jan. 11, 1937, 21.

25. Patrick Glenn Zander, *Right Modern: Technology, Nation, and Britain's Extreme Right in the Interwar Period* (London: Proquest, 2011), 273.

26. *Argus* (Melbourne), July 2, 1938, 10.

27. MEPO 3/902, Nov. 30, 1937, Rudolph Slavik to Procureur; MEPO 3/902, Dec. 24, 1937; MEPO 3/902, Jan. 8, 1938; MEPO 3/902, letter from Paris police (Feb. 8, 1938) describing the plight of Rudolph Slavik, barman.

28. MEPO 3/902, Dec. 28, 1937, Scotland Yard to Paris police; MEPO 3/902, Jan. 12, 1938, Letter and report of Paris police regarding Lonsdale and Élie Lévy; MEPO 3/902, Dec. 28, 1937, L'Inspecteur Général to The Commissioner of Police. MEPO 3/902, Jan. 8, 1938, CID to Chief Inspector, notes that the French had issued a warrant for Lonsdale's arrest on Dec. 10, 1937, for swindling a diamond ring worth 85,000 francs. The CID also stated there was no record of Souriat Chardanoff, née Chakoff, aged twenty-four, having been in Britain.

29. Élie Lévy escaped France with an unauthorized Salvadoran citizenship certificate, Jan. 11, 1944. Photo Archives, US Holocaust Memorial Museum, "Unauthorized Salvadoran citizenship certificate issued to Élie Lévy (b. January 29, 1890 in Paris), his wife Berti (née Hirsch) Lévy (b. March 15, 1903 in Cologne) and their children Gerard (b. June 16, 1929), Yvonne (b. September 22, 1931) and Eliane (b. November 15, 1937) by George Mandel-

Mantello, First Secretary of the Salvadoran Consulate in Switzerland and sent to their residence in Marseilles." Élie Lévy arrived in Switzerland on May 13, 1944, along with Berthe Lévy-Hirsch, Gerard, Yvonne, and Eliane. See http://collections.ushmm.org/search/catalog/pa1169122 (accessed Oct. 12, 2015).

30. *Daily Express*, Feb. 19, 1938, 3.

31. *Times*, Jan. 19, 1935, 8; see also www.ukwhoswho.com/view/article/oupww/whowaswho/U244542 (accessed Aug. 2, 2014).

32. See the *Times*, May 27, 1958, 10, on death, in Paris, Ontario, of Brigadier E. R. G. Wilmer.

33. *Sussex Agricultural Express*, July 22, 1910, 9.

34. On the death of Marjory Wilmer, see the *Times*, Jan. 4, 1947, 1.

35. *Evening Telegraph*, Dec. 15, 1938, 3.

36. *Cheltenham Chronicle*, May 11, 1935, 2; *Gloucestershire Echo*, Jan. 29, 1937, 6. The police made a point of Wilmer's status in labeling his file "Nephew of Lady Horsburgh-Porter."

37. *Times*, Apr. 30, 1935, 19.

38. She was living at 20 Victoria Grove when her husband died. *Times*, Feb. 8, 1940, 11; July 3, 1940, 1; May 23, 1942, 1; Mar. 30, 1951, 6.

39. On F. C. Wilmer awarded the Oundle school certificate and a cadetship at Sandhurst, see *Times*, Jan. 16, 1933, 8; Dec. 22, 1934, 4.

40. Born Oct. 1913 in Chelsea to Mrs. Wilmer, née Worsley. *England and Wales Birth Registration Index*, vol. 1A (1913): 704, line 90.

41. *Daily Express*, Feb. 19, 1938, 2.

42. Information provided by Elspeth Langsdale, Oundle School archivist; *Times*, Feb. 19, 1938, 17; Archivleiterin, Universitätsarchiv Heidelberg; Service immatriculation et mobilité, Université de Neuchâtel.

43. *News of the World*, Feb. 20, 1938, 13.

44. *Daily Express*, Feb. 19, 1938, 1.

45. *Times*, Feb. 19, 1938, 17.

46. *Daily Express*, Feb. 19, 1938, 3.

47. *Times*, Oct. 18, 1935, 1. Wilmer's parents were living at 20 Victoria Grove, W8.

48. *Evening Telegraph*, Mar. 18, 1938, 4; *Argus* (Melbourne), July 2, 1938, 10; *Times*, Nov. 2, 1939, 2.

49. MEPO 3/902, Dec. 22, 1937, Wilmer further Statement.

50. MEPO 3/902, Dec. 23, 1937, Newbury police to Scotland Yard; MEPO 3/902, Dec. 29, 1937, Newbury police to Scotland Yard.

51. *Daily Mail*, Feb. 19, 1938, 10.

52. *Daily Express*, Feb. 19, 1938, 3.

53. *Times*, Feb. 19, 1938, 17.

54. MEPO 3/902, Dec. 23, 1937, Hampshire Constabulary reports to Scotland Yard on Wilmer's scuffles.

55. Peter Martin Jenkins, *Mayfair Boy* (London: W. H. Allen, 1952).

56. "Great Marlborough Street Area," *Survey of London*, vols. 31–32: *St James Westminster*, part 2 (1963): 250–267. Jenkins's partner was Harold Cobb.

57. *Montreal Gazette*, Feb. 19, 1938, 12. His mother was Evelyn Jane Elder O'Brien.

58. Gerald Walter Jenkins, the eldest son, born at Harrow in 1910, worked as an accountant at Lester Parry and Company, also housed at 11 Great Marlborough Street. He married Clarrie Elizabeth, daughter of John William Motley, at St. Paul's Church, Portman Square, the Reverand J. Lowry Maxwell officiating. They lived at 18 Queensborough

Terrace, W2. *Times*, Mar. 7, 1949, 7; July 29, 1950, 6; MEPO 3/902, Dec. 23, 1937, Oxford police.

59. Information kindly provided by Angharad Meredith, Archivist, Harrow School.

60. *Times*, Feb. 8, 1935, 25. Walter Martin Jenkins died Dec.12, 1934.

61. After his father's death, Jenkins lived for a few months with Sir Ernest Graham-Little, a leading dermatologist and Independent MP representing the University of London. Jenkins, *Mayfair Boy*, 38.

62. *Daily Express*, Feb. 19, 1938, 5.

63. Jenkins, *Mayfair Boy*, 66. On pajamas worn by both men and women as evening attire, see Mary Louise Roberts, "Samson and Delilah Revisited: The Politics of Women's Fashion in 1920s France," *American Historical Review* 98, 3 (1993): 657–684.

64. Jenkins, *Mayfair Boy*, 53. And for a tabloid's assertion that Jenkins was the best looking and most "effeminate in manner" of the accused, see *News of the World*, Feb. 20, 1938, 13.

65. Jenkins, *Mayfair Boy*, 45.

66. Ibid., 57.

67. *Times*, Feb. 19, 1938, 17. A "life interest" refers to a person given an interest in a property and/or other assets for life or for a shorter period of time. When that interest ends, the interest "reverts" (passes) to other specified persons. Those other specified persons are said to have a "reversionary interest" in the property and/or other assets.

68. *Daily Express*, Feb. 19, 1938, 3.

69. An Eleanore Foster was born Nov. 3, 1909, in Lebanon, Pennsylvania. Passenger records show her sailing from New York City to San Diego in Nov. 1935; from San Francisco to New York City, July 14, 1936; from New York City to Southampton, May 31, 1937; from Le Havre to New York City, Oct. 14, 1937; and from Le Havre to New York City, Oct. 10, 1938. *New York Passenger and Crew Lists, 1925–1957*, https://familysearch.org/search/collection /results?count=20&query=%2Bgivenname%3Aeleanore~%20%2Bsurname%3Afoster~%20 %2Bgender%3AF&collection_id=1923888 (accessed Jan. 15, 2017).

70. *Daily Express*, Feb. 19, 1938, 1, 3. Journalist and biographer Ralph Hewins, who was a friend of Jenkins, wrote of his pursuit of an heiress. See *Daily Mail*, Feb. 19, 1938, 10.

71. *Daily Express*, Feb. 19, 1938, 2.

72. Ibid., 5

73. *News Chronicle*, Feb. 17, 1938, 1.

74. MEPO 3/902, Dec. 20, 1937, Description of Harley: "30–35, 5ft 10in hair brushed back brown, medium bld; dress, dark suit, light brown teddy bear overcoat (buff colour), no hat." Harley sometimes went as Michael Paul Robert Harley.

75. *Times*, Jan. 12, 1920, 15, Obituary of Colonel H. Kellett Harley, DSO, 7th Hussars, www.ukwhoswho.com/view/article/oupww/whowaswho/U197551 (accessed Aug. 20, 2014). His clubs were Whites and Cavalry. The family liked to believe they were descended from Robert Harley, Earl of Oxford, minister to Queen Anne.

76. Unfortunately, the same year he was declared insolvent due to bad investments.

77. *England and Wales Marriage Registration Index* 1A (1899): 1002, line 166; Divorce Court File: 9174, National Archives, *Records*, 1908, J77/961/9174.

78. England and Wales Marriage Registration Index, 1A (1910): 930 line 152.

79. Known also as Patrick Dennis, he died in 1980 in Westminster, London. *England and Wales Death Registration Index* 15 (1980): 2261 line 44.

80. The 1911 census shows one-year-old Peter Harley living with H. Kellett Harley.

81. He attended in 1935 the Bowring Toms dance, the St. Andrews Ball, and served as sub-warden of the Sherborne House Club for boys in Southwark. See *Times*, May 21, 1935, 19; Dec. 10, 1935, 19; June 13, 1938, 8.

82. *London Gazette*, June 9, 1949, 2826; June 12, 1958, 3535; Jan. 1, 1962, 45.

83. Jacintha Buddicom, *Eric and Us* (London: Frewin, 1974), 58.

84. Kevin Ingram, *Rebel: The Short Life of Esmond Romilly* (London: Weidenfeld & Nicolson, 1985).

85. Margaret Morley, *Larger Than Life: The Biography of Robert Morley* (London: Robson Books, 1979).

86. *Montreal Gazette*, Feb. 19, 1938, 12; *San Bernardino County Sun*, Feb. 20, 1938, 3.

87. James S. Kempling, "Birth of a Regiment, Princess Patricia's Canadian Light Infantry 1914–1919" (MA thesis, University of Victoria, 2011); MEPO 3/902, Jan. 12, 1938, Sergeant Tapsell to Chief Inspector, Information on Harley in Canada sought by cable from Officer in Charge of Records, Department of National Defense, Ottawa ("Defensor"); telegram from Ottawa, Canada, indicating that Harley served three years from October 1929 in the Princess Patricia's Light Infantry. He listed as next of kin his mother, Mrs. E. T. Harley of 18 Parkhurst Road, Bexhill, Sussex.

88. *Ottawa Citizen*, Mar. 1, 1938, 1; *Winnipeg Free Press*, Feb. 19, 1938, 2.

89. For a photo of Mrs. Robert Harley in court dress before her marriage, see *Daily Express*, Feb. 19, 1938, 5.

90. *Times*, Aug. 24, 1938, 13. Wheler served on the North West Frontier in 1917, was attached to the Indian Army between 1918 and 1920, and was recalled by the army in 1940. A game farmer between the wars, he served in the Kenya Police Reserve throughout the Mau Mau Emergency of 1953.

91. *New York Times*, July 27, 1936, 21. Michael Robert Harley arrived in New York City on the *Europa* in the summer of 1936 and returned to North America in the fall on the *Empress of Britain*. *New York Passenger and Crew Lists, 1925–1957*, https://familysearch.org/search/collection/results?count=20&query=%2Bgivenname%3A%22michael%20robert%22~%20%2Bsurname%3Aharley~%20%2Bgender%3AM&collection_id=1923888 (accessed Jan. 15, 2017).

92. *Times*, Jan. 22, 1937, 1. On the 1937 birth of Valerie P. Harley in Battle, Sussex, to a Mrs. Harley née Whightwick [*sic*], see *England and Wales Birth Registration Index*, vol. 2B (1937): 43 line 126.

93. *Portsmouth Evening News*, July 29, 1938, 9.

94. See photo of Robert Paul Harley dining out with a group of unidentified friends, circa 1935. *Daily Express*, Feb. 19, 1938, 1.

95. *Toronto Globe and Mail*, Feb. 19, 1938, 15.

96. *Evening Telegraph*, Feb. 19, 1938, 4.

97. *Winnipeg Tribune*, Dec. 23, 1937, 1; *Times*, Feb. 19, 1938, 17.

98. Sir William Traven Aitken was a Canadian-born British journalist and politician who wrote for the *Evening Standard* and was an MP for fourteen years, He was a nephew of Lord Beaverbrook (William Maxwell Aitken), owner of the *Evening Standard* and the *Daily Express*.

99. On the riots in Winnipeg, see Brian McKillop, "A Communist in City Hall," *Canadian Dimension*, April 1974, 43–46, and *Daily Mail*, Feb. 19, 1938, 10.

100. *Daily Express*, Feb. 19, 1938, 1.

101. Gerald Kersh, *Night and the City* (1938; reprint, New York: Simon & Schuster, 1946), 120.

102. *Daily Express*, Feb. 19, 1938, 3.

103. *Evening Telegraph*, Feb. 19, 1938, 4.

104. MEPO 3/902, Jan. 19, 1938, Miss Woolrich letter.

105. The case is reminiscent of the emergence of the concept of "affluenza." In December 2013, the lawyers of a wealthy sixteen-year-old who had killed four people in a Texas

drunk-driving accident successfully argued that his parents had indulged him to such a degree that he could not be held responsible for his actions. He purportedly suffered from "affluenza," an inability to appreciate the consequences of bad behavior. *New York Times*, Dec. 30, 2015, A3.

4: The Trial

1. James Agate, *Ego 3* (London: G. G. Harrup, 1938), 295.

2. *Chicago Tribune*, Feb. 18, 1938, 8.

3. *Daily Sketch*, Feb. 16, 1938, 11; *Ottawa Journal*, Mar. 8, 1938, 6.

4. *Times*, Jan. 28, 1938, 4.

5. *Times*, Feb. 10, 1938, 11.

6. In *R v Sussex Justices, Ex parte McCarthy* ([1924] 1 KB 256, [1923] All ER Rep 233).

7. George Buchanan McClure was prosecuting counsel to the Treasury, 1928–1942, and judge of the Mayor's and City of London Court, 1942–1953, and as such presided at Peter Martin Jenkins's 1945 trial.

8. Henry Elam, called to the Bar, Inner Temple, in 1927, served at the West Kent Quarter Sessions 1947–1953; Court of Quarter Sessions, Inner London, 1953–1976; and as a circuit judge, 1971–1976. He represented the Wolfe brothers in the complex 1933 Leopold Harris fire insurance fraud trial. See Angus McLaren, "Smoke and Mirrors: Willy Clarkson and the Role of Disguises in Interwar England," *Journal of Social History* 40, 3 (2007): 597–618.

9. *Daily Telegraph*, Feb. 16, 1938, 6, 7.

10. *Times*, Feb. 16, 1938, 18.

11. Ibid.; *Daily Telegraph*, Feb. 16, 1938, 6, 7.

12. *Daily Telegraph*, Feb. 16, 1938, 6, 7.

13. MEPO 3/902, Dec. 29, 1937, Statement of Frederick Cherrill.

14. Robert Jackson, *The Chief: The Biography of Gordon Hewart, Lord Chief Justice of England, 1922–40* (London: George G. Harrup, 1959), 319. The exchange is reminiscent of the role that gloves played in the 1995 O. J. Simpson trial in Los Angeles.

15. *Daily Express*, Feb. 17, 1938, 8, 9.

16. *Times*, Feb. 17, 1938, 9.

17. *Daily Telegraph and Morning Post*, Feb. 17, 1938, 6.

18. Ibid.; *Evening Standard*, Feb. 17, 1938, 13. For a photo of Toby Barry, see *Daily Mail*, Feb. 17, 1938, 7.

19. *Times*, Feb. 17, 1938, 9.

20. *Times*, Feb. 16, 1938, 18.

21. *Daily Telegraph and Morning Post*, Feb. 17, 1938, 6.

22. *Times*, Feb. 17, 1938, 9.

23. *Aberdeen Journal*, Feb. 17, 1938, 9.

24. *Daily Telegraph and Morning Post*, Feb. 17, 1938, 6.

25. *Times*, Feb. 17, 1938, 9.

26. Ibid.

27. H. Montgomery Hyde, *Norman Birkett: The Life of Lord Birkett of Ulverston* (London: Hamish Hamilton, 1964). William Arthur Fearnley-Whittingstall, QC 1949 and Recorder of Leicester from 1957 on, later represented the Soho pornographer Paul Raymond.

28. *Evening News*, Feb. 17, 1938, 9; *Times*, Feb. 18, 1938, 20.

29. A similarly orchestrated theft was described in George Dilnot, *Getting Rich Quick: An Outline of Swindles Old and New, with Some Account of the Manners and Customs of Confidence Men* (London: Geoffrey Bles, 1935), 174–176.

30. *Gloucestershire Echo*, Feb. 17, 1938, 1.

31. *Daily Express*, Feb. 18, 1938, 17.

32. *Hull Daily Mail*, Feb. 18, 1938, 1.

33. *Times*, Feb. 18, 1938, 20.

34. A. E. Bowker, *Behind the Bar* (London: Staples Press, 1951), 248.

35. *Times*, Feb. 18, 1938, 20.

36. *Daily Mail*, Feb. 18, 1938.

37. *Evening Standard*, Feb. 17, 1938, 1, 4, 12.

38. Fredman Ashe Lincoln later became Master of the Bench of the Inner Temple and chairman of the Association of Jewish ex–Service Men and Women. An active member of the Conservative Party, he encountered within it explicit anti-Semitic prejudices. His brother was the solicitor Ellis Lincoln. *Times*, Oct. 22, 1998, 29.

39. *Times*, Feb. 18, 1938, 20.

40. *Evening Standard*, Feb. 17, 1938, 1, 4, 12.

41. *Times*, Feb. 16, 1938, 18.

42. *Daily Express*, Feb. 18, 1938, 17. His full answer was that Lévy gave a ring to a man who gave it to a woman who sold two rings to Lonsdale, but he himself never dealt directly with Lévy.

43. Following the war, Christmas Humphreys led the prosecution in several famous criminal trials, including those of Ruth Ellis and Timothy Evans. His memoir, *Both Sides of the Circle: The Autobiography of Christmas Humphreys* (London: G. Allen & Unwin, 1978), mostly concerns his interest in Buddhism.

44. *Times*, Feb. 16, 1938, 18.

45. *Daily Worker*, Feb. 18, 1938, 3.

46. *Times*, Feb. 18, 1938, 20.

47. The authorities took precautions to keep Jenkins and Wilmer away from Harley.

48. *Times*, Feb. 19, 1938, 17; *Daily Express*, Feb. 19, 1938, 15.

49. *Times*, Feb. 19, 1938, 17.

50. Gerald Abrahams, *According to the Evidence: An Essay on Legal Proof* (London: Cassell, 1958), 159.

51. *Evening Telegraph*, Feb. 19, 1938, 4. Given Harley's admission that he had hidden rings, which he knew were stolen, the judge instructed him that he should plead guilty to receiving. On February 17, Harley did change his plea on receiving to guilty, which the jury formalized. *Times*, Feb. 18, 1938, 14; Jackson, *The Chief*, 319.

52. *Times*, Feb. 19, 1938, 17.

53. "Writer Fryniwyd Tennyson (Jesse) Harwood Writes to Her Friend GBH," Apr. 1, 1938, Huntington Digital Library, http://hdl.huntington.org/cdm/ref/collection/p15150coll7/id/5823 (accessed Sept. 16, 2015).

54. The enterprising were placing bets on the total number of years of imprisonment the judge would dole out. *Daily Mail*, Feb. 19, 1938, 6.

55. Lonsdale's argument was that all he did was discuss the idea of obtaining jewels by false pretenses or on credit; he did not conspire to rob. Mr. Justice Humphreys asked how Lonsdale could not be a conspirator when he suggested the hotel room be checked before the actual means of stealing were determined. Ashe Lincoln responded that there was a difference between stealing and false pretenses. Mr. Justice Charles conceded that the judge could have been clearer on this point, but there obviously was a conspiracy: it was inspired by Lonsdale's story, and his subsequent behavior incriminated him. *Times*, Feb. 26, 1938, 14; Mar. 23, 1938, 4; "Accessory before the Fact," *Journal of Criminal Law* 2 (1938): 219–221.

56. *Daily Express*, Feb. 19, 1938, 2.

57. *Daily Mail*, Feb. 19, 1938, 9.

58. *Daily Express*, Feb. 19, 1938, 1.

59. Ibid., 3.

60. "An Old Maidstonian" and "Prison Food," *Men Only*, May 1936, 48–51; *Sunday Graphic*, Feb. 20, 1938, 9; *News of the World*, Feb. 20, 1938, 13.

61. *Evening Telegraph*, Feb. 19, 1938, 4.

62. *Daily Express*, Feb. 19, 1938, 1.

63. *Hull Daily Mail*, Apr. 7, 1938, 13.

64. Hans Nadelhoffer, *Cartier* (London: Chronicle Books, 2007), 313. On Bellenger's fear that Britain did not recognize the danger posed by Germany, see his articles "A Frenchman's View of the Crisis," *Daily Mail*, Apr. 3, 1936, 14, and "I Say France Is Right," *Daily Mail*, Apr. 27, 1936, 12.

65. Jackson, *The Chief*, 321.

5: The Aftermath

1. Evelyn Waugh, *Decline and Fall* (1928; reprint, London: Everyman's Library, 1993), 161.

2. *Times*, July 8, 1939, 13. Even before his release, journalists were exploiting Lonsdale's notoriety. See the report in an Australian newspaper: "The first news John Christopher Mainwaring Lonsdale, one-time Mayfair 'man-about-town,' will hear when he comes out of prison shortly, will be the secret marriage of the girl to whom he was once engaged. She is attractive 25-year-old Miss Evelyn 'Moon' Wolsley, popular debutante of 1933, who has been married in Paris to M. de Garzuly, 45, member of the Budapest Foreign Office." *Newcastle Sun* (NSW), Apr. 27, 1939, 6.

3. *Aberdeen Journal*, July 8, 1939, 5. A year earlier he had penned "I Have Been a Fool: Confessions of John Christopher Mainwaring Lonsdale," *Empire News*, Feb. 20, 1938, 1; *Aberdeen Journal*, Feb. 19, 1938, 5.

4. On Nicholas Sidoroff, see *England and Wales Death Registration Index* 18 (1974): 1054 line 88.

5. *Times*, Sept. 12, 1938, 9.

6. *Ottawa Journal*, Oct. 8, 1938, 17.

7. Ibid.

8. Matthew Sweet, *West End Front: The Wartime Secrets of London's Grand Hotels* (London: Faber & Faber, 2011), 225–226.

9. *Ottawa Citizen*, July 22, 1939, 9.

10. Ibid., 229–230.

11. Pat O'Leary, "Stella Lonsdale aka Simone de Lavalliere aka Michael aka . . . ," www .conscript-heroes.com/Art08-Stella-Lonsdale-960.html (accessed Sept. 8, 2015).

12. Nigel West, *The Guy Liddell Diaries: Volume I: 1939–1942* (London: Routledge, 2005), 191. And see p. 199 regarding Lonsdale's sister, the actress Diana Vernon, being a good friend of Stella's.

13. One intelligence officer, while cloaking her identity, recalled she was "quite ravishing." J. M. Langley, *Fight Another Day* (London: Collins, 1974), 179.

14. Sweet, *West End Front*, 217–218.

15. West, *The Guy Liddell Diaries*, 203, 214.

16. Home Office: Defence Regulation 18B, Advisory Committee Papers. Detainees. LONSDALE, Stella Edith Howson. See also HO 45/25745, National Archives, London.

17. MEPO 3/902, Oct. 5, 1946, RMH forwarding of Fabian's report to Sir Frank Newsam at the Home Office.

18. A. W. Brian Simpson, *In the Highest Degree Odious: Detention without Trial in Wartime Britain* (Oxford: Clarendon, 1992), 217; Bradley W. Hart, *George Pitt-Rivers and the Nazis* (London: Bloomsbury, 2015), 168–171.

19. David Renton, "Rivers, George Henry Lane Fox Pitt- (1890–1966)," *Oxford Dictionary of National Biography* (Oxford: Oxford University Press, May 2005) www.oxforddnb.com /view/article/75512 (accessed Dec. 1, 2014). His eldest son, Michael Pitt-Rivers, gained notoriety in Britain in the 1950s when he was put on trial charged with buggery. His younger son, Julian Pitt-Rivers, a social anthropologist, attacked his father's racialist views.

20. Augustus Henry Lane Fox Pitt-Rivers, a father of modern archaeology, left part of his vast ethnology collection to Oxford, and the rest to his own private museum in Farnham, Dorset, where it was controlled by his eccentric grandson, George. Before dying in 1966, George willed his estate to Stella. Needing money to support herself and her lover, Raoul Maumen, "a conman from Marseille," Stella sold much of the collection to private buyers. She married Maumen, as French citizenship allowed her to export art pieces to France. See Nicholas Shakespeare, *Bruce Chatwin* (New York: Random House, 2010), 180–183.

21. On Walton's marriage, her presentation at court, and her London University BA in English, see *Times*, June 26, 1935, 19; June 27, 1935, 11; July 26, 1935, 20.

22. *Times*, Jan. 25, 1950, 8; *Edinburgh Gazette*, Jan. 27, 1950, 47; *London Gazette*, Jan. 24, 1950, 442.

23. *London Gazette*, Aug. 3, 1956, 4506.

24. Peter Jenkins, *Mayfair Boy* (London: W. H. Allen, 1952), 76.

25. Ibid., 83–90.

26. Jenkins wrote a friend that he was allowed to take German and shorthand classes but was afraid that on his release his friends would not rally round and that "I shall still have that abominable 'Mayfair Playboy' attached to my name as well." *Daily Mail*, Apr. 20, 1938, 9.

27. There were reports that Jenkins joined the army on his release but soon deserted. See *Milwaukee Sentinel*, Apr. 16, 1944, 21.

28. *Manchester Guardian*, Jan. 28, 1942, 6; MEPO 3/902, Oct. 5, 1946.

29. *Times*, Oct. 30, 1941, 2; Mar. 13, 1942, 2; *Toronto Globe and Mail*, Nov. 1, 1941, 7; Ina Zweiniger-Bargielowska, *Austerity in Britain: Rationing, Controls, and Consumption, 1939–1955* (Oxford: Oxford University Press, 2000), 185–189; Jenkins, *Mayfair Boy*, 111–113.

30. "Admiral Sir Francis Murray Austin, *Born* 1881; *m* Marjorie Jean Stewart, *d* of late Maj.-Gen. J. Stewart S. Barker, RA, CB; two *s*; *died* 19 June 1953. Served European War, 1914–19; Rear-Admiral in Charge and Admiral Superintendent, HM Dockyard, Gibraltar, 1932–35; Vice-Adm. and retired list, 1936. Club: United Service. Address: 8 Cardinal Mansions, Carlisle Palace, SW1." See www.ukwhoswho.com/view/article/oupww/whowaswho /U234247 (accessed Aug. 2, 2014). See also *Times*, Jun 22, 1953, 8.

31. *Times*, June 7, 1945, 2. The *Times* always referred to "Mrs Gillian Austin." Popular papers called her "Mrs Jill Austin."

32. Jenkins, *Mayfair Boy*, 132–133.

33. Curtis-Bennett made a specialty of taking on difficult cases. In 1945 he defended both Jenkins and the traitor William Joyce (Lord Haw-Haw); in 1950, atomic spy Klaus Fuchs; and in 1953, serial killer John Christie. *Times*, July 24, 1956, 8. He was the son of Sir Henry Curtis-Bennett, who defended Edith Thompson.

34. *Daily Mail*, June 2, 1945, 12.

35. *Times*, June 7, 1945, 2.

36. Jenkins, *Mayfair Boy*, 142.

37. MEPO 3/902, Oct. 5, 1946.

38. Jenkins, *Mayfair Boy*, 156.

39. Ibid., 159.

40. *Times*, Sept. 14, 1948, 2; Oct. 16, 1948, 3; *Daily Mail*, Oct. 16, 1948, 3.

41. Jenkins, *Mayfair Boy*, 176. For the account of an Australian convict who knew Jenkins when he was "doing bird" (in Cockney rhyming slang "doing bird" means "doing bird lime" or "time"), see Margaret Wentworth, *Hellbent: Ces Waters and Me: A Tale of Trust and Treachery* (Chippendale, NSW: Kerr, 1998).

42. *Daily Mail*, Nov. 20, 1952, 3. Asserting that a Sunday newspaper was hounding him, in 1952 Jenkins changed his name by deed poll to "Peter Trowbridge." Here he will continue to be referred to by his birth name. *Manchester Guardian*, Apr. 15, 1955, 9.

43. *Daily Mail*, Aug. 21, 1959, 7.

44. *Daily Mail*, Oct. 17, 1959, 7. A Peter M. Jenkins, age forty-nine, died September 1965, in Chelsea; *England and Wales Death Registration Index* 5A (1965): 614 line 131.

45. *Examiner* (Launceston, Tasmania), Oct. 29, 1938, 25.

46. *People*, July 2, 1939, 17.

47. *Daily Mail*, Feb. 21, 1938, 12.

48. MEPO 3/902, Jan. 6 1938. On Blacker-Douglas's social life, see *Times*, July 20, 1933, 15; July 25, 1933, 17; Sept. 27, 1933, 13; Mar. 1, 1938, 19; June 2, 1939, 7. On the death of his father in France on Dec. 13, 1943, see *Times*, Apr. 4, 1944, 1. On his marriage, see *Times*, May 24, 1948, 1.

49. Timothy Travers, *How the War Was Won: Command and Technology in the British Army on the Western Front, 1917–1918* (New York: Routledge, 1992), 6.

50. *Times*, July 2, 1934, 19; Mar. 28, 1934, 17. On her marriage, see *Times*, Jan. 11, 1939, 13.

51. Since she was still a minor the appeal was formally made by Hilary's guardian. Divorce Court File: 3840 (Appellant: Hilary Inez Elizabeth Wilmer; Respondent: David Wilmer), Records of the Supreme Court of Judicature and Related Courts, National Archives.

52. *Evening Telegraph*, Mar. 18, 1938, 4; *Times*, Mar. 19, 1938, 4; *Daily Mail*, Mar. 19, 1938, 5.

53. Cavendish Morton's photographic portrait of Patrick Gamble as a child is in the National Portrait Gallery.

54. MEPO 3/902, Dec. 22, 1937, David Wilmer further statement.

55. *Times*, Aug. 3, 1918, 9. Henry Reginald Gamble was for fourteen years vicar of Holy Trinity, Sloane Street (which had a large influential West End congregation), in 1916 Canon of Westminster, and in 1918 Dean of Exeter.

56. *Daily Mail*, Oct. 29, 1935, 16.

57. *Times*, Oct. 29, 1935, 5. Marter and Lady Mercy married in 1936.

58. "Romance in the Clink; or, What's to Become of London's Playboy Raffles?" *American Weekly*, Apr. 16, 1944, 5.

59. MEPO 3/902, Oct. 5, 1946, RMH writes Sir Frank Newsam at the Home Office.

60. "Captain Paul Phillimore, son of the Rev. Arthur Phillimore, was married on Wednesday to Miss Augusta Tredcroft, daughter of Colonel and the Hon. Mrs Tredcroft, of Glen Ancrum, Guildford." *Tablet*, Apr. 14, 1917, 12.

61. *Times*, Mar. 11, 1936, 19; May 4, 1936, 21; May 28, 1936, 19; May 7, 1937, 11.

62. "BEAUMONT, Baroness, 11th in line *cr* 1309. Mona Josephine Tempest Fitzalan-Howard; née Stapleton. *Born* Broughton Hall, Skipton, 1 Aug. 1894; *e d* of 10th Baron and late Ethel Mary, *d* of Sir Charles H. Tempest, 1st and last Bt of Heaton; *m* 1914, 3rd Baron

Howard of Glossop; four *s* four *d*. Roman Catholic; *died* 31 Aug. 1971." *Who Was Who*, www
.ukwhoswho.com/view/article/oupww/whowaswho/U152156 (accessed Sept. 17, 2015).

63. *Daily Mail*, Nov. 13, 1937, 11; *Times*, Nov. 12, 1937, 19.

64. *New York Post*, Mar. 3, 1939, 19; for the subsequent engagement of Richard Michael
Allye Clifton, son of John Talbot de Vere Clifton of Lytham Hall, Lytham St. Annes and
Annamary Corbet-Burcher, owners of purportedly the finest Georgian house in Lan-
cashire, see *Times*, Aug. 4, 1943, 7.

65. *Times*, Feb. 9, 1939, 17; Mar. 1, 1939, 19; *Daily Mail*, Mar. 7, 1939, picture gallery.

66. *Daily Mail*, Apr. 16, 1940, 7.

67. During the Dunkirk evacuation a Gilbert Eric Graham Cockburn of the Royal Irish
Fusiliers was reported as missing. It was later established that he was killed in action. *Times*,
July 23, 1940, 1. It is easy to confuse him with Pamela's husband, Gilbert Alastair William
Graham Cockburn. On the latter's involvement in a long-running libel action, see *Times*,
Apr. 12, 1956, 14; May 2, 1956, 1; and *Daily Mail*, June 22, 1957, 5.

68. *London Gazette*, July 21, 1944, 34427; Jan. 10, 1947, 245.

69. *England and Wales Marriage Registration Index* 1A (1945): 659, lines 78, 89, 99.

70. *Daily Mail*, Feb. 19, 1938, 9.

71. A Parisian paper quoted the *Star*'s account of Harley's punishment: "Harley a subi
son châtiment virilement. Toute la prison l'admire pour son courage." *Le Populaire*, Mar. 3,
1938, 5.

72. Frances H. Simon, *Prisoners' Work and Vocational Training* (London: Routledge,
2005), 5–6.

73. *Times*, May 15, 1940, 3; *Daily Mail*, May 15, 1940, 8; *Evening Telegraph*, May 15,
1940, 5.

74. *Daily Mail*, Feb. 22, 1938, 9; see also *Hull Daily Mail*, Feb. 21, 1938, 1, and *Gloucestershire Echo*, Feb. 21, 1938, 1.

75. See, e.g., *Milwaukee Sentinel*, Apr. 16, 1944, 21; *American Weekly*, Apr. 16, 1944, 5; *San
Antonio Light*, Apr. 16, 1944, 41; *World's News* (Sydney), July 22, 1944, 4.

76. The *Electoral Register* in 1946 had a Robert Paul Harley and a Dorothy E. Harley
living in Kensington at 9b Penywern Road, SW5; in 1948, at 35 Philbeach Gardens,
SW5.

77. MEPO 3/902, Oct. 5, 1946.

78. George Orwell, "Raffles and Miss Blandish" (which first appeared in *Tribune*,
Aug. 25, 1944), in *The Collected Essays* (London: Secker & Warburg, 1968), 3:214.

Part II. The Context

1. *King's Counsellor: Abdication and War: The Diaries of Tommy Lascelles*, ed. Duff Hart-
Davis (London: Weidenfeld & Nicolson, 2006), 110. Lascelles, who served Edward from
1920 to 1928, wrote up this summary in 1943.

6: Pain

1. H. Montgomery Hyde, *Norman Birkett: The Life of Lord Birkett of Ulverston* (London:
Hamish Hamilton, 1964), 466.

2. *Mail* (Adelaide), Feb. 19, 1938, 3.

3. *San Bernardino County Sun*, Feb. 20, 1938, 3.

4. For the legal community's noting that corporal punishment was "brought into prominence recently by the flogging of the 'Mayfair men,'" see *Solicitor: A Journal for Solicitors
and Their Managing Clerks* 5 (1938): 74.

5. On life in the Scrubs, see H. W. Wicks, *The Prisoner Speaks* (London: Jarrolds, 1938), and Richard Griffiths, "Anti-Semitic Obsessions: The Case of H. W. Wicks," *Patterns of Prejudice* 48, 1 (2014): 94–113.

6. *Times*, Feb. 28, 1938, 11; *Daily Mail*, Feb. 28, 1938, 13.

7. *Evening Telegraph*, Mar. 1, 1938, 1.

8. *Times*, Feb. 25, 1938, 9.

9. *Times*, Mar. 4,1938, 7.

10. *Montreal Gazette*, Mar. 2, 1938, 1; *Glasgow Herald*, Mar. 2, 1938, 7.

11. *Dundee Courier*, Mar. 2, 1938, 7.

12. The IP story appeared in American papers such as the *Bluefield* (WV) *Daily Telegraph*, Mar. 2, 1938, 1; *Ogden* (UT) *Standard-Examiner*, Mar. 1, 1938, 3; and *Altoona* (PA) *Tribune*, Mar. 2, 1938, 1.

13. *Le Populaire*, Mar. 3, 1938, 5.

14. *Times*, June 21, 1932, 5; Jan. 25, 1935, 6; Feb. 16, 1937, 13.

15. *Report of the Departmental Committee on Corporal Punishment*, Cmd. 5684 (London: HMSO, 1938), 52–54. In 343 cases between 1925 and 1934, 9 floggings were halted and 4 men needed to be hospitalized.

16. As the Home Office would not allow the taking of a new photograph of the triangle, the paper used an old one by Philippe Millet from *L'Illustration*. See *Sunday Pictorial*, Feb. 20, 1938, 3. For a 1926 first-person account of a Canadian lashing, see Jack Black, *You Can't Win* (Blacksburg, VA: Wilder Publications, 2010), 171–175.

17. *San Bernardino County Sun*, Feb. 20, 1938, 3.

18. *Times*, Feb. 4, 1930, 11; Feb. 6, 1930, 15. His inquest jury returned a verdict of "temporary insanity," insisting that Spiers's objection was not to flogging but to his long sentence.

19. *Times*, Nov. 30, 1934, 4.

20. *Times*, Dec. 7, 1934, 7; Dec. 12, 1934, 7.

21. *Toronto Globe and Mail*, Mar. 2, 1938, 13; Mar. 14, 1938, 15.

22. *Kingston Gleaner* (Jamaica), Mar. 25, 1938, 35.

23. *Times*, Feb. 16, 1938, 18.

24. On the end of flogging in the British navy in 1881, see Isaac Land, "Customs of the Sea: Flogging, Empire, and the 'True British Seaman' 1770 to 1870," *Interventions: International Journal of Postcolonial Studies* 3, 2 (2001): 169–185.

25. Michel Foucault, *Discipline and Punish: The Birth of the Prison*, trans. Alan Sheridan (New York: Vintage Books, 1995).

26. Youths continued to be birched, but here we restrict our discussion solely to the punishment of adults. But see Cyril Burt, *The Young Delinquent* (London: University of London Press, 1925); S. F. Hatton, *London's Bad Boys* (London: Chapman & Hall, 1931), Geoffrey Pearson, *Hooligan: A History of Respectable Fears* (London: Macmillan, 1983), 261n92; Stephen Humphries, *Hooligans or Rebels: An Oral History of Working-Class Childhood and Youth, 1889–1939* (Oxford: Basil Blackwell, 1981), 220–223.

27. Lucy Bland, *Banishing the Beast: English Feminism and Sexual Morality, 1885–1914* (London: Penguin, 1995), 298.

28. McLaren, *The Trials of Masculinity*, 13–36; Raymond L. Gard, *The End of the Rod: A History of the Abolition of Corporal Punishment in the Courts of England and Wales* (Boca Raton, FL: Brown Walker Press, 2009).

29. In a satiric novel a Scot notes: "If you assault a man in England and bash his teeth down his throat and kick him in the stomach, that's just playfulness and you'll get fourteen days in the jug. But if you lay a finger on him and pinch his watch at the same time, that's

robbery with violence, and you'll probably get eighteen strokes with the 'cat' and about three years in Dartmoor." A. G. MacDonell, *England, Their England* (London: Macmillan, 1933), 11–12.

30. A. Crocker and S. Pete, "Letting Go of the Lash: The Extraordinary Tenacity and Prolonged Decline of Judicial Corporal Punishment in Britain and Its Former Colonies in Africa: Part 1," *Obiter* 28, 2 (2007): 272.

31. *Report of the Departmental Committee on Corporal Punishment*, 130. Robbery with violence dropped from an annual average of 199 (1898–1903) to 73 (1931–1935), but the percentage of those found guilty of the crime who were flogged rose from 11.2 to 44.4 percent.

32. For the argument that the committee played down the extent of corporal punishment since it wanted to end it, see Gard, *The End of the Rod*, 102.

33. Mr. Justice Roche repeated the story that the lash put an end to garroting in Liverpool. *Times*, Feb. 8, 1930, 7.

34. *Report of the Departmental Committee on Corporal Punishment*, 84–85.

35. J. V. McAree "Official Report Condemns Flogging," *Toronto Globe and Mail*, Apr. 22, 1938, 6.

36. *Report of the Departmental Committee on Corporal Punishment*, 74.

37. Ibid., 57; see also E. Lewis-Faning, "Statistics Relating to the Deterrent Element in Flogging," *Journal of the Royal Statistical Society* 102, 4 (1939): 565–578.

38. *Evening Telegraph*, Mar. 18, 1938, 3.

39. *Spectator*, Mar. 25, 1938, 3.

40. *Spectator*, Feb. 25, 1938, 18.

41. Ian Gibson, *The English Vice: Beating, Sex and Shame in Victorian England and After* (London: Duckworth, 1978), 181.

42. Cicely M. Craven, "Flogging: The Last Chapter But One," *Howard Journal* 5, 2 (1938): 102–107.

43. George Benson and Edward Glover, *Corporal Punishment on Indictment* (London: Howard League for Penal Reform, 1931); George Benson, *Flogging: The Law and Practice in England* (London: Howard League for Penal Reform, 1931) and *Flogging: The Law and Practice in England*, rev. ed. (London: Howard League for Penal Reform, 1937). On his earlier Corporal Punishment Abolition Bill, see *Times*, Feb. 12, 1930, 8.

44. HC Deb 16 Nov. 1938, vol. 341, cc964.

45. The Cadogan committee found that Canada stood out with an average of 130 floggings a year (1932–1936). *Report of the Departmental Committee on Corporal Punishment*, 150.

46. E. Roy Calvert and Theodora Calvert, *The Lawbreakers* (London: Routledge, 1933); *New Statesman and Nation*, Feb. 26, 1938, 319.

47. *Spectator*, Mar. 11, 1938, 431.

48. HC Deb 7 Apr. 1936 vol. 310 cc2611; see also Linda Mahood, "'Give him a Doing': The Birching of Young Offenders in Scotland," *Canadian Journal of History* 37, 3 (2002): 439–457.

49. *Maxims for Revolutionists* is an appendix to Shaw's play *Man and Superman* (1903) and is supposedly a revolutionary manual written by John Tanner, the play's main character.

50. Gibson, *The English Vice*.

51. Henry S. Salt, *The Flogging Craze: A Statement of the Case against Corporal Punishment* (London: George Allen, 1916), 80.

52. Ibid.

53. George Bernard Shaw, *Misalliance*, in *Collected Works* (London: Constable, 1930), 13:56.

54. *Ogden Standard-Examiner,* Mar. 1, 1938, 3; see also Lisa Z. Sigel, *Making Modern Love: Sexual Narratives and Identities in Interwar Britain* (Philadelphia: Temple University Press, 2012), 166–169.

55. C. Gordon Clunn to the *New Statesman and Nation,* Feb. 26, 1938, 323–324.

56. *New Statesman and Nation,* Mar. 5, 1938, 361.

57. *Report of the Departmental Committee on Corporal Punishment,* 110.

58. *Times,* Nov. 30, 1938, 7.

59. *Times,* Nov. 6, 1931, 10.

60. *Times,* Dec. 16, 1930, 16.

61. *Times,* Mar. 4, 1932, 11.

62. *Times,* July 1, 1932, 9.

63. *Times,* Nov. 30, 1938, 7. Moore was an admirer of another animal lover, Adolf Hitler. See Moore's article "The Blackshirts Have What the Conservatives Need," *Daily Mail,* Apr. 25, 1934, 2.

64. *Report of the Departmental Committee on Corporal Punishment,* 91–92.

65. HC Deb 1 Dec. 1938 vol. 342 cc694.

66. *Dundee Courier,* Feb. 19, 1938, 6.

67. *Times,* Jan. 3, 1939, 7.

68. *Times,* Jan. 10, 1939, 17. In 1881 Parliament ended flogging in the army, but it was only suspended in the navy. Clive Emsley, *Soldier, Sailor, Beggarman, Thief: Crime and the British Armed Services since 1914* (Oxford: Oxford University Press, 2013), 20.

69. *Spectator,* Jan. 6, 1939, 7.

70. *Spectator,* Mar. 4, 1938, 366.

71. F. Mead, "Corporal Punishment," *National Review,* Sept. 1938, 359.

72. *Sunday Times* (Perth, WA), Apr. 17, 1938, 1.

73. *Spectator,* Mar. 4, 1938, 366.

74. Robert Armstrong-Jones, "Corporal Punishment," *Nineteenth Century,* Aug. 1938, 215. Robert Fabian would continue this tradition of belittling psychological interpretations. "They seem to think these days that because your nanny patted your bottom when you were two, it entitles you to run a razor over someone's face when you are 22." *Daily Mail,* Oct. 29, 1962, 6.

75. F. Mead, " Corporal Punishment," *National Review,* Sept. 1938, 355–360.

76. The article first appeared in the *Daily Telegraph and Morning Post,* Mar. 8, 1938, 15, and was reprinted in the *Kingston Gleaner* (Jamaica), Mar. 25, 1938, 35.

77. *Evening Post,* Aug. 5, 1939, 7.

78. It was a given that liberals opposed the lash. Malcolm Muggeridge recalled, as a neophyte, asking a *Manchester Guardian* colleague: "What's our 'line' on corporal punishment? The journalist replied: 'The same as capital, only more so.'" Malcolm Muggeridge, "The Great Liberal Death Wish," *Imprimis, the Monthly Journal of Hillsdale College* 8, 5 (May 1979).

79. *Evening Telegraph,* Mar. 18, 1938, 3.

80. *New Statesman and Nation,* Mar. 5, 1938, 361.

81. *Times,* Mar. 18, 1938: 17.

82. *Spectator,* Mar. 4, 1938, 347; see also "The Press and the 'Cat,'" *New Statesman and Nation,* Mar. 5, 1938, 364, and J. D. A., "The Case against Flogging," *Spectator,* Feb. 25, 1938, 314–315.

83. *Spectator,* Mar. 18, 1938, 471–472. On the elite's distaste for the sensationalism of the popular press, see D. L. LeMahieu, *A Culture for Democracy: Mass Communication and the*

Cultivated Mind in Britain between the Wars (Oxford: Oxford University Press, 1988), 110–112.

84. Only men were involved in such contests. The whipping of women had been ended in 1820 (1 Geo. 4, c. 57).

85. Gard, *The End of the Rod*, 105.

86. HC Deb 1 Dec. 1938 vol. 342 cc672.

87. Ibid., cc694.

88. *Times*, Mar. 12, 1946, 5.

89. HC Deb 15 July 1948 vol. 453 cc1560.

90. *Evening News*, July 23, 1948; *Daily Mail*, July 24, 1948, 3.

91. See 11 & 12 Geo. 6, c. 58.

92. Gibson, *The English Vice*, 182.

93. Though appointed by the Labour government, Lord Goddard, the Lord Chief Justice, espoused the line that in the absence of flogging, gangsterism and violence flourished. He was a peculiar man, and it has been claimed that "[i]t was the task of the Lord Chief Justice's clerk, Arthur Harris, to take a spare pair of the standard striped trousers to court on sentencing days. When condemning a youth to be flogged or hanged, Goddard always ejaculated." *Penguin Encyclopaedia of Crime* (London: Penguin, 1996), 574.

94. *Times*, Mar. 10, 1950, 8.

95. *Manchester Guardian*, Mar. 18, 1950, 6.

96. Robert Fabian, "Only the 'CAT' Holds Back the Brutes," *Empire News*, July 11, 1954, 6. In addressing the Anti-Violence League, Fabian indulged in the most violent fantasies. "Today a criminal can grind his heel in your face, slash you across the face, wipe a bicycle chain around your neck or wipe a sleeve lined with fishhooks down your face, and you must not lay a hand on him." *Sunday Times*, July 16, 1961, 4.

97. According to some accounts the men were not as repentant as Fabian claimed. "One of the Mayfair men became popular at parties where he took off his shirt to show the scars which would be there for life." Alan Jenkins, *The Thirties* (London: Stein & Day, 1976), 168.

98. Paul Lawrence, "Fabian, Robert Honey (1901–1978)," *Oxford Dictionary of National Biography* (Oxford: Oxford University Press, Sept. 2010), www.oxforddnb.com/view/article /77433 (accessed Nov. 24, 2014).

99. Grassroots Conservatives were so preoccupied by fears of hooligans and the need to give blackguards "a taste of their own medicine" that in 1960, despite government reluctance, a report was prepared for Rab Butler of the Home Office on the possible reintroduction of corporal punishment. Of the 3,500 letters the Advisory Council received, 77 percent were for flogging and 17 percent against. Nevertheless, the council concluded that the Cadogan committee was correct in finding such punishments ineffective, and the case was closed. *Corporal Punishment: Report to the Advisory Council on the Treatment of Offenders* (London: HMSO, 1960).

7: Masculinity

1. See, e.g., Lesley Hall, ed., *Outspoken Women: An Anthology of Women's Writing on Sex, 1870–1969* (London: Routledge, 2005).

2. *OED* Online, www.oed.com /view/Entry/145481?rskey=OOD6xZ&result=1 (accessed Aug. 29, 2015).

3. John Millington Synge, *The Playboy of the Western World* (New York: Mercier Press, 1990), 22, 40. For the observation that "[w]e have almost entirely lost the literature of roguery, the life of which has been prolonged in Ireland by the tradition of disrespect for foreign

law," see V. S. Pritchett, "The End of Gael," *The Complete Essays* (London: Chatto & Windus, 1991), 121.

4. David M. Kiely, *John Millington Synge: A Biography* (Dublin: Gill & Macmillan, 1994), 165.

5. *Playboy: A Portfolio of Art and Satire* 1 (1919): 5.

6. D. H. Lawrence to John Middleton Murry, Sept. 17, 1923, in *The Letters of D. H. Lawrence* (Cambridge: Cambridge University Press, 2002), 500. The *Times* referred to Irish Republicans' dream of a united Ireland as "playboyism." *Times*, Aug. 5, 1924, 11.

7. Mazo de la Roche, *Whiteoak Harvest* (Boston: Little, Brown, 1936), 160.

8. *Times*, Jan. 7, 1933, 9; Oct. 7, 1933, 13; *Daily Mail*, Nov. 3, 1928, 10.

9. Temple Bailey, "Playboy," *Good Housekeeping* 105 (Dec. 1935): 44–46, 197–203; Richard Connell, *Playboy* (New York: Putnam's, 1936).

10. Franklin D. Roosevelt, "On the Progress of the War," *Fireside Chat 20*, Feb. 23, 1942, www.presidency.ucsb.edu/ws/index.php?pid=16224 (accessed Jan. 17, 2017).

11. A batch of letters written by the Prince of Wales to his mistress Freda Dudley Ward revealed, according to the *New York Times*, "a man alarmingly spoiled, relentlessly misogynistic, caustically racist, and determined to avoid his ordained role in life at all costs." *New York Times*, June 8, 2003, 9.7.

12. "Mrs S.," wrote one courtier, "was no isolated phenomenon, but merely the current figure in an arithmetical progression that had been robustly maintained for nearly twenty years." Alan Lascelles, *King's Counsellor: Abdication and War: The Diaries of Tommy Lascelles*, ed. Duff Hart-Davis (London: Weidenfeld & Nicolson, 2006), 113; Philip Ziegler, *King Edward VIII: The Official Biography* (London: Collins, 1990), 150.

13. *New York Times*, May 24, 1931, SM 2; Apr. 28, 1935, BR3; *Washington Post*, Jan. 21, 1936, 1. His brother, Prince George, Duke of Kent, a bisexual playboy who died in a 1942 plane crash, had been targeted by extortionists. See Angus McLaren, *Sexual Blackmail: A Modern History* (Chicago: University of Chicago Press, 2002), 121.

14. Leonore Davidoff and Belinda Westover, "'From Queen Victoria to the Jazz Age': Women's World in England, 1880–1939," in *Our Work, Our Lives, Our Words: Women's History and Women's Work*, ed. Leonore Davidoff and Belinda Westover (London: Macmillan, 1986), 28.

15. Simon Szreter and Kate Fisher, *Sex before the Sexual Revolution: Intimate Life in England, 1918–1963* (Cambridge: Cambridge University Press, 2010), 328; Lesley Hall, ed., *Outspoken Women: An Anthology of Women's Writing on Sex, 1870–1969* (London: Routledge, 2005), 101–102.

16. McLaren, *Twentieth-Century Sexuality*, 51–52.

17. Bourne challenged the law against abortion by notifying the authorities that he had terminated the pregnancy of a fourteen-year-old girl whom a group of soldiers had gang-raped. Barbara Brookes and Paul Roth, "*Rex v. Bourne* and the Medicalization of Abortion," in *Legal Medicine in History*, ed. Michael Clark and Catherine Crawford (Cambridge: Cambridge University Press, 1992), 314–343.

18. The censorious were particularly appalled at the idea of women drinking to excess. A judge described the tipsy victim of one robbery as "loathsome," while the reviewer of the comedy *Kicking the Moon Around* wrote that the otherwise excellent film had one flaw: "The scene showing Pepper coming in drunk is an unfortunate episode, as it will certainly prove distasteful to some." *Daily Mail*, July 6, 1939, 5; *Monthly Film Bulletin*, Jan. 31, 1938, 66.

19. Adrian Bingham, *Gender, Modernity, and the Popular Press in Interwar Britain* (Oxford: Clarendon, 2004); Lucy Bland, *Modern Women on Trial: Sexual Transgression in the Age of the Flapper* (Manchester: Manchester University Press), 106–107.

20. On the argument that the history of masculinity focuses on such desires, see Graham Dawson, "The Blond Bedouin: Lawrence of Arabia, Imperial Adventure and the Imagining of English-British Masculinity," in *Manful Assertions: Masculinities in Britain since 1800*, ed. Michael Roper and John Tosh (London: Routledge, 1991), 118–119.

21. M. Collins, "The Fall of the English Gentleman: The National Character in Decline, c. 1918–1970," *Historical Research* 75 (2002): 93. The architect Edwin Luytens referred to the "masculine repose" of his chimneys. See Gabriel Koureas, *Memory, Masculinity and National Identity in British Visual Culture, 1914–1930* (Aldershot: Ashgate, 2007), 42.

22. Christine Grandy, *Heroes and Happy Endings: Class, Gender, and Nation in Popular Film and Fiction in Interwar Britain* (Manchester: Manchester University Press, 2014).

23. Ina Zweiniger-Bargielowska, "Building a British Superman: Physical Culture in Interwar Britain," *Journal of Contemporary History* 41 (2006): 595–610, 600–601.

24. Praseeda Gopinath, *Scarecrows of Chivalry: English Masculinities after Empire* (Charlottesville: University Press of Virginia, 2013).

25. For newspapers' assertion that the modern woman's brother was anemic, weary, feminine, bloodless, and "an exquisite without masculinity," see D. J. Taylor, *Bright Young People: The Rise and Fall of a Generation, 1918–1940* (London: Chatto & Windus, 2007), 53.

26. On the important point that "[w]hat is fascinating, if perhaps frustratingly ambiguous, is that the promotion of and resistance to romantic ideals in popular culture occurred simultaneously," see Stephen Brooke "'A Certain Amount of Mush': Love, Romance, Celluloid and Wax in the Mid-Twentieth Century," in *Love and Romance in Britain, 1918–1970*, ed. Alana Harris and Timothy Willem Jones (New York: Palgrave Macmillan, 2015), 84.

27. Laura King, *Family Men: Fatherhood and Masculinity in Britain, 1914–1960* (New York: Oxford University Press, 2015); Alison Light, *Forever England: Femininity, Literature and Conservatism between the Wars* (London: Routledge, 1991).

28. The American male consumer became fully formed during the economic boom of the 1920s and was an established figure by 1933, when *Esquire* magazine was launched. See Anna Gough-Yates and Bill Osgerby, eds., *Action TV: Tough-Guys, Smooth Operators and Foxy Chicks* (London: Routledge, 2001).

29. For Barbara Ehrenreich the traditional middle-class masculine breadwinner's ethos of thrift and family-based respectability gave way in 1950s America to the new Playboy ethics, which was more in step with the demands of an economy increasingly based on commodity consumption. Barbara Ehrenreich, *The Hearts of Men: American Dreams and the Flight from Commitment* (Garden City, NY: Anchor, 1983), 170–171.

30. Frank Mort, *Capital Affairs: London and the Making of the Permissive Society* (New Haven: Yale University Press, 2010).

31. Bill Osgerby, *Playboys in Paradise: Masculinity, Youth and Leisure-style in Modern America* (New York: Berg, 2001). It is worthy of note that in 1936, Hutton of Northampton advertised his newly designed crepe sole footwear as "Playboy shoes."

32. Bill Osgerby, "A Pedigree of the Consuming Male: Masculinity, Consumption and the American 'Leisure Class,'" *Sociological Review* 51, 1 (2003): 65. See also Tom Pendergast, *Creating the Modern Man: American Magazines and Consumer Culture, 1900–1950* (Columbia: University of Missouri Press, 2000).

33. Martin Green, *Children of the Sun: A Narrative of "Decadence" in England after 1918* (New York: Basic, 1976).

34. Osbert Sitwell, *Great Morning* (London: Macmillan, 1948); see also *Punch*, May 25, 1938, 580–581. Thomas Burke listed Swell, Johnny, Masher, Blood, K'nut, and Gigolo. *Daily Mail*, Apr. 6, 1934, 10. One might add boulevardier, exquisite, lady-killer, lounge lizard, and man-about-town.

35. See Daniel Statt, "The Case of the Mohocks: Rake Violence in Augustan London," *Social History* 20, 2 (1995): 179–199; Peter McNeil, "Macaroni Masculinities," *Fashion Theory*, 4, 4 (2000), 373–403.

36. Jenkins, *Mayfair Boy*, 66.

37. Philip Hoare, *Noël Coward: A Biography* (Chicago: Chicago University Press,1995).

38. Terry Castle, *Noël Coward and Radclyffe Hall: Kindred Spirits* (New York: Columbia University Press, 1996). See also Laura Doan, *Fashioning Sapphism: The Origins of a Modern English Lesbian Culture* (New York: Columbia University Press, 2001), 238n77.

39. Cecil Beaton, *The Glass of Fashion* (New York: Doubleday, 1954), 153.

40. Orson Welles, cited in Gene D. Phillips, *Beyond the Epic: The Life and Films of David Lean* (Lexington: University Press of Kentucky, 2006), 65. The play was written in 1939, performed in 1942, and filmed in 1944.

41. *Coward Plays: 4: Blithe Spirit; Present Laughter; This Happy Breed* (London: Bloomsbury, 1990), xiv.

42. Nell Murray, "Mayfair's Spoiled Young People," *Sunday Mail* (Brisbane), Mar. 20, 1938, 45.

43. Andrew Spicer, *Typical Men: The Representation of Masculinity in Popular British Cinema* (London: I. B. Taurus, 2001); Grandy, *Heroes and Happy Endings*, 177–198.

44. Cited in Michael Williams, *Ivor Novello: Screen Idol* (London: British Film Institute, 2003), 40.

45. *Yorkshire Evening Post*, Sept. 18, 1937, 5.

46. George Mikes, *How to Be an Alien* (London: Andre Deutsch, 1946), 22.

47. Nancy Mitford, *Highland Fling* (New York: Vintage, 2010), 13.

48. *Western Daily Press*, Nov. 15, 1937, 7.

49. Richard Aldington, *Death of a Hero* (London: Hogarth Press, 1984), 253.

50. *Aberdeen Journal*, Mar. 4, 1937, 6.

51. George Orwell, *An Age Like This: 1920–1940*, in *The Collected Essays, Journalism, and Letters*, ed. Sonia Orwell and Ian Angus (London: Harcourt, Brace & World, 1968), 1:226.

52. Adrian Bingham, *Gender, Modernity, and the Popular Press in Interwar Britain* (Oxford: Clarendon Press, 2004).

53. D. Todd, "Decadent Heroes: Dandyism and Masculinity in Art Deco Hollywood," *Journal of Popular Film and Television* 32, 4 (2010): 168–181.

54. Frank Mort, *Capital Affairs: London and the Making of the Permissive Society* (New Haven: Yale University Press, 2010), 74.

55. On middle-class worries about the feminization of British society, see Light, *Forever England*, 118.

56. Jill Greenfield, Sean O'Connell, and Chris Read, "Fashioning Masculinity: *Men Only*, Consumption and the Development of Marketing in the 1930s," *Twentieth-Century British History* 10, 4 (1999): 466; see also Harry Cocks, "'The Social Picture of Our Own Times': Reading Obscene Magazines in 1940s Britain," *Twentieth Century British History* 27, 2 (2016): 171–194.

57. *Men Only*, Dec. 1935, 13; Jan. 1938, 10.

58. Trevor Allen, *Underworld: The Biography of Charles Brooks, Criminal* (London: R. M. McBride, 1931), 258–259.

59. Psychoanalytical explanations of how smothering mothers putatively made sissified men were more common in the United States than in Britain. On such "limp and querulous" men, see Philip Wylie, *Generation of Vipers* (1942; reprint, New York: Holt, Rinehart & Winston, 1955), 208.

60. MEPO 3/902, Dec. 20, 1937, Statement of Henrietta Gordon.

61. Peter Bailey, "Fats Waller Meets Harry Champion: Americanization, National Identity and Sexual Politics in Interwar British Music Hall," *Cultural and Social History* 4, 4 (2007): 495–509.

62. Justin Bengry, "Courting the Pink Pound: *Men Only* and the Queer Consumer, 1935–39," *History Workshop Journal* 68, 1 (2009): 12. Harry Raymond, the famous black-mailer of homosexuals, was described as a handsome playboy in the *Mirror* (Perth) Jan. 8, 1938, 2; also see McLaren, *Sexual Blackmail*, 108–120. For a scabrous poetic presentation of an aging gay playboy, see "The Playboy of the Demi-World: 1938," in William Plomer, *Collected Poems* (London: Cape, 1973), 119–120.

63. *Daily Mail*, July 7, 1939, 7.

64. Robert Graves and Alan Hodge, *The Long Weekend: A Social History of Great Britain 1918–1939* (New York: Macmillan, 1941), 217; see also John Worby, *The Other Half: The Autobiography of a Spiv* (London: J. M. Dent, 1937), 165; Taylor Croft, *The Cloven Hoof: A Study of Contemporary London Vices* (London: Denis Archer, 1932), 63.

65. *Yorkshire Evening Post*, Feb. 6, 1937, 7.

66. In 2012 a 1934 teddy bear coat sold at auction for £20,400. "'Teddy' coats were all the rage in the 1930s when, despite the Depression, fashion was influenced by the escapist glamour of the 'golden age' of Hollywood." *Daily Mail*, Oct. 19, 2012.

67. Philip Hoare, "I Love a Man in a Uniform: The Dandy Esprit de Corps," *Fashion Theory: The Journal of Dress, Body & Culture* 9, 3 (2005): 275.

68. Peter Jenkins, *Mayfair Boy* (London: W. H. Allen, 1952), 120–129.

69. Ibid., 173.

70. Sali Löbel, *Glamour and How to Achieve It* (London: Hutchinson, 1938), 20. On the bankruptcy of Löbel's *Every Women's Health Movement*, see *The Times*, June 1, 1940, 11.

71. *Times*, Feb. 21, 1938, 12.

72. *Daily Mail*, Feb. 21, 1938, 12.

73. *Argus* (Melbourne), July 2, 1938, 10.

74. The code mothers purportedly used when exchanging information on eligible young men included NSIT (Not Safe in Taxis) or MTF (Must Touch Flesh) or VVSITPQ (Very Very Safe in Taxis Probably Queer). See Fiona MacCarthy, *Last Curtsey: The End of the Debutantes* (London: Faber & Faber, 2006), 71.

75. Sarah Churchill, *Keep on Dancing: An Autobiography* (London: Littlehampton, 1981), 60.

76. *Times*, Sept. 17, 1936; *New York Times*, Sept. 16, 1936, 27; Sept. 17, 1936, 25.

77. Mary Soames, *A Daughter's Tale: The Memoir of Winston Churchill's Youngest Child* (New York: Random House, 2012), 52–53.

78. When Churchill was told that though he had many burdens, they weren't as great as those of Hitler and Mussolini, he purportedly replied, "Ah! but Mussolini has this consolation, that he could shoot his son-in-law!" His barb could have been directed at either Vic Oliver or Duncan Sandys. Cecil King, *With Malice toward None: A War Diary* (London: Sidgwick & Jackson, 1970), 267.

79. Churchill, *Keep on Dancing*, 68–69.

80. Entry for Sept. 17, 1936, in *Diary of Robert Graves 1935–39 and Ancillary Material* (University of Victoria, 2002), http://graves.uvic.ca/graves/site/index.xml (accessed Jan. 15, 2017).

81. According to a police informer, Stewart Cappel and Tony Wheeler were criminal associates. On Wheeler, see Graves's account: "Then to Spotted Dog in Burton Mews. Met Pat Moran and Tony Wheeler. Tony Wheeler hardboiled, married, speaking against Jenny living alone without a 'background'—'you'd only get a chap like Pat if you wanted

to marry.'" Entry Nov. 24, 1936, *Diary of Robert Graves*; see also MEPO 3/902, Jan. 20, 1938, Metropolitan police telegrams 20 and 21 Jan. 1938.

82. Entry Dec. 1936, *Diary of Robert Graves*; see also Richard Perceval Graves, *Robert Graves: The Years with Laura 1926–40* (New York: Viking, 1990), 261–264, and Miranda Seymour, *Robert Graves: Life on the Edge* (London: Doubleday, 1995), 247–248.

83. Entry Dec. 23, 1937, *Diary of Robert Graves*.

84. *Daily Mail*, Feb. 21, 1938, 12.

85. *Dover Express*, Jan. 26, 1940, 8; *Times*, Jan. 19, 1940, 5; Mar. 12, 1940, 3.

86. *Times*, Jan. 19, 1940, 5.

87. *Daily Mail*, July 16, 1932, 7; July 19, 1932, 5; Mar. 16, 1936, 10; *Times*, Apr. 20, 1936, 17; *Daily Mirror*, Feb. 3, 1939, 13.

88. D. J. Taylor, *Bright Young People: The Rise and Fall of a Generation, 1918–1940* (London: Chatto & Windus, 2007).

89. *Times*, Oct. 20, 1932, 4.

90. See, e.g., "Motorist Killed. Narrow Escape for the Hon. Elizabeth Pelly. Mr. Gordon Russell, of Good Trees, Cowden, Kent, was killed yesterday in a motor accident near Maidstone." *Exeter and Plymouth Gazette*, July 6, 1931, 8.

91. *Ottawa Journal*, Aug. 24, 1940, 19; *Lincoln Evening Journal*, Feb. 13, 1939, 2; *Monthly Film Bulletin*, Jan. 1, 1941, 46; Jan. 1, 1938, 196; *New York Times*, Apr. 30, 1932, 19; *Times*, Oct. 6, 1943, 6.

92. MEPO 3/902, Jan. 18, 1938, Detective Constable W. Chamberlain and Detective Sergeant Heathfield of Kent County to Commissioner. See also MEPO 3/902, Metropolitan police telegrams Jan. 20 and 21, 1938.

93. MEPO 3/902, Jan. 24, 1938, Burt report on Miss Cappel; *Daily Mail*, Dec. 24, 1937, 7.

94. *Times*, June 8, 1939, 9; June 9, 1939, 9; June 20, 1939, 11; June 28, 1939, 11; July 5, 1939, 18; July 7, 1939, 16; July 11, 1939, 9.

95. James Burge defended Stephen Ward during the Profumo scandal, but he was best known for having been the barrister on whom John Mortimer based the character of Horace Rumpole. *Guardian*, Jan. 16, 2009.

96. *Times*, July 21, 1939, 8.

97. *Daily Mail*, July 27, 1939, 5; *Times*, July 25, 1939, 4; July 26, 1939, 4; July 27, 1939, 16.

98. *Times*, July 27, 1939, 16.

99. *Dundee Courier*, July 27, 1939, 7. The judge was presumably thinking of the May 1939 scuffle in a Turkish bath between Charles Smirke, the Aga Khan's jockey, and Derek Piggott, stepson of Sir Max Bonn, a wealthy American-born merchant banker and Jewish philanthropist. When the case came to court, Smirke's barrister succeeded in portraying Piggott as a well-known Mayfair playboy who lounged around West End bars. *Daily Mail*, May 23, 1939, 13; Dec. 1, 1939, 4.

100. *Times*, Nov. 10, 1944, 7; Nov. 2, 1945, 1.

101. Lawrence Stone, *Road to Divorce: England, 1530–1987* (Oxford: Oxford University Press, 1990), 99–100.

102. Beverley Nichols, *News of England* (New York: Doubleday, Doran, 1938), 163.

103. *Fresno Bee*, Apr. 21, 1936, 3.

104. *Daily Mail*, Apr. 16, 1936, 13; *Daily Times*, Apr. 22, 1936, 3; see also *Australian Women's Weekly*, Sept. 26, 1936, 35.

105. "The following announcement appears today as an agony advertisement: To all whom it may concern.—I, Paul Vincent Desgrand Mitchell, hereby give notice . . . (I am) not responsible for my wife's debts. Ann Mitchell, residing at the Splendide Hotel, Picca-

dilly." *Evening Telegraph*, Jan. 12, 1938, 1; *Times*, Jan. 12, 1938, 1; Walter Winchell, "On Broadway," *Syracuse Journal*, Feb. 7, 1938, 7.

106. *Courier-Mail* (Brisbane, Queensland), May 13, 1938, 5.

107. *Times*, July 28, 1938, 16.

108. *Times*, Dec. 22, 1938, 9. Mallory, an artist's model, who did not have a "good family," was to be supervised by a probation officer. See *Times*, July 30, 1938, 9; Aug. 8, 1938, 7; Sept. 17, 1938, 12; Jan. 12, 1939, 12.

109. *Daily Mail*, May 5, 1938, 13.

110. Mitchell was identified as a private and Jenkins as a signalman in the Royal Engineers. *Daily Mail*, Oct. 8, 1940, 3; Nov. 14, 1940, 3; *Hull Daily Mail*, Oct. 23, 1940, 6.

111. *Yorkshire Evening Post*, Dec. 16, 1938, 15. For a photo of Leggi, see *Daily Mail*, Dec. 17, 1938, 3.

112. Leggi arrived in New York City on Mar. 4, 1938, aboard the U.S. liner *Washington* and returned to Plymouth on May 10, 1938. *New York Passenger and Crew Lists 1938*, https://familysearch.org/search/collection/results?count=20&query=%2Bgivenname%3A%22sylvia%20doris%22~%20%2Bsurname%3Aleggi~%20%2Bgender%3AF&collection_id=1923888 (accessed Jan. 15, 2017).

113. *Dundee Courier*, Dec. 1, 1938, 7; *Yorkshire Post and Leeds Intelligencer*, Dec. 1, 1938, 3; *Times*, Dec. 1, 1938, 16; Dec. 17, 1938, 4.

114. Blood tests, which were beginning to be employed in British courts to determine paternity, were not helpful in this case. See "Blood Test Ends Paternity Claim," *Daily Mail*, May 17, 1938, 11; *Times*, Dec. 17, 1938, 4.

115. Skeffington was not called as a witness but admitted through his counsel, B. B. Gillis, that he had slept with Leggi. Gillis, while representing Harley in the 1938 Hyde Park Hotel trial, had savagely cross-examined Jenkins.

116. Note that in 1938 both Wilmer and Harley approached Reginald Thomas Philip Bennett of Speed and Company, solicitors, for an alibi.

117. *Yorkshire Evening Post*, Dec. 16, 1938, 15.

118. Pat Thane and Tanya Evans, *Sinners? Scroungers? Saints? Unmarried Motherhood in Twentieth-Century England* (Oxford: Oxford University Press, 2012), 78.

119. *Times*, Dec. 17, 1938, 4; *Evening Telegraph*, Dec. 16, 1938, 1. The boxer Max Baer was described as the "playboy of New York" because of several breach-of-promise suits brought against him. *Daily Mail*, May 15, 1934, 16.

120. *Times*, Mar. 15, 1939; Mar. 23, 1939, 1; Nov. 3, 1938, 17.

121. *Times*, Apr. 22, 1939, 4; Nov. 15, 1939, 3; *Evening Telegraph*, Nov. 14, 1939, 2. Skeffington succeeded his father in 1956. A member of the Carlton, Turf, and Royal Yacht Clubs; master of the Ashford Valley Fox hounds; and lord of Chilham Castle (Kent), he was the classic dotty peer. His speeches in the Lords were regarded as "bizarre." *Times*, Jan. 9, 1993, 15.

122. *Judicial Statistics* stopped including breach of promise suits in its reports in 1922 as courts now rarely compensated for emotional injury. See Ginger S. Frost, " 'I Shall Not Sit Down and Crie': Women, Class and Breach of Promise of Marriage Plaintiffs in England, 1850–1900," *Gender and History* 6, 2 (1994): 224–245; *Daily Mail*, Apr. 21, 1937, 11; Saskia Lettmaier, *Broken Engagements: The Action for Breach of Promise of Marriage and the Feminine Ideal, 1800–1940* (Oxford: Oxford University Press, 2010), 178–179.

123. HC Deb 5 Feb. 1937 vol. 319 cc1957.

124. McLaren, *Sexual Blackmail*, 176–179.

125. *Daily Express*, Feb. 15, 1935, 11.

126. Since she was still a minor the appeal was formally made by Hilary's guardian. Divorce Court File: 3840 (1937), J77/3736/3840, National Archives, London.

127. *Evening Telegraph,* Mar. 18, 1938, 4; *Times,* Mar. 19, 1938, 4; *Daily Mail,* Mar. 19, 1938, 5.

128. *Daily Mail,* Feb. 22, 1938, 9; see also *Hull Daily Mail,* Feb. 21, 1938, 1; *Gloucestershire Echo,* Feb. 21, 1938, 1.

129. O. R. McGregor, *Divorce in England: A Centenary Study* (London: Heinemann, 1957).

130. Lawrence Stone, *Road to Divorce: England 1530–1987* (Oxford: Oxford University Press, 1990), 396; see also Colin S. Gibson, *Dissolving Wedlock* (London: Routledge, 1994), 85–98.

131. *Daily Mail,* Mar. 17, 1937, 13; see also Nov. 26, 1936, 11.

132. Bryan Guinness provides a fictional portrait of his failed marriage to Diana Mitford and the dreary divorce proceedings that resulted when she left him for Oswald Mosley in *Singing Out of Tune* (London: Putnam, 1933).

133. British censors banned four films dealing with collusive divorce and A. P. Herbert never succeeded in obtaining permission for the filming of his novel *Holy Deadlock*. Jeffrey Richards, "The British Board of Film Censors and Content Control in the 1930s: Images of Britain," *Historical Journal of Film, Radio and Television* 1, 2 (1981): 34–35.

134. *Times,* Mar. 11, 1937, 4; *Daily Mail,* Mar. 17, 1937, 13.

135. Noting the Byzantine complexities of divorce law, a solicitor in the novel states: "Whenever I explain certain sections of the law my clients conclude that I must be mad or drunk." A. P. Herbert, *Holy Deadlock* (London: Methuen, 1934), 29. Because of his concern for pub workers, Lady Astor (a prohibitionist) called Herbert the "playboy of the drink world." *Daily Mail,* Mar. 7, 1936, 8.

136. *Daily Mail,* Nov. 23, 1935, 6. See also Reginald Pound, *A. P. Herbert: A Biography* (London: Michael Joseph, 1976), 135–148.

137. *Times,* Oct. 27, 1938, 4; *Daily Mail,* Dec. 14, 1939, 3. And on the tensions between modern marriage and traditional restraints, see Frank Mort, "Love in a Cold Climate: Letters, Public Opinion and Monarchy in the 1936 Abdication Crisis," *Twentieth Century British History* 25, 1 (2014): 30–62.

138. *Daily Mail,* June 11, 1938, 11.

139. S. E. Karminski was the author of *Some Aspects of the Development of English Personal Law in the Last Century* (Jerusalem: Magnes Press, 1963).

140. *Times,* July 30, 1938, 3.

141. *Evening Telegraph,* Feb. 6, 1939, 5.

142. Ralph G. Martin, *The Woman He Loved* (New York: Simon & Schuster, 1973), 199–202.

143. *Daily Mail,* Apr. 17, 1939, 6.

144. MEPO 3/902, Dec. 22, 1937, Wilmer further statement.

145. *Times,* Nov. 2, 1939, 2.

146. *Daily Mail,* Nov. 7, 1939, 1. Shortly thereafter Hilary and Gamble married in West Ashford, Kent. See *England and Wales Marriage Registration Index* 2A (1939): 4847, line 139.

147. *Times,* Nov. 2, 1939, 2.

148. Films that followed some variant of the reformist plot with the hedonist finally seeing the evil of his ways include *It Happened One Night* (1934, dir. Frank Capra), *No More Ladies* (1935, dir. Edward H. Griffith), *You Can't Beat Love* (1937, dir. Christy Cabanne), *For You Alone* (1937, dir. Robert Riskin), *The Playboy* (1938, dir. Walter Forde), *Love Affair* (1939, Leo McCarey), *Millionaire Playboy* (1940, dir. Leslie Goodwins), and *Heaven Can Wait* (1943, dir. Ernst Lubitsch).

8: Crime

1. Patrick Hamilton, *The West Pier* (1951; London: Kaye & Ward, 1974), 120. Gorse is a social climber and, unlike the Mayfair men, has to work at passing for upper-middle class.

2. Margery Allingham, *Crime and Mr. Campion* (New York: Doubleday, 1937).

3. Matt Houlbrook, "Commodifying the Self Within: Ghosts, Libels, and the Crook Life Story in Interwar Britain," *Journal of Modern History* 85, 2 (2013): 325.

4. Christine Grandy, "'Avarice' and 'Evil Doers': Profiteers, Politicians, and Popular Fiction in the 1920s," *Journal of British Studies* 50, 3 (2011): 667–689.

5. Ian Hacking, *Historical Ontology* (Cambridge, MA: Harvard University Press, 2002).

6. *Daily Mirror*, July 6, 1939, 5; *Daily Mail*, July 7, 1939, 7.

7. *Times*, July 7, 1939, 11.

8. Coop wrote anti-Labour government songs such as "The Left Honourables" for a postwar stage review. See *Daily Mail*, Dec. 7, 1946, 3.

9. Victor became the sixth Marquess of Bristol in 1960. See *Daily Sketch*, July 7, 1939; Michael De-la-Noy, *The House of Hervey: A History of Tainted Talent* (London: Constable, 2001); Marcus Scriven, *Splendour and Squalor: The Disgrace and Disintegration of Three Aristocratic Dynasties* (London: Atlantic Books, 2009), 65–95.

10. *Daily Mail*, May 27, 1929, 12.

11. *Times*, July 7, 1939, 11.

12. *Daily Mail*, Sept. 21, 1935, 9.

13. Scriven, *Splendour and Squalor*, 85–86; *Times*, Mar. 23, 1937, 5.

14. *Daily Mail*, June 25, 1937, 7.

15. Scriven, *Splendour and Squalor*, 86–87; *Daily Mail*, Oct. 12, 1940, 3; Anne de Courcy, "Curse of the House of Hervey," *Daily Mail*, Apr. 14, 2001, 32–33.

16. *Daily Mail*, Apr. 18, 1939, 17; *Times*, Apr. 18, 1939, 7.

17. Pauline Daubeny, the twenty-six-year-old daughter of the White Russian Princess Nicolas Galitzine, was in the midst of divorcing her husband, Reginald Daubeny. *Daily Mail*, Apr. 22, 1939, 6.

18. Walter had gone to the same school as Prince Yurka Galitzine, Pauline Daubeny's half-brother. *Manchester Guardian*, May 17, 1939, 14.

19. *Times*, May 2, 1939, 11; *Daily Mail*, May 10, 1939, 16.

20. *Times*, May 2, 1939, 11.

21. *Daily Mail*, May 10, 1939, 16.

22. In 1939 Eustace Hoey was fined for selling spirits without an excise license at the Nest nightclub. The magistrate said it was "a bad place, exercising a bad influence." *Ottawa Journal*, Feb. 11, 1939, 20.

23. *Daily Mail*, May 2, 1939, 6.

24. For the story headlined "Robbed Woman was 'Pretty Drunk,'" see *Daily Mail*, May 10, 1939, 16.

25. Scriven, *Splendour and Squalor*, 93.

26. *Daily Mail*, July 4, 1939, 3; *Times*, July 4, 1939, 4.

27. *Daily Mail*, July 6, 1939, 5.

28. *Daily Mail*, July 7, 1939, 7.

29. *Times*, July 7, 1939, 11.

30. A year later Michael A. V. Walter, twenty-one, married Mrs. Gabrielle Burley and was interviewed in her luxurious Park Lane flat. See "Gem Trial Man Weds Hostess," *Daily Mail*, Mar. 23, 1940, 5.

31. *Daily Mail*, July 21, 1939, 4. See *Sunday Dispatch*, July 9, 1939, 5; July 16, 1939, 5; July 23, 1939, 5; July 30, 1939, 15; Aug. 6, 1939, 15.

32. Christopher Andrew, *Defense of the Realm: The Authorized History of MI5* (London: Allen Lane, 2008), 217. The story of Hervey robbing a Mayfair jeweller is repeated in Ben MacIntyre, *Spy among Friends: Kim Philby and the Great Betrayal* (London: Bloomsbury, 2014).

33. When he was released on license in 1941 Hervey established a film company, but the police (and Chief Inspector Fabian in particular) still viewed him with suspicion. Shunned by many of his peers, he could at least count on the support of the eccentric John Whyte-Melville Skeffington, a fellow member of the Monarchist League. Scriven, *Splendour and Squalor*, 95, 102.

34. P. G. Wodehouse, *Quick Service* (1940; reprint, New York: Overlook Press, 1968), 115.

35. P. G. Wodehouse, *The Mating Season* (1947; reprint, London: Everyman, 2001), 164.

36. *Sydney Morning Herald*, Aug. 20, 1937, 12. The Dame of Sark, Sybil Mary Hathaway, was the daughter of W. F. Collings, seigneur of Sark. Dick Beaumont was her son by her first husband, Dudley Beaumont. See Barbara Stoney, *Sybil, Dame of Sark: A Biography* (London: Hodder & Stoughton, 1978), 119, 215–216.

37. *Times*, Aug. 27, 1937, 9.

38. *Daily Mail*, Sept. 3, 1937, 17.

39. *Times*, Aug. 5, 1939, 9.

40. *Daily Mail*, July 20, 1937, 10.

41. Hugh G. Edwards, "Confessions of a Mayfair Playboy," *Sunday Pictorial*, Apr. 7, 1940, 18–19.

42. *Times*, May 5, 1939, 11. The *Times* only used the term "Mayfair Playboy" from 1939 on.

43. *Daily Mail*, Feb. 21, 1938, 12.

44. John Bowlby, "Forty-four Juvenile Thieves: Their Characters and Home-life," *International Journal of Psychoanalysis* 25 (1944): 116.

45. *Times*, Feb. 3, 1938, 13.

46. Adrian Bingham, *Family Newspapers: Sex, Private Life and the British Popular Press 1918–1978* (Oxford: Oxford University Press, 2009).

47. On aristocratic habits of indebtedness, see Margot Finn, *The Character of Credit: Personal Debt in English Culture, 1740–1914* (Cambridge: Cambridge University Press, 2010).

48. The essay first appeared in *Passing Show*, Feb. 23, 1929. See "Careers for Our Sons," in *The Essays, Articles and Reviews of Evelyn Waugh*, ed. Donat Gallagher (London: Methuen, 1983), 47–52.

49. Dorothy L. Sayers, *Murder Must Advertise* (1933; reprint, London: New English Library, 1969), 22.

50. Ngaio Marsh, *Surfeit of Lampreys* (London: Collins, 1941), 31.

51. *Times*, Mar. 18, 1938, 11; Mar. 19, 9; Mar. 22, 13; *Daily Mail*, Mar. 18, 1938, 11.

52. *Evening Telegraph*, Jan. 20, 1938, 5.

53. *Ottawa Journal*, Dec. 19, 1936, 19. His mother (the well-known actor June van Buskirk) was quoted as saying: "It is a shame that such young men as my son, with good family connections, should be the prey of certain people." *Daily Mail*, Dec. 3, 1936, 14.

54. *Daily Mail*, Dec. 13, 1935, 14. In 1926, when only nineteen, he married Dorothy, a dance hostess daughter of Kate Meyrick, the notorious owner of the 43 Club on Gerard Street. See Michael John Law, "Speed and Blood on the Bypass: The New Automobilities of Interwar London," *Urban History* 39, 3 (2012): 490–509.

55. Agatha Christie, *And Then There Were None* (1939; reprint, New York: William Morrow, 2011), 55.

56. Valentine Cunningham, *British Writers of the Thirties* (Oxford: Oxford University Press, 1988), 161.

57. Wolfgang Sachs, *For Love of the Automobile: Looking Back into the History of Our Desires* (Berkeley: University of California Press, 1992), 112–115.

58. Graham Greene, *Brighton Rock* (1938; reprint, London: Everyman's Library, 1993), 122. In the 1920s the Jordan Motor Company of Cleveland produced a swanky roadster called the "Playboy."

59. *New York Times*, July 16, 1937, 22; *Times*, Aug. 2, 1937, 8.

60. *Times*, Oct. 29, 1938, 9.

61. *Derby Daily Telegraph*, Nov. 18, 1938, 5.

62. *Daily Mail*, Nov. 18, 1938, 13.

63. *Dover Express*, Nov. 2, 1934, 8. Traffic laws caused unprecedented friction between the middle class and the police. See Clive Emsley, "'Mother, What Did Policemen Do When There Weren't Any Motors?' The Law, the Police and the Regulation of Motor Traffic in England, 1900–1939," *Historical Journal* 36, 2 (1993): 357–381.

64. *Hull Daily Mail*, Oct. 4, 1934, 12; *Times*, Oct. 4, 1934, 9.

65. *Daily Mail*, Nov. 18, 1938, 13.

66. Miller's father also killed himself. See *Daily Mail*, Nov. 19, 1938, 9.

67. *Times*, Dec. 19, 1939, 4; Jan. 19, 1940, 5; Mar. 12, 1940, 3; *Nottingham Evening Post*, Jan. 16, 1940, 6; *Gloucestershire Echo*, Jan. 18, 1940, 1.

68. *Daily Mail*, June 29, 1939, 9.

69. Scriven, *Splendour and Squalor*, 101.

70. *Times*, July 7, 1939, 11.

71. *Exeter and Plymouth Gazette*, July 6, 1931, 8; *Daily Mail*, July 27, 1931, 5.

72. Martin Francis, *The Flyer: British Culture and the Royal Air Force, 1939–1945* (Oxford: Oxford University Press, 2008).

73. *Times*, Sept. 28, 1938, 13; Jan. 6, 1983, 12.

74. His wife, Amy Johnson, broke some of his records. They divorced in 1938, and she was killed in 1941 ferrying aircraft. His drinking led to his pilot's license being revoked in 1953. James Mollison, *Playboy of the Air* (London: M. Joseph, 1937); *Aberdeen Journal*, Sept. 13, 1937, 10; Ronald Bythe, *The Age of Illusion: England in the Twenties and Thirties, 1919–1940* (London: Hamish Hamilton, 1963), 83–102.

75. *Daily Sketch*, Feb. 18, 1938, 4.

76. David Edgerton, *England and the Aeroplane: Militarism, Modernity and Machines* (Hampshire: Macmillan, 1991), 47–49; Valentine Cunningham, *British Writers of the Thirties* (Oxford: Oxford University Press, 1988), 187; Mark Rawlinson, *British Writing of the Second World War* (Oxford: Clarendon Press, 2000), 61.

77. *Empire News*, Mar. 6, 1938, 5; Brett Holman, *The Next War in the Air: Britain's Fear of the Bomber, 1908–1941* (Aldershot: Ashgate, 2014), 2–3.

78. *Daily Mail*, Feb. 21,1938, 12.

79. *Derby Daily Telegraph*, Nov. 18, 1938, 5.

80. *News Chronicle*, Feb. 19, 1938, 1, 3, 5.

81. Leonore Davidoff, *The Best Circles: Society, Etiquette and the Season* (London: Croom Helm, 1973); D. J. Taylor, *Bright Young People: The Rise and Fall of a Generation, 1918–1940* (London: Chatto & Windus, 2007), 73; Stephen Graham, *London Nights* (London: John Lane, 1925) and *Twice Round the London Clock* (London: Benn, 1933).

82. The press made a few references to playboys' use of drugs. One journalist noted: "It is hard to tell if they dope, as they boast they do." *Daily Mail*, Feb. 21, 1938, 12. On the police cleanup of "Mayfair's so-called 'playboys'" with raids on night clubs and bottle parties and the impounding of the passports of those suspected of "peddling dope," see *Daily Mail*, June 13, 1938, 2.

83. Blythe, *Age of Illusion*, 37.

84. Matt Houlbrook, *Queer London: Perils and Pleasures in the Sexual Metropolis, 1918–1957* (Chicago: University of Chicago Press, 2005), 70–75; Horace Wyndham, *Nights in London: Where Mayfair Makes Merry* (London: Bodley Head, 1926).

85. On Halsey's prosecution, see *Times*, July 8, 1933, 9.

86. Judith Walkowitz, *Nights Out: Life in Cosmopolitan London* (New Haven: Yale University Press, 2012), 229–230.

87. *Times*, July 14, 1936, 13.

88. *Daily Mail*, Dec. 22, 1939, 3. See also *Times*, Oct. 1, 1935, 4.

89. *Times* Apr. 20, 1938, 12.

90. Allison Jean Abra, "On with the Dance: Nation, Culture, and Popular Dancing in Britain, 1918–1945" (Ph.D. diss., University of Michigan, 2009), 204; Julia Laite, *Common Prostitutes and Ordinary Citizens: Commercial Sex in London, 1885–1960* (Basingstoke: Palgrave Macmillan, 2012), 139–140, 160–161; Louise Settle, "The Kosmo Club Case: Clandestine Prostitution during the Interwar Period," *Twentieth-Century British History* 25, 4 (2014): 562–584.

91. Amy Milne-Smith, *London Clubland: A Cultural History of Gender and Class in Late-Victorian Britain* (New York: Palgrave Macmillan, 2011), 205.

92. The club was destroyed in the blitz of October 1940. Stephen Bourne, *Mother Country: Britain's Black Community on the Home Front, 1939–45* (London: History Press, 2010).

93. Sidney Theodore Felstead, *The Underworld of London* (London: John Murray, 1923), 1, 3, 14; also see Lucy Bland, *Modern Women on Trial: Sexual Transgression in the Age of the Flapper* (Manchester: Manchester University Press, 2013), 55–101.

94. *Daily Mail*, Dec. 3, 1936, 17.

95. On Lonsdale, see *Empire News*, Feb. 20, 1938, 1.

96. *Daily Mail*, June 5, 1936, 9; Oct. 26, 1936, 13.

97. *Daily Mail*, Aug. 23, 1937, 9.

98. *The Times*, June 8, 1939, 9; June 20, 1939, 11.

99. *Daily Mail*, July 27, 1939, 5.

100. *Daily Mail*, Mar. 7, 1941, 1.

101. *Daily Mail*, Nov. 5, 1948, 1; Dec. 24, 1948, 3; Jan. 10, 1949, 3.

102. *Daily Mail*, Sept. 21, 1953, 5.

103. Stephen Knight, "Radical Thrillers," in *Watching the Detectives: Essays in Crime Fiction*, ed. Ian A. Bell and Graham Daldfy (London: Macmillan, 1990), 176. The Raffles stories first appeared in the *Strand Magazine* and subsequently in an 1899 collection. Additional stories appeared in *The Black Mask* (1901) and *A Thief in the Night* (1905). Hornung ultimately made amends for Raffles's misdeeds by having him die heroically in the Boer War.

104. E. W. Hornung, *The Amateur Cracksman* (Toronto: Morang, 1899), 40.

105. George Smithson, *Raffles in Real Life* (London: Hutchinson 1930), which was puffed in "Confessions of a Real Raffles," *Daily Mail*, May 23, 1930, 5. On his last job, see his "Burglar's Confession," *Daily Mail*, July 28, 1923, 4. He claimed to have taken £50,000 of booty in his last twelve months and admitted to thirty-six breakings and entries from 1922 to 1930.

106. Eloise Moss, "'How I had liked this villain! How I had admired him!': A. J. Raffles and the Burglar as Transnational British Icon, 1898–1939," *Journal of British Studies* 53, 1 (2014): 136–161.

107. Hornung, *The Amateur Cracksman*, 88.

108. Ibid., 44, 69.

109. "A Costume Piece," cited in Colin Watson, *Snobbery with Violence* (London: Eyre & Spottiswoode, 1971), 44–45.

110. While the adventure novelists declared their hatred of the effeminate, they felt free in a pre-Freudian age to laud male attractiveness. Bunny admitted his jealousy when Raffles flirted with a German girl. Roger Pocock described his rugged hero as having shoulders and thighs "all of gigantic strength and beauty, a sight that would have appealed to any athlete as beyond the loveliness of women." Graham Greene spoofed these conventions in imagining Bunny in Reading Gaol with Oscar Wilde. Hornung, *The Amateur Cracksman*, 80, 262; Roger Pocock, *The Blackguard* (London: Ward, Lock, 1897), 6; Graham Greene, *The Return of A. J. Raffles* (London: Bodley Head, 1975).

111. C. J. Cutliffe Hyne, *Honour of Thieves* (London: Chatto & Windus, 1895).

112. Christine Grandy, "The Empire and 'Human Interest': Popular Empire Films, the Colonial Villain, and the British Documentary Movement 1926–39," *Twentieth Century British History* 25, 4 (2014): 509–532.

113. Pocock, *The Blackguard*, 124.

114. *The People*, May 3, 1925, 15.

115. George Orwell, "Raffles and Miss Blandish," in *The Collected Essays* (London: Secker & Warburg, 1968), 3:212–221.

116. M. Collins, "The Fall of the English Gentleman: The National Character in Decline, c.1918–1970," *Historical Research* 75 (2002): 90–111. On the elite's fear of cultural commercialization and Americanization, see D. L. LeMahieu, *A Culture for Democracy: Mass Communication and the Cultivated Mind in Britain between the Wars* (Oxford: Oxford University Press, 1988).

117. *New York Times*, Dec. 23, 1937, 13.

118. *Times*, Aug. 5, 1930, 8; see also Federico Pagello, "A. J. Raffles and Arsène Lupin in Literature, Theatre, and Film: On the Transnational Adaptations of Popular Fiction (1905–30)," *Adaptation* 6, 3 (2013): 268–282. For the observation that in the "1939 remake when the code was being strictly enforced, David Niven's Raffles had to give himself up," see Neil McDonald, "The Romance of the Jewel Thief," *Quadrant* 56, 10 (2012): 96.

119. *New York Times*, Feb. 23, 1933, 20.

120. *Times*, May 4, 1936, 12.

121. Sigmund Freud, who arrived in London on January 6, 1938, asserted that the jewel box symbolized the female genitalia. Apparently no British film critic took up the idea. See Sigmund Freud, *Dora: An Analysis of a Case of Hysteria* (New York: Simon & Schuster, 1997), 62.

122. *Times*, Jan. 10, 1938, 10. For a similar real life case, see "Convict Alleges Jewel Raid was 'Staged,'" *Daily Mail*, Apr. 7, 1933, 9; "Judge Finds £13,000 Hold-Up a Fake," Apr. 8, 1933, 7; "Broker Acquitted," Sept. 22, 1933, 9.

123. *Times*, Mar. 30, 1936, 10.

124. *Times*, May 31,1937, 12.

125. *Times*, Mar. 25, 1940, 4. But on the censors' defense of the police, see Christine Grandy, *Heroes and Happy Endings: Class, Gender, and Nation in Popular Film and Fiction in Interwar Britain* (Manchester: Manchester University Press, 2014), 188.

126. On the assertion of Conservative MPs that attacks on jewelers by smash-and-grab raiders were attributable to "the growth of Socialist and Communist ideas of disregard for

private property," see Keith Laybourn and David Taylor, *Policing in England and Wales, 1918–39: The Fed, Flying Squads and Forensics* (New York: Palgrave Macmillan, 2011), 187.

127. For the argument that such films can "open up a certain cultural space within which contradictory subject positions and identities may be taken up, however provisionally," see Tony Bennett and Janet Woollacott, *Bond and Beyond: The Political Career of a Popular Hero* (London: Macmillan, 1987), 5.

128. Matt Houlbrook, "Fashioning an Ex-crook Self: Citizenship and Criminality in the Work of Netley Lucas," *Twentieth Century British History* 24, 1 (2013): 1–30.

9: Class

1. West does not locate George's behavior in its social context but simply attributes his failings to his innate character flaws. Rebecca West, *The Modern "Rake's Progress"* (London: Hutchinson, 1934).

2. *Chicago Tribune*, Feb. 18, 1938, 9.

3. For the assertion that the trial revealed "a side of London's social life so far only partly exposed," see *Daily Sketch*, Feb. 19, 1938, 10.

4. Frank Mort, *Capital Affairs: London and the Making of the Permissive Society* (New Haven: Yale University Press, 2010), 5.

5. *Clovis* (NM) *News Journal*, Apr. 24, 1938, 13; *Times Recorder* (Zanesville, OH), Apr. 24, 1938, 15.

6. *Spokesman Review*, Dec. 24, 1937, 18.

7. *Times*, Feb. 19, 1938, 13.

8. *Times*, Feb. 18, 1938, 20; HC Deb 21 Feb. 1956 vol. 549 cc177.

9. *Clovis News Journal*, Apr. 24, 1938, 13; *Times*, Feb. 16, 1938, 18.

10. Robert Graves and Alan Hodge, *The Long Weekend: A Social History of Great Britain* (New York: Macmillan, 1941), 56.

11. John Hilton, *Rich Man, Poor Man* (London: Allen & Unwin, 1944), 52; see also William D. Rubinstein, "Britain's Elites in the Interwar Period, 1918–1939: Decline or Continued Ascendancy?" *British Scholar* 3, 1 (2010): 5–23.

12. G. D. H. Cole and M. I. Cole, *The Condition of Britain* (London: Victor Gollancz, 1937), 64.

13. Noreen Branson and Margot Heinemann, *Britain in the Nineteen Thirties* (London: Weidenfeld & Nicolson, 1971), 154.

14. Cole and Cole, *The Condition of Britain*, 61–63, 75.

15. Hilton, *Rich Man, Poor Man*, 87.

16. Bill Brandt, *A Night in London* (London: Country Life, 1938), 42–43.

17. Ross McKibben, *Classes and Cultures: England 1918 to 1951* (Oxford: Oxford University Press, 1998), 39.

18. *Daily Mail*, Oct. 20, 1919, 7.

19. *Times*, Mar. 11, 1933, 15.

20. Graves and Hodge, *The Long Weekend*, 56.

21. *Times*, Aug. 13, 1932, 5.

22. *Sunday Mail* (Brisbane), Dec. 17, 1939, 6.

23. *Sunday Chronicle and Sunday Referee*, July 9, 1939, 6.

24. *Advertiser* (Adelaide), Dec. 25, 1937, 12.

25. *Lincolnshire Echo*, Feb. 18, 1938, 1.

26. *Daily Sketch*, Feb. 16, 1938, 11.

27. *Daily Mail*, Dec. 24, 1937, 7.

28. *Brooklyn Daily Eagle*, Dec. 26, 1937, 2. But note that society women also attended the sensational trials of lower-class women like Edith Thompson. See Lucy Bland, *Modern Women on Trial: Sexual Transgression in the Age of the Flapper* (Manchester: Manchester University Press, 2013), 103–104.

29. Paul Cohen-Portheim, *England, the Unknown Isle*, trans. Alan Harris (London: Duckworth, 1930), 117.

30. Graves and Hodge, *The Long Weekend*, 55–56.

31. Patrick Balfour, *Society Racket: A Critical Survey of Modern Social Life* (London: John Long, 1933).

32. McKibben, *Classes and Cultures*, 23.

33. She also had a sharp tongue. "When Somerset Maugham—whose homosexuality was never mentioned—left one of Emerald Cunard's parties early, explaining, 'I have to keep my youth,' she retorted: 'Then why don't you bring him with you.'" Carol Kennedy, *Mayfair: A Social History* (London: Hutchinson, 1986), 219.

34. Branson and Heinemann, *Britain in the Nineteen Thirties*, 155.

35. Driberg, a Communist in his youth, later claimed that he deliberately exaggerated the decadence of the upper classes in order to fan the flames of class warfare. Tom Driberg, *Ruling Passions* (London: Jonathan Cape, 1977). See also Sarah Newman, "Gentleman, Journalist, Gentleman-Journalist: Gossip Columnists and the Professionalisation of Journalism in Interwar Britain," *Journalism Studies* 14, 5 (2013): 698–715.

36. Balfour, *Society Racket*, 266.

37. *Daily Mail*, Aug. 19, 1932, 10.

38. Brian Howard was one of the inspirations for the character of Anthony Blanche in Evelyn Waugh's *Brideshead Revisited*. See D. J. Taylor, *Bright Young People: The Rise and Fall of a Generation 1918–1940* (London: Chatto & Windus, 2007), 314, and Marie-Jacqueline Lancaster, ed., *Brian Howard: Portrait of a Failure* (London: Blond, 1968).

39. Clarence Rook, *Highways and Byways in London* (London: Macmillan, 1902), 166.

40. Kennedy, *Mayfair*, 179.

41. Judith Walkowitz, *Nights Out: Life in Cosmopolitan London* (New Haven: Yale University Press, 2012), 222.

42. Thomas Burke, *English Night-Life* (London: Batsford, 1941), 137–138.

43. E. F. Benson, *The Freaks of Mayfair* (London: T. N. Foulis, 1916).

44. John Buchan, *Three Hostages* (London: Thomas Nelson, 1946).

45. Michael Arlen, *The Green Hat: A Romance for a Few People* (London: W. Collins & Sons, 1924).

46. HC Deb 4 Dec. 1933 vol. 283 cc1310.

47. Kennedy, *Mayfair*, 190–191.

48. *Daily Mail*, Sept. 30, 1930, 9.

49. Graves and Hodge, *The Long Weekend*, 56. In the film *The Man in Possession* (1937, dir. W. S. Van Dyke), the comic Barnett Parker gave, according to the critics, a side-splitting portrayal of the Mayfair accent. *Monthly Film Bulletin*, Jan. 1, 1937, 82.

50. HC Deb 7 Apr. 1930 vol. 237 cc1802.

51. *John Bull*, Jan. 27, 1945, 8.

52. *News Chronicle*, Feb. 19, 1938, 8. In 1939 a writer of a letter to the editor asked why the papers described three young men who appeared in court as "Mayfair Men": "He pointed out that all three lived somewhere else, and wanted to know why possession of gentility fixed a man's geography." *Newspaper World and Advertising Review* 2138–2163 (1939): 13.

53. *Daily Mail*, July 16, 1931, 9.

54. Most films about Mayfair were comedies. An exception was *Mayfair Girl* (1933, dir. George King), in which a young American woman is framed for killing a cad while drunk. *Daily Mail*, May 10, 1933, 5.

55. Mark Glancy, *Hollywood and the Americanization of Britain from the 1920s to the Present* (London: I. B. Tauris, 2013), 109–143.

56. Jeffrey Richards, *The Age of the Dream Palace: Cinema and Society in 1930s Britain* (London: Routledge & Kegan Paul, 1984), 109–121, 172–173.

57. The film was based on the novel by J. C. Snaith, *The Crime of Constable Kelly* (London: Nelson, 1924).

58. *Monthly Film Bulletin*, Jan. 1, 1937, 54.

59. *Monthly Film Bulletin*, Jan. 1, 1938, 66.

60. Critics declared it "dull and vulgar." Ibid., 95.

61. Ibid., 158.

62. For the view that the film was supposed to be light and gay but was in fact plagued by wooden dialogue, see *Monthly Film Bulletin*, Jan. 1, 1949, 115.

63. On American movies' portrayal of the myth of a classless society, see Andrew Bergman, *We're in the Money: Depression America and Its Films* (New York: New York University Press, 1971); and on British stereotypical views of America, see Sian Nicholas, "American Commentaries: News, Current Affairs and the Limits of Anglo-American Exchange in Interwar Britain," *Cultural and Social History* 4, 4 (2007): 461–479.

64. Raymond Chandler pointed out that English, in England, was a class language. "The English writer is a gentleman first and a writer second." Dorothy Gardiner and Katherine Sorley Walker, eds., *Raymond Chandler Speaking* (Berkeley: University of California Press, 1997), 82; see also Ken Worpole, *Dockers and Detectives* (London: Verso, 1983). For the argument that English viewers preferred American films for aesthetic rather than political reasons, see Jeffrey Richards, "Modernism and the People: The View from the Cinema Stalls," in *Rewriting the Thirties: Modernism and After*, ed. Keith Williams and Steven Mathews (London: Routledge, 2014), 188.

65. Some reviewers felt that the film presented an idealized view of English undergraduates. *Times*, Apr. 1, 1938, 14; Richards, *The Age of the Dream Palace*, 316.

66. J. B. Priestley, *English Journey* (1934; reprint, London: W. Heinemann, 1949), 401.

67. McKibben, *Classes and Cultures*, 523–527.

68. Alan O'Shea, "English Subjects of Modernity," in *Modern Times: Reflections on a Century of English Modernity*, ed. Mica Nava and Alan O'Shea (London: Routledge, 1996).

69. *Daily Telegraph and Morning Post*, Feb. 19, 1938, 9.

70. "An older stereotype of the 'hooligan' was increasingly eclipsed by the more modern, and more dangerous, figure of the 'gangster.'" Theodora Benson and Betty Askwith, *Foreigners; or, the World in a Nutshell* (London: Victor Gollancz, 1935), 111; *Daily Mail*, Feb. 19, 1938, 8.

71. *San Bernardino County Sun*, Jan. 16, 1938, 4; *Times*, Jan. 15, 1938, 7; Feb. 11, 1938, 7.

72. *Times*, May 20, 1942, 3. The judge ordered that one of the troopers be given twelve strokes of the cat. See also David Reynolds, *Rich Relations: The American Occupation of Britain, 1942–1945* (New York: Random House, 1995), 146.

73. Bowker, assistant to Norman Birkett, recalled that all London was eager to witness the examination of the four youths coming from "respectable families." A. E. Bowker, *Behind the Bar* (London: Staples Press, 1951), 249.

74. Deborah Cohen, *Family Secrets: Living with Shame from the Victorians to the Present Day* (Oxford: Oxford University Press, 2013), 8.

75. *News of the World*, Feb. 20, 1938, 13.

76. Sept. 19, 1932 entry from the unpublished diary of Arthur Ponsonby, cited in Taylor, *Bright Young People*, 271.

77. Catherine Horwood, *Keeping Up Appearances: Fashion and Class between the Wars* (London: Sutton, 2005).

78. Cole and Cole, *The Condition of Britain*, 312.

79. *New York Times*, Feb. 19, 1938, 6.

80. Cited in H. G. Woodward, "Mayfair Lepers," *Sign of the Times* 65, 18 (May 3, 1938), 4, 14.

81. David Turner, *The Old Boys: The Decline and Rise of the Public School* (Hartford: Yale University Press, 2015), 185.

82. In addition, a degree of anti-Semitism fed on the belief that Jews were too intellectual and individualistic to immerse themselves fully in the athletics and arcane rituals so beloved by the schools. Anthony Julius, *Trials of the Diaspora: A History of Anti-Semitism in England* (Oxford: Oxford University Press, 2010), 377–378; Jeffrey Richards, *Happiest Days: The Public Schools in English Fiction* (Manchester: Manchester University Press, 1988).

83. Graham Greene, *The Old School: Essays by Divers Hands* (London: Jonathan Cape, 1934), 9.

84. Alec Waugh, *The Loom of Youth* (London: Richards, 1917); H. G. Wells, *The World of William Clissold* (London: Benn, 1926); George Orwell, "Such Such Were the Joys," in *The Collected Essays, Journalism and Letters of George Orwell*, ed. Sonia Orwell and Ian Angus (London: Secker & Warburg, 1968), 4:330–369.

85. Jonathan Gathorne-Hardy, *The Old School Tie: The Phenomenon of the English Public School* (New York: Viking, 1977), 210.

86. Horwood, *Keeping Up Appearances*, 122–123.

87. *Daily Mail*, Aug. 1, 1936, 7.

88. *Daily Mail*, Jan. 21, 1938, 7.

89. *Daily Mail*, July 15, 1935, 10.

90. *Men Only*, May 1936, 15–19.

91. "The Old School Tie," www.youtube.com/watch?v=JmCNtG2HL4M (accessed Sept. 11, 2015).

92. The *Times* judged their mockery "admiringly affectionate." *Times*, Aug. 19, 1969, 10.

93. *Times*, Feb. 19, 1938, 17.

94. *Times*, Aug. 5, 1937, 6.

95. *Times*, Mar. 11, 1933, 15.

96. Harold J. Laski, *The Danger of Being a Gentleman and Other Essays* (London: Allen & Unwin, 1939), 13–31.

97. Douglas Reed, *A Prophet at Home* (London: Cape, 1941), http://archive.org/stream /AProphetAtHome_27/prophet_djvu.txt (accessed Sept. 11, 2015). See also Tony Kushner, *The Persistence of Prejudice: Anti-Semitism in British Society during the Second World War* (Manchester: Manchester University Press, 1989), 99–100, and Julius, *Trials of the Diaspora*, 410–411.

98. Arthur Marwick, "Class," in *A Companion to Contemporary Britain*, ed. Paul Addison and Harriet Jones (Oxford: Blackwell, 2005), 78; David Cannadine, *The Rise and Fall of Class in Britain* (New York: Columbia University Press, 1999), 138.

99. *Daily Mirror*, Feb. 19, 1938, 3.

10: Fascism

1. Oswald Mosley, *My Life* (London: Nelson, 1968), 302; see also John Harvey, *Men in Black* (Chicago: Chicago University Press, 1995), 239–242.

2. See A. P. Herbert's taunt: "I shall never be drawn by any political movement whose main idea seems to be to wear underclothes of a particular colour. As between the Black-shirts and the Redshirts, I am among those who cry, 'A plague on both your blouses!' In the old days a political party took its name from its ideas and ideals. Now we have leaders who name themselves after their lingerie—black shirts or blue braces, pink pants or dirty draw-ers." HC Deb 10 July 1936 vol. 314 cc1606.

3. J. Baxendale and C. Pawling, *Narrating the Thirties: A Decade in the Making, 1930 to the Present* (London: Macmillan, 1996).

4. *New York Post*, Mar. 19, 1938, 2; *New York Times*, Mar. 20, 1938, 46; *Times*, Mar. 21, 1938, 14.

5. On Mrs. Trewartha (Esther Surle), see *Daily Mail*, May 23, 1922, 7.

6. *Daily Mail*, Aug. 21, 1923, 4; *Times*, Dec. 6, 1923, 15; Dec. 17, 1923, 15.

7. *Times*, May 28, 1926, 11.

8. *Daily Mail*, Apr. 26, 1924, 5; In 1927, Enid was given a three-year driving ban. *Daily Mail*, Sept. 10, 1927, 9.

9. *Times*, June 11, 1925, 13.

10. *Times*, Mar. 13, 1925, 17.

11. *Times*, July 31, 1926, 4.

12. *Times*, Oct. 7, 1926, 15; Mar. 3, 1927, 9; Nov. 2, 1927, 5.

13. Heather Shore, "'Constable Dances with Instructress': The Police and the Queen of Nightclubs in Interwar London," *Social History* 38, 2 (2013): 183–202.

14. *Daily Mail*, June 7, 1928, 9.

15. Walkowitz, *Nights Out*, 212. As noted in chapter 8, Dorothy, another of Kate Meyrick's daughters, married Edward Russell, Lord de Clifford, a supporter of Sir Oswald Mosley and the British Union of Fascists.

16. His first wife, the Countess Kinnoull, went in the opposite direction. In 1928 she converted to Catholicism and used her enormous wealth to benefit the church. She financed the White Fathers' missions in Africa, funded the *Catholic Herald*, and supported Franco's anticommunist crusade. Like Evelyn Waugh, a defender of the traditional mass, she finan-cially aided Archbishop Lefebvre's campaign against modernism. "In Memory of Lady Kin-noull," *Regina Coeli Report* 220 (Apr. 2010): 5.

17. *Daily Express*, July 24, 1929; *New York Times*, July 24, 1929, 52; *Times*, May 9, 1934, 7; Kinnoull said he would prefer an elected upper house to what was in effect a "Committee of the Conservative Party."

18. On his driving offenses, see *Daily Mail*, May 14, 1932, 5.

19. *Times*, Mar. 7, 1934, 8.

20. *Times*, Nov. 17, 1932, 7; HL Deb 16 Nov. 1932 vol. 85 cc1350.

21. *Times*, Mar. 1, 1934, 7. Viscount Esher replied that the left was as bad as the right, and if he had to choose, he would opt for Oswald Mosley over Sir Stafford Cripps.

22. *Times*, July 7, 1933, 8.

23. *Times*, Dec. 2, 1936, 7; HL Deb 1 Dec. 1936 vol. 103 cc510–514; see also HC Deb 21 Apr. 1936 vol. 311 cc18–19.

24. *Times*, Jan. 26, 1937, 11.

25. *Times*, Nov. 20, 1936, 18.

26. See the leaflet "Food for the Spanish People," Warwick Digital Collection, http://contentdm.warwick.ac.uk/cdm/ref/collection/scw/id/7788 (accessed Oct. 12, 2015); *Ottawa Journal*, Dec. 22, 1936, 15; Jim Fyrth, *The Signal Was Spain: The Spanish Aid Movement in Britain, 1936–1939* (London: Lawrence & Wishart 1986), 244.

27. *Daily News* (Perth, WA), July 31, 1933, 5; *Daily Mail*, Mar. 21, 1938, 9.

28. Cyril Connolly, *Enemies of Promise* (London: Routledge & Kegan Paul, 1938), 102–103.

29. Jeremy Lewis, *Cyril Connolly: A Life* (New York: Random House, 2012).

30. *Manchester Guardian*, Dec. 17, 1925, 34.

31. HC Deb 2 May 1938 vol. 335, cc584.

32. *Yorkshire Post and Leeds Intelligencer*, June 16, 1936, 9; *Exeter and Plymouth Gazette*, Mar. 18, 1938, 11.

33. *New Statesman and Nation*, Mar. 5, 1938, 365–366. In his essay "What Is Fascism?" (1944), George Orwell, agreed with Waugh that the word was overused. His conclusion was, however, less categorical. "Even the people who recklessly fling the word 'Fascist' in every direction attach at any rate an emotional significance to it. By 'Fascism' they mean, roughly speaking, something cruel, unscrupulous, arrogant, obscurantist, anti-liberal and anti-working-class. Except for the relatively small number of Fascist sympathizers, almost any English person would accept 'bully' as a synonym for 'Fascist.' That is about as near to a definition as this much-abused word has come." *The Collected Essays, Journalism and Letters*, 3:114.

34. Selina Hastings, *Evelyn Waugh: A Biography* (London: Sinclair-Stevenson, 1994).

35. Martin Stannard, *Evelyn Waugh: The Early Years 1903–1939* (Toronto: Fitzhenry & Whiteside, 1986), 458.

36. A right-wing apologist for conservative Catholicism, Heygate attended the 1935 Nuremberg Rally with the nature writer Henry Williamson. Heygate committed suicide in 1976. *Times*, Mar. 20, 1976, 16.

37. Michael Davie, ed., *The Diaries of Evelyn Waugh* (Boston: Little, Brown, 1976), 527.

38. See David Garnett in the *New Statesman and Nation*, Nov. 7, 1936, 735; Rose Macaulay, "Evelyn Waugh," *Horizon* 14, 84 (Dec. 1946): 370; Martin Stannard, *Evelyn Waugh: The Critical Heritage*. (London: Routledge & Kegan Paul, 1984), 188–190, 192–193.

39. Evelyn Waugh, *Robbery under Law* (London: Chapman & Hall, 1939), 17, 44, 75. On fascism, see Stannard, *Evelyn Waugh*, 458–460.

40. *New Statesman and Nation*, Mar. 5, 1938, 366.

41. *Empire News*, Mar. 6, 1938, 5.

42. James K. Hopkins, *Into the Heart of the Fire: The British in the Spanish Civil War* (Stanford: Stanford University Press, 1998).

43. Judith Keene, *Fighting for Franco: International Volunteers in Nationalist Spain during the Spanish Civil War, 1936–39* (London: Leicester University Press, 2001), 46–47.

44. Michael B. Miller, *Shanghai on the Métro: Spies, Intrigue, and the French between the Wars* (Berkeley: University of California Press, 1994), 114; on British condemnations of the arms trade, see David Edgerton, *Warfare State: Britain, 1920–1970* (Cambridge: Cambridge University Press, 2005), 26–26, and Richard Overy, *The Morbid Age: Britain between the Wars* (London: Allen Lane, 2009), 191–194.

45. *Daily Express*, Feb. 19, 1938, 5.

46. Marcus Scriven, *Splendour and Squalor: The Disgrace and Disintegration of Three Aristocratic Dynasties* (London: Atlantic Books, 2009), 85–86; Anthony Haden-Guest, "The End of the Peer," *Observer*, Jan. 22, 2006, magazine section, 32.

47. Such frauds were not uncommon. "In one instance the Madrid government paid eight million crowns for Finnish stocks that were totally obsolete." Miller, *Shanghai on the Métro*, 116. Michael Corrigan, a friend of Victor Hervey, received a two-year sentence for defrauding a Chinese group seeking to purchase arms; see *Daily Mail*, Nov. 16, 1938, 16, and Jan. 31, 1939, 11.

48. Kent Trust Ltd. sued Lonsdale for the £230 due on a promissory note for £100 signed by Lonsdale and Victor Hervey. Accompanied to court by a warder, Lonsdale argued

that the interest rate of 90 percent per annum was "harsh and unconscionable." Kent Trust responded that both men were bad risks. Hervey, a bankrupt, was not sued, and Lonsdale bitterly noted that his partner was enjoying life in Paris: "The George V Hotel there [you will] always find him." Ashe Lincoln's assertion that Lonsdale was not heavily involved with other moneylenders did not help. Mr. Justice Asquith ruled that, as Lonsdale freely agreed to the loan, the interest rate was reasonable. He awarded the total amount, costs, and interest to Kent. *Western Gazette*, July 22, 1938, 14.

49. *Times*, Mar. 23, 1937, 5.

50. Gerald Howson, *Arms for Spain: The Untold Story of the Spanish Civil War* (London: John Murray, 1998), 219–220.

51. Edward Arthur Donald St. George Hamilton Chichester, sixth Marquess of Donegall, was a product of Eton and Oxford who for many years wrote a column for the *Sunday Dispatch* under the byline "Almost in Confidence."

52. The Marquess of Donegall's story in the *Sunday Dispatch*, Apr. 18, 1937, 1, was reprinted in many papers; see, e.g., *Escanaba* (MI) *Daily Press*, May 27, 1937, 26, and *Toronto Globe and Mail*, Apr. 21, 1937, 10.

53. *Vapaa Sana* (*Free Press*, Toronto), Apr. 21, 1937, 1, 3; see also *Toronto Globe and Mail*, Apr. 21, 1937, 10.

54. HC Deb 31 May 1937 vol. 324 cc654–657.

55. *Daily Mail*, July 10, 1937, 10.

56. John Sutherland Northcliffe, *Stephen Spender: A Literary Life* (Oxford: Oxford University Press, 2004), 227.

57. Valentine Cunningham, *British Writers of the Thirties* (Oxford: Oxford University Press, 1988), 419, 422.

58. In a review of H. G. Wells's *The Holy Terror* (1939) Waugh reasserted that the "proletarian movement" represented by both fascism and communism posed a threat to traditional values. According to him, Wells "refuses to be misled by the preposterous distinctions of Left and Right that make nonsense of contemporary politics." *Spectator*, Feb. 10, 1939, 234; Humphrey Carpenter, *The Brideshead Generation: Evelyn Waugh and His Friends* (Boston: Houghton Mifflin, 1990), 312–313, 320.

59. Tom Villis, *British Catholics and Fascism: Religious Identity and Political Extremism between the Wars* (London: Palgrave Macmillan, 2013), 160.

60. Douglas Jerrold, *Georgian Adventures* (London: Collins Pall Mall, 1937), 354, 369–373.

61. *Empire News*, Aug. 20, 1939, 7.

62. Tom Buchanan, *Britain and the Spanish Civil War* (Cambridge: Cambridge University Press, 1997), 88–89.

63. Phillimore was also president of the Central Landowners' Association, which in 1943 heard the rural revivalist Rolf Gardiner call for a "conference of heirs of estates" to ward off "commissars and bureaucrats." *Times*, July 31, 1943, 2.

64. *Times*, Mar. 24, 1938, 9; Mar. 30, 1939, 16.

65. Michael Walsh, *The Martyrdom of William Joyce* (Sussex: Historical Review Press, 2002), 3.

66. Richard Griffiths, *Patriotism Perverted: Captain Ramsay, the Right Club, and British Anti-Semitism, 1939–40* (London: Constable, 1998); Robin Saikia, *The Red Book: The Membership List of the Right Club, 1939* (London: Foxley Books, 2010).

67. On Prince Yurka Galitzine, see the epilogue.

68. Reginald Daubeny, her first husband, was prosecuted during the war for talking about Operation Torch. Though not understanding the seriousness of leaking information

about the Second Front, he was cashiered and sentenced to twelve months imprisonment. Pauline's second husband (also a member of the Right Club), Colin Dennistoun Sword of the Gordon Highlanders, was reported missing in action in June 1940. Nigel West, *The Guy Liddell Diaries* (London: Routledge, 2005), 1:310, 2:14; *Times*, June 29, 1940, 1; Aug. 10, 1948, 1.

69. MEPO 3/902, Jan. 4, 1938, Philip John Ridout statement.

70. Leese was interned in 1940. See Robert Benewick, *The Fascist Movement in Britain* (London: Allen Lane, 1972), 44–45, and Richard Griffiths, "Anti-Semitic Obsessions: The Case of H. W. Wicks," *Patterns of Prejudice* 48, 1 (2014): 94–113.

71. *Times*, Oct. 8, 1937, 11.

72. Sherman Kadish, "Jewish Bolshevism and the 'Red Scare' in Britain," *Jewish Quarterly* 34, 4 (1987): 16–17.

73. Harry Defries, *Conservative Party Attitudes to Jews, 1900–1950* (New York: Psychology Press, 2001), 135.

74. *Portsmouth Evening News*, Apr. 4, 1938, 12; *Times*, Apr. 5, 1938, 8.

75. Nicholas Mosley, *Beyond the Pale: Sir Oswald Mosley and Family, 1933–1980* (London: Secker & Warburg, 1983); Beverley Nichols, *News of England* (New York: Doubleday, Doran, 1938), 261–267.

76. Matthew Worley, *Oswald Mosley and the New Party* (London: Palgrave Macmillan, 2010).

77. Colin Cross, *The Fascists in Britain* (New York: St. Martin's, 1963), 145–150.

78. Villis, *British Catholics and Fascism*, 161.

79. Storm Jameson, *In the Second Year* (New York: Macmillan, 1936), 108.

80. Stephen Dorrill, *Black Shirt: Sir Oswald Mosley and British Fascism* (London: Viking, 2006), 15.

81. Before Mosley's swing to the right, the *Manchester Guardian* in 1925 called the National Fascisti "Dangerous Play-Boys." See Janet Dack, " 'It Certainly Isn't Cricket': Media Responses to Mosley and the BUF," in *Varieties of Anti-Fascism in the Interwar Period*, ed. Nigel Copsey and Abdrzej Olechnowicz (London: Palgrave Macmillan, 2010), 143.

82. Robert Skidelsky, *Oswald Mosley* (New York: Holt, Rinehart & Winston, 1975), 109.

83. Raymond Postgate, *The Life of George Lansbury* (London: Longmans Green, 1951), 252.

84. Julie Gottlieb, "The Marketing of Megalomania: Celebrity, Consumption, and the Development of Political Technology in the British Union of Fascists," *Journal of Contemporary History* 41, 1 (2006): 40.

85. *Daily Mail*, Dec. 14, 1926, 9.

86. A. G. MacDonell, *The Autobiography of a Cad* (London: Macmillan, 1938), 245.

87. Harvey, *Men in Black*, 239–243.

88. Julie Gottlieb, "Body Fascism in Britain: Building the Blackshirt in the Interwar Period," *Contemporary European History* 20, 2 (2011): 53.

89. Aldous Huxley, *Point Counter Point* (1928; reprint, London: Penguin, 1967), 346, 347, 371; Patrick Hamilton, *Hangover Square* (1941; reprint, London: Penguin, 2001), 128.

90. Mosley, *My Life*, 168.

91. Skidelsky, *Oswald Mosley*, 164.

92. Anne de Courcy, *The Viceroy's Daughters* (New York: Orion, 2012), 173–174; Nicholas Mosley, *Rules of the Game* (London: Secker & Warburg, 1982); for an intimate account of the life of a contemporaneous "playboy politician," see *The Duff Cooper Diaries*, ed. John Julius Norwich (London: Weidenfeld & Nicolson, 2005).

93. Douglas Goldring, *Marching with the Times, 1931–1946* (London: Nicholson & Watson, 1947), 70.

94. *Observer,* Dec. 7, 1980, 11.

95. In the 1950 general election Jill Craigie called Randolph Churchill a "Mayfair play-boy." *Western Morning News,* Feb. 21, 1950, 5. Craigie was a documentary film director, screenwriter, and feminist married to the Labour Party MP Michael Foot.

96. Laura E. Nym Mayhall, "The Prince of Wales versus Clark Gable: Anglophone Celebrity and Citizenship between the Wars," *Cultural and Social History* 4, 4 (2007): 529–543; Stephen Gundle, *Glamour: A History* (Oxford: Oxford University Press, 2008), 151–153.

97. Julie V. Gottlieb, "Britain's New Fascist Men: The Aestheticization of Brutality in British Fascist Propaganda," in *The Culture of Fascism: Visions of the Far Right in Britain,* ed. Julie V. Gottlieb and Thomas P. Linehan (London: I. B. Tauris, 2004), 98.

98. Adrian Weale, *Roger Casement, John Amery, and the Real Meaning of Treason* (New York: Viking, 2001), 97–110; David Faber, *Speaking for England: Leo, Julian, and John Amery, the Tragedy of a Political Family* (New York: Free Press, 2005), 190.

99. *Daily Mail,* Sept. 14, 1932, 3; May 27, 1933, 7; Dec. 19, 1936, 5.

100. Faber, *Speaking for England,* 200.

101. *Daily Mail,* Aug. 23, 1932, 11.

102. "Freely" is perhaps the wrong word. Whereas his father provided John with an al-lowance of £10 a week, his Nazi minders gave him £30 a week plus expenses. Weale, *Roger Casement,* 213. See also Horst J. P. Bergmeier and Rainer E. Lotz, *Hitler's Airwaves: The In-side Story of Nazi Radio Broadcasting and Propaganda Swing* (New Haven: Yale University Press, 1999), 115–118.

103. Faber, *Speaking for England,* 519; *Daily Mail,* Nov. 20, 1942, 4; W. D. Rubenstein, "The Secret of Leopold Amery," *History Today* 49, 2 (1999): 17–23.

104. Leonard Burt, *Commander Burt of Scotland Yard* (London: William Heinemann, 1959), 7; on the Amerys' network of supporters, see Jimmy Burns, *Papa Spy: Love, Faith, and Betrayal in Wartime Spain* (London: Bloomsbury, 2009), 311–318.

105. Faber, *Speaking for England,* 508.

106. See, e.g., *Daily Mirror,* Nov. 29, 1945, 3; see also Judith Keene, *Treason on the Air-waves: Three Allied Broadcasters on Axis Radio during World War II* (Westport, CT: Praeger, 2009), 44.

107. Rebecca West, *The Meaning of Treason* (New York: Viking, 1947), 215. On West's concern to spare the feelings of the Amery family, see Bonnie Klime Scott, ed., *Selected Let-ters of Rebecca West* (New Haven: Yale University Press, 2000), 218–219.

108. Keene, *Treason on the Airwaves,* 77; see also Faber, *Speaking for England,* 502.

Epilogue

1. Hal Higdon, *Leopold and Loeb: The Crime of the Century* (New York: Putnam, 1975); Simon Baatz, *For the Thrill of It: Leopold, Loeb, and the Murder That Shocked Chicago* (New York: HarperCollins, 2008).

2. Patrick Hamilton, *Rope: A Play* (London: Constable, 1929).

3. Hamilton's characters repeatedly refer to situations and relationships as "queer." On the portrayal of homosexuality, see Amy Lawrence, "Jimmy Stewart Is Being Beaten: *Rope* and the Postwar Crisis in American Masculinity," *Quarterly Review of Film and Video* 16, 1 (1997): 41–58, and Jordan Schildcrout, "Queer Justice: The Retrials of Leopold and Loeb," *Journal of American Culture* 34, 2 (2011): 175–179.

4. *Rope* (1948), starring James Stewart and Farley Granger, was one of Hitchcock's less successful films. David Sterritt, "Morbid Psychologies and So Forth: The Fine Art of

Rope," in *Hitchcock at the Source: The Auteur as Adapter,* ed. R. Barton Palmer and David Boyd (Albany: State University of New York Press, 2011), 159–172.

5. Paul Willetts, ed., *Julian Maclaren-Ross: Selected Letters* (London: Black Spring, 2008), 10.

6. Eric Capon, "The Strange Case of Patrick Hamilton," *Theatre Today* 3 (Dec. 1946): 6; Nigel Jones, *Through a Glass Darkly: The Life of Patrick Hamilton* (New York: Scribner's, 1991), 157–158; see also Sean French, *Patrick Hamilton: A Life* (London: Faber & Faber, 1993).

7. Warwick Deeping, *Portrait of a Playboy* (London: Cassell, 1947), 4, 13.

8. Sax Rohmer, *Hangover House* (1949; reprint, London: Strauss, 2008), 99.

9. Mort, *Capital Affairs,* 56. Even during the war, Americans were so impressed by the comforts Mayfair offered British officers that they spoke of them countering the German Blitzkrieg with their own "Ritzkrieg." *New York Times,* Jan. 17, 1944, 5.

10. Andrew Lycett, *Ian Fleming* (London: Weidenfeld & Nicolson, 1995), 9–11, 14–22, 28, 46–56, 99. According to Malcolm Muggeridge, British intelligence employed the same favoritism in choosing its secretaries. "They were girls of good family, the idea being (so very English) that coming from rectories or Roedean (a girl's school) they would be less likely to betray secrets to the enemy. If they had come from humbler homes, the temptation might be greater." *Toronto Globe and Mail,* June 4, 1965, 7.

11. Paul Johnson, "Sex, Snobbery, and Sadism," *New Statesman,* Apr. 5, 1958, 430; Gopinath Praseeda, *Scarecrows of Chivalry: English Masculinities after Empire* (Charlottesville: University Press of Virginia, 2013), 154; James Chapman, "Bond and Britishness," in *Ian Fleming and James Bond: The Cultural Politics of James Bond,* ed. Edward P. Comentale, Stephen Watt, and Skip Willman (Bloomington: Indiana University Press, 2005), 133.

12. Music hall audiences demonstrated their knowingness by laughing at such frauds. Peter Bailey, *Popular Culture and Performance in the Victorian City* (Cambridge: Cambridge University Press, 1998), 109, 147; Judith R. Walkowitz, *City of Dreadful Delight: Narratives of Sexual Danger in Late-Victorian London* (Chicago: University of Chicago Press, 1992), 42–44. The "spiv"—the flashy black market profiteer—represented this type in the 1940s and '50s. See Mark Roodhouse, *Black Market Britain, 1939–1955* (Oxford: Oxford University Press, 2013), 225–252, and Paul Elliott, "The Weak and the Wicked: Non-conscripted Masculinities in 1940s British Cinema," in *The Home Front in Britain: Images, Myths and Forgotten Experiences since 1914,* ed. Maggie Andrews and Janis Lomas (London: Macmillan, 2014), 180–182.

13. On Profumo, see Gillian Swanson, *Drunk with Glitter: Space, Consumption and Sexual Instability in Modern Urban Culture* (London: Routledge, 2007), 48, and Mort, *Capital Affairs.* On Lucan, see Patrick Marnham, *Trail of Havoc: In the Steps of Lord Lucan* (New York: Viking, 1987), and Laura Thompson, *A Different Class of Murder: The Story of Lord Lucan* (London: Head of Zeus, 2014).

14. Steven Watts, *Mr. Playboy: Hugh Hefner and the American Dream* (Hoboken, NJ: John Wiley & Sons, 2008), 64. Founded in 1965, *Mayfair* was *Playboy*'s chief rival in the United Kingdom.

15. Elizabeth Fraterrigo, *Playboy and the Making of the Good Life in Modern America* (Oxford: Oxford University Press, 2009). See the similar crude consumerism in Fleming's description of a villain's lair having "the most expensive type of intercom" and "an expensive desk-lighter," air that held "a slight expensive fragrance," and secretaries who looked liked "assistants in the most expensive American beauty-parlors." Ian Fleming, *Dr. No* (1957; reprint, London: Penguin, 2002), 173, 174.

16. *Le Matin*, Feb. 20, 1938, 3; *Le Figaro*, Feb. 19, 1938, 3; *El Mundo* (San Juan, Puerto Rico), Mar. 20, 1938, 15.

17. *Alkmaarsche Courant*, Jan. 22, 1938, 1.

18. Robert Graves and Alan Hodge, *The Long Weekend: A Social History of Great Britain 1918–1939* (New York: Macmillan, 1941), 403.

19. Malcolm Muggeridge, *The Thirties: 1930–1940* (1940; reprint, London: Collins, 1971), 300.

20. *Daily Mail*, Dec. 7, 1945, 2; *Times*, Dec. 10, 1945, 8. See also *The Day Will Dawn* (1942, dir. Harold French), in which a playboy journalist turned secret agent guides bombers to destroy a U-boat base. *Times*, May 6, 1942, 6; *Monthly Film Bulletin*, May 31, 1942, 57.

21. *New York Times*, May 29, 1946, 18; Nov. 14, 1946, 49. Rex Harrison made a career out of playing middle-class rogues; women were attracted by his louche charm while men envied his daring. Andrew Spicer, *Typical Men: The Representation of Masculinity in Popular British Cinema* (London: I. B. Tauris, 2001), 120.

22. Spicer, *Typical Men*, 9. On the war years as the "golden age" of British cinema, see James Chapman, *Past and Present: National Identity and the British Historical Film* (London: I. B. Tauris, 2005).

23. *Times*, Sept. 4, 1942, 6; Anthony Aldgate, and Jeffrey Richards, *Britain Can Take It: The British Cinema in the Second World War* (Edinburgh: Edinburgh University Press, 1994), 187–217. A later critic states: "It now looks impossibly patronizing, the epitome of stiff upper lip as Coward's captain graciously condescends to his forelock-touching crew like an indulgent auntie. Interesting chiefly as a reminder of the structures of snobbery and privilege in the services which were largely responsible for Labour's postwar election victory." John Pym, ed., *Time Out Film Guide* (London: Penguin, 2004), 577.

24. *Toronto Globe*, June 12, 1943, 14.

25. He left an estate of £105,349. *Portsmouth Evening News*, Nov. 3, 1942, 1.

26. *Times*, Jan. 1, 1944, 1.

27. He is buried at Banneville-la-Campagne, Calvados. See http://francecrashes39-45 .net/page_fiche_av.php?id=5003 (accessed Sept. 17, 2015).

28. *Daily Mail*, Jan. 21, 1938, 7; Aug. 13, 1947, 3.

29. *Times*, July 29, 1944, 1.

30. *Daily Mail*, Nov. 18, 1938, 13.

31. *Daily Mail*, Mar. 16, 1949, 5.

32. *Times*, Aug. 13, 1942, 8.

33. *Times*, Oct. 21, 1942, 1.

34. He married Mrs. Renee Mayall in Secunderabad, India. *Times*, May 2, 1947, 1. Her father, Sir Clive Burn, was an Oxford cricket blue, steeplechaser, and solicitor employed as secretary to the Duchy of Cornwall; her brother, Michael Burn, journalist, commando, writer, and friend of the Cambridge spy Guy Burgess, wrote, *Turned toward the Sun: An Autobiography* (London: Michael Russell, 2003), where he mentions his sister Renee's three marriages but says nothing about her husbands. F. C. Wilmer was her second.

35. Richard Griffiths, *Patriotism Perverted: Captain Ramsay, the Right Club, and British Anti-Semitism, 1939–40* (London: Constable, 1998), 156; Lorie Charlesworth, "2 SAS Regiment, War Crimes Investigations, and British Intelligence: Intelligence Officials and the Natzweiler Trial," *Journal of Intelligence History* 6, 2 (2006): 13–60.

36. On the "low dishonest decade," see W. H. Auden, "September 1, 1939," in *Another Time: Poems* (New York: Random House, 1940), 98.

37. Geoff Eley, "Finding the People's War: Film, British Collective Memory and World War Two," *American Historical Review* 105 (2001): 821.

38. Monica Charlot, "Mythes de guerre," in *La Société anglaise en guerre, septembre 1939–août 1945*, ed. Jean-Paul Pichardie (Le Havre: University of Rouen, 1996), 131. When Mass Observation began its chronicling of everyday life in 1937, some labeled its investigators snoopers and "society playboys." *Mass-Observation, First Year's Work, 1937–1938* (London: Lindsay Drummond, 1938), 63.

39. On the wartime coalition and consensus politics, see Angus Calder, *The People's War: Britain, 1939–1945* (London: Jonathan Cape, 1969) and *The Myth of the Blitz* (London: Jonathan Cape, 1991); Paul Addison, *The Road to 1945: British Politics and the Second World War* (London: Cape, 1975); and Kenneth O. Morgan, *The People's Peace: British History, 1945–1989* (Oxford: Oxford University Press, 1990). For a critique of this perspective, see Stephen Brooke, *Labour's War: The Labour Party and the Second World War* (Oxford: Clarendon Press, 1992), and J. Baxendale and C. Pawling, *Narrating the Thirties: A Decade in the Making, 1930 to the Present* (London: Macmillan, 1996).

40. Austin Vernon Mitchell, *Election '45: Reflections on the Revolution in Britain* (London: Fabian Society, 1995), 12. Bruce, a Labour MP from 1945 to 1950, was in 1975 made a life peer as Baron Bruce of Donington.

41. Penny Summerfield, *Women Workers in the Second World War: Production and Patriarchy in Conflict* (London: Croom-Helm, 1984).

42. Though the King's Regulations called for the expulsion of homosexuals from the army, senior officers could use their own discretion. John Costello, *Love, Sex and War: Changing Values, 1939–45* (London: Guild Publishing, 1985), 157–158, 158–173 . On gay subtexts in films, see Stephen Bourne, *Brief Encounters: Lesbians and Gays in British Cinema, 1930 to 1971* (London: Cassell, 1996).

43. Houlbrook, *Queer London*, 273–274; on the relationship of sexual reform and socialism, see Stephen Brooke, *Sexual Politics: Sexuality, Family Planning, and the British Left from the 1880s to the Present Day* (Oxford: Oxford University Press, 2011).

44. Sonya Rose, *Which People's War?: National Identity and Citizenship in Britain, 1939–1945* (Oxford: Oxford University Press, 2003), 151–197, and "Temperate Heroes: Concepts of Masculinity in Second World War Britain," in *Masculinities in Politics and War: Gendering Modern History*, ed. Stefan Dudink et al. (Manchester: Manchester University Press, 2004), 177–198.

45. Fryniwyd Tennyson Jesse and Harold Marsh Harwood, *London Front: Letters Written to America, 1939–1940* (New York: Doubleday Doran, 1941), 19.

46. Martin Francis, *The Flyer: British Culture and the Royal Air Force, 1939–1945* (Oxford: Oxford University Press, 2008), 17; for the argument that "[a]viation reinvented the glamour of war," see Mark Rawlinson, *British Writing of the Second World War* (Oxford: Clarendon Press, 2000), 58.

47. For example, Squadron Leader John "Chips" Carpenter had "Chez Nina" inscribed on the side of his plane. Francis, *The Flyer*, 23.

48. For the argument that after the war some of those portraying the RAF pilot came to regard his charmingly debonair façade as veering toward "oiliness and spivery," see Mark Connelly, *We Can Take It!: Britain and the Memory of the Second World War* (Harlow: Longman, 2004), 104, and Francis, *The Flyer*, 5.

49. W. O. Bentley, *My Life and My Cars* (London: Hutchinson, 1967), 109, cited in Martin Pugh, "Bentley Boys (act. 1919–1931)," *Oxford Dictionary of National Biography* (Oxford University Press, May 2013), www.oxforddnb.com/view/article/101179 (accessed Nov. 5, 2016).

50. "Children of the Ritz," from *Words and Music* (1932), in Noël Coward, *The Lyrics of Noël Coward* (London: Heinemann, 1965), 121.

51. See Matt Houlbrook, "Commodifying the Self Within: Ghosts, Libels, and the Crook Life Story in Interwar Britain," *Journal of Modern History* 85, 2 (2013): 321–363.

52. By 1937 the economy was beginning to recover from the slump, though in the north of England unemployment rates remained high. On the complexity of the finely graded divisions within the classes, see David Cannadine, *The Rise and Fall of Class in Britain* (New York: Columbia University Press, 1999), 139–140. In the south the standard of living actually improved due to the fall in prices in the 1920s and the salary increases of the 1930s. In an age of suburban house construction and electrification, those with jobs and income could take advantage of a range of cheap consumer goods, from motorcars to radios. Arthur Marwick, *Britain in the Century of Total War: War, Peace and Social Change, 1900–1967* (London: Bodley Head, 1970), 216–220; Jill Greenfield, Sean O'Connell, and Chris Read, "Fashioning Masculinity: *Men Only*, Consumption and the Development of Marketing in the 1930s," *Twentieth Century British History* 10, 4 (1999): 460.

53. Once Labour was in office after 1945 it suffered similar attacks. "The press regularly attacked Aneurin Bevan for his 'champagne socialism', dubbing him the 'Bollinger Bolshevik' and the 'Playboy of the West End World.'" Mark Roodhouse, "The 1948 Belcher Affair and Lynskey Tribunal," *Twentieth Century British History* 13, 4 (2002): 390.

Index

Page numbers in *italics* refer to illustrations.